the Annotated McGuffey

the Annotated McGuffey

Selections from the McGuffey Eclectic Readers
1836-1920

Stanley W. Lindberg

VNR VAN NOSTRAND REINHOLD COMPANY
NEW YORK   CINCINNATI   ATLANTA   DALLAS   SAN FRANCISCO

Van Nostrand Reinhold Company Regional Offices:
New York   Cincinnati   Atlanta   Dallas   San Francisco

Van Nostrand Reinhold Company International Offices:
London   Toronto   Melbourne

Library of Congress Catalog Card Number: 76-9845
ISBN: 0-442-24810-5

Manufactured in the United States of America

Published by Van Nostrand Reinhold Company
450 West 33rd Street, New York. N.Y. 10001

Published simultaneously in Canada by Van Nostrand Reinhold Ltd.

15 14 13 12 11 10 9 8 7 6 5 4 3 2 1

Library of Congress Cataloging in Publication Data

McGuffey, William Holmes, 1800–1873.
   The annotated McGuffey.

   Bibliography: p.
   Includes index.
   1. Readers—1800–1870.   2. Readers—1870–1950.
3. McGuffey, William Holmes, 1800–1873.   I. Lindberg,
Stanley W.   II. Title.
PE1117.A1M28 1976   428'.6   76-9845
ISBN 0-442-24810-5

for Carl and Leah Lindberg

Preface

Among the world's more influential books are many that are frequently alluded to but seldom actually read today—and the *McGuffey Eclectic Readers* certainly belong to that group. The major intent of this volume is to provide a closer look at these famous American schoolbooks, to examine their selections in an objective historical perspective, and to briefly assess the impact they had on the American culture. Although I elected to omit some longer, oft-anthologized poems like Gray's famous "Elegy" and Bryant's "Thanatopsis," the lessons included here represent well, I believe, the wide range of subject matter and quality characterizing the *McGuffey Readers* from 1836 to 1920. Since many of the lessons here were deleted in later editions, this volume is clearly not a simple abridgment of the 1920 *McGuffeys* (which are still available in print). Nor is it merely a selection of "old favorites" from the popular *Readers*, although there are certainly many of these sentimental choices included. It is instead an honest attempt to capture the essence of the *McGuffey Eclectic Readers* during the more than seventy-five years when they held and shaped the minds of most American youth.

My work on this book has received the kind assistance and support from more people than I can properly acknowledge. I am especially grateful to Jeanne Heller Lindberg for her advice and loyal support at every stage of the project, and to Sterling Cook, Curator of the McGuffey Museum in Oxford, Ohio, for his invaluable assistance and cooperation. Express thanks also go to Mrs. Helen C. Ball, Curator of Miami University's Special Collections, and to all the staff of Ohio University's Alden Library, especially Richard W. Ryan and Robert W. McDonnell in Special Collections. Mr. Emmert W. Bates and Miss Maxine Henderson of Litton Educational Publishing were instrumental in the initial conception of this book, and my colleagues Jack Matthews and Wayne Dodd contributed rigorous yet encouraging critical assessments of my manuscript, for which I am much indebted. For their kindness and help in various matters I again thank John Lindberg, Thomas Lindberg, Barbara Little, Cathy and David Mann, Norman Schmidt, and Catherine H. Horr.

All photographs included here, unless specifically otherwise credited, were provided from the files of the McGuffey Museum and the Public Information Office of Miami University, and are used by permission. The facsimile reproductions of the *McGuffey* lessons were photographed from the *Readers* in the Maude Blair Collection, now housed in the McGuffey Museum.

My early research on the *McGuffey Readers* was supported by a summer grant from the Ohio University Research Committee. Subsequent institutional encouragement and support came from Dean Norman S. Cohn, Director of Research, and Adam J. Marsh, Director of Ohio University's Research Institute. To these and all others who offered assistance and cooperation, I remain deeply grateful.

S. W. L.
Athens, Ohio

Contents

FOURTH READER

FIFTH READER

SIXTH READER

Note: Names in [brackets] received no attribution in the McGuffeys, but are shown here by the present author.

the Annotated McGuffey

Introduction

As the only textbooks recognizable by name to most Americans, the *McGuffey Eclectic Readers* are clearly among America's most impressive historical, cultural, and educational monuments. First published in 1836, they dominated the schoolbook market for over seventy-five years, holding and shaping the minds of several generations of Americans. Although they were used in nearly every state and territory, the *McGuffeys* enjoyed a popularity west of the Alleghenies and south of the Mason-Dixon line exceeded only by that of the Bible. Over 122,000,000 copies of the *Readers* were published before their use began to decline in the 1920's, and most of these copies (if one can judge by the survivors) passed through the hands of at least five or six students. Largely supplanted by more progressive school books after World War I, the *McGuffeys* have never actually gone out of print, and are currently experiencing something of a revival in response to the "back-to-basics" trend in American schools.

Yet the *McGuffey Readers* stand today as an ambiguous symbol—denounced by some as anathema, and regarded by others with reverence and nostalgia. While they are often referred to disparagingly or even jokingly by many professional educators, they are frequently the texts called for by outraged parents and other critics who are alarmed by the fact that so many of today's students are little better than functional illiterates. Distorted claims and charges alike often reveal that, while the name of the *McGuffey Readers* may be known to most Americans, very few people have a real understanding of just what these books were, and indeed still are.

I

The basic set of *McGuffey Eclectic Readers* consists of a *Primer* and six "graded" *Readers*, but even such a simple statement requires immediate qualifying explanations. First of all, the *Readers* were not graded for what we conceive of as "first grade," "second grade," etc.; they were simply arranged in order of increasing difficulty. Most classes were held in one-room schoolhouses (with children from six to the late teens under a single teacher), and every child used the *First Reader*

until he or she qualified for the *Second*, which might have been at age seven or possibly as late as fourteen. The length of the school year was not the same for all pupils, since many children simply could not attend during harvesting season or spring planting. "Graduation" varied too. Most nineteenth-century students finished at least the *Second Reader*, but many left school permanently before completing the *Third*. And for many years anyone who had finished the *Fourth Reader* was considered very well educated indeed. The practice of grading the *Readers* at a level corresponding more closely to our present school grade-levels was accomplished by the *McGuffey Eclectic Readers* only in 1879.

In addition to the best known *Primer* plus six *Readers*, however, there were several other *McGuffey* textbooks produced by the publishers. One of these, the *McGuffey Eclectic Speller*, received wide use for many years, but most of the others were fairly short-lived attempts to capitalize on the fame of the series and were of limited success. Such titles as *McGuffey's Eclectic Speaker*, *McGuffey's Eclectic Juvenile Speaker*, and *McGuffey's High School Reader* all appeared later in the century, and all were prepared by the publisher's assignees with no participation by anyone named McGuffey. Although the fact that they existed is evidence of the incredible popularity of the *McGuffeys*, their use and impact were relatively slight, and they are not normally regarded as part of the basic *McGuffey* series. Usually excluded as well are Dr. James Baldwin's 1901 *New McGuffey Readers*, which attempted to use the McGuffey name on what was essentially an entirely new series of lessons.

Even after we agree upon what books comprise the *McGuffeys*, however, confusion still exists. Extensive revisions at all levels occurred in 1844, 1857, and 1879, with less sweeping changes in individual *Readers* introduced at other times (particularly in 1841, 1853, and 1866). Although a number of the original selections manage to survive through all the later revisions, the 1920 edition of the *McGuffeys* that is still circulating today is a much different set of textbooks from the originals. Throughout the years over 1,200 different lessons appeared at least once within the pages of the *McGuffeys*, with many of the lessons being added, deleted, or revised because of such profound influences as the Temperance Movement, Darwin's theory of evolution, and the Civil War. To be sure, a constant religious and moral philosophy informs all of the editions, but enough other elements change in focus or intensity to seriously qualify many of the current generalizations often heard about the *McGuffey Readers*.

Let it be conceded immediately that some of the most persistent criticisms of the *McGuffeys* are well founded. The *Readers* do, in fact, contain most of the expected outrages of our Victorian heritage, and a look back through their pages will cast a glaring spotlight on some of the tangled values and hypocrisies of their times. Like their world, the *Readers* were often artlessly moralistic, heavily didactic, and fulsomely repetitious. They were aimed almost exclusively at a conventional white, Protestant, middle-class audience. They were highly selective in their endorsement of social reforms during their era (endorsing the Temperance Movement, for instance, but studiously avoiding the touchy slavery issue or the trade union movement). In constantly reflecting and explicitly endorsing the stereotyped roles for women held in the nineteenth century, they helped insure the continuation of those values for additional generations by stamping them into young minds. Similarly, in reflecting so pervasively the increasing sentimentality of the later nineteenth century, they helped to perpetuate its influence on American writing much longer than it might otherwise have lasted. In short, as the novelist Jack Matthews has noted, "It is strange to think that such an incubus of pedagogy did not destroy every precious flower of morality and intellect that was struggling to come forth in that day, but the fact is that an uncomfortably large number of gifted people were to emerge. . . ."

For all of these now notable excesses and weaknesses, however, the *McGuffey Eclectic Readers* offered a number of corresponding strengths—as judged by both the values of their own era and those that most Americans think of as ours today. The moral values most heavily inculcated by the *Readers*—honesty, industry, courage, kindness, courtesy, and obedience—are among those values whose absence in contemporary society is so eloquently lamented by social critics and serious commentators. And the *McGuffeys'* emphasis on "basics" in education (particularly reading, spelling, punctuation, and enunciation) suddenly appears more attractive to many Americans,

WILLIAM HOLMES McGUFFEY, 1800–1873. (From an 1836 portrait by Horace Harding)

including an increasing number of educators.

There can be little question that the *McGuffey Readers*—particularly in the earlier editions—were far more demanding and challenging than most present-day school texts. The subject range was greater too, with many lessons on farming, science, history, and biography—in addition to the literary selections. And the subject of *death* (often taboo in twentieth-century texts, at least until its recent popularization by the media) was confronted directly and frequently in the *Readers*. There was no room for the coddling of young pupils in the thinking of William Holmes McGuffey. As he wrote in an early "Preface": "[The author] has long been of opinion that a mischievous error pervades the public mind, on the subject of juvenile understanding. Nothing is so difficult to be understood as 'nonsense.' Nothing so clear and easy to comprehend as the simplicity of wisdom."

Especially in the upper-level *Readers* the major focus was on literature, and it is here that changed critical tastes will find them most dated. Overly represented, by today's standards, are such writers as Longfellow, Whittier, James Russell Lowell, and Oliver Wendell Holmes—all of whose reputations were enhanced by the *Readers*, but are now in decline. And the *McGuffeys* can easily be faulted for omitting Walt Whitman and Mark Twain—two of America's greatest writers—as well as for allotting brief space (and that only in the latest editions) to such eminent figures as Poe, Emerson, and Thoreau. It must also be conceded that the literary selections generally include far too many works by third- and fourth-rate writers (especially American poetasters). In some respects the *McGuffey Readers* represented all too well the popular literary tastes of their era.

It should be noted, however, that the *Readers* also provided numerous poetic selections of much higher order, including many from the Bible and from writers such as Shakespeare, Dr. Johnson, Hawthorne, and Wordsworth—passages which even today might well be chosen as "Elegant Extracts in Prose and Poetry, from the Best American and English Writers" (as the early *Fourth Readers* were subtitled). And along with lessons from American authors like Washington Irving, William Cullen Bryant, and James Fenimore Cooper, one can find a healthy number from such British writers as Sir Walter Scott, Dickens, Goldsmith, Byron, and Tennyson. The British authors are represented more than adequately, in fact, to disprove the traditional charges against (or occasional claims for) the *McGuffeys'* supposedly parochial or nationalistic attitude.

HARRIET SPINNING McGUFFEY, 1809–1850. William's first wife and—according to family legend—compiler of the *Eclectic Primer*. (From an 1836 portrait by Horace Harding)

All in all, the *McGuffey Eclectic Readers* introduced their users to a wider range of literature than that offered many of our students today. And much of what was provided was good literature—by today's or any day's standards. Students may have tasted only fragments from Shakespeare and other important writers, but they *were* being introduced to them. Furthermore, those young minds were being exposed to the *Readers* without such distractions as radio, television, and movies; the impact of textbooks then was doubtless much greater than it is today. It was perhaps in this respect that the *McGuffeys* made their most significant contribution to American culture. As Henry Steele Commager so accurately observes: "They gave to the American child of the nineteenth century what he so conspicuously lacks today—a common body of allusions, a sense of common experience and of common possession."

II

Among the myths that have developed over the years are many concerning the man whose name appears on the *Readers:* William Holmes McGuffey. Sometimes represented as having almost singlehandedly dragged America out of the swamps of ignorance, McGuffey himself never assumed such a larger-than-life pose. He knew, for instance, that there were at least two McGuffeys involved, the second being Alexander Hamilton McGuffey, William's younger brother. (William's wife Harriet may have had a part too; according to oft-repeated but unconfirmed family stories, she supposedly compiled the little *Primer*, but modestly—or shrewdly—asked that it be published under her husband's more famous name.) And almost from the start there were yet other hands shaping the *Readers*, since the editors hired by the publishers took an active role in the subsequent revised editions. As the famous *McGuffey Readers* appear today, they are clearly much more than the work of any single individual.

The man who did start it all, however, was William Holmes McGuffey—now sometimes praised as the "Schoolmaster to Our Nation," but more often thought of as a book than as a person. Born in Washington County, Pennsylvania, on 23 September 1800, McGuffey spent most of his youth in Ohio. He was only two years old when his Scotch-Irish, Presbyterian family moved into the newly-opened Northwest Territory, and settled near what is now Youngstown. He returned to

WILLIAM HOLMES McGUFFEY (From a daguerreotype by W. L. Retzler of Virginia. c. 1847).

Pennsylvania in 1820 to attend Washington (now Washington & Jefferson) College, and then taught a private school in an abandoned smokehouse near Paris, Kentucky, until he was selected in 1826 to become Professor of Ancient Languages at the new Miami University in Oxford, Ohio. While at Miami, McGuffey married, was ordained a Presbyterian minister, argued with the college president until he was allowed to teach the classes in moral philosophy, and compiled the earliest of the textbooks that were soon to make his name famous.

The *Eclectic Readers* were initiated in the mid-1830's at the request of the Cincinnati publishing firm of Truman & Smith, who desired to offer a "Western" series of texts to compete in the growing market for school books in Ohio, Kentucky, and Indiana. They selected McGuffey for the job only after their first choice, Catherine Beecher (daughter of the famous Rev. Lyman Beecher), had declined. And they drove a hard bargain, for in 1836 they got McGuffey to sign a contract obliging him to compile a series of four "graded" readers, with royalties of 10% on all copies sold to a total of $1,000, *after which all profits reverted to the publishers*. The first two *Readers* were released in 1836; the *Third* and *Fourth* appeared the following year, accompanied by the small *Primer*.

Even before the success of the *Readers* was assured, McGuffey had left Miami University, and had in 1836 assumed the presidency of the newly-formed Cincinnati College. (The move prompted Truman & Smith to alter the title pages, presenting not only his new rank, but also the amusing description "formerly professor at Oxford"—clearly calculated to suggest grander academic credentials than were usually accorded the institution at Oxford, *Ohio*.) The new Cincinnati College quickly assembled an impressive faculty and seemed to be off to a promising start, but the financial panic of 1837 doomed the venture. In 1839 McGuffey resigned, and the school closed shortly thereafter.

Almost immediately, however, McGuffey had another chance—this time as president of Ohio University in Athens, Ohio. Once again things started out well: the enrollment increased, and the reassessments of rental fees on university-owned property promised a more secure financial base for the land-grant school. But the townspeople of Athens, angered over the reassessments, persuaded the Ohio legislature to rescind them; and McGuffey's Calvinistic disciplinary measures quickly wiped out enrollment gains. At that point McGuffey further infuriated the residents of Athens by fencing in the college campus—in part to protect the new elm trees he had planted, but primarily to keep Athenian pigs and cows from grazing up to the doorsteps of the college buildings. When a torchlight parade failed to convince McGuffey to reconsider his actions, the youngsters of the town (encouraged by their parents) began to throw mudballs at the college president whenever he appeared. Despite his manly response of lashing back with a long, red-leather horsewhip, he evidently lost often enough that, one day in 1843, an exasperated and mud-covered McGuffey came home and instructed his wife to pack immediately. Moreover, according to the legend, he left hurriedly, not even pausing to write his resignation until he and his family were well out of Athens.

The rest of William Holmes McGuffey's life was much less exciting. In 1845 he became professor of moral philosophy at the University of Virginia, where he lived until his death on 4 May 1873. Although the royalty payments from his famous *Readers* had ceased long before he went to Virginia, McGuffey evidently received some additional reimbursement for later revisions. And after the Civil War the grateful publishers also gave him an annuity: a barrel of "choice smoked hams" every Christmas.

Although most of the credit for the *Readers* has been given to William Holmes McGuffey, a surprising amount of the work was actually done by his brother, Alexander Hamilton McGuffey (1816–1896). Sixteen years younger than William, Alexander was the one who had the initial responsibility for the *McGuffey Rhetorical Guide* (1844), almost immediately retitled *McGuffey's Fifth Eclectic Reader*. He also did major work on the *McGuffey Eclectic Speller* in 1846 and was the only McGuffey who had any voice in the *Sixth Reader*, which the publishers decided to add in 1857. Although he taught English for a while in a Cincinnati academy, Alexander concentrated most of his efforts on the practice of law, which ultimately brought him a reasonable degree of success and wealth. His contributions to the *Readers* have been unjustly ignored or underestimated, partly because in the 1850's the publishers reduced Alexander's credit line to "A. H. McGuffey"—and set it in a flourishing script that positively invited a misreading of the "A. H." as "W. H.". This subterfuge rubbed Alexander's pride enough that he insisted his name be removed completely in subsequent editions. The publishers complied, apparently without protest, furnishing no author credit for a few years; but by 1866 they actually started crediting the *Fifth* and *Sixth*

ALEXANDER HAMILTON McGUFFEY, 1816-1896.

Readers (mostly Alexander's editorial product) to "Wm. H. McGuffey, LL.D."—despite William's total lack of involvement with those books. As far as is known, Alexander didn't get any Christmas hams, either.

III

The unsung Alexander certainly deserves more credit than history has allotted, but there were others who remained even more hidden in the saga of the *McGuffey Readers*—particularly the publishers and their editors. Most important of these was Winthrop B. Smith (1808–1885) in the firm of Truman & Smith, the one who first conceived the idea of the *Readers* and

commissioned W. H. McGuffey to start the series in 1836. Smith's faith in the *Readers'* potential was such that one morning in 1843 he supposedly divided all of the firm's assets into two uneven stacks: a small one containing the *McGuffey Readers* and *Ray's Arithmetics;* the other containing all the many other books published by the firm *together with* the total cash reserve. He then proposed to Truman that they dissolve their partnership, with Truman to have his choice of the divided assets. Truman, according to the legend, selected the wrong pile and faded into oblivion; Smith was left with the textbooks that ultimately made him a millionaire. The dissolution of the firm may not actually have occurred as dramatically as the legend suggests, but the division of assets did follow those lines, with Smith acquiring exclusive copyright of the *McGuffeys* as part of the settlement.

The *McGuffey Readers*, however, were not markedly different from most other reading textbooks of the time (in fact, nearly all the textbooks "borrowed" heavily from the same sources and each other). The major reason the *McGuffeys* gained ascendancy was not because of any unique content or pedagogical approach, but because of the skillful promotion and marketing practices of W. B. Smith and the publishers who followed him. Even before the *McGuffeys* began to be published over his name alone, Smith had taken important steps to establish a secure base for his firm and to elevate *his* series of *Readers* above those of his competitors. Certainly the contract offered W. H. McGuffey is one indication of Smith's astute business practices. Even more important, however, were his fortuitous use of the label "*eclectic*," and his exploitation of regional rivalries in promoting the *Readers*.

In later years McGuffey's name itself served to distinguish these texts from competing titles, but initially the prime identifying factor was the catchy word *eclectic*, a term then very much in vogue. Deriving from the tenets of Victor Cousin (a French philosopher who was trying to chart a middle road between the idealism of Kant and the empiricism of Descartes and Locke), the term was quickly absorbed into educational jargon. W. B. Smith had already sensed the slogan's drawing powers when he published Joseph Ray's *Eclectic Arithmetic* in 1834, and it was logical for the *McGuffey Readers* to carry the phrase, too. As the 1837 *Third Reader* announced to "The Friends of Education":

> The *Eclectic* System of Instruction now predominates in Prussia, Germany, and Switzerland. 'It is in these countries that

the subject of education has been deemed of paramount importance. The art of teaching, particularly, has there been most ably and minutely investigated.'

The Eclectic System, '*aims at embodying all the valuable principles of previous systems, without adhering slavishly to the dictates of any master, or the views of any party. It rejects the undue predilection for the mere expansion of mind, to the neglect of positive knowledge and practical application.*'

These were well received words at the time . . . obviously calculated to appeal to pragmatic American minds which were confused by the foreign-sounding Pestalozzian system, but distrusted or rejected humanistic rhetoric about "the mere expansion of mind." Here was a "system" that was based on common sense—one that in a typically American way melded the best ideas from all possible educational worlds. And Smith, recognizing this clearly, made the most of it; within the next twenty years America was to see *Eclectic Histories, Eclectic Geographies*, even *Eclectic Shorthand* and *Eclectic Music* textbooks.

Smith also learned to cultivate to his advantage the growing regional pride of the West, especially prevalent in Cincinnati. Almost from the beginning, the *Readers* carried advertisements similar to this 1838 announcement:

The above works have been prepared by a few untiring laborers in the cause of Education (President M'Guffey and others,) *for the purpose of furnishing the South and West* with a complete, uniform, and improved set of school books, commencing with the alphabet; and which might obviate the constant difficulties and perplexities occasioned by the too frequent changes in School Books. The effort has been successful. The fact that SIX HUNDRED THOUSAND of the Eclectic School Books have been disposed of during the short time they have been before the public, is the best evidence of their superior excellency. *They have gone into GENERAL USE, and have become the Standard School Books of the WEST and South.*

As the *McGuffey Eclectic Readers* achieved a more national distribution, such regional puffs became less common and were often replaced by statements actually disclaiming regional ethnocentrism. The 1844 *Fourth Reader*, for instance, stresses that "NO SECTIONAL matter, reflecting upon the local institutions, customs, or habits of any portion of the United States, is to be found among their contents, and hence they are extensively used at the South and at the North, in the East as well as the West." Since the more blatantly pro-West lessons

had been removed, the claim appears sincere and fairly accurate. When one realizes, however, that the phrase "local institutions, customs, or habits" is primarily a euphemism for *slavery* (then under attack in some New England textbooks), it becomes clear that Smith's cultivation or exploitation of regionalism has only become more subtle. It continued to be successful for some years, and the *McGuffeys* began to receive more and more adoptions in the South.

When the Civil War broke out, however, W. B. Smith and his associates were suddenly caught with a vastly reduced market and a large number of uncollectible accounts. The official embargo on trade with the South signaled rough times ahead, and some publishing firms were going bankrupt. The embargo had, of course, halted trade not only of the *McGuffey Readers*, but of its competitors as well. And this gave W. B. Smith the chance he needed, since the Confederacy contained no textbook publishers within its borders. Someone would have to supply that market, and somehow (the term *smuggling* is probably too harsh) the stereotyped printing plates for the *McGuffey Eclectic Readers* found their way to the Methodist Book Concern in Nashville, Tennessee. Soon the *McGuffeys* were being distributed widely throughout the Confederacy— and by the end of the war they enjoyed what approached a monopoly south of the Mason-Dixon line. It is still unknown whether W. B. Smith & Co. or its successor shared in the Methodist Book Concern's war-time profits, but one point is very clear: the *McGuffeys'* pre-war market was not only preserved but considerably expanded. And as the Federal Army occupied additional portions of the South, orders flowed into Cincinnati for new supplies of *Readers*. The Methodists, we now see, had helped to provide the textbooks of a Presbyterian minister the market domination and moral influence they were to enjoy for the rest of the century.

By the end of the Civil War, W. B. Smith had retired and the publishers of the *McGuffeys* had changed imprints again. From the original Truman & Smith in 1836 (W. B. Smith & Co. after 1843) the firm's name changed in 1863 to Sargent, Wilson, and Hinkle. That imprint was succeeded in 1868 by Wilson, Hinkle and Company; in 1877 by Van Antwerp, Bragg and Company; and finally in 1890 by The American Book Company. Regardless of the publishing imprint, however, the aggressive and shrewd promotion of the *Readers* begun by W. B. Smith remained a constant. There were always new textbooks coming out, but none could supplant the *McGuffeys*.

Charges were made by competitors that agents promoting the *Eclectic Readers* bribed school board members, offered special introductory rates, and instigated ceremonial book-burnings of the texts they replaced. And there is enough evidence to indicate that some of these charges were probably true. Such practices were evidently considered common in the late nineteenth century, however, and the *McGuffey Readers* salesmen could well afford to laugh when disgruntled competitors assigned Van Antwerp, Bragg and Company the dubious label of "*Van Ante-up, Grabb and Company*."

For these reasons, then, as well as for their merits, the *McGuffey Readers* flourished magnificently throughout the nineteenth century, with revised editions appearing only as necessary to hold the market. Although both William and Alexander McGuffey were offered near-token consulting roles in the early revisions, the *Readers* now belonged to the publishers, and most of the editorial revisions were carried out by their assignees. The people who actually decided the contents were such now-forgotten figures as Dr. Timothy S. Pinneo, Daniel G. Mason, Obed J. Wilson, Henry H. Vail, and others. (And after Obed J. Wilson became a partner in the firm, he let his wife revise the 1863 edtion of the *First Reader*, inserting the names of her favorite nephews and nieces in many of the lessons.) The books still carried the name of McGuffey, but they were now the product of many hands . . . in nearly all respects an institution in themselves.

IV

The *McGuffey Eclectic Readers* began to lose their dominant market control after World War I, and support for their use continued to erode during the 1920's. It was at this time that McGuffey Alumni Societies began to form across the midwestern states, motivated by both nostalgia and some sincere reservations about the progressive textbooks that were supplanting the *McGuffeys*. Another intangible element was involved in these societies, too—a rather fierce pride in the accomplishments of the *McGuffey* "graduates" that probably also included resentment of the exclusive clubs like those for Harvard, Yale, or Princeton men. Ultimately, many of these groups combined in 1935 into the Federated McGuffey Societies of America, which still meets annually in Oxford, Ohio—near the brick home McGuffey built in 1833. That home itself has become the McGuffey Museum, housing the most complete collection of the *Readers* extant, along with an impressive collection of other nineteenth-century textbooks and McGuffey memorabilia.

The McGuffey heritage lives on in other places, too—with buildings carrying the name at both Ohio University and the University of Virginia, as well as at Miami University; and McGuffey streets, lanes, drives, and avenues abound throughout the American heartland. The log cabin in which W. H. McGuffey was born in Washington County, Pennsylvania, now stands restored in Henry Ford's Greenfield Village in Dearborn, Michigan; and Ford—despite his famous declaration that "history is bunk"—also purchased the McGuffey family home near Youngstown, Ohio, and used the materials to build a McGuffey schoolhouse in Greenfield Village. An enthusiastic supporter of the McGuffey Societies during the 1920's and 1930's, Ford joined with such luminaries of the time as Hamlin Garland, Mark Sullivan, James M. Cox, and John Studebaker to lobby for continued use of the *Eclectic Readers* in American schools.

The *McGuffey Readers* are clearly of value today, if for no other reason than their symbolic importance as curious historical artifacts. In many respects they offer a fascinating survey of American nineteenth-century life and values (with a few curious historical omissions, such as the glamour of the river steamboats and the California gold rush). But their legacy is much more significant than this, even if harder to measure. Wielding an influence second only to the Bible over millions of minds, they played a major role in establishing the moral, social, and literary values of several generations. In so doing, the *McGuffey Eclectic Readers* served as a major force in shaping the present consciousness of what we now call Middle America.

the Annotated McGuffey

First Reader

THE SUBJECT OF PLAYING, ESPECIALLY IN THE EARLIEST EDITIONS, was rarely treated directly. Instead, as in this selection from the first edition of the First Reader, *playing is quickly subordinated to instruction in proper behavior. This lesson appeared only in the 1836 and 1841 editions, being replaced in 1844 by "The Boys and the Kite," in which playing outdoors serves as both ostensible and actual subject.*

LESSON XI.

Boys at Play.

Can you fly a kite ?   See how the boy flies his kite.   He holds the string fast, and the wind blows it up.

Now it is high in the air, and looks like a bird.   When the wind blows hard, you must hold fast, or your kite will get away.

Boys love to run and play.

But they must not be rude.   Good boys do not play in a rude way, but take care not to hurt any one.

You must not lie. Bad boys lie, and swear, and steal.

When boys are at play they must be kind, and not feel cross. If you are cross, good boys will not like to play with you.

When you fall down, you must not cry, but get up, and run again. If you cry, the boys will call you a baby.

Some boys use bad words when they are at play. The Bible says that you must not use bad words ; and you must mind what the Bible says, for it is God's book. You must not play with boys that speak bad words or tell lies.

kite	holds	wind	high
string	fast	blows	looks
bird	when	boys	ba-by
words	play	you	not
speak	bad	book	but
bi-ble	hurt	rude	take
care	one	they	cry
get	up	run	a-gain
kind	not	feel	cross
must	mind	good	says
boys	lie	swear	steal

B 2

Although few lessons present sexual stereotypes as blatantly as this, a number of them remind boys that males do not cry. And in the progression here (from playing to moral instruction, and then to religious instruction) "Boys at Play" is a good representative of the earliest McGuffey lessons.

McGuffey's earliest editions were clearly designed more for boys than for girls, but "The Good Girl" was present from the start in 1836. It remained in the McGuffeys through the various editions (moving up to the Second Reader in 1857) until 1879, when it was quietly dropped.

LESSON XIII.

sew	best	wish	seam	child
yes	here	what	help	bring
hem	join	wear	made	stool
new	nice	wash	turn	lit-tle
may	soil	wipe	girl	la-dy
use	said	your	frill	moth-er

THE GOOD GIRL.

MOTH-ER, may I sew to-day?

Yes, my child; what do you wish to sew?

I wish to hem a frill for your cap.   Is not this a new cap? I see it has no frill.

You may make a frill for me; I shall

like to wear a frill that you have made. Here is a bit of cloth which will make a nice frill. You must hem it. I will turn it down for you; but take care not to soil it.

Wash your hands, and take care to wipe them dry. Now sit down on your low stool. Now you may go on. You will see best here by my side.

You must join these two bits with a seam; and when you have done as far as this pin, bring it to me to look at.

Jane sat down upon her stool and sew-ed like a lit-tle la-dy. In a short time she said, Moth-er, I have done as far as you told me; will you look at it?

Yes, my child, it is well done; and if you take pains, as you have done to-day, you will soon sew well.

I wish to sew well, Moth-er, for then I can help you to make caps and frocks, and I hope to be of some use to you.

Not only did this lesson teach girls how to be "little ladies," but it also reinforced the traditional role of women in the minds of both male and female readers. The most favorable roles a girl could hope for in the McGuffeys were those of a dutiful mother and a benefactress to the poor; roles of moral and physical courage were reserved for boys. It is worth noting, perhaps, that William Holmes McGuffey never taught girls in his 38 years of classroom teaching.

LESSON XVI.

day	come	give	shade	fruit	wash-es
hot	cool	rich	beats	roots	sum-mer
out	meet	dark	heads	brook	up-ward
run	soft	swim	thick	raise	branch-es
sea	warm	move	green	sleep	cur-tain
air	grow	worm	trees	praise	pleas-ant

THE COOL SHADE.

COME, let us go into the thick shade, for it is noon-day, and the sum-mer sun beats hot upon our heads.

The shade is pleas-ant and cool; the branch-es meet a-bove our heads, and shut out the sun, as with a green cur-tain.

ORIGINALLY ENTITLED "THE THICK SHADE" (IN THE 1836 AND 1841 editions), this lesson was also transferred to the Second Reader in 1857 and then removed from the series in the 1879 revision. It presents a common image of nature in nineteenth-century textbooks: nature as the primary evidence for the existence of a Creator.

The grass is soft to our feet, and the clear brook wash-es the roots of the trees.

The sheep and cows can lie down to sleep in the cool shade, but we can do bet-ter; we can praise the great God who made us.

He made the warm sun, and the cool shade; the trees that grow up-ward, and the brooks that run along.

The plants and trees are made to give fruit to man.

All that live get life from God. He made the poor man as well as the rich man.

He made the dark man, as well as the fair man. He made the fool, as well as the wise man. All that move on the land are his; and so are all that fly in the air, and all that swim in the sea.

The ox' and the worm are both the work of his hand. In him they live and move. He it is that doth give food to them all, and when he says the word, they all must die.

The parallel structure here (rich, fair, *and* wise VERSUS poor, dark, *and* fool) *reveals a value system that is deeply embedded in the language, and probably reflects no deliberate racism or class consciousness; but such statements can exert a strong subliminal influence, leading toward less subtle discriminations. This possibility becomes even more likely in a textbook series like the* McGuffeys, *where there were practically no other references to Negroes or black slavery.*

ILLUSTRATIONS IN THE EARLIEST EDITION WERE ALL OF BRITISH ORIGIN, some of them of questionable relevance to the stories they accompanied. But by 1853 the McGuffey Readers *included nearly all American-produced woodblock engravings, most of them created for specific lessons. The lesson reproduced here is from the 1844 edition, although it was one of McGuffey's original selections in 1836 and continued in use until the massive 1879 revision. The illustration is British, and was replaced in the 1848 edition.*

LESSON XXI.

day	went	came	arms	dress
man	take	same	each	bound
and	walk	then	warm	great
saw	town	back	once	ground
one	home	lift	been	pit-y
own	hurt	pain	pray	lit-tle

THE LAME DOG.

ONE day a man went to take a walk in the town, and on his way home he saw a lit-tle dog which had hurt his leg.

The poor dog was so lame he could not lift his foot off the ground with-out great pain.

When this kind man saw there was no one to take pit-y on the poor dog, he took him in his arms, and brought him home, and bound up his leg. Then he fed him, and made a warm place, and kept him in his house for two days.

He then sent the dog out of his house, to his old home; for, as it was not his own dog, he had no right to keep him; but each day the dog came back for this kind man to dress his leg. And this he did till he was quite well.

In a few weeks the dog came back once more, and with him came a dog that was lame.

The dog that had been lame, and was now well, first gave the man a look, and then he gave the lame dog a look, as much as to say:

"You made my lame leg well, and now pray do the same for this poor dog that has come with me."

Then the kind man took care of this dog al-so, and kept him in his house till his leg was quite well, and he could go home.

Many of McGuffey's selections embody a moral lesson in kindness through the action of animals. Other values were easily assimilated as well, in this case including a reminder that the dog remained the property of his owner, regardless of the deserts of his benefactor.

THIS STORY, EXPLOITING A NARRATIVE CLICHÉ AT LEAST AS OLD AS
Tom Jones, *underwent a number of revisions from 1836 until it
was omitted in the 1879 edition. Originally entitled "Mr. Post
and the Little Girls" in 1836, it dropped the inaccurate
plural and became "Mr. Post and the Little Girl" in 1841;
in 1844 (the lesson reproduced here) it was labeled simply
"Mr. Post," a title it retained until 1857, when it was moved
to the* Second Reader *and became "Mr. Post and Mary."
Until 1844 it was preceded by a curious lesson, "About
Mr. Post," which described him as a very poor man living in
New York. That lesson portrayed him as being very popular
with small children and also offered—without further
elaboration—the following description: "When he was young,
he went to the wars, and had his leg shot off. But he had a
leg made of wood, and can walk very well on it."*

LESSON XXVII.

care	gate	work	large	o-pen
cold	grew	know	heard	Ma-ry
babe	goat	noise	where	ta-ken
died	name	could	thought	na-med
arms	warm	where	strange	lit-tle

MR. POST.

ONE cold night, aft-er old Mr. Post
had gone to bed, he heard a noise at the
door.   So he got up, and went out.

And what do you think he found?
A dog? No.   A goat? No: he found a
lit-tle babe on the steps.

10

Some bad per-son had left it there, and if Mr. Post had not ta-ken it in-to the house, it might have died with cold.

He held it to the fire until it was warm, and then took it in his arms, and went to bed. How kind old Mr. Post was. He did not know what to do with the lit-tle babe, but he could not let it die.

When Mr. Post's lit-tle friends came to see him the next day, they thought it ver-y strange to see him have a lit-tle babe with him. He told them where he found the babe, and they all said that they would bring it milk, and some-times come and help him to take care of it.

The lit-tle girl was na-med Ma-ry, and was soon ver-y fond of Mr. Post, and call-ed him fa-ther. In a short time she grew so large that she could run out and o-pen the gate for her fa-ther when he was going out.

Mr. Post taught her to read, and at night Ma-ry would read the Bi-ble to her fa-ther; and when Mr. Post got so old that he could not work, Ma-ry took care of him.

PETER PINDAR WAS THE PSEUDONYM OF JOHN WOLCOT (1738–1819), A British physician and writer. His story here, originally entitled "The Snow Dog and the Boy" when it first appeared in the McGuffeys, was one of the lessons most commonly found in nineteenth-century textbooks. It has been part of the Readers *from 1836 to the present, although it was shifted to the* Second Reader *in 1857 and subsequent editions. In all editions it is preceded by the lesson "The Story Teller," which describes Peter Pindar as an old man who loves to tell stories. To preserve the transition from that lesson into the story itself, the earlier editions open this lesson with the line: "After the old man had wiped the sweat from off his face, he went on with his story." In 1844, however, Peter stopped sweating.*

LESSON XXIX.

one	hour	hair	close	heard
star	weak	when	child	could
seen	walk	drew	stiff	shrill
lain	coat	quite	there	good
blew	sure	arms	might	length

PE-TER PIN-DAR'S STO-RY.

ONE sad cold night, when the snow fell fast, and the wind blew loud and shrill, and it was quite dark, with not a star to be seen in the sky, these good men sent out a dog to hunt for those who might want help.

In an hour or two the dog was heard at the gate; and, on look-ing out, they saw the dog there, with a boy on his back.

The poor child was stiff with cold, and could but just hold on to the dog's back.

He told the men that he had lain a long time in the snow, and was too ill and weak to walk, and the snow fell fast on him. At length, he felt some-thing pull him by the coat, and then he heard the bark of a dog close to him.

The boy then put out his hand, and he felt the hair of the dog; and then the dog gave him one more pull. This gave the poor boy some hope, and he took hold of the dog, and drew him-self out of the snow; but he felt that he could not stand or walk.

He then got up-on the dog's back, and put his arms round the dog's neck, and thus he held on. He felt sure the dog did not mean to hurt him; and thus he rode on the dog's back, all the way to the good men's house, who took care of the boy till the snow was gone, when they sent him to his own home.

The "good men" who send their dog out are, of course, Benedictine monks, but McGuffey quietly divorces their humanitarian act from any direct association with the Catholic Church. Anti-Catholic feelings were strong during much of the nineteenth century, and McGuffey's editorial changes certainly reflect that sentiment somewhat. In comparison with their competition, however, the McGuffey Readers exhibit little of the overt Nativism and anti-Catholicism present in many of the texts then; in fact, the McGuffeys actually display a relatively high level of religious tolerance.

The Preface to the 1843 edition of the Third Reader announced the following:

NO SECTARIAN matter has been admitted into this work. It has been submitted to the inspection of highly intelligent clergymen and teachers of the various Protestant and Catholic denominations, and nothing has been inserted, except with their united approbation. While the instruction imparted through works of this kind should be decidedly moral and religious in its tendency, it is believed that nothing of a denominational character should be introduced.

Some anti-Catholic sentiments, however, were difficult to erase immediately. The articulation exercises in the Fifth Reader, for instance, continued until 1857 to carry the practice sentence: "He cannot tolerate a papist."

THE CREDIT FOR THIS FAMOUS NURSERY RHYME BELONGS TO MRS.
Sarah Josepha Hale, editor of Godey's Lady's Book *and one of*
the most influential American women of her time (see pages
231–32). The lines first appeared in print over her initials in
the Juvenile Miscellany *of September, 1830, and were*
almost immediately reprinted in her Poems for Our Children
later that year. The McGuffey Readers appropriated the
poem (as usual, without authorial attribution) in the 1844
First Reader, *transferring it to the* Second Reader *in 1857,*
and then—for no apparent reason—dropping it in 1879.

Mrs. Hale reportedly acknowledged that the lines were
based on a "partly true" incident, and most of her proud de-
scendants went further, claiming the poem to be entirely the
product of her fertile imagination. But throughout the century
new claimants came forth (even including her son, Horatio
Hale!); and periodically, debate over the identities of the
real Mary and her historian occupied American magazines
and newspapers. The dispute had little bearing on the
popularity of the rhyme itself, however, as it quickly reached
Mother Goose status. And its immortality was insured in
1877 when Thomas Edison's first words on a phonograph
were "Mary had a little lamb . . . ."

The original Mary—or at least the girl who got the most
mileage out of that claim—was Mary Elizabeth Sawyer (1806–
1889), whose story was told in full in a book, Mary Had a
Little Lamb *(New York: Frederick A. Stokes Co., 1902).*
According to that account, her pet lamb followed her to
school one day in 1817, and the next day she was given
the first three stanzas of the poem as it now stands, written
by another student: John Roulstone, Jr. (who died a few
years later while a student at Harvard). In her old age, this
Mary (now Mrs. Mary Tyler) sold for charity a number
of souvenir cards containing bits of yarn supposedly un-
raveled from stockings knit with wool from the lamb.
The poor little lamb, she reported, had met its untimely
end on the horns of an angry cow.

LESSON XLIV.

rule	lamb	where	fol-low
love	what	fleece	a-gainst
sure	harm	school	wait-ed
that	made	ea-ger	ap-pear
snow	laid	Ma-ry	ev-er-y
near	white	gen-tle	an-i-mal
went	laugh	a-fraid	pa-tient-ly
made	makes	teach-er	lin-ger-ed

MA-RY'S LAMB.

MA-RY had a lit-tle lamb,
Its fleece was white as snow,
And ev-er-y where that Ma-ry went,
The lamb was sure to go.

He went with her to school one day—
    That was a-gainst the rule—
It made the chil-dren laugh and play,
    To see a lamb at school.

So the teach-er turn-ed him out,
    But still he lin-ger-ed near,
And wait-ed pa-tient-ly a-bout,
    Till Ma-ry did ap-pear.

And then he ran to her, and laid
    His head up-on her arm,
As if he said—I'm not a-fraid—
    You'll keep me from all harm.

" What makes the lamb love Ma-ry so?"
    The ea-ger chil-dren cry;
"O Ma-ry loves the lamb, you know,"
    The teach-er did re-ply.

"And you each gen-tle an-i-mal
    To you, for life, may bind,
And make them fol-low at your call,
    If you are al-ways *kind*."

Mary Sawyer's claim for herself and John Roulstone might well have been forgotten now, if it hadn't been for Henry Ford. In the 1920's Ford began buying up large chunks of Americana (subsequently moving many of them to Greenfield Village in Dearborn, Michigan). One of his unmoved purchases was the Wayside Inn referred to by Longfellow, which happened to be located not too far from the school that Mary Sawyer (and her lamb) had attended. Naturally, Ford bought the little red schoolhouse too, and had it reconstructed. Then, to insure that he had placed his money on the right lamb, he had literary and historical experts study the matter and compile "the facts" for publication. The result was a forty-page book entitled: The Story of Mary and Her Little Lamb as told by Mary and her Neighbors and Friends; To which is added a critical analysis of the Poem: Now put in print for the Old Schoolhouse which Mary attended and which now stands near the Wayside Inn at Sudbury, Massachusetts, and which was made famous by Longfellow's "Tales of a Wayside Inn." *It was published by Mr. and Mrs. Henry Ford at Dearborn in 1928.*

Ford's experts make a fairly persuasive case for John Roulstone, suggesting that there is a definite "seam" between the first three stanzas (claimed for Roulstone) and the last three (freely given to Mrs. Hale). They also point out the strong likelihood that the verse circulated orally for some years before it appeared in print, and that Mrs. Hale—who lived just across the state line—probably heard it first in that fashion. Their claim, of course, is less for Roulstone than for Mary and that schoolhouse, but they clearly believe that Sarah Josepha Hale should share half her crown with John Roulstone, Jr. Most other authorities remain unconvinced, or at least maintain a noble silence.

This lesson and its conclusion in the following selection were among those lessons originally compiled by McGuffey in 1836. They appeared in the various editions of the First Reader until 1857, when they were combined, with only minor modifications, into a single lesson and placed in the Second Reader. The major 1879 revision, however, dropped "The Little Chimney Sweep" from its inclusions— an unpopular decision with many of the long-time McGuffey supporters. Protests over the omission of this and other favorites were strong enough that the publishers found it necessary in 1885 to reprint the earlier 1866 edition and offer it in addition to their highly publicized 1879 revision.

LESSON LII.

rich	sweep	shall	found	chim-ney
hide	seals	hands	watch	cham-ber
what	thief	sweet	could	blank-et
down	could	might	thought	kitch-en

THE LIT-TLE CHIM-NEY SWEEP.

SOME time a-go, there was a lit-tle chim-ney sweep, who had to sweep a chim-ney in the house of a ver-y rich la-dy. The lit-tle sweep went up at the kitch-en fire place, and came down in the cham-ber.

When he got in-to the cham-ber, he found him-self all a-lone. He stop-ped a mo-ment to look round up-on the rich things he saw there. As he look-ed on the top of the ta-ble, he saw a fine gold watch, with gold seals to it.

He had nev-er seen a-ny thing so beau-ti-ful be-fore, and he took it up in his hands. As he list-en-ed to hear it tick, it be-gan to play sweet mu-sic. He then thought, that if it was on-ly his own, how rich he would be; and then he thought he might hide it in his blank-et.

"Now," said he, "if I take it, I shall be a thief—and yet no bod-y sees me. No bod-y! Does not God see me? Could I ev-er a-gain be good? Could I then ev-er say my pray-ers a-gain to God? And what should I do when I came to die?"

LESSON LIII.

fear	steal	leave	own-ed	small-est
jail	while	would	for-get	trem-bled
grew	knees	school	al-ways	yes-ter-day
crept	years	thieves	rob-bers	com-mand-ment

MORE A-BOUT THE CHIM-NEY SWEEP.

WHILE the lit-tle sweep was think-ing a-bout tak-ing the la-dy's watch, he felt cold all o-ver, and trem-bled with fear.

"No," said he, "I can not take this watch. I would rath-er be a sweep and al-ways be poor, than steal." And down he laid the watch and crept up the chim-ney.

Now the la-dy who own-ed the watch was just in the next room, and she could look through, and see and hear all that

THIS BRIEF STORY ANTICIPATES DELIGHTFULLY THE BASIC PLOT OF the Horatio Alger "rags-to-riches" novels that were later to become so popular in the second half of the nineteenth century and into the twentieth. Eternal rewards and punishments in a life after death are assumed without question throughout the Readers; but instant earthly rewards and punishments are usually found as well. The subject of this tale is merely one of the earliest and brightest examples of those boys (and occasionally girls) who receive instant gratification for having acted virtuously.

pass-ed. She did not say a-ny thing to the boy then, but let him go a-way.

The next day she sent for him, and when he came, she said to him, ".Well, my lit-tle friend, why did you not take my watch yes-ter-day?" The lit-tle sweep then fell up-on his knees and told the la-dy all a-bout it.

Now, as the lit-tle sweep did not steal the gold watch, nor tell a-ny sto-ries a-bout it, the la-dy let him stay and live in her house. For ma-ny years she sent him to school, and when he grew up, he be-came a good man, and nev-er for-got the com-mand-ment which says, "Thou shalt not steal."

Had he ta-ken the la-dy's watch, he would have sto-len. Then he would have been sent to jail.

Let no lit-tle boy or girl ev-er take things with-out leave, for it is steal-ing; and they who steal are thieves.

You can not steal the small-est pin, with-out its be-ing a sin, nor with-out be-ing seen by that eye which nev-er sleeps.

Although the moral is quite clear as it appears in this 1844 version, earlier editions stress the point even more vividly. Until 1844, for instance, after reiterating the point about God's omniscience, the lesson closed: "It is by stealing small things that children become robbers, and have to be put in prison."

18

LESSON LV.

bush   eŭn′ning   plāce   shōw

find   brō′ken   ō′ver   brĭng

a ḡain′ (a ḡĕn′)   fàs′ten (fàs′n)

"Come here, Rose. Look down
into this bush."

"O Willie! a bird's nest! What

FAIRLY EXTENSIVE REVISIONS OF THE McGUFFEYS HAD OCCURRED IN 1844 and 1857, with some minor changes in individual texts at other times, but the revision of 1879 was probably the most sweeping in scope. Pressured by increased competition—particularly from the Appleton Readers—the publishers of the McGuffeys hired a team of educators to revise the series, and then commissioned illustrations from the best artists and engravers. The result, with only minimal modifications in 1920, is essentially the same edition still being printed today.

The illustration here, representative of the new prints introduced in 1879, reflects the more sophisticated photo-engraving process not previously available. Also, it is signed—both by the engraver, Harley, and the artist, H. F. Farney.

ALTHOUGH THIS LESSON AND ITS CONTINUATION WERE WRITTEN *specifically for the 1879/1920 editions, they bear a close relationship to earlier lessons (used from 1836 until 1857) in the* Second Reader. *The topic was clearly one of McGuffey's personal concerns, present in many of the early lessons. But note the markedly different tone and approach in such earlier treatments as:*

> *God takes care of birds. Not a sparrow falls to the ground without his care. He has forbidden us to rob bird's nests. Let us not disobey him.*

and

> *. . . who can describe her distress, when she returns to feed her helpless charge, and spread over them her sheltering wings! How will she complain, in a mournful song, of the injustice and cruelty of the boy who has robbed her of all that was dear to her!*

cunning, little eggs! May we take it, and show it to mother?"

"What would the old bird do, Rose, if she should come back and not find her nest?"

"Oh, we would bring it right back, Willie!"

"Yes; but we could not fasten it in its place again. If the wind should blow it over, the eggs would get broken."

LESSON LVI.

strŏng round drȳ bĭll wõrked
sĕndṣ c̶lạwṣ flĭt Gŏd sprĭng

"How does the bird make the nest so strong, Willie?"

"The mother bird has her bill and her claws to work with, but she would not know how to make the nest if God did not teach her. Do you see what it is made of?"

"Yes, Willie, I see some horse-hairs and some dry grass. The old bird must have worked hard to find all the hairs, and make them into such a pretty, round nest."

"Shall we take the nest, Rose?"

"Oh no, Willie! We must not take it; but we will come and look at it again, some time."

SLATE WORK.

God made the little birds to sing.
And flit from tree to tree;
'Tis He who sends them in the spring
To sing for you and me.

The slate work exercises were not introduced until 1879, when some of the regular lessons were also produced in written script. The style here (a reprint of the 1920 edition) represents a change throughout the edition from the more flourishing Spencerian style of the late nineteenth century.

Second Reader

The dating of the creation here is based approximately upon the calculations of the Irish prelate James Ussher (1581-1656), who had used biblical chronology to date the moment of Creation in 4,004 B.C. This date was so commonly accepted that mathematics textbooks in McGuffey's era often included such problems as "How many minutes have passed since the creation of the world?"

The McGuffey Readers *continued to employ Bishop Ussher's date from the first edition in 1836 through the 1850's—despite the new geological hypotheses of Sir Charles Lyell and the discoveries of the bones of prehistoric monsters. After Darwin's* Origin of The Species *(1859), however, a modification became necessary. So, in the 1865 edition the reference to "Six thousand years ago" became merely "Many thousand years ago . . . ." And in 1879, the entire lesson was silently removed from the series.*

LESSON XLIV.
How the World was Made.

1. When we look on the pleasant earth, we see the green grass and the gay flowers. We look around us and see the tall trees and the lofty hills. Between them rolls the bright river, and down their sides flow the clear streams.

2. If we raise our eyes when the sky is clear, we look through the light thin air away to where the bright sun is placed, that shines down upon our world to give it light and to make it pleasant.

3. These things were not always so. Six thousand years ago there was no pleasant earth; and then the bright sun was not made. But the Great God lived then, and there never was a time when he did not live.

4. When the time came that the Creator was pleased to make this world, he made it all out of nothing. When our world was first created, it had nothing beautiful upon it; but it was all dark and empty. When God wanted light, he said, "Let there be light, and there was light." God made the air that spreads all around our earth. He made the grass to grow, the lovely flowers, the useful herbs, and all the trees that bear the delicious fruit.

5. After all these things were made, the earth was silent as the grave. There were no cattle to eat the grass, or birds, or the smallest insect to fly through the air. When the fourth day came, He made the glorious sun to shine by day, and the moon and stars to give light by night. When the fourth day ended, the sun set upon a

silent world. And when the fair moon arose and the stars shone in the sky, there was not a man living on all the earth to behold them.

6. The next day came, and the waters brought forth fish, the birds flew through the soft air, and sung among the trees. On the sixth day, God created the beasts of the field: and last of all, he made man in his own image, and breathed into him the breath of life, and man became a living soul.

QUESTIONS.—1. What do we see as we look around us? 2. Were these always so? 3. How long is it since the earth was made? 4. By whom was the earth made? 5. What was made on the fourth day? 6. What on the fifth? 7. What on the sixth? 8. What was last made? 9. What is the nobler part of creation? 10. Why is man more noble than the beasts and the birds? 11. For what should man use these powers?

earth	tall	light	a-round	pleas-ed
look	trees	make	loft-y	emp-ty
green	hills	world	riv-er	want-ed

thous-and	small-est	wa-ters
cre-a-ted	glo-ri-ous	liv-ing
flow-ers	be-hold	breath-ed

LESSON XLV.
The Bear in a Stage Coach.

1. Two travelers set out from their inn in London, early on a December morning. It was dark as pitch; and one of the travelers not feeling very sleepy, and wishing to talk a little, endeavored to enter into conversation with his neighbor.

2. He accordingly began: "A very dark morning, sir." "Shocking cold weather for traveling." "Slow going in these heavy roads, sir."

THE POINTED QUESTIONS FOLLOWING EACH LESSON HAD SEVERAL objectives. Most obviously, of course, they attempted to insure that the student had not only read the passage, but read it with comprehension. Also they served as a strong reinforcement of the lesson's moral and/or religious application, removing what little doubt a slow reader might have had. But in addition, they made the teacher's job a little easier— particularly since many teachers in one-room schoolhouses had to use their older students extensively to supervise the younger pupils' recitations.

One of McGuffey's original selections, this fable appeared with essentially no changes from 1836 until the 1879 revision, when it was removed. Both the story and the illustration here (from the 1841 edition) are British in origin. A complete Americanization of the lesson would have altered corn *to read* wheat, *but this was seldom done—even with lessons where the word caused significant confusion. There was usually no footnote, for instance, to accompany Keats's famous description of the biblical Ruth standing "in tears amid the alien corn." Nor is annotation provided for Thomas Hood's takeoff on Keats's line: "She stood breast-high amid the corn."*

The story goes that one nineteenth-century Indiana lad, when asked to paraphrase this line, sensibly concluded that Ruth was a lonely giantess.

QUESTIONS. 1. Why is it dangerous to hang on behind a carriage? 2. Why is it unkind? 3. What anecdotes are told in this lesson? 4. What is the Golden Rule? 5. In what book do you find this rule?

LESSON XXXI.

corn	young	cous'-ins	reap'-ers
hear	field	un'-cles	crea'-tures
reap	brood	al'-most	neg-lect'
fail	flight	ab'-sence	neigh'-bors
next	chirp	be-lieve'	kins'-men
work	fright	re-solves'	farm'-er
ones	friends	for'-ward	our-selves'

THE LARK AND THE FARMER.

1. An old lark once had a nest of young ones in a field of corn which was almost ripe. She was rather afraid the reapers would be set to work before her lovely brood were fledged enough to be able to remove from the place.

2. One morning, therefore, before she took her flight, to seek for something to feed them with, " My dear little creatures," said she, " be sure that in my absence, you take the strictest notice of every word you hear, and do not fail to tell me as soon as I come home."

3. Sometime after she was gone, in came the owner of the field and his son. " Well, George," said he, " this corn, I think, is ripe enough to be cut down; so, to-morrow morning, go as soon as you can see, and desire our friends and neighbors to come and help us; and tell them that we will do as much for them, when they want us."

4. When the old lark came back to her nest, the young ones began to nestle and chirp about her: beg-

ging her, after what they had heard, to remove them as soon as she could.

5. "Hush!" said she, "hold your silly tongues; if the farmer depends upon his friends, and his neighbors, you may take my word for it, that his corn will not be reaped to-morrow." The next morning, therefore, she went out again, and left the same orders as before.

6. The owner of the field came soon after, to wait for those he had sent to; but the sun grew hot, and not a single man came to help him. "Why, then," said he to his son, "I'll tell you what, my boy; you see, those friends of ours have forgotten us, you must therefore run to your uncles and cousins, and tell them that I shall expect them to-morrow, early, to help us to reap."

7. Well, this also the young ones told their mother as soon as she came home; and in a sad fright they were. "Never mind it, children," said the old one; "for if that be all, you may take my word for it, that his brethren and kinsmen will not be so forward to assist him as he seems willing to believe. But mark,"

said she, " what you hear the next time ; and let me know without fail."

8. The old lark went abroad the next day as before, but when the poor farmer found that his kinsmen were as backward as his neighbors, " Why, then," said he, " since your uncles and cousins so neglect us, do you get," said he to his son, " a couple of good sickles against to-morrow morning, and we will reap the corn ourselves, my boy."

9. When the young ones told their mother this, she said, " Now, my little dears, we must indeed be gone : for when a man resolves to do his own work himself, you may then depend upon it that it will be done."

QUESTIONS. 1. Who had a nest of young ones ? 2. What did she say one morning ? 3. Who came to the field after she was gone ? 4. What did he say ? 5. What did the young birds then wish ? 6. Did the old bird think there was much danger ? 7. When did she think the corn would be reaped ? 8. What may we learn from this story ?

LESSON XXXII.

knew	po'-ny	gath'-er	qui'-et-ly
went	en-joy'	mead'-ow	how-ev'-er
reach	hal'-ter	whith'-er	re-mem'-ber
quite	bri'-dle	feed'-ing	sud'-den-ly
sieve	troub'-le	pranc'-ing	can'-ter-ing

HOW TO CATCH A PONY.

1. WILLY went to unfasten his pony ; but when he came to the tree to which he had tied him, he found that Coco had unfastened himself, and had gone prancing away, he knew not whither.

2. After hunting about for some time, he saw him at a distance, quietly feeding on the grass. Willy ran

LESSON LXIX.

Father William.

1. You are old, Father William, Theophilus cries,
    The few locks which are left you are gray :—
You appear, Father William, a healthy old man ;
    Now tell me the reason, I pray.

2. When I was a youth, Father William replied,
    I remembered that youth would fly fast ;
I abused not my health and my vigor at first,
    That I never might need them at last.

3. You are old, Father William, Theophilus said,
    And pleasures, with youth, pass away ;
And yet you repent not the days that are gone ;—
    Now tell me the reason, I pray.

4. When I was a youth, Father William replied,
    I remembered that youth could not last ;
I thought of the future, whatever I did,
    That I never might grieve for the past.

5. You are old, Father William, the young man still cries,
    And life is swift hastening away ;
You are cheerful, and love to converse upon death !
    Come tell me the reason, I pray.

6. I am cheerful, young man, Father William replied,
    Let the cause your attention engage ;
In the days of my youth I remembered my God !
    And he hath not forgotten my age.

QUESTIONS.—1. Who is it that speaks to Father William ?
2. What does he wish to know ? 3. How had the old gentleman preserved his health so well ? 4. What is it to abuse our health ? 5. Why was Father William so cheerful ? 6. What is it to remember God ?

death	cheer-ful	ap-pear	en-gage
young	con-verse	rea-son	a-way
youth	vig-or	health-y	a-bu-sed

Will-iam	at-ten-tion	re-pli-ed
The-oph-i-lus	for-got-ten	at-ten-tive
re-mem-ber-ed	meas-ures	what-ev-er

THIS ADAPTATION OF ROBERT SOUTHEY'S FAMILIAR VERSE WAS A standard in many American readers in the nineteenth century, but McGuffey used it only in the 1836, 1838, and 1841 editions. Although the publisher's editors took an increasingly active role in later revisions, McGuffey was still very much involved with the Readers *when "Father William" was first omitted, and he must have had a voice in the decision to drop it. No reason for its departure was ever given, but quite possibly it was removed because it was so easily parodied. Not the first, but certainly one of the more famous parodies of "Father William" is that by Lewis Carroll in* Alice in Wonderland, *which begins:*

"You are old, father William," the young man said,
"And your hair has become very white;
And yet you incessantly stand on your head—
Do you think, at your age, it is right?"

"In my youth," father William replied to his son,
"I feared it might injure the brain;
But, now that I'm perfectly sure I have none,
Why, I do it again and again."

WILLIAM HOLMES McGUFFEY APPARENTLY DID NOT POSSESS MUCH of a sense of humor, so moments consciously inviting laughter are rather rare in those Readers in which he had a hand. This is one of those moments. If the humor here seems rather cruel, we should remember that to the stern McGuffey such indolence was a legitimate target for derisive laughter.

QUESTIONS. 1. What animal did the tigers first attack? 2. What did the keeper try to do when he came in? 3. What did the tigress do then? 4. How was the keeper saved from the tigress? 5. What became of the tiger?

LESSON XL.

worse	les'-son	pock'-ets	Ken'-ne-bec
drone	for'-tune	quar'-rel	in'-do-lent
snail	fa'-ther	drawl'-ed	syl'-la-ble
chance	de-fine'	laugh'-ing	com'-i-cal
learn	an'-swer	scar'-let	nav'-i-ga-ble

THE IDLE SCHOOLBOY.

1. I WILL tell you about the laziest boy you ever heard of. He was indolent about every thing. When he played, the boys said he played as if the teacher told him to; and when he went to school, he went creeping along like a snail. The boy had sense enough; but he was too lazy to learn any thing.

2. When he spelled a word, he drawled out one syllable after another, as if he were afraid the syllables would quarrel, if he did not keep them a great ways apart. Once when he was reciting a lesson in geography, the teacher asked him, "What is said of Hartford?" He answered, "Hartford is a flourishing *comical* town."

3. He meant that it was "a flourishing *commercial* town;" but he was such a drone, that he never knew what he was about. When asked how far the river Kennebec was navigable, he said, "it was navigable for *boots* as far as Waterville." The boys all laughed, and the teacher could not help laughing too. The idle boy colored like scarlet.

4. "I say it is so in my book," said he; and when one of the boys showed him the book, and pointed

to the place, where it was said that the Kennebec was navigable for *boats* as far as Waterville, he stood with his hands in his pockets, and his mouth open, as if he could not understand what they were all laughing at.

5. Another day, when the boys were reciting a lesson from the dictionary, he made a mistake worse than all the rest. The word A-CEPH'-A-LOUS, was printed with syllables divided as you see; the definition of the word was, "without a head."

6. The idle boy had often been laughed at for being so slow in saying his lessons; this time he thought he would be very quick and smart; so he spelled the word before the teacher had a chance to put it out. And how do you think he spelled it?

7. "A-C-E-P-H, ACEPH," said he "a louse without a head." The boys laughed at him so much about this, that he was obliged to leave school. The teacher said, "he was a drone, and the working bees stung him out of the hive."

8. You can easily guess what luck this idle boy had. His father tried to give him a good education, but he *would* be a dunce; not because he was a fool, but because he was too lazy to give his attention to anything. He had some fortune left him; but he was too lazy to take care of it, and now he goes about the streets, begging his bread.

9. And now, he often wishes that he had been more attentive to his books, when young; but he cannot live over again the time he has spent so badly, and he must be a poor, ignorant fellow for the rest of his life.

QUESTIONS. 1. What is this lesson about? 2. How did the idle boy play? 3. What did he say about Hartford? 4. What did he say about the Kennebec river? 5. How did he spell and define 'acephalous?' 6. Can you spell it rightly? 7. What became of the lazy boy?

This lesson—a favorite of older McGuffey fans—was among those dropped in 1879, perhaps because of an increasing number of drones in American society, but probably because it was more openly didactic than the later editors desired. As in the case of such positive examples as "The Little Chimney Sweep," this poor dunce receives his deserts quickly and inevitably.

Not added until the 1844 edition, "The Little Lord and the Farmer" remained part of the series for over thirty years, moving from the Second *to the* Third Reader *in 1857. Its origin is clearly British, but it had obvious appeal to an American audience.*

LESSON LXXV.

what	sil'-ly	po-lite'	vin'-e-gar
shoes	sau'-cy	tumb'-led	en-ra'-ged
brook	a-way'	down'-cast	a-sham'-ed
frock	hast'-y	stur'-dy	prof'-fer-ed
field	re-ply'	child'-ish	man'-ful-ly
choose	be-yond'	lord'-ship	gen'-tle-man

THE LITTLE LORD AND THE FARMER.

1. A LITTLE lord engaged in play,
Carelessly threw his ball away;
So far beyond the brook it flew,
His lordship knew not what to do.

2. By chance, there passed a farmer's boy,
Whistling a tune in childish joy;
His frock was patched, and his hat was old,
But his manly heart was very bold.

3. "You little chap, pick up my ball!"
His saucy lordship loud did call;
He thought it useless to be polite,
To one, whose clothes were in such a plight.

4. "Do it yourself, for want of me,"
The boy replied right manfully;
Then quietly he passed along,
Whistling aloud his fav'rite song.

5. His little lordship furious grew,—
For he was proud and hasty too;
"I'll break your bones," he rudely cries,
While fire flashed from both his eyes.

6. Now heedless quite which way he took,
He tumbled plump into the brook;

And, as he fell, he lost his bat,
And next, he dropped his beaver hat.

7. " Come, help me out," enraged he cried ;
   But the sturdy farmer thus replied ;
   " Alter your tone, my little man,
   And then I'll help you all I can."

8. " There are few things I would not dare,
   For gentlemen who speak me fair ;
   But for rude words, I do not choose
   To wet my feet, and soil my shoes."

9. " Please help me, then," his lordship said ;
   " I'm sorry I was so ill-bred."
   " 'Tis all forgot," replied the boy,
   And gave his hand with honest joy.

10. The proffered aid his lordship took,
   And soon came safely from the brook
   His looks were downcast and aside,
   For he felt ashamed of his silly pride.

This fine lesson in pride deflated has more than its share of class-consciousness and anti-urban sentiments as well. In fact, given the predominantly rural audience of the McGuffey Readers, *the selection (ostensibly attacking the sin of pride, while implicitly appealing to the pride of the farm boys) was both canny and—probably unconsciously—ironic.*

11. The farmer brought his ball and bat,
    And wiped the wet from his dripping hat;
    And mildly said, as he went away,
    "Remember the lesson you've learned to-day."

12. "Be kind to all you chance to meet,
    In field, or lane, or crowded street;
    Anger and pride are both unwise,
    Vinegar never catches flies."

QUESTIONS. 1. How did the little lord speak to the boy? 2. What was the boy's answer? 3. What advice did the farmer give the lord as he was leaving?

LESSON LXXVI.

coat	sec'-ond	piec'-es	of-fi'-cers
dream	ru'-ler	treat'-ed	char'-i-ot
meant	col'-ors	show'-ed	Pha'-ra-oh
young	pris'-on	mer'-chant	re-bu'-ked
would	fam'-ine	young'-er	Ben'-ja-min

How many regular sounds has the vowel O? Which sound of O is heard in *sec-ond?* Which in *do-min-ion? Pha-ra-oh* is pronounced as if it were spelled *Fa'-ro.*

STORY OF JOSEPH.

1. JACOB had twelve sons. He loved one of them very much, and made for him a coat of many colors. But Joseph's brethren hated him, because he was the favorite of their father.

2. One day, when he came to them, as they were keeping their flocks in the field, they took him and sold him for a slave, to some merchants who were going down into Egypt. And they sold him to one of the king's officers in Egypt.

3. Whilst he was in this great man's house, he was falsely accused, and thrown into prison. Soon after

6. Then let your little heart, my love,
   Its grateful homage pay
To that kind Friend, who, from above,
   So gently guides you every day.

QUESTIONS.— Who made all things? Who supplies all our wants? Should we not remember God, who has been so kind? What is *"paying homage?"*

ARTICULATION.

In this and the succeeding exercises, utter the combined consonants as *one sound*, and give the *sound*, and not the *name*, of each single letter and dipthong, thus: not be–el–a, but bl-a, bla; not be–er–a, but br-a, bra; not be–er–a–de, but br-a-d, brad; not be–el–o–i, but bl-oi, bloi. Pronounce each syllable *forcibly* and *distinctly*. The teacher should go through the whole, and the pupil should follow him, step by step, until he can perform the exercise alone.

Bl. bla, ble, bli, blo, blu, bloi, blou.
Br. bra, bre, bri, bro, bru, broi, brou.
    brad, bled, brik, blab, bred, cabl, fabl.

LESSON XX.

done	laugh	Su'-san	a-gain'	av'-e-nue
pain	month	liv'-ed	peo'-ple	pro-vi'-ded
bring	throw	un-tie'	sur'-geon	feath'-er-ed
spilt	should	be-gan'	sprain'-ed	gen'-tle-man
lives	sport	no -ses	sprawl'-ing	fright'-en-ed
bleed	be-lieve'	go'-ing	thought'-less	dan'-de-li-ons

The Thoughtless Boys.

1. WILLIAM and Edward were two clever little boys, and not at all ill-natured, but they were very fond of sport, and they did not care whether people were hurt or not, provided they could have a laugh.

IN THE EARLIEST EDITIONS OF THE READERS THERE WERE VERY FEW exercises of this type furnished, and those few appeared in the prefatory pages. By the middle of the century, however, such articulation exercises were integrated evenly throughout the books. This particular set appeared in the 1853 edition.

2. One fine summer's day, when they had finished their lessons, they took a walk through the long grass in the meadows. William began to blow the dandelions, and the feathered seeds flew in the wind like arrows.

3. But Edward said, "Let us tie the grass. It will be very good sport to tie the long grass over the path, and to see people tumble upon their noses as they run along, and do not suspect any thing of the matter."

4. So they tied it in several places, and then hid themselves to see who would pass. And presently a farmer's boy came running along, and down he tumbled, and lay sprawling on the ground; however, he had nothing to do but to get up again; so there was not much harm done this time.

5. Then there came Susan the milk-maid tripping along with her milk upon her head, and singing like a lark. When her foot struck against the place where the grass was tied, down she came with her pail rattling about her shoulders, and her milk was all spilt upon the ground.

6. Then Edward said, "Poor Susan! I think I

should not like to be served so myself; let us untie the grass." "No, no," said William, "if the milk is spilt, there are some pigs that will lick it up; let us have some more fun: I see a man running along as if he were running for a wager. I am sure he will fall upon his nose."

7. And so the man did. William and Edward both laughed; but when the man did not get up again, they began to be frightened, and went to him, and asked him if he was hurt.

8. "O masters," said the man, "some thoughtless boys, I do not know who they are, have tied the grass together over the path, and as I was running with all my might, it threw me down, and I have sprained my ankle so, that I shall not be able to walk for a month."

9. "I am very sorry," said Edward; "do you feel much pain?" "O yes," said the man, "but that I do not mind; but I was going in a great hurry to bring a surgeon, to bleed a gentleman who is in a fit, and they say he will die if he is not bled."

10. Then Edward and William both turned pale, and said, "Where does the surgeon live? We will go for him; we will run all the way." "He lives at the next town," said the man, "but it is a mile off, and you can not run so fast as I should have done; you are only boys."

11. "Where must we tell the surgeon to come?" said William. "He must come to the white house, at the end of the long chestnut avenue," said the man; "he is a very good gentleman that lives there."

12. "Oh, it is our dear father! it is our dear father!" said the two boys. "Oh, father will die! what must we do?"

13. I do not know whether their father died or not; I believe he got well again; but I am sure

The moral lessons in prudence and consideration for others are here reinforced strongly by an almost predictable twist of fate that places the life of the boys' father in jeopardy. Like so many lessons in the Readers, *this one unequivocally emphasizes the principle that one's actions usually have immediate consequences.*

37

of one thing, that Edward and William never tied the grass to throw people down again as long as they lived.

QUESTIONS.—What is this story about? What did William and Edward do? Was this right? What was the consequence? When we begin to do mischief, can we tell where we shall stop? What did these boys learn from this occurrence?

LESSON XXI.

aim	swam	spear	tongue	twen'-ty	sur-rounds'
oil	yields	dives	midst	sur'-face	knock'-ed
air	whale	smell	throat	har-poon'	di-rec'-tion
float	beast	watch	thrown	pic'-ture	di-rect'-ly
foes	large	casks	an'-gry	blub'-ber	un-pleas'-ant
state	great	foam	fu'-ry	catch'-ing	dan'-ger-ous

Whale Catching.

1. A WHALE is a large fish. There is no beast so large as a whale; they have been seen of so large a size that they look like land, as they float on the surface of the sea.

2. They have a large mouth, but a small throat, so that they can not eat large fish. The tongue is a lump of fat, which yields a great deal of oil; their eyes are small and have lids to them; they have fins and a large tail, which they lash when in a rage or pain, and the sea is then all foam for some way round.

3. Men kill whales with a sharp iron spear or harpoon. This they throw at the whale with great force. When the whale is struck, it dives down into the sea, quite out of sight; but it soon comes up to the top for want of air.

4. The men are on the watch for this; and as soon as they see it rise, they strike it with their harpoons till it dies.

5. The men tie ropes to their harpoons, which

are made fast to the boat, so that they may not be lost when they miss their aim. When the whale is dead, it is cut up; and those parts which yield the oil are put into casks.

6. Directly under the skin, lies the blubber or fat. This surrounds the whole body, and is from ten to twenty inches thick. In its fresh state it has no unpleasant smell. The oil which we burn in our lamps is made from this.

7. Catching whales is very dangerous. Sometimes the whales get angry and plunge about with great fury. In the picture you see the whale has thrown the boat into the air, and the men have been knocked in every direction.

8. A whale with one of its young, was once left by the tide close to the shore, where the sea was not deep enough for them to get out. The men who saw them, took their harpoons and got into their boats to go and kill them; for they were a rich prize.

9. The whales were soon much hurt; but the old one was strong, and with one bold push got clear of her foes, and swam out to the deep sea.

10. She had not long been there, when she

*In the early editions of the **Readers** one finds a number of factual and even technical accounts of natural objects and events. It should be remembered that the **McGuffeys** served as repositories for much information other than literature in the days when a student's textbooks consisted only of a reader, a speller, and a math book. As the century progressed, textbooks in history, geography, etc., became more common, and the need for the **Readers'** inclusiveness diminished. This particular selection was retired from use in 1857.*

40

found her poor young one was not with her. She swam back into the midst of her foes to seek it; and they both had the good fate to be borne back by the flow of the tide, to their safe and wide home in the deep sea.

QUESTIONS.—Where do whales live? How large is the whale? What do men use to kill whales with? What do we use that comes from the whale? What story is told of a whale?

ARTICULATION.

Dl. dla, dle, dli, dlo, dlu, dloi, diou.
Dr. dra, dre, dri, dro, dru, droi, drou.
drab, drill, dred, dry, droll, dreer, ladl.

LESSON XXII.

wear	poor	noise	girls	peo'-ple	cot'-tage
wait	knows	break	thank	par'-ents	re-mem'-bers
tear	coach	deal	speaks	serv'-ants	veg'-et-a-bles

The Rich Boy.

1. THE good boy whose parents are rich, has fine clothes to wear; he rides on a pretty horse, or in a coach, and has servants to wait upon him. But, for all that, he does not think that he is better than other boys.

2. He knows that rich people are not all good; and that God gives a great deal of money to some persons, in order that they may assist those who are poor.

3. He speaks kindly to all his father's servants, and does not call them to wait upon him, when he sees that they are busy; and he always remembers to thank them for what they do for him.

4. He never gives them any trouble that he can

avoid. He is careful not to make a noise in the house, or to break any thing, or to put it out of its place, or to tear his clothes. When any of the servants are sick, he often thinks of them; he likes to go and see them, and ask how they do.

5. He likes to go with his parents to visit poor people, in their cottages, and gives them all the money he can spare. He often says: "If I were a man, and had plenty of money, I think no person who lived near me should be very poor.

6. "I would build a great many pretty cottages for poor people to live in, and every cottage should have a garden and a field, in order that the people might have vegetables, and might keep a cow, and a pig, and some chickens; they should not pay me much rent. I would give clothes to the boys and girls who had no money to buy clothes with, and they should all learn to read and write, and be very good."

QUESTIONS.—Do riches make one person better than another? What does? How does a good boy treat the servants? How does he feel toward poor people? What does he think he would do, if he were a man?

LESSON XXIII.

does	word	swear	steal	or'-der	fin'-ish-ed
lose	spare	wants	should	ac-counts'	em-ploy'-ed
work	write	bread	streets	naught-y	hap'-pi-er
road	store	fight	mon'-ey	reck'-on	gen'-tle-men

The Poor Boy.

1. THE good boy whose parents are poor, rises very early in the morning; and, all day long, does as much as he can to help his father and mother.

2. When he goes to school he walks quickly, and does not lose time on the road. "My parents," says he, "are very good, to save some of

PRACTICAL ECONOMICS CONCERNED McGUFFEY A GREAT DEAL, AND (as both this lesson and the next demonstrate) it is often incorporated into the reading. Benevolence—always a favorite virtue in the McGuffeys—becomes the primary obligation of the rich boy. Humble acceptance of one's situation, whatever its state, is pretty much left to the poor.

their money, in order that I may learn to read and write; but they can not give much, nor can they spare me long: therefore I must learn as fast as I can; if any body has time to lose, I am sure I have not.

3. "I should be very sorry when I am a man, not to know how to read in the Bible, and other good books; and when I leave my parents, not to be able to read their letters, and to write them word where I am, and how I do.

4. "I must also learn accounts; for when I grow up I shall have many things to reckon, about my work, and what I buy: I shall perhaps have bills to make out, as my father has; and perhaps I shall be employed in a store."

5. When he has finished his lessons, he does not stay to play, but runs home; he wants to see his father and mother, and to help them.

6. He often sees naughty boys in the streets, who fight, and steal, and do many bad things; and he hears them swear, and call names, and tell lies; but he does not like to be with them, for fear they should make him as bad as they are; and lest any body who sees him with them should think that he too is naughty.

7. When he is at home, he is very industrious. He takes care of the little children, weeds his father's garden, and hoes, and rakes it, and sows seed in it.

8. Sometimes he goes with his father to work; then he is very glad; and though he is but a little fellow, he works very hard, almost like a man.

9. When he comes home to dinner, he says, "How hungry I am! and how good this bread is, and this bacon! Indeed, I think every thing we have is very good. I am glad I can work: I hope that I shall soon be able to earn all my clothes, and my food too."

10. When he sees little boys and girls riding on pretty horses, or in coaches, or walking with ladies and gentlemen, and having on very fine clothes, he does not envy them, nor wish to be like them.

11 He says, "I have often been told, and I have read, that it is God who makes some poor, and others rich; that the rich have many troubles which we know nothing of; and that the poor, if they are but good, may be very happy: indeed, I think that when I am good, nobody can be happier than I am."

QUESTIONS.—What is this lesson about? What feelings does he have toward his parents? What does he do when he has finished his lessons? What does he do when he is at home? To whom should we look as the giver of all our blessings? What is better than riches?

ARTICULATION.

Bw.   bwă, bwē, bwĭ, bwŏ, bwŭ, bwoi, bwou.
Dw.   dwă, dwē, dwĭ, dwŏ, dwŭ, dwoi, dwou.

LESSON XXIV.

fall	coat	beast	un-less'	serv'-i-ces
door	hurt	tricks	at-tract'	af-fec'-tion
took	when	strange	cham'-ber	com-pan'-ion
room	meet	suf'-fer	anx'-ious	im-port'-ant
once	tried	ceil'-ing	thou'-sand	suf-fi'-cient
head	drive	bark'-ing	per-sua'-ded	op-por-tu'-ni-ty

The Little Dog Fido.

1. A LITTLE dog was once very anxious to obtain the favor of his master, and tried all the little arts in his power to attract his notice. Whenever his master came near the house, Fido, for that was the name of the dog, would run to meet him, lick

CLASS AND ECONOMIC DISTINCTIONS ARE RECOGNIZED HERE, BUT ANY *serious discussion of them is avoided or short-circuited by citing the Deity. That economic and class inequities exist is not McGuffey's point here; the emphasis remains on the moral and religious elements of life.*

43

THIS FAMOUS ANECDOTE ABOUT GEORGE WASHINGTON WAS THE imaginative product of Mason Locke Weems (c. 1760–1825), an Episcopalian clergyman who was one of America's most talented and colorful rogues. Parson Weems, as he is better known, appears never to have had a regular charge, although he claimed to have been rector of the Mount Vernon parish (a nonexistent parish) before the Revolutionary War. In his later years he was a traveling entertainer, preacher, and bookseller in the South, often promoting books he had written. A few of his many titles are God's Revenge Against **Gambling**, *a Life of Benjamin Franklin with Essays, a Life of William Penn, and a curious book entitled Hymen's Recruiting Serjeant (a serious attempt to encourage marriage and the raising of little Christians to populate the waiting wilderness of America—an entertaining piece of reading today). Many of his writings—including the supposedly factual biographies—are largely fictional.*

LESSON LXI.

nail	cof'-fin	a-void'	re-ceive'	he-ro'-ic
eyes	in-vite'	es-teem'	ques'-tion	qual'-i-ty
dread	ly'-ing	lone'-ly	chop'-ping	fa'-vor-ite
truth	au'-thor	prat'-tle	con'-scious	gen'-er-al
pains	pleas'-ed	con-ceal'	thou'-sand	ac'-ci-dent
youth	hatch'-et	brave'-ly	trans'-ports	re-la'-tions

George and the Hatchet.

1. NEVER, perhaps, did a parent take more pains, than did the father of General Washington to inspire his son George with an early love of TRUTH. "Truth, George," said he, "is the most lovely quality of youth. I would ride fifty miles, my son, to see the boy whose heart is so honest, and whose lips so pure, that we may depend on every word he says.

2. "How lovely does such a child appear in the eyes of every body! His parents dote on him. His relations glory in him. They praise him before their children, and wish them to follow his example. They often invite him to visit them, and when he comes, they receive him with joy, and treat him as one whose visits they esteem the greatest favor.

3. "But oh! George, how far from this is the case with the boy who is given to lying! Good people avoid him wherever he goes; and parents dread to see him in company with their children.

4. "Oh, George, my son, rather than see you come to this pass, dear as you are to me, gladly would I assist to nail you up in your little coffin, and follow you to your grave.

5. "Hard, indeed, it would be to me to give up my son, whose feet are always so ready to run about with me, and whose smiling face and sweet prattle make so large a part of my happi-

ness. But still I would give him up, rather than see him a common liar."

6. "Father," said George, with tears in his eyes, "do I ever tell lies?"

7. "No, George; I thank God you do not, my son; and I rejoice in the hope you never will. Whenever, by accident, you do any thing wrong, which must often be the case, as you are but a little boy yet, you must never say what is not true, to conceal it, but come bravely up, my son, like a little man, and tell me of it."

8. When George was about six years old, he was made the owner of a little hatchet, with which he was much pleased, and went about chopping every thing that came in his way. One day, when in the garden, he unluckily tried the edge of his hatchet on the body of a fine young English cherry-tree, which he barked so badly as to destroy it.

9. The next morning, the old gentleman, finding out what had befallen his favorite tree, came into the house, and with much warmth, asked who was the author of the mischief. Nobody could tell him any thing about it. At this moment, in came George with his hatchet.

Best known of Weems's many books was, of course, his Life of Washington *(1800), which went through more than 70 editions by mid-nineteenth century. Parson Weems was the myth-maker of the popular Washington, with such famous fabrications as the cherry-tree incident (which, it should be noted, did not appear in the* Life *until 1806, in the fifth edition). This is only one of several Weems-created anecdotes concerning the "father of our country"—all of them very popular in the nineteenth century, nearly all of them now viewed as apocryphal.*

Even this favorite passage, an original McGuffey selection, failed to make it past the editors of the 1879 edition. After over fifty years of service in the Readers *(having been moved up to the* Third Reader *in 1857), Parson Weems's famous tree and hatchet were retired.*

10. "George," said his father, "do you know who killed that fine cherry-tree yonder, in the garden?" This was a hard question; George was silent for a moment; and then, looking at his father, his young face bright with conscious love of truth, he bravely cried out, "I can't tell a lie, father; you know I can't tell a lie. I cut it with my hatchet."

11. "Come to my arms, my dearest boy!" cried his father, in transports; "come to my arms! you killed my cherry-tree, George, but you have now paid me for it a thousand-fold. Such proof of heroic truth in my son, is of more value than a thousand trees, though they were all of the purest gold."

QUESTIONS.—What is this story about? Who was George Washington? What did Mr. Washington teach his son? Did George attempt to conceal what he had done? What should we always do when we have done wrong? How did George's father feel toward him when he had confessed his fault? What did he say to him?

ARTICULATION.

Mt. ămt, ĕmt, ĭmt, ŏmt, ŭmt, oimt, oumt.
Mts. ămts, ĕmts, ĭmts, ŏmts, ŭmts, oimts, oumts.

LESSON LXII.

dai'-ly	heav'-en	por'-tion	tempt-a'-tion
hum'-ble	hal'-low	king'-dom	com-pas'-sion
par'-dons	boun'-ty	weak'-ness	trans-gres'-sions

The Lord's Prayer.

1. Our Father in heaven,
   We hallow thy name!
   May thy kingdom holy
   On earth be the same!

They found a great deal of gold and silver. They used the natives of the country very cruelly, in hopes that they would tell them of still more gold and silver than they had found.

QUESTIONS. — What is this story about? Where was Columbus born? What did he wish to do? What kings would not assist him? What did the king of Spain do for Columbus? What land did Columbus first discover? What did he discover on his second voyage? How did the Spaniards treat the natives of South America?

ARTICULATION.

Sp. spa, spe, spi, spo, spu, spoi, spou,
asp, esp, isp, osp, usp, oisp, ousp.

Sk. ska, ske, ski, sco, scu, skoi, skou,
ask, esc, isc, osk, usk, oisc, ousk.

LESSON LXXX.

ma′-ny	fight′-ing	en′-vi-ed	Vir-gin′-i-a
pass′-ed	Will′-iam	vil′-la-ges	A-mer′-i-ca
set′-tlers	hard′-ships	cov′-er-ed	Phil-a-del′-phi-a
hun′-ger	James′-town	cul′-ti-va-ted	Penn-syl-va′-ni-a

Settlement of America.

1. AFTER the discoveries of Columbus, the kings and people of other countries sent out ships to America, till, in time, it was all known to the people of Europe. People came from different countries of Europe to different parts of America.

2. They found neither towns, nor pleasant fields, nor fine gardens; they found only woods, and wild men, and wild animals. The men they called Indians, because they looked a little like the people who live in India, a country in Asia. There were

THIS LESSON IN THE 1853 EDITION APPEARED BETWEEN OTHER LESSONS entitled "Story About Columbus" and "The American Revolution." Thus in a few pages, McGuffey provided a capsule history from the discovery and colonization of America through the end of the eighteenth century. In contrast to the jingoistic passages in many of the competing textbooks, the McGuffey lesson is remarkably balanced, objective in both content and tone.

a great many Indians then; but now there are but very few.

3. As the white people increased, the Indians were driven away or killed; often with rum. The Spaniards were not only cruel to the poor Indians, but cruel to Columbus, who discovered America; and they put him in prison, and let him die of want.

4. After this, many people came over from Europe to live in America. And in the year 1607, they came from England and settled at Jamestown, in Virginia. The Indians killed many. The settlers had many hardships to endure, and in six months, only a few men were left out of six hundred.

5. Many went to New England to live. Pennsylvania was settled by Swedes, in 1627, and William Penn came here in 1681, one hundred and sixty-five years ago. He came to this country, and a great many more, who were Quakers, came with him, because they could not worship God in their own country.

6. Very little good is ever got by fighting, and William Penn did not wish to fight with the

Indians, and take their land from them, though the king of England had granted it to him. He came without any army, and a great many Indian chiefs met him under a large elm tree, near Philadelphia.

7. He bought as much land from them as he wanted. This was much better than to try to drive them away or kill them, or make them drunk with rum, and then cheat them, as many white men have since done.

8. Many of the first settlers, in some parts of our country, died of hunger, and more were murdered by the Indians, and all had much suffering to endure. Then the dark forests covered the land, and the savage Indians hunted the deer, and danced around their fires, and sung their songs of war.

9. But we can now look around on our rich, cultivated, sunny hills, covered with pasture, and waving with golden grain. We live in splendid cities. Beautiful villages are spread over our country, thick as the stars in an evening sky.

10. After our fathers had passed through a great many trials, the Lord blessed their labors and smiled upon them; then there were some who envied them, and the king of England began to oppress them. There were many good people in England who loved the Americans, and who did not wish to do them any harm.

11. But there were others there who did not know or care any thing about our country, and thought the people here were almost the same as Indians.

QUESTIONS.—How was America first settled? Why were the natives of America called Indians? What was the first settlement in North America? What has been our treatment of the Indians? What did William Penn do? What did our forefathers endure? Who brought them through their trials and protected them?

The role of New England in the colonization of America seems rather consciously downplayed in this account. This should not be too surprising, since the folks in the West, especially in Cincinnati, distrusted the intellectual dominance of New England. Such curt treatment here, however, was probably the result of a desire to give more attention to the laudatory example of William Penn. Even in historical lessons, the moral and religious objectives remain dominant.

Inspirational verses, such as this selection from the 1857 edition, appear steadily in the McGuffeys *from the first edition to the present. Usually the author is unidentified, but legend (supported by quality, perhaps) suggests that at least some of the verses appearing in the early editions were written by McGuffey's neighbors and friends in Cincinnati and Oxford, Ohio.*

The God pictured throughout the Readers *is unquestionably omnipotent, usually benevolent (especially as the century progressed), but always omniscient. The controlling metaphor in much of this verse (as well as many of the prose selections) is God as an all-seeing eye, recording all moral indiscretions.*

50

LESSON XXXVII.

fear	paths	fields	an-gels	pray-er
ones	brood	pow-er	re-gard	help-less
flood	storm	clothes	cho-sen	spar-row
pours	Christ	ten-der	ob-jects	chil-dren
hours	guides	naught	a-broad	fond-ness
world	guards	ra-vens	heav-en	num-bers

FEAR NOT.

1. FEAR not, fear not, lit-tle ones;
    There is in heav-en an eye,
That looks with ten-der fond-ness down
    On all the paths you try.

2. 'T is He who guides the spar-row's wing,
    And guards her lit-tle brood;
Who hears the ra-vens when they cry,
    And gives them all their food.

3. 'T is He who clothes the fields with flow-ers,
    And pours the light a-broad;
'T is He who num-bers all your hours,
    Your Fa-ther and your God.

4. You are the cho-sen of his love,
    The ob-jects of his care;
And will he guide the help-less dove,
    And not re-gard your pray-er?

5. Then, fear not, fear not, lit-tle ones;
  There is in heav-en an eye,
That looks with ten-der fond-ness down
  On all the paths you try.

6 He'll keep you, when the storm is wild,
  And when the flood is near;
O trust him, trust him, as a child,
  And you have naught to fear.

---

1. A lit-tle child who loves to pray,
  And read his Bi-ble too,
Shall rise a-bove the sky one day,
  And sing as an-gels do;
Shall live in heav-en, that world a-bove,
Where all is joy, and peace, and love.

2. Look up, dear chil-dren, see that star,
  Which shines so bright-ly there;
But you shall bright-er shine by far,
  When in that world so fair;
A harp of gold you each shall have,
And sing the pow-er of Christ to save.

QUESTIONS.—Whose eye looks down upon us in love? How does God show his kindness? From what danger will he guard us, if we trust him? Who will rise above the sky and sing as angels? Of what will they sing?

This short verse is unusual not in its general didacticism, which it shares with much of the verse in the McGuffeys, but in its fairly literal location and description of heaven ("above the sky" and with "harps of gold"), and its specific reference to Christ. Religion in the McGuffey Readers may be confidently assumed to mean Christianity, and it is usually well within the Protestant tradition; but seldom is Christ mentioned specifically.

ARTICULATION.

In this and the succeeding exercises, utter the combined consonants as *one sound*, and give the *sound* and not the *name* of each single letter and dipthong, thus: not be–el–a, but bl–a, bla; not be–er–a, but br–a, bra; not be–er–a–de, but br–a–d, brad; not be–el–o–i, but bl–oi, bloi. The teacher should go through the whole, and the pupil should follow him, step by step, until he can perform the exercise alone.

Bl.   bla,   ble,   bli,   blo,   blu,   bloi,   blou.

Br.   bra,   bre,   bri,   bro,   bru,   broi,   brou.

brad,   bled,   brik,   blab,   bred,   cabl,   fabl.

LESSON LII.

lose	u-sed	will-ing	of-fend-ed
does	Sa-rah	com-fort	a-sha-med
place	se-cret	be-cause	else-where
wants	bor-row	thim-ble	de-pend-ed

A PLACE FOR EV-ER-Y THING.

Mary. I wish you would lend me your thim-ble, Sa-rah. I can nev-er find mine.

Sarah. And why can you not find it?

Mary. How can I tell? But if you will not lend me, I can bor-row else-where.

THE PRACTICE OF INSERTING HYPHENS BETWEEN THE SYLLABLES OF *all multisyllable words was common in most editions of the* First Reader, *but was not extended to the* Second *and* Third Reader *until the 1857 edition. The experiment was discontinued in 1865.*

Sarah. I am will-ing to lend you. But I should like to know why you al-ways come to me to bor-row.

Mary. Be-cause you nev-er lose any of your things, and al-ways know where to find them.

Sarah. And how, do you think, I al-ways know where to find my things?

Mary. How do I know? If I knew, I might some-times find my own.

Sarah. I will tell you the se-cret. I have a place for ev-er-y thing, and when I have done with it, I al-ways put it in its place.

Mary. But who wants to run and put a-way a thing, as soon as she has u-sed it, as if her life de-pend-ed on it.

Sarah. Your life does not de-pend up-on it, but your com-fort does. How much more time will it take to put a thing in its place, than to hunt for it, or bor-row?

Mary. Well, I will nev-er bor-row of you a-gain, you may de-pend up-on it.

Sarah. You are not of-fend-ed, I hope.

Mary. No, Sa-rah. But I am a-sha-med. Be-fore night, I will have a place for ev-er-y thing, and then I will keep ev-er-y thing in its place.

This selection entered the Second Reader *in 1844 and—except for being juggled within the lesson sequence—remained in every edition since then with no significant changes. It was one of the earliest lessons to be set in dialogue form instead of the almost unvarying expository prose format common to the first editions of the* Readers. *The moral lesson here is hardly lost in the dramatic vehicle, but the use of dialogue did help to add variety to the* Readers *and was increasingly employed in later editions.*

LESSON XLIX.

toys	dodge	dol'lar	fear'ed	skip'ping
eight	George	miss'ed	bro'ken	throw'ing
might	bus'y	press'es	gath'ers	cov'er-ed
bright	sil'ver	stop'ped	be-tween'	an-oth'er

THE BROKEN WINDOW.

1. GEORGE ELLET had a fine New-year's gift. What do you think it was? A bright silver dollar! A merry boy was George.

2. He thought of all the fine things he might buy with it. When the sun began to warm the air, he put on his cap, and ran into the street.

AMONG THE MOST POPULAR OF MCGUFFEY SELECTIONS, THIS SERIES of lessons entered the First Reader *in 1841, was moved up to the* Second Reader *in the 1857 edition, and has been retained at that level in all subsequent editions. Revisions of it occurred, however, in 1879, when it was condensed into two lessons from the three lessons included here (reproduced from the 1865 edition). At that time a number of small editorial changes were also made, with the chief result being a slightly reduced level of reading difficulty.*

3. The ground was covered with snow; but the sun shone out, and every thing looked bright.

4. As George went skipping along, he met some boys, throwing snow-balls. This is fine sport, and George was soon as busy as the rest.

5. See how he gathers up the snow, and presses it between his hands.

6. Now he has hit James Mason. But the ball was soft, and James is not hurt.

7. Now he has made another ball, and if James does not dodge, George will hit him again.

8. Away goes the ball! But it missed James, and broke a window on the other side of the street.

9. George feared that some one would come out of the house and whip him. So he ran off, as fast as he could.

10. As soon as he got round the next corner, he stopped, because he was very sorry for what he had done.

11. Just then he saw a man with a box, full of pretty toys. As George was only eight years old, he soon forgot the broken window, and ran after the toyman.

In the early nineteenth century, George might well have had cause to fear a whipping, but in 1879 that sentence was revised to read: "George feared some one would come out of the house and find him." The discipline of the young was perhaps already deteriorating.

LESSON L.

glass	break	pock′et	ask′ed	in-tend′
doors	ought	mon′ey	turn′ed	e-nough′
takes	thought	beat′en	start′ed	mis′chief
threw	hon′est	him-self′	scold′ed	chim′neys

MORE ABOUT THE BROKEN WINDOW.

1. GEORGE was about to buy a little house with doors and chimneys.

2. But as he felt in his pocket for the money, he thought of the broken window.

3. He said to himself, "I have no right to spend this dollar for a toy-house. I ought to go back, and pay for the glass I broke with my snow-ball."

IN THE 1879 VERSION GEORGE LOSES HIS EXCUSE OF BEING ONLY EIGHT years old (no age is given), and the whole episode of temptation by the toyman is removed. In the revised version, remorse and recriminations begin immediately with classic inevitability.

4. So he gave back the house, and turned round; but he was afraid of being scolded or beaten, and did not know what to do.

5. He went up and down the street, and felt very badly. He wished very much to buy something nice. He also wished to pay for the broken glass.

6. At last he said, "It was wrong to break the window, though I did not mean to do it. I will go and pay for it at once.

7. "If it takes all my money, I will try not to be sorry. I do not think the man will hurt me, if I pay for the mischief I have done."

8. He then started off, and felt much happier for having made up his mind to do what was right.

9. He rang the door bell. When the man came out, George said, "Sir, I threw a snow-ball through your window. But I did not intend to do it.

10. "I am very sorry, and wish to pay you. Here is the dollar my father gave me as a New-year's gift.'

11. The man took the dollar, and asked George if he had any more money. George said he had not. "Well," said he, "this will be enough."

12. So, after asking George his name, and where he lived, he called him an honest lad, and shut the door.

<hr>

ARTICULATION.

Th. thin², thick², both¹, duth², hath², pith².

Th. than², then², with², that², lathe¹, this².

Ng. bang², hang², rang², sang², pang², tang².

<hr>

LESSON LI.

eyes	school	months	want'ed	mer'chant
years	bright	brought	part'ner	mer'ri-ly
knew	wrong	ros'y	be-came'	an-oth'er
whose	thinks	play'ed	fore'noon	hon'est-ly

<hr>

MORE ABOUT THE BROKEN WINDOW.

1. WHEN George had paid the man, he ran away, and felt very happy; for he had done what he knew was right.

2. He played merrily all the forenoon, although he had no money to spend.

3. He went home at dinner time, with a face as rosy, and eyes as bright, as if nothing had gone wrong.

4. At dinner, Mr. Ellet asked George what he had bought with his money.

5. George very honestly told him all about the broken window, and said he felt very well without any money to spend.

6. When dinner was over, Mr. Ellet told George to go and look in his hat. He did so, and found two silver dollars.

7. The man, whose window had been broken, had been there, and told Mr. Ellet about it. He also gave back George's dollar, and another one with it.

8. A few months after, the man came, and told Mr. Ellet, that he wanted a good boy to stay in his store.

9 He said he would like to have George as soon as he left school, for he was sure that George was an honest boy.

10. George went to live with this man, who was a rich merchant.

11. In a few years, he became the merchant's partner, and is now rich.

12. George often thinks of the BROKEN WINDOW.

EXERCISES.—Relate the whole story of George and the broken window. What did George become?

THE TYPICAL McGUFFEY PATTERN IS HERE MAINTAINED, WITH GEORGE receiving as compensation for his honesty both an instant doubling of his money and a long-term reward as well. Like "The Little Chimney Sweep," this tale clearly anticipates— by more than twenty-five years—the stereotyped plot structures of Horatio Alger's success stories. Alger (1834–1899) may not have been directly influenced by the McGuffey Readers, but he certainly owed them a debt of thanks for preparing, even softening, the market he later exploited with over 130 separate juvenile novels.

LESSON XIV.

sup pōrt'   a lŏng'   bo͞ots

be lŏng'   dŏl'lar   yēarṣ

măn'aġe

taught

eôr'ner

nŏ'tĭçe

mŏn'ey

blăck'ing

ġĕn'ṭle men

hŏn'est (ŏn'est)   quīte   buȳ   ẽarned

HENRY, THE BOOT-BLACK.

1. Henry was a kind, good boy. His father was dead, and his mother was very poor. He had a little sister about two years old.

2. He wanted to help his mother, for she could not always earn enough to buy food for her little family.

3. One day, a man gave him a dollar for finding a pocket-book which he had lost.

4. Henry might have kept all the money, for no one saw him when he found it. But his mother had taught him to be honest, and never to keep what did not belong to him.

5. With the dollar he bought a box, three brushes, and some blacking. He then went to the corner of the street, and said to every one whose boots did not look nice, "Black your boots, sir, please?"

6. He was so polite that gentlemen soon began to notice him, and to let him black their boots. The first day he brought home fifty cents, which he gave to his mother to buy food with.

7. When he gave her the money, she said, as she dropped a tear of joy, "You are a dear, good boy, Henry. I did not know how I could earn enough to buy bread with, but now I think we can manage to get along quite well."

HERE IS ANOTHER LESSON WITH SIMILARITIES TO THE HORATIO ALGER paradigm, but this selection didn't enter the Readers *until the 1879 edition. By that time Alger had already cornered the "success market," and it would have been difficult for Henry to compete within the space of only a few pages. His success, then, is of a milder form, but the actual moral lesson is probably clearer here than if he had married his benefactor's daughter or become a millionaire.*

8. Henry worked all the day, and went to school in the evening. He earned almost enough to support his mother and his little sister.

LESSON XV.

trĕad	whĭs'per	sŏft'ly
tạlk	chēer fụl	eâre'fụl

DON'T WAKE THE BABY.

Baby sleeps, so we must tread
Softly round her little bed,
And be careful that our toys
Do not fall and make a noise.

We must not talk, but whisper low,
Mother wants to work, we know,
That, when father comes to tea,
All may neat and cheerful be.

LESSON XVI.

full	lōad	hĕav′y	mid′dle	hĕav′i er
slĭp	wrŏng	hăn′dle	brŏth′er	de çēived′

A KIND BROTHER.

1. A boy was once sent from home to take a basket of things to his grand-mother.

2. The basket was so full that it was very heavy. So his little brother went with him, to help carry the load.

ORIGINALLY ENTITLED "THE GOOD BOY," THIS LESSON APPEARED IN the McGuffeys for the first time in the 1857 edition. Although several different illustrations were used in subsequent editions (this one, for instance, is from the 1879 edition), the lesson itself underwent only minor changes. It is still part of the Second Reader today.

3. They put a pole under the handle of the basket, and each then took hold of an end of the pole. In this way they could carry the basket very nicely.

4. Now the older boy thought, "My brother Tom does not know about this pole.

5. "If I slip the basket near him, his side will be heavy, and mine light; but if the basket is in the middle of the pole, it will be as heavy for me as it is for him.

6. "Tom does not know this as I do. But I will not do it. It would be wrong, and I will not do what is wrong."

7. Then he slipped the basket quite near his own end of the pole. His load was now heavier than that of his little brother.

8. Yet he was happy; for he felt that he had done right. Had he deceived his brother, he would not have felt at all happy.

Earlier versions of this lesson ended with the sentence: "We may be sure that we shall always be happy, when we do right." In this 1879 revision, however, such absolute assurance is no longer explicitly offered.

LESSON LVII.

dīned	g̅ā̆y′ly	dŏe′tor	g̅lŭt′ton
nēedṣ	līve′ly	ā′eornṣ	rēad′erṣ
tāstes	Lạu′rà	g̅rēed′y	tĕm′perṣ

THE GREEDY GIRL.

Laura English is a greedy little girl. Indeed, she is quite a glutton. Do you know what a glutton is? A glutton is one who eats too much, because the food tastes well.

2. Laura's mother is always willing she should have as much to eat as is good for her; but sometimes, when her mother is not watching, she eats so much that it makes her sick.

3. I do not know why she is so silly. Her kitten never eats more than it needs. It leaves the nice bones on the plate, and lies down to sleep when it has eaten enough.

4. The bee is wiser than Laura. It

PERHAPS THE COINCIDENTAL ALLITERATION OF GREEDY AND GLUTTON with girl dictated the sex of the offender in this negative moral lesson, although McGuffey's selection may have been deliberate—another reminder that he was (at least originally) writing primarily for boys. At any rate, all fat girls and all girls named Laura were forced to live with this lesson for many years. One of McGuffey's original 1836 selections, "The Greedy Girl," has been present in every edition of the **Second Reader.**

flies all day among the flowers to gather honey, and might eat the whole time if it pleased. But it eats just enough, and carries all the rest to its hive.

5. The squirrel eats a few nuts or acorns, and frisks about as gayly as if he had dined at the king's table.

6. Did you ever see a squirrel with a nut in his paws? How bright and lively he looks as he eats it!

7. If he lived in a house made of acorns, he would never need a doctor. He would not eat an acorn too much.

8. I do not love little girls who eat too much. Do you, my little readers?

9. I do not think they have such rosy cheeks, or such bright eyes, or such sweet, happy tempers as those who eat less.

The withholding of love as punishment for a gluttonous child would not be what most psychologists, teachers, and parents would recommend today. But this lesson does confront greed directly—without merely calling it a sin—and presents practical objections. "The Greedy Girl" is a good representative of the negative moral lessons in the McGuffeys.

Third Reader

THIS DIALOGUE WAS USED IN THE McGUFFEYS ONLY FIFTEEN YEARS, appearing in the first edition of the Third Reader *(classified as prose) and in the 1843 and 1853 editions (classified as poetry). Death was a familiar subject in the* Readers, *as it was in the lives of most students at that time. This particular selection was unusual, however, in that most discussions of death in the early editions are religiously oriented, focusing on life after death.*

Here the child's naive questions are left essentially unanswered by his father, with no religious consolation being offered.

LESSON XXVII.

The Dead Mother.

RULE.—This kind of composition is called *Dialogue*, and requires more care in reading, than any other. The tones should not be *too* familiar, yet still *conversational*.

1. *Fath.* Touch not thy mother, boy—Thou canst not wake her.

2. *Child.* Why, Father? She still wakens at this hour.

3. *Fath.* Your mother's dead, my child.

4. *Child.* And what is dead?
   If she be dead, why, then, 'tis only sleeping,
   For I am sure she sleeps. Come, mother, rise—
   Her hand is very cold!

5. *Fath.* Her *heart* is cold.
   Her limbs are bloodless, would that mine were so!

6. *Child.* If she would waken, she would soon be warm.
   Why is she wrapt in this thin sheet? If I,
   This winter morning, were not covered better,
   I should be cold like her.

7. *Fath.* No—not like her:
   The fire might warm *you*, or thick clothes—but *her*—
   Nothing can warm again!

8. *Child.* If I could wake her,
   She would smile on me, as she always does,
   And kiss me. Mother! you have slept too long—
   Her face is pale—and it would frighten me,
   But that I know she loves me.

9. *Fath.* Come, my child.

10. *Child.* Once, when I sat upon her lap, I felt
    A beating at her side, and then she said
    It was her heart that beat, and bade me feel
    For my own heart, and they both beat alike,
    Only mine was the quickest—and I feel
    My own heart yet—but hers—I cannot feel—

11. *Fath.* Child! child!—you drive me mad—come hence, I say.

12. *Child.* Nay, father, be not angry ! let me stay
Here till my mother wakens.

13. *Fath.* I have told you,
Your mother cannot wake—not in this world—
But in another she *will* wake for us.
When we have slept like her, then we shall see her.

14. *Child.* Would it were night, then !

15. *Fath.* No, unhappy child !
Full many a night shall pass, ere thou canst sleep
That last, long sleep. Thy father soon shall sleep it ;
Then wilt thou be deserted upon earth ;
None will regard thee ; thou wilt soon forget
That thou hadst natural ties—an orphan lone,
Abandoned to the wiles of wicked men.

16. *Child.* Father ! Father !
Why do you look so terribly upon me,
You will not hurt me ?

17. *Fath.* Hurt thee, darling ? no !
Has sorrow's violence so much of anger,
That it should fright my boy ? Come, dearest, come.

18. *Child.* You are not angry, then ?

19. *Fath.* Too well I love you.

20. *Child.* All you have said, I cannot now remember,
Nor what is meant—you terrified me so.
But this I know, you told me—I must sleep
Before my mother wakens—so, to-morrow—
Oh, father ! that to-morrow were but come !

———

QUESTIONS.—1. What is this species of composition called ? 2. How should it be read ? 3. What mark is after cold ? 4. What is its use ?

ERRORS.—*Tetch* for touch ; *close* for clothes ; *slep* for slept ; *sayd* for said ; *tur-ri-bly* for ter-ri-bly.

SPELL AND DEFINE—10. beating ; 15. orphan ; abandoned ; 16. terribly ; 17. violence.

And if you do not improve the advantages you enjoy, you sin against your Maker.

> " With books, or work, or healthful play,
> Let your first years be past,
> That you may give, for every day,
> Some good account at last."

QUESTIONS.—1. What is the subject of this lesson? 2. In what respect was Charles Bullard different from George Jones? 3. Which of them do you think most worthy of imitation? 4. For what are you placed in this world? 5. Should you not then be diligent in your studies? 6. How should you sit or stand when you read?

ERRORS.—*Bout* for a-bout; *dil-a-gent* for dil-i-gent; *in-stid* for in-stead; *gin-ral-ly* for gen-er-al-ly; *se-si-e-ty* for so-ci-e-ty; *stud-id* for stud-i-ed; *in-va-ra-bly* for in-va-ri-a-bly.

SPELL AND DEFINE—1. History; 2. game; 3. preceptor; 5. review, tranquil; 7. graduated; 8. universally; 9. invariably; 10. advantages.

LESSON V.

Punctuality and Punctuation.—WORCESTER.

RULE.—Be careful to learn and remember the Stops and Marks so well, that you will know their uses whenever you meet with them.

1. Perhaps my young readers may think that *punctuality* and *punctuation* mean the same thing; but I will soon show that there is a great difference. *Punctuality* means, *Doing things at the proper time;* but *punctuation* means, *Placing the proper Stops and Marks in sentences:* thus, you see, these words mean very different things.*

2. Have you learned all the Stops and Marks that have been used in the foregoing Lessons? ' No, sir, not half of them.'† You have n't indeed! Well, I am sorry that you are not more punctual. If you had learn-

---

* The learner will observe that there are four different stops in this sentence ; and he will notice the other stops and marks in other parts of the Lesson.

† Notice all the marks that are here used.

THIS LESSON HAD A SINGLE APPEARANCE IN THE McGUFFEYS: *IN THE first edition of the* **Third Reader** *(1837). It differs significantly in tone from most lessons in the series, but its combination of morality with subject matter is certainly familiar enough. The passage was taken from a competitor's book—the* Worcester Reader, *compiled by Samuel Worcester and published by Richardson, Lord and Holbrook of Boston. Borrowing material from competing textbooks was very common practice at that time (indeed, such cross-fertilization was almost expected), and McGuffey's attribution of the lesson to Worcester by name was actually more rigorously honest than was customary. Nevertheless, a lawsuit charging infringement of*

ed every one when it was used, you would not be so
troubled now when they all come upon you together.‡

3. When we omit to do things at the proper time,
we can never have every thing in its proper place.   The
scholar who is not ready to read and spell when his
turn comes, is not punctual, and he ought to stand
                            word
aside, like a   that forgot to take its proper place.
            ∧

4. A scholar who has not learned his lesson, stands
like an ellipsis, that is denoted by stars, * * *, or by
dots, ..., or by a dash, ——, to show that something is omitted.   He will read, limping along, and
hesitating how to call his words, as if he were saying, Mr. B . . . . gave five dollars to N * * * to buy
a —— for M. ——

5. If you go over the whole country, you will find
that men, and women, and children, do their head-work
and their hand-work, and all sorts of work, without proper regard to punctuality.   If one promises to meet
you at 10 o'clock, it is not likely that he will come till
11; and then he may make the wicked excuse, that it is
ten till eleven.

6. It is the fashion of every one to be making excuses for want of punctuality.   The shoemaker, the tailor, the blacksmith, the carpenter, the book-maker, the
printer, the book-binder, the book-seller, the reader, and
all sorts of workmen, neglect to fulfil their promises;
and then they make excuses.   I believe it was Dr.
Franklin who said ☞ ' A man who is good at making
excuses, is good for nothing else.' He meant that those
who try to fulfil their promises, are very seldom obliged
to break them, and, therefore, they have no occasion
to learn how to make excuses; but those who break
their promises often, have to study to make such excuses as will make others think them innocent: and such
men are not to be trusted.

7. Now, my young friends, I would have you consider this matter well.   Sometimes you cannot be punc-

---

‡ Sometimes there are other marks used to refer to notes in the mar-
gin or bottom of the page.   The scholar will easily understand them if
he looks carefully.

copyright was brought against *McGuffey and his publishers in
1838, leading to a flurry of activity—with angry charges and
countercharges being aired in the newspapers.*

*Many of the lessons in question had appeared in various
other textbooks even before Worcester's, and were thus viewed
by McGuffey as common property. But with the threat of
an injunction to stop circulation of the* McGuffeys *and the
prospects of a long legal battle, the wisest course of action was
obviously to avoid debating the actual issues. So, the* McGuffey
Readers *were quickly revised to expunge all lessons in question (including this one), and an out-of-court settlement (in
which McGuffey's publishers paid the plaintiffs $2,000)
closed the matter. Although the plagiarism charges against
McGuffey caused a temporary furor at the time, they now appear to have been only another aspect of the bitter, although fairly common wars among textbook publishers.*

In the hastily revised "Improved Edition" of the Third Reader (1838), a special Preface informs the readers of the legal causes for the revision—and at the same time strikes a typical regional posture:

These compilers [i.e., Worcester] have resorted to the law, and an effort is now making, not only to force their own books into the Western market, but to wrest from Western talent, and Western enterprise, the legitimate fruits of a persevering toil.

They mistake the spirit of the West, however, who think they can thus force it into any channel. It has the intelligence to choose well; and having thus chosen, no combination can move it from its purpose.

The whole incident with the Worcester Readers was an unpleasant interruption in the growth of the McGuffeys, but it was only a minor setback. And it didn't help the Worcester Readers much either; they had a relatively short and inconspicuous life, never approaching the dominance achieved by the McGuffeys.

tual in doing what you have promised, or proposed, or have been told to do; but it is certainly true that you cannot be in the habit of breaking your promises, or delaying and neglecting your duties, without very great sin.

‖ *Want of punctuality is want of economy.*

8. ¶ I have said that want of punctuality is sin; and this is the proper reason why you should be as punctual as possible in all things. But I now say also, that those persons who are not punctual, waste their time and their money.

9. [The Reason.] The reason why want of punctuality is want of economy, is that every thing is confused and comes out of time and place, when you neglect it at its proper season; and then it takes much time, (and time is money,) to set right what you have suffered to go wrong.

10. If, therefore, you mean to be honest men and women, and live comfortably with others, and have enough of the good things of life, be *punctual* in performing all your duties.

> If others promise—and neglect to do,
> (Their fault is surely no excuse for you)
> They'll trouble many—and be loved by few.

———

QUESTIONS.—1. What does *punctuality* mean? 2. What is *punctuation?* 3. Name the stops in the fourth paragraph? 4. What do the asterisk, obelisk, and section refer to? 5. What is a caret? 6. What do stars, dots, and a dash show? 7. What is a hyphen? 8. What is an apostrophe? 9. What is an index? 10. What is a quotation? 11. What is a section used for? 12. What is a paragraph used for? 13. What are brackets used for? 14. What is the use of the brace? 15. What is the use of the dash? 16. What rule is at the beginning of the Lesson?

ERRORS.—*Lar-ned* for learn-ed; *lim-pin* for limp-ing; *chil-durn* for chil-dren.

SPELL AND DEFINE—1. Punctuality; 2. punctuation; 4. ellipsis; 7. proposed; 9. economy; 19. performing.

C

LESSON XXXI.

On Speaking the Truth.—ABBOTT.

RULE.—Too much pains cannot be taken to acquire familiarity with the stops.

1. A little girl once came into the house, and told her mother a story about something which seemed very improbable.

2. The persons who were sitting in the room with her mother did not believe the little girl, for they did not know her character. But the mother replied at once, "I have no doubt that it is true, for I never knew my daughter to tell a lie." Is there not something noble in having such a character as this?

3. Must not that little girl have felt happy in the consciousness of thus possessing her mother's entire confidence? Oh, how different must have been her feelings from those of the child whose word cannot be believed, and who is regarded by every one with suspicion? Shame, shame on the child who has not magnanimity enough to tell the truth.

4. There are many ways of being guilty of falsehood without uttering the lie direct, in words. Whenever you try to deceive your parents, in doing that which you know they disapprove, you do in reality tell a lie. Conscience reproves you for falsehood.

5. Once when I was in company, as the plate of cake was passed around, a little boy who sat by the side of his mother, took a much larger piece than he knew she would allow him. She happened, for the moment, to be looking away, and he broke a small piece off, and covered the rest in his lap with his handkerchief. When his mother looked, she saw the small piece, and supposed he had taken no more. He intended to deceive her. His mother has never found out what he did.

6. But God saw him at the time. And do you not think that the boy has already suffered for it? Must he not feel mean and contemptible, whenever he thinks that, merely to get a little bit of cake, he would deceive

JACOB ABBOTT (1803–1879) WAS A CONGREGATIONAL MINISTER, EDUCA-tor, and juvenile writer. His best known writings were a juvenile series, the Rollo Books, *but he contributed extensively to the early issues of* Harper's Monthly, *and—as did so many educators then—he also compiled school readers. His little sermon-like lessons were used not only by McGuffey but by many other textbook compilers of the time.*

his kind mother? If that little boy had one particle of honorable or generous feeling remaining in his bosom, he would feel reproached and unhappy whenever he thought of his meanness. If he was already dead to shame, it would show that he had by previous deceit acquired such a character.

7. And can any one love or esteem a child who has become so degraded? And can a child, who is neither beloved nor respected, be happy? No! You may depend upon it, that when you see a person guilty of such deceit, he does, in some way or other, even in this world, suffer a severe penalty. A frank and open-hearted child is the only happy child. Deception, however skilfully it may be practised, is disgraceful, and ensures sorrow and contempt.

8. If you would have the approbation of your own conscience, and the approval of friends, never do that which you shall desire to have concealed. Always be open as the day. Be above deceit, and then you will have nothing to fear. There is something delightful in the magnanimity of a perfectly sincere and honest child. No person can look upon such a one without affection. With this, you are sure of friends, and your prospects of earthly usefulness and happiness are bright.

9. But we must not forget that there is a day of most solemn judgment near at hand. When you die, your body will be wrapped in the shroud, and placed in the coffin, and buried in the grave. And there it will remain and moulder in the dust, while the snows of unnumbered winters, and the tempests of unnumbered summers, shall rest upon the cold earth which covers you. But your spirit will not be there. Far away beyond the cloudless skies, and blazing suns, and twinkling stars, it will have gone to judgment.

10. How awful must be the scene which will open before you, as you enter the eternal world! You will see the throne of God: how bright, how glorious, will it burst upon your sight! You will see God, the Savior, seated upon that majestic throne. Angels, in number more than can be counted, will fill the universe with their glittering wings, and their rapturous songs. Oh, what a

---

In the higher Readers, *where rhetoric is more consciously a part of the subject matter, passages such as this are common. In the lower-level* Readers, *however, such pulpit oratory is rare. Furthermore, the descriptions here of death, heaven, and hell are far more specific than usual in the* McGuffeys. *Similar specifics, however, were offered in another lesson by Abbott, "The Lost Child," which also appeared in early editions of the* Third Reader:

> *The child was in danger of being torn by the claws and teeth of a bear—a pang which would be but for a moment; but the sinner must feel the ravages of the never-dying worm; must be exposed to the fury of the inextinguishable flame.*

"The Lost Child" has been found in all editions of the McGuffeys, *but the passage quoted here was omitted when the lesson was moved up to the* Fourth Reader *in 1857.*

scene to behold! And then you will stand in the presence of this countless throng, to answer for every thing you have done while you lived.

11. Every action and every thought of your life will then be fresh in your mind. You know it is written in the Bible, "God will bring every work into judgment, with every secret thing, whether it be good or whether it be evil." How must the child then feel who has been guilty of falsehood and deception, and who sees it then all brought to light! No liar can enter the kingdom of heaven. Oh, how dreadful must be the confusion and shame, with which the deceitful child will then be overwhelmed! The angels will all see your sin and your disgrace.

12. And do you think they will wish to have a liar enter heaven, and be associated with them? No! They will turn from you with disgust. The Savior will look upon you in his displeasure. Conscience will rend your soul. And you must hear the awful sentence, "Depart from me, into everlasting fire, prepared for the devil and his angels."

13. Oh, it is a dreadful thing to practice deceit. It will shut you out from heaven. Though you should escape detection as long as you live; though you should die, and your falsehood not be discovered, the time will soon come when it will be brought to light, and when the whole universe—men and angels will be witnesses of your shame.

———

QUESTIONS.—1. What is the subject of this Lesson? 2. What did the little girl do? 3. What did the company think? 4. What did her mother say of her? 5. How must the little girl have felt when her mother said she could not doubt her word? 6. What did the boy do? 7. What is degrading? 8. Should we ever resort to deception?— 9. If we escape detection for falsehood here, when shall we be detected?

ERRORS.—*Set-ting* for sit-ting; *dah-ter* for daugh-ter; *diff-runt* for dif-fer-ent; *fur-git* for for-get.

SPELL AND DEFINE—2. character; 3. consciousness; confidence; 4. falsehood; 6. contemptible; 7. disgraceful; 8. magnanimity; 10. rapturous; 11. deceitful.

This lesson was one of the original McGuffey selections and was used until the 1843 revision—the revision announcing that its contents had been inspected by "highly intelligent clergymen and teachers of the various Protestant and Catholic denominations" to prohibit anything of a "denominational character" (see page 13). Whether or not it was objected to on these grounds is uncertain, but it disappeared from the McGuffeys at this time.

The 1843 edition also cut a lesson entitled "Character of Martin Luther"—and here the motives for the deletion are clear. Although the account was reasonably balanced in terms of describing Luther (noting his arrogance and obstinance, as well as his abilities, zeal, industry, etc.), it was written with a bias that allowed phrases such as: "The account of his death filled the Roman Catholic party with excessive as well as indecent joy...."

THE ANONYMOUS AUTHOR HERE IS ACTUALLY MRS. LYDIA HOWARD *Huntley Sigourney (1791–1865). One of early America's most prolific writers, she authored or co-authored over forty books and contributed more than 2,000 pieces—mainly verse—to approximately 300 periodicals. Her major books of verse include* Pocahontas *(1841),* Scenes in My Native Land *(1844), and* Voice of Flowers *(1845). As Mrs. Sigourney's fame grew, her work in later editions of the* McGuffeys *was allowed to carry a credit-line.*

LESSON LXVII.

The Dying Boy.—ANONYMOUS.

RULE.—In solemn pieces of this kind, you should read slower and more softly than usual.

1.   It must be sweet, in childhood, to give back
    The spirit to its Maker; ere the heart
    Has grown familiar with the paths of sin,
    And sown—to garner up its bitter fruits.
    I knew a boy whose infant feet had trod
    Upon the blossoms of some seven springs,
    And when the eighth came round, and called him out
    To revel in its light, he turned away,
    And sought his chamber, to lie down and die.

2. 'Twas night : he summoned his accustomed friends,
    And on this wise bestowed his last bequest.
            'Mother—I'm dying now !
    There's a deep suffocation in my breast,
    As if some heavy hand my bosom pressed :—
            And on my brow
            I feel the cold sweat stand ;
    My lips grow dry and tremulous, and my breath
    Comes feebly on.   Oh! tell me, is this death ?

3.   Mother, your hand—
            Here—lay it on my wrist,
    And place the other thus beneath my head,
    And say, sweet mother, say, when I am dead,
            Shall I be missed ?
            Never beside your knee,
    Shall I kneel down again at night to pray ;
    Nor with the morning wake, and sing the lay
            You taught me ?

4.   Oh, at the time of prayer,
    When you look round, and see a vacant seat,
    You will not wait then for my coming feet—
            You'll miss me there.
            Father, I'm going home !
    To the good home you spoke of, that blest land,
    Where it is one bright summer always, and
            Storms do never come.

5.   I must be happy then:
From pain and death you say I shall be free,
That sickness never enters there, and we
    Shall meet again.

    Brother—the little spot
I used to call my garden, where long hours
We've stayed to watch the budding things, and flowers,
    Forget it not!

6.   Plant there some box or pine,
Something that lives in winter, and will be
A verdant offering to my memory,
    And call it mine!

7.   Sister—my young rose tree,
That all the spring has been my pleasant care,
Just putting forth its leaves so green and fair,
    I give to thee;

    And when its roses bloom,
I shall be far away, my short life done;
But will you not bestow a single one
    Upon my tomb?

8.   Now, mother, sing the tune
You sang last night; I'm weary, and must sleep.
Who was it called my name? Nay, do not weep,
    You'll all come soon!'

Morning spread over earth her rosy wings.
And that meek sufferer, cold and ivory pale,
Lay on his couch asleep. The gentle air
Came through the open window, freighted with
The savory odors of the early spring—
He breathed it not; the laugh of passers by,
Jarred like a discord in some mournful tune,
But wak'ned not his slumber. He was dead.

———

QUESTIONS.—1. What is the subject of this piece? 2. What is said of childhood? 3. What did the little boy exclaim, as he addressed his mother? 4. How did he say he felt? 5. What did he ask his mother to do with her hand? 6. Was not this very affectionate? 7. How did the little sufferer feel in view of death? 8. What is it that will enable us to triumph over death?

One of the most sentimental of the early selections, "The Dying Boy" treats life after death without the religious specifics used earlier by the Rev. Jacob Abbott, and perhaps that accounts for its longer life in the series (from 1837 until 1879). Many of the same specifics were implied, of course, but they were left here to be developed by the teacher, particularly in responding to the final study question.

JOHN AIKIN (1747–1822) WAS AN ENGLISH PHYSICIAN AND WRITER WHOSE popular Evenings at Home *(6 vols., 1792–1795) contained a number of instructive family readings that were widely appropriated by American textbook compilers. "The Colonists" was a particular favorite, especially before the Civil War. The "Mr. Barlow" in this lesson was probably intended to be recognized as the teacher, rather than the literal father, of all "his children." A man with sixteen sons would have been unusual—even in an age when large families were common.*

LESSON XVI.

SPELL AND DEFINE

Pro-fes'-sion, a man's business or trade.
Col'-o-nists, people who go to live together in a new country.
Found'-er, one from whom any thing originates.
Mill'-wright, one who builds mills.

Forge, a place where iron is beaten into form.
Em-ploy'-ment, business, occupation.
Law'-yer, one who practices law.
O-be'-di-ent, doing what is directed.

THE COLONISTS. — *Dr. Aikin.*

RULE. — Read this dialogue, as if you were talking to each other, under the circumstances here described.

[*Note.*—Mr. Barlow one day invented a play for his children, on purpose to show them what kind of persons and professions are the most useful in society, and particularly in a new settlement. The following is the conversation which took place between himself and his children.]

Mr. Barlow. Come, my boys, I have a new play for you. I will be the founder of a colony; and you shall be people of different trades and professions, coming to offer yourselves to go with me. What are you, Arthur?

Arthur. I am a farmer, sir.

Mr. Barlow. Very well. Farming is the chief thing we have to depend upon. The farmer puts the seed into the earth, and takes care of it when it is grown to ripe corn; without the farmer we should have no bread. But you must work very diligently; there will be trees to cut down, and roots to dig out, and a great deal of hard labor.

Arthur. I shall be ready to do my part.

Mr. Barlow. Well, then I shall take you willingly, and as many more such good fellows as I can find. We shall have land enough, and you may go to work as soon as you please. Now for the next.

James. I am a miller, sir.

Mr. Barlow. A very useful trade! Our corn must be ground, or it will do us but little good. But what must we do for a mill, my friend?

James. I suppose we must make one, sir.

Mr. Barlow. Then we must take a *mill-wright* with us, and carry mill-stones.   Who is next?

Charles. I am a carpenter, sir.

Mr. Barlow. The most necessary man that could offer. We shall find you work enough, never fear.   There will be houses to build, fences to make, and chairs and tables besides.   But all our timber is growing; we shall have hard work to fell it, to saw boards and planks, and to frame and raise buildings.   Can you help us in this?

Charles. I will do my best, sir.

Mr. Barlow. Then I engage you, but you had better bring two or three able assistants along with you.

William. I am a blacksmith.

Mr. Barlow. An excellent companion for the carpenter. We cannot do without either of you. You must bring your great bellows, anvil, and vise, and we will set up a forge for you as soon as we arrive.   By the by, we shall want a mason for that.

Edward. I am one, sir.

Mr. Barlow. Though we may live in log houses at first, we shall want brick work, or stone work, for chimneys, hearths, and ovens, so there will be employment for a mason. Can you make bricks, and burn lime?

Edward. I will try what I can do, sir.

Mr. Barlow. No man can do more.   I engage you. Who comes next?

Francis. I am a shoemaker, sir.

Mr. Barlow. Shoes we cannot well do without, but I fear we shall get no leather.

Francis. But I can dress skins, sir.

Mr. Barlow. Can you?   Then you are a useful fellow. I will have you, though I give you double wages.

George. I am a tailor, sir.

Mr. Barlow. We must not go naked; so there will be work for a tailor.   But you are not above mending, I hope, for we must not mind wearing patched clothes, while we work in the woods.

George. I am not, sir.

Mr. Barlow. Then I engage you, too.

Henry. I am a silversmith, sir.

Mr. Barlow. Then, my friend, you cannot go to a worse place than a new colony to set up your trade in.

The importance of agriculture, along with occupations supporting agriculture, is stressed in many of the early McGuffey selections. The farmer is the first listed here, emphasizing the fact that agriculture is "the chief thing we have to depend upon." Other trades are also evaluated almost exclusively on pragmatic grounds.

As a class, lawyers are seldom pictured favorably in the Readers; their motives are nearly always suspect, and they are often portrayed as being more self-serving than members of any other profession. Thus, the rejection of the lawyer's offer is not surprising. Aikin's treatment of the schoolmaster also reflects views common at that time, and familiar even today, revealing a popular distrust of the intellectual, except as he is able and willing to confine himself to teaching the basic skills. A current of anti-intellectualism runs throughout the McGuffeys, despite an abundance of rhetoric praising education; a basic education is viewed as desirable on practical grounds, but it is sometimes implied that higher education is unnecessary, even dangerous or subversive. Common sense and hard work are regularly shown to be more than adequate substitutes for any advanced "book learning."

Henry. But I understand clock and watch making too.

Mr. Barlow. We shall want to know how the time goes, but we cannot afford to employ you. At present you had better stay where you are.

Jasper. I am a barber and hair-dresser.

Mr. Barlow. What can we do with you? If you will shave our men's rough beards once a week, and crop their hairs once a quarter, and be content to help the carpenter the rest of the time, we will take you. But you will have no ladies' hair to curl, or gentlemen to powder, I assure you.

Louis. I am a doctor, sir.

Mr. Barlow. Then, sir, you are very welcome; we shall some of us be sick, and we are likely to get cuts, and bruises, and broken bones. You will be very useful. We shall take you with pleasure.

Maurice. I am a lawyer, sir.

Mr. Barlow. Sir, your most obedient servant. When we are rich enough to go to law, we will let you know.

Oliver. I am a schoolmaster.

Mr. Barlow. That is a very respectable and useful profession; as soon as our children are old enough, we shall be glad of your services. Though we are hard working men, we do not mean to be ignorant; every one among us must be taught reading and writing. Until we have employment for you in teaching, if you will keep our accounts, and at present read sermons to us on Sundays, we shall be glad to have you among us. Will you go?

Oliver. With all my heart, sir.

Mr. Barlow. Who comes here?

Philip. I am a soldier, sir; will you have me?

Mr. Barlow. We are peaceable people, and I hope we shall not be obliged to fight. We shall have no occasion for you, unless you can be a mechanic or farmer, as well as a soldier.

Richard. I am a dancing-master, sir.

Mr. Barlow. A *dancing-master?* Ha, ha! And pray, of what use do you expect to be in the "back-woods?"

Richard. Why, sir, I can teach you how to appear in a drawing-room. I shall take care that your children know precisely how low they must *bow* when saluting company.

In short, I teach you the *science*, which will distinguish you from the savages.

Mr. Barlow. This may be all very well, and quite to *your* fancy, but *I* would suggest that we, in a new colony, shall need to pay more attention to the raising of corn and potatoes, the feeding of cattle, and the preparing of houses to live in, than to the cultivation of this elegant " *science*," as you term it.

John. I, sir, am a politician, and would be willing to edit any newspaper you may wish to have published in your colony.

Mr. Barlow. Very much obliged to you, Mr. Editor; but for the present, I think you had better remain where you are. We shall have to labor so much for the first two or three years, that we shall care but little about other matters than those which concern our farms. We certainly must spend some time in reading, but I think we can obtain suitable books for our perusal, with much less money than it would require to support you and your newspaper.

Robert. I am a gentleman, sir.

Mr. Barlow. A *gentleman!* And what good can you do us?

Robert. I intend to spend most of my time in walking about, and overseeing the men at work. I shall be very willing to assist you with my *advice*, whenever I think it necessary. As for my support, that need not trouble you much. I expect to shoot game enough for my own eating; you can give me a little bread and a few vegetables; and the barber shall be my servant.

Mr. Barlow. Pray, sir, why should we do all this for you?

Robert. Why, sir, that you may have the credit of saying that you have one gentleman, at least, in your colony.

Mr. Barlow. Ha, ha, ha! A fine gentleman, truly! When we desire the honor of your company, sir, we will send for you.

QUESTIONS.—1. What is the subject of this lesson? 2. What play did Mr. Barlow propose? 3. What was Arthur's occupation? 4. Of what use is the farmer? 5. Of what use is the miller? 6. Who builds houses? 7. What are the principal implements that the blacksmith has need of? 8. What was Francis'

In roughly equating the lawyer, soldier, dancing master, politician/journalist, and gentleman, Aikin suggests that all of these professions would be parasites on the real workers of the new colony. The implication, of course, is that they are largely superfluous in any society. Other than the poor example of the dancing master, no artists are represented here; musicians, painters, writers, etc., are evidently such weak candidates for the new society that they deserve no mention.

trade? 9. Did Mr. Barlow think he would be useful to the colonists? 10. What did Mr. Barlow think about Henry's business? 11. Did Mr. Barlow engage Maurice? 12. Why not? 13. Do you think the new colonists could live comfortably without Richard or John? 14. What did Mr. Barlow say to Robert, and what did he think of him? 15. Which trade, do you think, would be most useful in a new colony?

ERRORS. — *Dif'rent* for dif-fer-ent ; *com-in'* for com-ing ; *willin'-ly* for will-ing-ly ; *ne'sa-ry* for nec-es-sa-ry ; *'n-gage* for en-gage ; *s'gest* for sug-gest ; *col'ny* for col-o-ny ; *o-bleeg-ed* for o-blig-ed ; *veg'ta-bles* for veg-et-a-bles ; *I 'x-pect* for I ex-pect.

LESSON XVII.

SPELL AND DEFINE

1. Cel'-e-bra-ted, praised, honored.
2. Il-lus'-tri-ous, famous, highly distinguished.
   Sub-du'-ed, overcame, conquered.
3. Ex-pe-di'-tion, enterprise, undertaking.   [power of another.
4. Sub-jec'-tion, the being under the
5. Vic'-to-ries, conquests, superiority in war.

6. Hel'-les-pont, the name of a strait east of Europe.   [Asia.
   Gran'-i-cus, the name of a river in
8. En-coun'-ter, to meet in battle.
12. Ban'-quet, a feast.
14. In-tem'-per-ance, the excessive drinking of intoxicating liquors

ALEXANDER THE GREAT. — *Anonymous.*

RULE. — 1. Emphasis belongs both to words and to whole clauses of sentences.

2. Sometimes, in order to bring out fully the meaning of a passage, it is necessary to give emphasis to several successive words, or to a considerable part of the whole sentence.

1. Macedon was, for a long time, a small state in Greece, not celebrated for any thing, except that its kings always governed according to the laws of the country, and that their children were well educated.

2. At length, after many kings had reigned over Macedon, one named Philip came to the throne, who determined to render his kingdom as illustrious as other kingdoms. He

would still bless and take care of the widow and the or-phan.

LESSON XIII.

wires	a-piece	bar-gain	o-pen-ed
fly-ing	French	peep-ing	re-solv-ed
try-ing	set-tled	sur-prise	pris-on-ers

THE BIRDS SET FREE.

1. A MAN was walk-ing one day through
the streets of a cit-y. He saw a boy with
a num-ber of small birds for sale, in a cage.

2. He look-ed with sad-ness up-on the
lit-tle pris-on-ers, fly-ing a-bout the cage,
peep-ing through the wires, and try-ing to
get out.

3. He stood, for some time, look-ing at
the birds. At last, he said to the boy,
"How much do you ask for your birds?"

4. "Fif-ty cents a-piece, sir," said the
boy. "I do not mean how much a-piece,"
said the man, "but how much for all of
them. I want to buy them all."

*"THE BIRDS SET FREE" WAS ONE OF THE SELECTIONS ADDED IN 1857—THE
last edition before the outbreak of the Civil War. Ostensibly
another lesson teaching kindness to animals, the analogies between the birds and the slaves were almost certainly calculated.
But the lesson stands so well on its own that it has been retained in all subsequent editions.*

5. The boy be-gan to count, and found they came to five dol-lars. "There is your mon-ey," said the man. The boy took it, well pleas-ed with his morn-ing's trade.

6. No soon-er was the bar-gain set-tled, than the man o-pen-ed the cage door, and let all the birds fly a-way.

7. The boy, in great sur-prise, cried, "What did you do that for, sir? You have lost all your birds."

8. "I will tell you why I did it," said the man. "I was shut up three years in a French pris-on, as a pris-on-er of war, and I am re-solv-ed nev-er to see a-ny thing in pris-on which I can make free."

QUESTIONS.—How much did the man give for the birds? What did he do with them? Why did he set them at liberty?

The issue of slavery is never discussed directly in the McGuffey Readers, but here—despite the distancing suggested by setting the prison experience in France—the abolitionist theme was certainly transparent to many anti-slavery readers. At the same time, however, the lesson was probably not too offensive to southern students, many of whom would hardly have viewed the institution of slavery in terms of such literal imprisonment.

LESSON XX.

sees	friend	ac-tions	heav-en
sight	guards	wick-ed	false-hood
hates	pray-er	de-light	re-mem-ber
saves	whis-per	pun-ish	for-give-ness

RE-MEM-BER.

1. RE-MEM-BER, child, re-mem-ber,
   That God is in the sky;
   That he looks on all we do,
   With an ev-er wake-ful eye.

2. Re-mem-ber, O! re-mem-ber,
   That all the day and night,
   He sees our thoughts and ac-tions,
   With an ev-er watch-ful sight.

3. Re-mem-ber, child, re-mem-ber,
   That God is good and true;
   That he wish-es us to be,
   Like him in all we do.

4. Re-mem-ber that he hates
   A false-hood or a lie;
   Re-mem-ber he will pun-ish
   The wick-ed, by-and-by.

ORIGINALLY ENTITLED "THINGS TO REMEMBER," THIS VAPID VERSE HAS occupied a slot in the McGuffey Readers from 1836 until the present. Initially located in the Second Reader, it was moved up to the Third in 1857 and has remained at that level in subsequent editions.

Although God's omniscience is still the major attribute stressed, this verse also portrays God as kind, understanding, and "like a friend"—a less Calvinistic deity than pictured in early New England texts. In general, the benevolence of God receives more emphasis in later editions, while lessons are dropped which stress the sinful nature of man and the likelihood of eternal punishment. Typical of those lessons omitted is "The Importance of a Well Spent Youth," which emphasized that "The soil of the human heart is naturally barren of every thing good, though prolific of evil . . . And what if you should die young?"

5. Re-mem-ber, O! re-mem-ber,
    That he is like a friend,
And wish-es us to be
    Good, and hap-py in the end.

6. Re-mem-ber, child, re-mem-ber,
    To pray to Him in heav-en;
And if you have done wrong,
    Oh! ask to be for-giv-en.

7. Be sor-ry, in your lit-tle pray-er,
    And whis-per in his ear;
Ask his for-give-ness and his love,
    And he will sure-ly hear.

8. Re-mem-ber, child, re-mem-ber,
    That you love, with all your might,
The God who lives in heav-en,
    And gives us each de-light,
Who guards us all the day,
    And saves us in the night.

QUESTIONS.—Who is it that looks on all we do? What does God hate? What must we do, if we have done wrong?

TO TEACHERS.

The Spelling Lists at the head of the Reading Lessons, are given merely as examples of the manner in which spelling should be taught, in connection with reading. The teacher should add all the important words of the lesson.

LESSON LI.

thief	peo-ple	vi-o-lent	re-ceiv-ed
Pil-fer	larg-est	or-an-ges	break-fast
bri-dle	faith-ful	hon-est-y	sprawl-ing
re-store	step-ped	neigh-bor	re-ward-ed
slip-ped	prom-ise	guard-ing	hap-pen-ed

THE TEACHER will observe, that in this, and in some of the following lessons, a *few* of the emphatic words are in *italics*, though by no means *all* of them.

HON-EST-Y RE-WARD-ED.

1. CHARLES was an hon-est boy, but his neigh-bor, Jack Pil-fer, was a *thief*. Charles would never take any thing which did not *be-long* to him. But Jack would take what-ev-er he could *get*, and when he found what was *lost*, he would never *re-store* it.

2. One sum-mer's morning, as Charles was go-ing to school, he met a man by the pub-lic house, who had or-an-ges to sell. The man wished to stop and get his break-fast, and asked Charles if he would hold his horse while he went into the house.

3. But he first asked the land-lord, if he knew Charles to be an hon-est boy, as he would not like to trust his or-an-ges with him, if he was *not*.

ORIGINALLY ENTITLED "THE HONEST BOY AND THE THIEF." THIS selection—used initially in the Second Reader—*appeared in the* McGuffeys *from 1836 until 1879. The thief here, Jack Pilfer, is a marvelously named villain—one of the best in McGuffey's rogues' gallery—but he carries a relatively innocuous name when compared to a nasty like "Lazy Slokins," who inhabits a number of lessons in Marcius Willson's* Second Reader *later in the century. Of course, all such examples of wickedness and sloth, regardless of name, get their appropriate come-uppance.*

90

4. "Yes," said the land-lord; "I have known Charles all his life, and have never known him to *lie* or *steal*. All the neigh-bors know him to be an hon-est boy, and I will prom-ise that your or-an-ges will be as safe with *him* as with *your-self*."

5. The or-ange man then put the bri-dle into Charles's hand, and went into the house to eat his break-fast.

6. Very soon Jack Pil-fer came along the road, and see-ing Charles hold-ing the horse, he asked him whose horse he had there, and what was in the bas-kets on the horse. Charles told him that the own-er of the horse was in the house, and there were or-an-ges in the bas-kets.

7. As soon as Jack found there were or-an-ges in the bas-kets, he re-solv-ed to have one. Go-ing up to the bas-ket, he slip-ped in his hand, and took out one of the larg-est, and was go-ing away with it.

8. But Charles said, "Jack, you shall not steal these or-an-ges, while *I* have care of them. So you may just put that one back into the bas-ket."

9. "Not I," said Jack, "as I am the *larg-est*, I shall do as I please." But Charles

was not afraid of him, and ta-king the or-ange out of his hand, he threw it back.

10. Jack then turn-ed to go round to the other side, and take one from the *other* bas-ket. But as he stepped too near the horse's heels, he re-ceiv-ed a vi-o-lent kick, which sent him sprawl-ing to the ground.

11. His cries soon brought out the peo-ple from the house, and when they learned what had hap-pen-ed, they said that Jack was *right-ly served.*

12. The or-ange man, taking Charles's hat, filled it with or-an-ges, and said, as he had been so faith-ful in *guard-ing* them, he should have all these for his *hon-est-y.*

QUESTIONS.—Relate this story. How can boys secure a good name? What advantage is there in having one?

Just as the heroes in McGuffey's lessons often reap instant rewards for virtuous deeds, the villains usually receive their deserts quickly as well. And no sympathy is wasted on the wounded Jack Pilfer, who evidently had to watch in pain as Charles accepted the rewards for his honesty.

ARTICULATION.

THE EXERCISES IN ARTICULATION are a continuation of those in the New Second Reader. They should be *carefully* and *thoroughly* practiced, until a distinct and perfect articulation is secured. The *sounds* alone, and not the *names* of the letters, should be uttered.

Lt. $\overset{2}{a}$lt, $\overset{2}{e}$lt, $\overset{2}{i}$lt, $\overset{2}{o}$lt, $\overset{2}{u}$lt,   oilt,   oult.

Lts. $\overset{2}{a}$lts, $\overset{2}{e}$lts, $\overset{2}{i}$lts, $\overset{2}{o}$lts, $\overset{2}{u}$lts,   oilts,   oults.

$\overset{2}{m}$elt, $\overset{2}{m}$elts, $\overset{2}{t}$ilt, $\overset{2}{t}$ilts, $\overset{2}{b}$elt, $\overset{2}{b}$elts, $\overset{2}{p}$elt, $\overset{2}{p}$elts.

LESSON II.

hire	o-bey′	con′duct	in-stead′
school	guilt′y	man′age	wa′ter-y
known	tru′ant	reach′ed	reg′u-lar
clothes	mon′ey	run′ning	ig′no-rant
thrown	les′sons	mind′ing	strug′gled
i′dle	play′ing	drown′ed	strug′gling

THE TRUANT.

1. JAMES BROWN was ten years old, when his parents sent him to school. It was not far from his home, and therefore they sent him by himself.

2. But, instead of going to school, he was in the habit of playing truant. He would go into the fields, or spend his time with idle boys.

"THE TRUANT" WAS A LATE-ARRIVAL IN THE READERS, NOT MAKING ITS first appearance until the 1857 edition. It has remained un-changed in all subsequent editions.

3. But this was not all. When he went home, he would tell his mother that he had been to school, and had said his lessons very well.

4. One fine morning, his mother told James to make haste home from school; for she wished, after he had come back, to take him to his aunt's.

5. But, instead of minding her, he went off to the water, where there were some boats. There he met a plenty of idle boys.

6. Some of these boys found that James had money, which his aunt had given him. He was led by them to hire a boat, and to go with them upon the water.

7. Little did James think of the danger he was running into. Soon, the wind began

Truancy must have been a major problem in McGuffey's time, since it appears frequently as a subject. Often—as here— the truant's actions lead him into lying, subsequent acts of disobedience, and dangerous situations. The subject of truancy was also denounced in a number of verses, such as this sample from a lesson following "The Truant":

Haste thee, school-boy, haste away,
Join no more the idler's play;
Quickly speed your steps to school,
And there mind your teacher's rule;
Haste thee, school-boy, haste away,
Join no more the idler's play.

James Brown is not the only (or even the first) child in the pages of the Readers who faces near death because of his disobedience. In fact, he is luckier than some, in that he lives to repent. Death—often by drowning—is frequently pictured in the McGuffeys as a possible consequence of disobedience.

to blow, and none of them knew how to manage the boat.

8. For some time, they struggled against the wind and tide. At last, they became so tired, that they could row no longer.

9. A large wave upset the boat, and they were all thrown into the water. Think of James Brown, the truant, at this time.

10. He was far from home, known by no one. His parents were ignorant of his danger. He was struggling in the water, on the point of being drowned.

11. Some men, however, saw the boys, and went out to them in a boat. They reached them just in time to save them from a watery grave.

12. They were taken into a house, where their clothes were dried. After a while, they were sent home to their parents.

13. James was sorry for his conduct, and was never guilty of the same thing again.

14. He became regular at school, learned to attend to his books, and, above all, to obey his parents.

EXERCISES.—What was James Brown in the habit of doing? What would he tell his mother? How was he at last punished? How was he saved? What effect did this have on him?

LESSON XXVIII.

chief	a'pron	pitch'er	mis'chief
tease	plăc'ed	be-lieve'	con-fin'ed
tricks	say'ing	pas'sage	car'ry-ing
trick'y	slip'ped	chăng'ed	de-serv'ed
screams	de-light'	laugh'ing	pun'ish-ment

THE TRICKY BOY.

1. GEORGE NORTON was very fond of playing tricks.

2. He thought it was fine fun to tie a rope across a passage, and see some one fall over it, or to pin a little girl's apron to the chair, so that it would tear when she rose.

3. He did not think or care about the danger of being hurt by the fall, or of the trouble of mending clothes that were torn.

4. As his chief delight was to tease others, he was not liked by any one. At last, however, he met with a punishment which he richly deserved.

5. One morning, he met a little girl with a pitcher of milk. Being tired of carrying it in her hand, she asked him to put it on her head.

"THE TRICKY BOY" HAD A SHORT LIFE IN THE McGUFFEYS, APPEARing only from 1857 until 1879. It may have been removed because—at least in the early part of the lesson—it suggests tricks some of the duller students may not yet have thought of. A more probable reason for its departure, however, lies in its being such a long negative example.

6. "With all my heart," said George. He thought it would be fine fun to throw it down, and make her believe that she had let it fall.

7. "Come here. Stand very still, and when I have lifted the pitcher, be sure that you take hold of the handle."

8. "Thank you," said the little girl. "My arm is ready to drop off. I have been a great way, and my little brothers and sisters can have no dinner till I get home."

9. "Very well," said George. "Now then, stand still." So saying, the moment he had placed the pitcher on her head, he took care to let go, before she could take hold of it.

96

10. As George wished, the pitcher fell to the ground, and was broken in pieces, and the milk lost.

11. The poor girl burst into tears; but George stood laughing, and asked her, why she did not take hold of the handle. But his laughing was very soon changed into screams.

12. The milk had made the ground so soft, that, in turning to run away, George's foot slipped, and he fell with his leg under him, and broke it.

13. Nobody could be very sorry for him. He was confined to his bed three months, and every one said, "So much the better. The lesson will do him good, and he will be out of the way of mischief."

EXERCISES.—Relate the story of the boy who loved to play tricks. Why could nobody be very sorry for him? How must we behave if we wish others to love us?

TO TEACHERS.

It should be remembered, that the *Spelling Exercises* connected with the reading lessons in this book, are, by no means, designed as a substitute for the *indispensable drill of the Spelling-book*, but merely as auxiliary to that. A very careful attention to this exercise is recommended, especially for young pupils; as youth is the time, when, if ever, the foundation is laid for correct spelling.

Like Jack Pilfer and other villains pictured in the McGuffeys, *George Norton receives little sympathy when his dastardly trick backfires. Unlike many of the other lessons, however, the victim of the trick is apparently left without compensation—although this may have been an editorial oversight, rather than an attempt toward realism.*

22. "The urn, too, would have come tumbling down; and then, all the hot water would have run out, and wet the room, and might have scalded me. I am very glad, mother, that I did as you bid me."

EXERCISE.—Relate the story of Frank and the table.

ARTICULATION.

Rt, rts.	art,	ort,	urt,	arts,	orts,	urts.
	hart,	harts,	dart,	darts,	hurt,	hurts.
	start,	starts,	cart,	carts,	part,	parts.

LESSON XXXII.

touch	bas'ket	re-joice'	for-sake'
bread	tap'ped	reach'ed	del'i-cate
bunch	pin'ned	match'es	fa'ther-ly
toss'ed	mod'est	stran'ger	care'less-ly
pen'ny	blank'et	build'ing	in'no-cence

MARY DOW.

1. "COME in, little stranger," I said,
   As she tapped at my half-open door;
   While the blanket pinned over her head,
   Just reached to the basket she bore.

"MARY DOW" IS AN EXAMPLE OF THE MORE SENTIMENTAL VERSE THAT was incorporated into the Readers *in the later half of the nineteenth century. This lesson first appeared in the 1857 edition and has been part of all subsequent editions of the* Third Reader.

2. A look full of innocence, fell
    From her modest and pretty blue eye,
As she said, "I have matches to sell,
    And hope you are willing to buy.

3. "A penny a bunch is the price,
    I think you'll not find it too much;
They are tied up so even and nice,
    And ready to light with a touch."

4. I asked, "What's your name, little girl?"
    "'T is Mary," said she, "Mary Dow;"
And carelessly tossed off a curl,
    That played on her delicate brow.

5. "My father was lost on the deep;
    The ship never got to the shore;
And mother is sad and will weep,
    To hear the wind blow and sea roar.

Much of the verse in the McGuffeys *reminds one of the description of Emmiline Grangerford in Mark Twain's* Adventures of Huckleberry Finn. *According to her proud brother Buck,*

. . .she could rattle off poetry like nothing. She didn't ever have to stop to think . . . she would slap down a line, and if she couldn't find anything to rhyme with it she would just scratch it out and slap down another one, and go ahead. She warn't particular, she could write about anything you choose to give her to write about, just so it was sadful.

Mary's situation is a fairly common one in these lessons: father dead, mother poor, brother (or sister) ill, but her faith in God undaunted. The importance of charity is constantly stressed, especially in the first three Readers. Here the narrator happens to be an adult who illustrates charity. More often it is a child with whom the young scholars can identify . . . one who acts charitably toward someone less fortunate, and usually—though not always—receives a parental reward for having so acted.

6. "She sits there at home without food,
     Beside our poor sick Willy's bed;
   She paid all her money for wood,
     And so I sell matches for bread.

7. "I'd go to the yard and get chips,
     But then it would make me too sad
   To see the men building the ships,
     And think they had made one so bad.

8. "But God, I am sure, who can take
     Such fatherly care of a bird,
   Will never forget nor forsake
     The children who trust in his word.

9. "And now, if I only can sell
     The matches I brought out to-day,
   I think I shall do very well,
     And we shall rejoice at the pay."

10. "Fly home, little bird," then I thought,
      "Fly home, full of joy, to your nest;"
    For I took all the matches she brought,
      And Mary may tell you the rest.

EXERCISES.—What had Mary to sell? Why did she sell them? Why did she not go the ship-yard to get chips? Who, did she think, would take care of her? Why? Point out the commas in this lesson. The semicolons. The periods. The interrogation marks.

100

LESSON XL.

friend	al-low'	old'est	neigh'bor
wheat	mon'ey	hunt'er	there'fore
brought	har'vest	hunt'ing	re-turn'ing

SPELL AND DEFINE.

2. Es'ti-mate; a value set.   3. Re-pay'; to pay back.

THE HONEST MAN.

1. A FARMER called, one day, upon a rich neighbor, who was very fond of hunting, and told him that his wheat had been so much cut up by the hunter's dogs, that, in some parts, there would be no crop.

2. "Well, my friend," said the hunter, "I know that we have often met in that wheat field. If you will give me an estimate of your loss, I will repay you."

3. The farmer said, that with the help of a friend, he had made an estimate. They thought that one hundred dollars would not more than repay him.

4. The hunter gave him the money. As the harvest came on, however, the farmer found, that the wheat in that place was the strongest and best in the field.

"THE HONEST MAN" STANDS AS ANOTHER EXAMPLE OF THE MANY LESsons in the McGuffeys emphasizing the value of honesty. As is so often the case in these lessons, being honest clearly pays. Although this particular lesson was employed for only twenty years (in the 1857 and 1865 editions), the theme itself has been a vital part of every McGuffey Reader ever published.

5. He called again, and said, "I have come about that wheat, of which I spoke to you some time since."

6. "Well, my friend," said the hunter, "did I not allow you enough for the loss?"

7. "O yes," said the farmer, "I find there will be no loss at all.   Where the dogs most cut up the land, the crop is the best.   I have therefore brought back the money."

8. "Ah," cried the hunter, "that is what I like.   This is what ought to be between man and man."

9. He then went into another room, and returning, gave the farmer five hundred dollars.

10. "Take care of this," said he, "and when your oldest son is twenty-one years old, give it to him, and tell him how it came into your hands."

EXERCISES.—What did the farmer tell the hunter?   What did the hunter say?   What did the hunter do?   What did the farmer do when he found there would be no loss?   What did the hunter say and do?

TO TEACHERS.

It is of the utmost importance that the pupil should understand thoroughly *all* that he reads.   A spirit of inquiry should be encouraged; and questions, in addition to those given, should be often put by the teacher, to stimulate the mind of the learner.

Although the McGuffey Readers *have sometimes been criticized as texts that encouraged teaching primarily through memorization and recitation, all editions stress the importance of helping pupils to acquire a thorough understanding of what they were reading. In the 1836* Second Reader, *McGuffey's "Suggestions to Teachers" were even stronger:*

Nothing can be more fatiguing to the teacher, nor irksome to the pupil, than a recitation conducted on the plan of "verbatim answers, to questions not always the most pertinent nor perspicuous." And even if the questions found in the book were the most pertinent, still it would be but little more than an exercise of memory, to the neglect of other faculties, to confine the examinations exclusively to these.

LESSON LXXII.

frol'ic   ap-pear'   cheer'ful   boun'ces
vil'lage   as-cends'   pleas'ure   march'ing

SPELL AND DEFINE.

5. Deck'ed; gaily dressed.   5. Lac'es; fine thread-work.

THE VILLAGE GREEN.

1. On the cheerful village green,
   Scattered round with houses neat,
All the boys and girls are seen,
   Playing there with busy feet.

2. Now they frolic, hand in hand,
   Making many a merry chain;
Then they form a happy band,
   Marching o'er the level plain.

PICTURES OR DESCRIPTIONS OF CHILDREN PLAYING ARE RELATIVELY rare within the Readers—*particularly in the early editions. This lesson, for instance, was not added until 1857—but even here (as the next page shows) the subject is not* play itself, *but the moral lesson that can be drawn from further reflection on those happy moments.*

And here that moral lesson is obvious; furthermore, in its emphasizing the need to be content with one's station, it is a familiar McGuffey theme. The questions that follow, however, are somewhat unusual, in that they encourage movement of the discussion far beyond the lesson's verse, even into Socratic matters.

3. Then ascends the merry ball;
    High it rises in the air,
Or, against the cottage wall,
    Up and down, it bounces there.

4. Or the hoop, with even pace,
    Runs before the cheerful crowd:
Joy is seen in every face,
    Joy is heard in shoutings loud.

5. For, among the rich and gay,
    Fine, and grand, and decked in laces,
None appear more glad than they,
    With happier hearts, or happier faces.

6. Then contented with my state,
Let me envy not the great;
Since true pleasure may be seen,
On a cheerful village green.

EXERCISES.—What sports are described in this lesson? Why are children so much happier than most older persons? Upon what does happiness depend?

ARTICULATION.

Ft, Fts.

Drift,	drifts:	sift,	sifts:	gift,	gifts.
Lift,	lifts:	toft,	tofts:	loft,	lofts.
Croft,	crofts:	tuft,	tufts:	theft,	thefts.

ARTICULATION.

Ks, (x), Kst, (xt).

[*Ck* has merely the sound of *K*.]

Lacks, lackst: packs, packst: clacks, clackst.
Cracks, crackst: tracks, trackst: stacks, stackst.
Tax, taxt: wax, waxt: box, boxt.

LESSON LXXVII.

meant	se′cret	yield′ed	fam′i-ly
la′bor	prof′its	re-quest′	in′dus-try
ex-act′	look′ing	treas′ure	gath′er-ed

INDUSTRY A TREASURE.

1. A WEALTHY old farmer, seeing that he must soon die, called together his sons to his bedside.

2. "My dear children," said he, "I leave it you as my last request, not to part with the farm, which has been so long in our family.

3. "To make known to you a *secret* which I had from my father, there is a *treasure* hid somewhere in the ground, though I could never find the *exact spot*.

come to acknowledging the tremendous excitement generated across the country by the California Gold Rush (which began in 1849). With the drilling of the first oil well near Titusville, Pennsylvania, in 1858, another boom rush began—and the lesson had another point of topical application, although neither is ever specifically pointed out or developed.

4. "However, as soon as the harvest is got in, spare no pains in the search. I am *sure* that you will not lose your labor."

5. The wise old man was no sooner laid in his grave, and the harvest gathered in, than his sons began to look for the treasure.

6. With great care, they turned up, again and again, nearly every foot of ground on the farm; but, though they did not find what they were looking for, their farm yielded a much larger crop than ever.

7. At the end of the year, when the sons were counting their great profits, one of them, *wiser* than the *others*, said, "I do believe, that *this* was the treasure my father *meant*.

8. "I am sure, at least, that we have found out this, that *industry* is itself a *treasure*."

Exercises.—What did the old man say to his sons? What did they do? What was the consequence? To what conclusion did they come?

ARTICULATION.

Lm, Ls, Lst.

elm,	helm:	ells,	cells:	ellst,	sellst.
ilm,	film:	ills,	rills:	illst,	killst.
ulm,	culm:	ulls,	mulls:	ullst,	hullst.

LESSON XIII.

wolf	grieved	sleeve	neigh'bors	ear'nest
ăx'eş	elŭbş	ôr'der	sĭn'ġle	de stroy'

THE WOLF.

1. A boy was once taking care of some sheep, not far from a forest. Near by was a village, and he was told to call for help if there was any danger.

2. One day, in order to have some fun, he cried out, with all his might, "The wolf is coming! the wolf is coming!"

3. The men came running with clubs and axes to destroy the wolf. As they saw nothing they went home again, and left John laughing in his sleeve.

4. As he had had so much fun this time, John cried out again, the next day, "The wolf! the wolf!"

5. The men came again, but not so many as the first time. Again they saw no trace of the wolf; so they shook their heads, and went back.

6. On the third day, the wolf came in earnest. John cried in dismay, "Help! help!

THIS FAMILIAR MORAL TALE IS ONE OF THE BEST KNOWN OF AESOP'S Fables, supposedly the product of a black Samian slave named Aesop who lived in the sixth century B.C. Actually, it is impossible now to determine exactly which tales were Aesop's— or indeed if there really was such an historical figure. Nearly all the fables known to Western civilization have been grouped under Aesop's name at one time or another, and it is likely that many of them existed in an oral tradition prior to Aesop's time. As Thackeray wrote in The Newcomes: *"So the tales were told ages before Aesop; and asses under lions' manes roared in Hebrew; and sly foxes flattered in Etruscan; and wolves in sheep's clothing gnashed their teeth in Sanskrit, no doubt." No doubt. But Aesop—the most famous Uncle Remus of all time—should have received author's attribution here: this is one of the oldest of those attributed to him.*

In contrast with many of the competing textbooks of the time, the McGuffeys include relatively few of Aesop's Fables. This one, however, entered the Readers in 1857 and has remained in use to the present. It differs significantly from standard translations only in that here the boy has a name and he suffers an emotional and personal loss—his pet lamb—in addition to the destruction of the other sheep.

the wolf! the wolf!" But not a single man came to help him.

7. The wolf broke into the flock, and killed

a great many sheep. Among them was a beautiful lamb, which belonged to John.

8. Then he felt very sorry that he had deceived his friends and neighbors, and grieved over the loss of his pet lamb.

The truth itself is not believed,
From one who often has deceived.

12. " Then, my dear, show your sorrow by deeds of kindness. The good alone are really beautiful."

LESSON XXV.

a void'	pre vĕnt'	for g̅ĭve'	rĭ§e	g̅uīde
dūr'ing	pout'ing	pro tĕe'tion	slăm	măn'ner
pee'vish	howl'ing	săt'is fīed	trŭst	ăṉ'g̅ry

THINGS TO REMEMBER.

1. When you rise in the morning, remember who kept you from danger during the night. Remember who watched over you while you slept, and whose sun shines around you, and gives you the sweet light of day.

2. Let God have the thanks of your heart, for his kindness and his care; and pray for his protection during the wakeful hours of day.

3. Remember that God made all creatures to be happy, and will do nothing that may prevent their being so, without good reason for it.

4. When you are at the table, do not eat in a greedy manner, like a pig. Eat quietly,

3. 5

CARRYING THE TITLE "THINGS TO REMEMBER IN THE MORNING" WHEN McGuffey *first used it in the 1838 edition of the* Second Reader, *this lesson was elevated to the* Third Reader *in 1857. With the exception of the minor title change, it has remained essentially unchanged in all editions from 1838 until the present.*

If there is any single lesson in the McGuffeys that incorporates most of the do's and don't's of the time, this is it— comprising a children's addenda to the Ten Commandments. Once again, the divine attribute being stressed is the omniscience of God, although this lesson goes further than many in also discussing God's benevolence.

and do not reach forth your hand for the food, but ask some one to help you.

5. Do not become peevish and pout, because you do not get a part of everything. Be satisfied with what is given you.

6. Avoid a pouting face, angry looks, and angry words. Do not slam the doors. Go quietly up and down stairs; and never make a loud noise about the house.

7. Be kind and gentle in your manners; not like the howling winter storm, but like the bright summer morning.

8. Do always as your parents bid you. Obey them with a ready mind, and with a pleasant face.

9. Never do anything that you would be afraid or ashamed that your parents should know. Remember, if no one else sees you, God does, from whom you can not hide even your most secret thought.

10. At night, before you go to sleep, think whether you have done anything that was wrong during the day, and pray to God to forgive you. If any one has done you wrong, forgive him in your heart.

11. If you have not learned something useful, or been in some way useful, during

the past day, think that it is a day lost, and be very sorry for it.

12. Trust in the Lord, and He will guide you in the way of good men. The path of the just is as the shining light that shineth more and more unto the perfect day.

13. We must do all the good we can to all men, for this is well pleasing in the sight of God. He delights to see his children walk in love, and do good one to another.

This illustration appeared in the 1857 edition of the Third Reader, *accompanying the next lesson included here: "The New Year." A capsule history of the evolution of McGuffey illustrations may be seen in comparing this plate with the 1865 illustration (next page) and then with the 1879/1920 plate (within the text of "The New Year" on the following pages).*

This is Edward dispensing charity in the 1865 edition. The engraving here emerges with a sharper focus, evidently having been made specifically for this lesson. Note, for instance, that the three foreign children are clearly pictured, whereas in the earlier edition it appears that a third child was hastily added to bring the engraving in line with the text.

LESSON XXVII.

Ed'ward	re çēive'	wrĕtch'ed	thou'ṣand	ḡrăt'i tūde
re pēat'	lăn̄'ḡuaġe	shĭv'er ing	Gẽr'man	ŭn der stōōd'

THE NEW YEAR.

1. One pleasant New-year morning, Edward rose, and washed and dressed himself

in haste. He wanted to be first to wish a happy New Year.

2. He looked in every room, and shouted the words of welcome. He ran into the

In the 1879 edition, the illustration captures better the relative affluence of young Edward, and it also makes better use of background and perspective to draw the viewer into a more realistic setting.

street, to repeat them to those he might meet.

3. When he came back, his father gave him two bright, new silver dollars.

4. His face lighted up as he took them. He had wished for a long time to buy some pretty books that he had seen at the bookstore.

For over twenty years after this lesson first appeared (in 1857), the poor family in the story was Swiss, rather than German. The change occurred in the 1879 revision, for reasons that cannot now be determined with certainty. One possible explanation is that the Swiss are regularly stereotyped in nineteenth-century American textbooks as fiercely independent—so the picture of a Swiss man begging might have seemed dramatically incongruous to some. Another possible explanation is that the McGuffey Readers were still being published in Cincinnati at this time, and the "Queen City of the West" had a high percentage of German-Americans within its population; it remained a terminal point for German immigrants for the rest of the century.

5. He left the house with a light heart, intending to buy the books.

6. As he ran down the street, he saw a poor German family, the father, mother, and three children shivering with cold.

7. "I wish you a happy New Year," said Edward, as he was gayly passing on. The man shook his head.

8. "You do not belong to this country," said Edward. The man again shook his head, for he could not understand or speak our language.

9. But he pointed to his mouth, and to the children, as if to say, "These little ones have had nothing to eat for a long time."

10. Edward quickly understood that these poor people were in distress. He took out his dollars, and gave one to the man, and the other to his wife.

11. How their eyes sparkled with gratitude! They said something in their language, which doubtless meant, "We thank you a thousand times, and will remember you in our prayers."

12. When Edward came home, his father asked what books he had bought. He hung his head a moment, but quickly looked up.

13. "I have bought no books," said he, "I gave my money to some poor people, who seemed to be very hungry and wretched.

14. "I think I can wait for my books till next New Year.   Oh, if you had seen how glad they were to receive the money!"

15. "My dear boy," said his father, "here is a whole bundle of books.   I give them to you, more as a reward for your goodness of heart than as a New-year gift.

16. "I saw you give the money to the poor German family.   It was no small sum for a little boy to give cheerfully.

17. "Be thus ever ready to help the poor, and wretched, and distressed; and every year of your life will be to you a happy New Year."

LESSON XXVIII.

stŏck	spĭr'it	hŭm'ble	glōōm'y	sŭn'dī al
fŏl'ly	stee'ple	stū'pid	bōast'ing	mŏd'es ty

THE CLOCK AND THE SUNDIAL.
A FABLE.

1. One gloomy day, the clock on a church steeple, looking down on a sundial, said,

Once again the McGuffey ethic is maintained. Edward receives not only personal (and probably heavenly) satisfaction for his act of charity, but an instant earthly reward as well. The bundle of books, incidentally, would have indeed been viewed as a reward by many in the nineteenth century—by more, one fears, than would view it so today.

LESSON XLII.

BEWARE OF THE FIRST DRINK.

1. "Uncle Philip, as the day is fine, will you take a walk with us this morning?"

2. "Yes, boys. Let me get my hat and cane, and we will take a ramble. I will tell you a story as we go. Do you know poor old Tom Smith?"

3. "Know him! Why, Uncle Philip, everybody knows him. He is such a shocking drunkard, and swears so horribly."

4. "Well, I have known him ever since we were boys together. There was not a more decent, well-behaved boy among us. After he left school, his father died, and he was put into a store in the city. There, he fell into bad company.

5. "Instead of spending his evenings in reading, he would go to the theater and to balls. He soon learned to play cards, and of course to play for money. He lost more than he could pay.

6. "He wrote to his poor mother, and told her his losses. She sent him money to pay his debts, and told him to come home.

DESPITE SUCH EARLY PUBLICATIONS AS BENJAMIN RUSH'S AN INQUIRY into the Effects of Spirituous Liquors on the Human Mind and Body *(1784), the temperance movement did not really get organized until early in the nineteenth century. Most prominent of the early leaders was the Rev. Mr. Lyman Beecher of Boston, whose sermons led in 1826 to the formation of The American Society for the Promotion of Temperance. (Beecher, incidentally, moved to the Cincinnati area in 1832, immediately becoming a major intellectual figure in the West. It was here that he met and clearly influenced—well before the* Readers *were compiled—both William Holmes McGuffey and his younger brother, Alexander.)*

This particular lesson, entitled simply, "The First Drink" when it initially entered the Readers *in 1857, is more fictionalized than the earlier lessons on the subject. But it is typical of many lessons in its development of the "falling domino" effects of the evil life in "the city." Theatre life and dancing lead to gambling—and they in turn lead to drinking, crime, deterioration, and destruction. One need not be an abstainer, however, to acknowledge that drunkenness was one of the most appalling social problems America had during the nineteenth*

7. "He did come home. After all, he might still have been useful and happy, for his friends were willing to forgive the past. For a time, things went on well. He married a lovely woman, gave up his bad habits, and was doing well.

8. "But one thing, boys, ruined him forever. In the city, he had learned to take strong drink, and he said to me once, that when a man begins to drink, he never knows where it will end. 'Therefore,' said Tom, 'beware of the first drink!'

9. "It was not long before he began to follow his old habit. He knew the danger, but it seemed as if he could not resist his desire to drink. His poor mother soon died of grief and shame. His lovely wife followed her to the grave.

10. "He lost the respect of all, went on from bad to worse, and has long been a perfect sot. Last night, I had a letter from the city, stating that Tom Smith had been found guilty of stealing, and sent to the state prison for ten years.

11. "There I suppose he will die, for he is now old. It is dreadful to think to what an end he has come. I could not but think,

century. It is within that context that Tom Smith's story was told, and it should be recognized that the problem then was deadly serious—not just the exaggerated rhetoric of the militant reformers.

The temperance movement quickly gained strength, and by 1834 over one million Americans had signed "the pledge." The name of the movement was actually misleading, however, since almost from the beginning its evangelistic campaign was conducted not for temperance, but for total abstinence from the use of alcoholic beverages. The movement remained a strong influence in America for nearly 100 years—until the Great Experiment of Prohibition was ended with the repeal of the 18th Amendment to the Constitution.

The illustration in the 1879 edition showed "poor old Tom Smith" standing in disheveled embarrassment before a judge. In the 1920 edition, however, Tom was reillustrated in meticulous detail, as shown here. Although penal practices have undergone enough reforms to render this portrayal rather humorous to a contemporary reader, its effect on a child fifty years ago was probably striking. Even more than the verbal lesson, the illustration shortens the distance between cause and effect.

as I read the letter, of what he said to me years ago, 'Beware of the first drink!'

12. "Ah, my dear boys, when old Uncle Philip is gone, remember that he told you

the story of Tom Smith, and said to you, 'Beware of the first drink!' The man who does this will never be a drunkard."

DEFINITIONS.—3. Hŏr′ri bly, *in a dreadful manner, terribly.* 4. Dē′çent, *modest, respectable.* 9. Re ṣïst′, *withstand, overcome.* 10. Sŏt, *an habitual drunkard.* Guïlt′y, *justly chargeable with a crime.*

3, 8.

LESSON XLIII.

SPEAK GENTLY.

1. Speak gently; it is better far
   To rule by love than fear:
Speak gently; let no harsh words mar
   The good we might do here.

2. Speak gently to the little child;
   Its love be sure to gain;
Teach it in accents soft and mild;
   It may not long remain.

3. Speak gently to the aged one;
   Grieve not the careworn heart:
The sands of life are nearly run;
   Let such in peace depart.

4. Speak gently, kindly, to the poor;
   Let no harsh tone be heard;
They have enough they must endure,
   Without an unkind word.

5. Speak gently to the erring; know
   They must have toiled in vain;
Perhaps unkindness made them so;
   Oh, win them back again.

VERY LITTLE IS KNOWN ABOUT THE AUTHOR OF THIS OFT-ANTHOLO-
*gized verse. It is usually, as here, attributed to David Bates
(1809–1870), who resided in Philadelphia and published at least
two books:* The Aeolian, a Collection of Poems *(1848), and
his* Poetical Works *(1870). But when the selection originally entered the* Readers *(in the 1857 edition) it was credited to
George Washington Langford, a figure whose claim to this
poem is evidently the only mark he left in this world. Another
claimant is one W. V. Wallace, about whom even less is known.*

*"Speak Gently" is one of the contemporary poems parodied
by Lewis Carroll in* Alice in Wonderland:

> *Speak roughly to your little boy,*
>   *And beat him when he sneezes:*
> *He only does it to annoy,*
>   *Because he knows it teases.*

6. Speak gently: 't is a little thing
    Dropped in the heart's deep well;
The good, the joy, which it may bring,
    Eternity shall tell.
David Bates.

DEFINITIONS.—1. Mär, *injure, hurt.* 2. Ae′çents, *language, tones.* 4. En dūre′, *bear, suffer.* 5. Err′ing (ēr′-), *sinning.* 6. E tĕr′ni ty, *the endless hereafter, the future.*

LESSON XLIV.

THE SEVEN STICKS.

1. A man had seven sons, who were always quarreling. They left their studies and work, to quarrel among themselves. Some bad men were looking forward to the death of their father, to cheat them out of their property by making them quarrel about it.

2. The good old man, one day, called his sons around him. He laid before them seven sticks, which were bound together. He said, "I will pay a hundred dollars to the one who can break this bundle."

3. Each one strained every nerve to break the bundle. After a long but vain trial, they all said that it could not be done.

THIS FAMILIAR TALE IS ONE OF THE OLDEST OF THOSE ATTRIBUTED to Aesop (as transcribed by Babrius, c. 230 A.D.). Its origins, however, are undoubtedly buried deep in the oral tradition that was old before the fabulous Aesop's birth, with some anticipations even in written literature. Note, for instance, this passage from Ecclesiastes (IV: 9–12):

> *Two are better than one; because they have good reward for their labour. For if they fall, the one will lift up his fellow: but woe to him that is alone when he falleth; for he hath not another to help him up. Again, if two be together, then they have heat: but how can one be warm alone? And if one prevail against him, two shall withstand him: and a threefold cord is not quickly broken.*

4. "And yet, my boys," said the father, "nothing is easier to do." He then untied the bundle, and broke the sticks, one by one, with perfect ease.

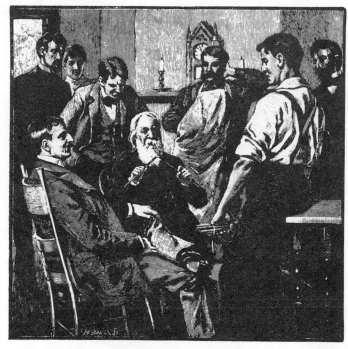

5. "Ah!" said his sons, "it is easy enough to do it so; anybody could do it in that way."

6. Their father replied, "As it is with these sticks, so is it with you, my sons. So

This moral tale, with relatively little variation, appears within the famous collections of fables and apologues of both L'Estrange and LaFontaine. Whether or not either of them used Aesop's Fables as the source is difficult to determine, however, since they might well have seen a similar story as told by Plutarch about a king of Scythia. Indeed, almost exactly the same incident supposedly occurred with Genghis Khan as the father-figure (recorded in Harkon's Armenian History of the Tartars).

A bundle of rods bound together was, of course, the emblem of not only union but authority to the ancient Romans, who called them fasces *(derived from the Latin* fascis, *meaning bundle). The emblem has been adopted for various ends over the centuries—serving, for instance, as a respected symbol for union on the backs of United States "Liberty" (or "Mercury") dimes from 1916 to 1946. But the symbol became tarnished in the 1930's and 1940's—when the Italian Fascists gave it notoriety—and it still carries negative connotations for many Americans today.*

long as you hold fast together and aid each other, you will prosper, and none can injure you.

7. "But if the bond of union be broken, it will happen to you just as it has to these sticks, which lie here broken on the ground."

Home, city, country, all are prosperous found,
When by the powerful link of union bound.

DEFINITIONS.—1. Chēat, *deceïve, wrong.* Prŏp′er ty, *that which one owns—whether land, goods, or money.* 2. Bŭn′dle, *a number of things bound together.* 3. Nērve, *sinew, muscle.* 6. Prŏs′per, *succeed, do well.* 7. Un′ion (ūn′yun), *the state of being joined or united.*

LESSON XLV.

THE MOUNTAIN SISTER.

1. The home of little Jeannette is far away, high up among the mountains. Let us call her our mountain sister.

2. There are many things you would like to hear about her, but I can only tell you now how she goes with her father and brother, in the autumn, to help gather nuts for the long winter.

LESSON XLVI.

HARRY AND THE GUIDEPOST.

1. The night was dark, the sun was hid
   Beneath the mountain gray,
   And not a single star appeared
   To shoot a silver ray.

2. Across the heath the owlet flew,
   And screamed along the blast;
   And onward, with a quickened step,
   Benighted Harry passed.

3. Now, in thickest darkness plunged,
   He groped his way to find;
   And now, he thought he saw beyond,
   A form of horrid kind.

4. In deadly white it upward rose,
   Of cloak and mantle bare,
   And held its naked arms across,
   To catch him by the hair.

5. Poor Harry felt his blood run cold,
   At what before him stood;
   But then, thought he, no harm, I'm sure,
   Can happen to the good.

ALTHOUGH THE VERSE ITSELF REMAINS UNCHANGED FROM ITS FIRST appearance in the Second Reader *in 1844 until this 1920 edition of the* Third Reader, *the title underwent several alterations (from "The Hand-Post" to "The Guide Post" and finally to that shown here). The opening stanzas reflect some of the Gothic elements that (although never present in force) were more common in some of the earlier editions, but weeded out gradually in the later 1800's.*

Harry's experience is but one of many anti-ghost lessons in the McGuffeys. *Most of them end on humorous notes with a frightened boy discovering that what he feared was merely a pillow hanging as a swing, or a lame goose struggling in the darkness.*

On at least one occasion, however, a lesson in the First Reader *attempted both to disprove the existence of ghosts and to dissuade children from pretending to be ghosts. That lesson, entitled "Never Do Mischief," describes two boys who dress under sheets and successfully frighten their playmate into mental derangement. It ends with the victim "a perfect idiot" who still cries out at night with horror, "Oh, they are coming! They are coming!" It was one of McGuffey's original selections, representative in its emphasizing strongly that all actions have consequences, but it was removed after the 1841 edition.*

6. So, calling all his cour-
    age up,
  He to the monster went;
  And eager through the
    dismal gloom
  His piercing eyes he bent.

7. And when he came well nigh the ghost
    That gave him such affright,
  He clapped his hands upon his side,
    And loudly laughed outright.

8. For 't was a friendly guidepost stood,
    His wandering steps to guide;
  And thus he found that to the good,
    No evil could betide.

9. Ah well, thought he, one thing I 've learned,
Nor shall I soon forget;
Whatever frightens me again,
I 'll march straight up to it.

10. And when I hear an idle tale,
Of monster or of ghost,
I 'll tell of this, my lonely walk,
And one tall, white guidepost.

DEFINITIONS.—2. Hēath, *a place overgrown with shrubs.*
Be nīght'ed, *overtaken by the night.* 3. Grōped, *felt his way
in the dark.* Hŏr'rid, *hideous, frightful.* 6. Mŏn'ster, *a
thing of unnatural size and shape.* Dĭṣ'mal, *dark, cheerless.*
Piĕr'çing, *sharp, penetrating.* 7. Ghōst (gōst), *a frightful
object in white, an apparition.* 8. Guīde'pōst, *a post and
sign set up at the forks of a road to direct travelers.* Be tīde',
befall, happen. 10. I'dle, *of no account, foolish.*

LESSON XLVII.

THE MONEY AMY DIDN'T EARN.

1. Amy was a dear little girl, but she was
too apt to waste time in getting ready to do
her tasks, instead of doing them at once as
she ought.

*"Harry and the Guide Post" is reproduced here from the 1920
edition, primarily because most of the earlier editions provided no illustration with this lesson. They did, however, furnish
auxiliary material that is missing here, such as study questions like "Are there such things as ghosts?" and "Does not God
always protect the good?"*

A NUMBER OF THE LESSONS IN THE McGUFFEYS ATTEMPT TO DEFINE and illustrate acts of real moral courage (as opposed especially to rash acts of mere physical bravado). This particular lesson epitomizes that objective and has always been a part of the series. Originally included in the first edition of the Second Reader, it was transferred to the Third Reader in 1857 and has remained at that level since.

One of the main results of the 1857 revised edition was the elevation of a number of lessons to higher level Readers. The reassessment appears to have been based mainly on close evaluation of each lesson's degree of reading difficulty. Obviously, pragmatic as well as idealistic motives helped form the McGuffeys. Even moved up to the Third Reader, however, this particular lesson still needed to be worked on, and a number of minor changes were made, most of which reduced the lesson's "hard words." In the last line of the first paragraph, for instance, the word good replaces the original amiable.

LESSON LII.

TRUE COURAGE.

One cold winter's day, three boys were passing by a schoolhouse. The oldest was a bad boy, always in trouble himself, and trying to get others into trouble. The youngest, whose name was George, was a very good boy.

George wished to do right, but was very much wanting in courage. The other boys were named Henry and James. As they walked along, they talked as follows:

Henry. What fun it would be to throw a snowball against the schoolroom door, and make the teacher and scholars all jump!

James. You would jump, if you should. If the teacher did not catch you and whip you, he would tell your father, and you would get a whipping then; and that would make you jump higher than the scholars, I think.

Henry. Why, we would get so far off, before the teacher could come to the door, that he could not tell who we are. Here is a snowball just as hard as ice, and George

would as soon throw it against the door as
not.

James. Give it to him, and see. He would
not dare to throw it.

Henry. Do you think George is a coward? You do not know him as well as I do.

Here, George, take this snowball, and show
James that you are not such a coward as he
thinks you are.

George. I am not afraid to throw it; but
I do not want to. I do not see that it

Yielding to the taunts of peers gets a number of children (particularly boys) into trouble throughout the pages of the McGuffey Readers. Nearly always it results in embarrassment and punishment, sometimes in near death (usually by drowning). Little George is actually treated rather kindly here by escaping with only a whipping for his rash action.

will do any good, or that there will be **any** fun in it.

James. There! I told you he would not dare to throw it.

Henry. Why, George, are you turning coward? I thought you did not fear anything. Come, **save** your credit, and throw it. I know you are not afraid.

George. Well, I am not afraid to throw. Give me the snowball. I would **as** soon throw it as not.

Whack! went the snowball against the door; and the boys took to their heels. Henry was laughing as heartily as he could, to think what a fool he had made of George.

George had a whipping for his folly, as he ought to have had. He was such a coward, that he was afraid of being called a coward. He did not dare refuse to do as Henry told him, for fear that he would be laughed at.

If he had been really a brave boy, he would have said, "Henry, do **you** suppose that I am so foolish as to throw that snowball, just because you want to have me? You may throw your own snowballs, if you please!"

Henry would, perhaps, have laughed at him, and called him a coward.

But George would have said, " Do you think that I care for your laughing? I do not think it right to throw the snowball. I will not do that which I think to be wrong, if the whole town should join with you in laughing."

This would have been real courage. Henry would have seen, at once, that it would do no good to laugh at a boy who had so bold a heart. You must have this fear-less spirit, or you will get into trouble, and will be, and ought to be, disliked by all.

DEFINITIONS.—Sehŏl'arṣ, *children at school.* Whĭp'ping, *punishment.* Dâre, *have courage.* Crĕd'it, *reputation.* Heärt'i-ly, *freely, merrily.* Re fūṣe', *decline.* Fēar'less, *bold, brave.* Dis līked', *not loved.*

LESSON LIII.

THE OLD CLOCK.

1. In the old, old hall the old clock stands,
   And round and round move the steady hands;
   With its tick, tick, tick, both night and day,
   While seconds and minutes pass away.

The original closing read as follows: "And you must have this fearlessness of spirit, or you will be continually involved in trouble, and will deserve and receive contempt." By revising it to the form shown in the version here—a decision evidently made by the publisher's editors, not McGuffey himself—the lesson clearly becomes less difficult to read. At the same time, however, a more simplistic, even absolute, set of values is introduced.

THIS FAMILIAR POEM—STILL ANTHOLOGIZED TODAY IN COLLECTIONS of comfortable verse—was first included in the McGuffeys in 1879 (the edition from which this lesson is reproduced).

LESSON LVII.

WHICH LOVED BEST?

"I love you, mother," said little John;
Then, forgetting work, his cap went on,
And he was off to the garden swing,
Leaving his mother the wood to bring.

2. "I love you, mother," said rosy Nell;
"I love you better than tongue can tell;"

Then she teased and pouted full half the day,
Till her mother rejoiced when she went to play.

3. "I love you, mother," said little Fan;
"To-day I'll help you all I can;
How glad I am that school does n't keep!"
So she rocked the baby till it fell asleep.

4. Then, stepping softly, she took the broom,
And swept the floor, and dusted the room;
Busy and happy all day was she,
Helpful and cheerful as child could be.

5. "I love you, mother," again they said—
Three little children going to bed;
How do you think that mother guessed
Which of them really loved her best?

Joy Allison.

LESSON LVIII.

JOHN CARPENTER.

1. John Carpenter did not like to buy toys
that somebody else had made. He liked the
fun of making them himself. The thought
that they were his own work delighted him.

2. Tom Austin, one of his playmates,
thought a toy was worth nothing unless it
cost a great deal of money. He never tried
to make anything, but bought all his toys.

"Joy Allison" was the pseudonym of Mary A. Cragin (later Mrs. Mary A. Gillette). This poem is her major claim to fame, although she published at least three prose books. Two of these sound like conventional period pieces: Kate Jameson and Her Friends *(1872), and* David Kent's Ambition *(1877). The third, however, carries the more inviting title of* Conrad and the House Wolf *(1884).*

10. "Fly home, little bird," then I thought,
　　　"Fly home, full of joy, to your nest;"
　　For I took all the matches she brought,
　　　And Mary may tell you the rest.

DEFINITIONS.—1. Blăn′ket, *a square of loosely woven woolen cloth.* 2. Mătch′eṣ, *small splints of wood, one end of which has been dipped in a preparation which will take fire by rubbing.* 3. Pĕn′ny, *cent.* 4. Dĕl′i cate, *soft and fair.* 8. For sāke′, *leave, reject.*

LESSON LXVI.

THE LITTLE LOAF.

1. Once when there was a famine, a rich baker sent for twenty of the poorest children in the town, and said to them, "In this basket there is a loaf for each of you. Take it, and come back to me every day at this hour till God sends us better times."

2. The hungry children gathered eagerly about the basket, and quarreled for the bread, because each wished to have the largest loaf. At last they went away without even thanking the good gentleman.

3. But Gretchen, a poorly-dressed little girl, did not quarrel or struggle with the rest,

THIS LESSON DID NOT ENTER THE McGUFFEYS UNTIL THE 1879 EDITION, when a number of lessons were added that combined a rather sweet sentimentality with the dual moral injunctions to exercise charity and to be content with one's economic station, whatever it might be. All things considered, this is quite a juggling act of didactic writing.

but remained standing modestly in the distance. When the ill-behaved girls had left, she took the smallest loaf, which alone was left in the basket, kissed the gentleman's hand, and went home.

4. The next day the children were as ill-behaved as before, and poor, timid Gretchen received a loaf scarcely half the size of the one she got the first day. When she came home, and her mother cut the loaf open, many new, shining pieces of silver fell out of it.

5. Her mother was very much alarmed, and said, "Take the money back to the good gentleman at once, for it must have got into the dough by accident. Be quick, Gretchen! be quick!"

6. But when the little girl gave the rich man her mother's message, he said, "No, no, my child, it was no mistake. I had the silver pieces put into the smallest loaf to reward you. Always be as contented, peaceable, and grateful as you now are. Go home now, and tell your mother that the money is your own."

DEFINITIONS.—1. Făm'ĭne, *a general scarcity of food.* Lōaf, *a molded mass of regular shape* (as of bread or cake). 3. Grĕtch'en, *a girl's name—the shortened form, or pet name, for Marguerite.* Re māined', *staid.* Dĭs'tançe, *place which is far off.* Ill-be hāved', *rude, having bad manners.* 5. Ae'çi-dent, *mistake.* 6. Mĕs'sage, *word sent, communication.* Pēaçe'-a ble, *quiet, gentle.*

Fourth Reader

PRESENTED FIRST IN THE EARLY EDITIONS OF THE FOURTH READER, *"Ginevra" was transferred to the* Fifth Reader *in 1857, and then moved to the* Sixth Reader *for the 1879 and subsequent editions. It is one of fifty-two anecdotes and impressions (most of them in blank verse) published by Samuel Rogers under the title of* Italy *in successive volumes from 1822 to 1830. Although the poetic quality of* Italy *is generally poor, it was clearly one of the most popular poems during the early 1800's. The version reproduced here is from the 1841 edition and is—particularly in the opening lines—severely abridged.*

LESSON VI.

RULE.—Be careful to pronounce every syllable distinctly, and not to join the words together.

EXERCISES UNDER THE RULE.   To be read over several times by all the pupils.

The *range of* the valleys is his.
He was the *first ambassador sent.*
Swords and pens were both employed.
I do not *flinch from* the argument.
He never *winced, for* it hurt him not
Do not *singe your* gown.
Pluck'd from its native tree.
Nipt in the bud.
Thou *found'st me* poor, and *keep'st me* so.

Ginevra.—ROGERS.

1.   If ever you should come to Modena,
Stop at a palace near the Reggio-gate,
Dwelt in of old by one of the Donati.
Its noble gardens, terrace above terrace,
And rich in fountains, statues, cypresses,
Will long detain you—but, before you go,
Enter the house—forget it not, I pray you—
And look awhile upon a picture there.

2.   'Tis of a lady in her earliest youth,
The last of that illustrious family;
Done by Zampieri—but by whom I care not.
He, who observes it—ere he passes on,
Gazes his fill, and comes and comes again,
That he may call it up when far away.

3.   She sits, inclining forward as to speak,
Her lips half open, and her finger up,
As though she said, "Beware!" her vest of gold
Broidered with flowers and clasped from head to foot,
An emerald stone in every golden clasp;
And on her brow, fairer than alabaster,
A coronet of pearls.

4   But then her face,
So lovely, yet so arch, so full of mirth,

The overflowings of an innocent heart—
It haunts me still, though many a year has fled,
Like some wild melody!

5   Alone it hangs
Over a mouldering heir-loom ; its companion,
An oaken chest, half-eaten by the worm,
But richly carved by Antony of Trent
With scripture-stories from the life of Christ ;
A chest that came from Venice, and had held
The ducal robes of some old ancestors—
That by the way—it may be true or false—
But don't forget the picture ; and you will not,
When you have heard the tale they told me there.

6. She was an only child—her name Ginevra,
The joy, the pride of an indulgent father ;
And in her fifteenth year became a bride,
Marrying an only son, Francesco Doria,
Her playmate from her birth, and her first love.

7. Just as she looks there, in her bridal dress,
She was, all gentleness, all gayety,
Her pranks the favorite theme of every tongue.
But now the day was come, the day, the hour ;
Now, frowning, smiling for the hundredth time,
The nurse, that ancient lady, preached deco′rum ;
And, in the luster of her youth, she gave
Her hand, with her heart in it, to Francesco.

8. Great was the joy ; but at the nuptial feast,
When all sate down, the bride herself was wanting.
Nor was she to be found !   Her father cried,
"'Tis but to make a trial of our love !"
And filled his glass to all ; but his hand shook,
And soon from guest to guest the panic spread.

9. 'Twas but that instant she had left Francesco,
Laughing and looking back and flying still,
Her ivory tooth imprinted on his finger.
But now, alas ! she was not to be found ;
Nor from that hour could any thing be guessed,
But that she was not !

Samuel Rogers (1763–1855) was acknowledged as one of the leading literary figures and arbiters of taste in London during the first half of the nineteenth century. In fact, after Wordsworth's death in 1850, Rogers was offered the poet laureateship, but declined (the honor was subsequently bestowed upon Tennyson). His most famous poems are Pleasures of Memory *(1792) and* Italy, *the collection from which this lesson is taken. His total poetic canon is small—he wrote very little after* Italy—*and his reputation declined rapidly after his death. Rogers is seldom read today.*

This romantic tale exercised a haunting power over American textbook compilers, being included in nearly all of the advanced nineteenth-century readers. Concerning the basic plot, Rogers noted: "This story is, I believe, founded on fact; though time and place are uncertain. Many of the houses in England lay claim to it."

10.   Weary of his life,
Francesco flew to Venice, and embarking,
Flung it away in battle with the Turk.
Donati lived—and long might you have seen
An old man wandering as in quest of something,
Something he could not find—he knew not what.
When he was gone, the house remained awhile
Silent and tenantless—then went to strangers.

11. Full fifty years were past, and all forgotten,
When on an idle day, a day of search
Mid the old lumber in the gallery,
That mouldering chest was noticed; and 'twas said
By one as young, as thoughtless as Ginevra,
" Why not remove it from its lurking-place?"
'Twas done as soon as said; but on the way
It burst, it fell; and lo! a skeleton
With here and there a pearl, an emerald-stone,
A golden clasp, clasping a shred of gold.
All else had perished—save a wedding-ring,
And a small seal, her mother's legacy,
Engraven with a name, the name of both—
" Ginevra."

12. —There then had she found a grave!
Within that chest had she concealed herself,
Fluttering with joy, the happiest of the happy;
When a spring-lock, that lay in ambush there,
Fastened her down for ever!

———

QUESTIONS.- 1. Where is Modena? 2. Who was the painter of the picture? 3. Describe the attitude and dress. 4. What lies beneath the picture? 5. Relate the story which gives interest to the chest and picture.

ERRORS.—*Reg-gi-o* for Red-ge-o; *hont* for haunt (pronounced *hant*); *an-cient* for ān-cient; *sred* for shred.

SPELL AND DEFINE.—1. statues, terrace, cypresses; 2. illustrious; 3. broidered, emerald; 4. overflowing; 5. mouldering, ancestors, heirloom; 6. indulgent, ancient; 8. nuptial; 9. imprinted; 10. embarking; 11. engraven, emerald; 12. ambush.

LESSON LXX.

RULE.—Let the pupil stand at as great a distance from the teacher as possible, and then try to read so loud and distinctly that the teacher may hear each syllable.

America.—PHILLIPS.

1. I appeal to History! Tell me, thou reverend chronicler of the grave, can all the illusions of ambition realized, can all the wealth of a universal commerce, can all the achievments of successful heroism, or all the establishments of this world's wisdom, secure to empire the permanency of its possessions? Alas! Troy thought so once; yet the land of Priam lives only in song!

2. Thebes thought so once; yet her hundred gates have crumbled, and her very tombs are as the dust they were vainly intended to commemorate! So thought Palmyra—yet where is she? So thought the countries of Demosthenes and the Spartan; yet Leonidas is trampled by the timid slave, and Athens insulted by the servile, mindless and enervate Ottoman!

3. In his hurried march, Time has but looked at their imagined immortality; and all its vanities, from the palace to the tomb, have, with their ruins, erased the very impression of his footsteps! The days of their glory are as if they had never been; and the island, that was then a speck, rude and neglected in the barren ocean, now rivals the ubiquity of their commerce, the glory of their arms, the fame of their philosophy, the eloquence of their senate, and the inspiration of their bards!

4. Who shall say, then, contemplating the past, that England, proud and potent as she appears, may not, one day, be what Athens is, and the young America yet soar to be what Athens was! Who shall say, that, when the European column shall have mouldered, and the night of barbarism obscured its very ruins, that mighty continent may not emerge from the horizon to rule, for its time, sovereign of the ascendant! * *

5. Sir, it matters very little what immediate spot may have been the birthplace of such a man as WASHINGTON. No people can claim, no country can appropriate him. The boon of Providence to the human race, his fame is eternity, and his residence creation. Though it was the defeat of our arms, and the disgrace of our policy, I almost bless the convulsion in which he had his origin.

6. If the heavens thundered, and the earth rocked, yet, when the storm had passed, how pure was the climate that

THE PHILLIPS WHO WROTE THIS WAS PROBABLY CHARLES PHILLIPS *(1787–1859), an Irish barrister, author, and would-be orator. His speeches were printed and available in America, especially the volumes,* Speeches Delivered at the Bar and on Several Public Occasions in Ireland and England *(1817) and* Speeches of Phillips, Curran, and Grattan *(1831). Although this selection appeared only in the two 1837 editions of the* Fourth Reader, *it became a popular lesson in competing textbooks—primarily because such prophetic-sounding praise coming from England appealed to American pride. The hyperbolic treatment of the hallowed Washington was, of course, also well received.*

McGuffey's reasons for deleting this lesson after 1837 are unknown, but they may well have been governed in part by reservations about Phillips' style—considered "excessive" even by the standards of that time. The Edinburgh Review, *for instance, wrote regarding Phillips: "If he learns to think of his subject; to regard the sense always, even in ornamental passages; to speak plainly and rationally; to use figures only when they come naturally in, and then to use them as not*

abusing them—we will venture to promise him very consider-
able success in the arduous pursuit of oratorical renown."
No small order. And Sir James Mackintosh wrote in an 1832
issue of the North American Review *of "Counsellor Phillips (or*
O'Garnish, as he is nicknamed here)": "O'Garnish's style is
pitiful to the last degree. He ought by common consent to be
driven from the bar." Phillips did receive some critical praise,
although it was somewhat qualified. Blackwood Magazine's
usually acerbic critic "Christopher North" (John Wilson)
noted, "...In the midst of his most tedious and tasteless exag-
gerations, you still feel that Charles Phillips has a heart...."

it cleared! how bright, in the brow of the firmament, was the planet which it revealed to us! In the production of Washington, it does really appear as if Nature was endeavoring to improve upon herself, and that all the virtues of the ancient world were but so many studies preparatory to the patriot of the new.

7. Individual instances, no doubt, there were, splendid exemplifications, of some singular qualification: Cæsar was merciful, Scipio was continent, Hannibal was patient; but it was reserved for Washington to blend them all in one, and, like the lovely masterpiece of the Grecian artist, to exhibit, in one glow of associated beauty, the pride of every model, and the perfection of every master.

8. As a general, he marshaled the peasant into a veteran, and supplied by discipline the absence of experience; as a statesman, he enlarged the policy of the cabinet into the most comprehensive system of general advantage; and such was the wisdom of his views, and the philosophy of his counsels, that, to the soldier and the statesman, he almost added the character of the sage!

9. A conqueror, he was untainted with the crime of blood; a revolutionist, he was free from any stain of treason; for aggression commenced the contest, and his country called him to the command. Liberty unsheathed his sword, necessity stained, victory returned it. If he had paused here, history might have doubted what station to assign him, whether at the head of her citizens, or her soldiers, her heroes, or her patriots. But the last glorious act crowns his career, and banishes all hesitation.

10. Who like Washington, after having emancipated a hemisphere, resigned its crown, and preferred the retirement of domestic life to the adoration of a land he might be said almost to have created!

11. Happy, proud America! The lightnings of heaven yielded to your philosophy! The temptations of earth could not seduce your patriotism!

QUESTIONS.—1. What is the testimony of history on the permanence of national greatness? 2. What is said of the character of Washington? 3. How does he compare with Cæsar, Scipio, Hannibal, Bonaparte?

ERRORS.—*his-try* for his-to-ry; *en'-er-vate* for en-er'-vate; *Le-on-a-das* for Le-on-i-das.

SPELL AND DEFINE.—1. chronicler, achievements, establishments, permanency; 2. crumbled, commemorate, enervate; 3. immortality, impression; 4. contemplating, emerge, ascendant; 5. appropriate, convulsion; 6. firmament, endeavoring, preparatory; 8. marshaled, discipline, comprehensive; 9. revolutionist, aggression; 10. hemisphere, patriotism.

LESSON XCII.

RULE.—Be careful to speak such little words as *the, of, a, in, from, at, by,* etc., very distinctly, and yet not to dwell on them so long as on the other more important words.

The Wife.—W. IRVING.

1. I have often had occasion to remark the fortitude with which women sustain the most overwhelming reverses of fortune. Those disasters which break down the spirit of a man, and prostrate him in the dust, seem to call forth all the energies of the softer sex, and give such intrepidity and elevation to their character, that at times it approaches to sublimity.

2. Nothing can be more touching, than to behold a soft and tender female, who had been all weakness and dependence, and alive to every trivial roughness, while treading the prosperous paths of life, suddenly rising in mental force to be the comforter and supporter of her husband under misfortune, and abiding, with unshrinking firmness, the most bitter blasts of adversity.

3. As the vine, which has long twined its graceful foliage about the oak, and been lifted by it into sunshine, will, when the hardy plant is rifted by the thunderbolt, cling around it with its caressing tendrils, and bind up its shattered boughs; so is it beautifully ordered by Providence, that woman, who is the mere dependent and ornament of man in his happier hours, should be his stay and solace when smitten with sudden calamity; winding herself into the rugged recesses of his nature, tenderly supporting the drooping head, and binding up the broken heart.

4. I was once congratulating a friend, who had around him a blooming family, knit together in the strongest affection. " I can wish you no better lot," said he, with enthusiasm, " than to have a wife and children. If you are prosperous, there they are to share your prosperity; if otherwise, there they are to comfort you."

5. And, indeed, I have observed, that a married man, falling into misfortune, is more apt to retrieve his situation in the world than a single one; partly, because he is more stimulated to exertion by the necessities of the helpless and beloved beings who depend upon him for subsistence; but chiefly, because his spirits are soothed and relieved by do-

As the first American writer to achieve international fame, Washington Irving (1783–1859) was a popular author with the textbook compilers. There are more selections from his writings in the McGuffey Readers *than from any other single author, British or American. Although this passage would be regarded as sexist by today's standards, Irving seems to reflect accurately the values of his time. Most "soft and tender females" then probably read this as Irving intended it: honest respect, tinged with flattery, rather than chauvinistic condescension. No excuse will be offered, however, for his purple prose style.*

Irving's respect for women is perhaps more honest than that of D. V. Mitchell, whose description of "The Good Wife" is anthologized in an 1866 National Reader:

"She gains a mastery over your sterner nature, by very contrast; and wins you unwittingly to her slightest wish. And yet her wishes are guided by that delicate tact, which avoids conflict with your manly pride; she subdues by seeming to yield. . . ." Etc.

Marriage was often recognized in the popular literature of the West as a desirable civilizing influence, a vital social institution. Furthermore, having a large family was important on the frontier—almost a necessity if the land were to be successfully managed—since children growing into extra workers were always needed. The purpose of Question #6, then, is somewhat more loaded than it may appear at first glance, although it is clearly more subtle than Parson Weems's approach in Hymen's Recruiting Serjeant.

mestic endearments, and his self-respect kept alive by finding, that though all abroad is darkness and humiliation, yet there is still a little world of love at home, of which he is the monarch.

6. Whereas, a single man is apt to run to waste and self-neglect; to fancy himself lonely and abandoned, and his heart to fall to ruin, like some deserted mansion, for want of an inhabitant.

———

QUESTIONS.—1. What is said of the fortitude of the female sex? 2. What effect is produced on the mind by the view of this trait? 3. To what natural object is it beautifully compared? 4. Why should man have a family? 5. What is apt to be the case with the single man, as to character and comfort? 6. Do married persons generally *live longer* than unmarried?

ERRORS.—*of'n* for of-ten; *o-ver-wel-min'* for o-ver-whelm-ing; *fortin* and *for-chune* for fort-une.

SPELL AND DEFINE.—1. fortitude, overwhelming, disasters, intrepidity, sublimity; 2. dependence, roughness, unshrinking, adversity; 3. foliage, thunderbolt, rifted, shattered, beautifully, solace, recesses, rugged, tendrils; 4. congratulating, enthusiasm, prosperous; 5. stimulated, retrieve, necessities, subsistence, domestic; 6. abandoned.

———

LESSON XCIII.

RULE.—Be careful to give all the consonants their full sound in each word.

Duty of the American Orator.—GRIMKE.

1. One theme of duty still remains, and I have placed it alone : because of its peculiar dignity, sacredness and importance.   Need I tell you that I speak of the union of the states ? Let the American orator discharge all other duties but this, if indeed it be not impossible, with the energy and eloquence of John Rutledge, and the disinterested fidelity of Robert Morris, yet shall he be counted a traitor, if he attempt to dissolve the union.

2. His name, illustrious as it may have been, shall then be gibbeted on every hill-top throughout the land, a monument of his crime and punishment, and of the shame and grief of his country. If indeed he believe, and doubtless there may be such, that wisdom demands the dissolution of

the union, that the south should be severed from the north, the west be independent of the east, let him cherish the sentiment, for his own sake, in the solitude of his breast, or breathe it only in the confidence of friendship.

3. Let him rest assured, that as his country tolerates the monarchist and the aristocrat of the old world she tolerates him ; but should he plot the dismemberment of the union, the same trial, judgment, and execution await him as would await them, should they attempt to establish the aristocracy of Venice, or the monarchy of Austria on the ruins of our confederacy. To him as to them she leaves freedom of speech ; and the very licentiousness of the press : and permits them to write, even in the spirit of scorn, and hatred, and unfairness.

4. She trembles not at such effort, reckless and hostile as they may be. She smiles at their impotence ; while she mourns over their infatuation. But let them lift the hand of parricide, in the insolence of pride, or the madness of power, to strike their country, and her countenance, in all the severity and terrors of a parent's wrath shall smite them with amazement and horror. Let them strike, and the voices of millions of freemen from the city and hamlet, from the college and the farm-house, from the cabins amid the western wilds, and our ships scattered around the world, shall utter the stern irrevocable judgment, self banishment for life, or ignominious death.

5. Be it then among the noblest offices of American Eloquence to cultivate, in the people of every state, a deep and fervent attachment to the union. The union is to us the marriage-bond of states ; indissoluble in life, to be dissolved, we trust, only on that day when nations shall die in a moment, never to rise again. Let the American orator discountenance, then, all the arts of intrigue and corruption, which not only pollute the people and dishonor republican institutions, but prepare the way for the ruin of both—how secretly, how surely, let history declare   Let him banish from his thoughts, and his lips, the hypocrisy of the demagogue, equally deceitful and degraded,

> " With smooth dissimulation, skill'd to grace
> A devil's purpose, with an angel's face."

6. Let that demagogue and those arts, his instruments of power, be regarded as pretended friends, but secret and dangerous enemies of the people. Let it never be forgotten that to him and to them we owe all the licentiousness and violence, all the unprincipled and unfeeling persecution of

This impassioned plea for union was written by Thomas Smith Grimké (1786–1834) of South Carolina and delivered to the Western Literary Institute in Cincinnati (originally named the "College of Teachers," the first important teachers' association in America and a group in which W. H. McGuffey was prominent). Grimké was a reformer's reformer, speaking forcefully for such assorted causes as temperance, tariff reform, Sunday schools, and pacifism. He regularly opposed the teaching of the classics and mathematics in schools, arguing instead for more training in religion and his own system of "fonetic" spelling.

Grimkě's oratory remained within the Readers *from the first edition of the* Fourth Reader *in 1837 until the 1879 revision, having been moved up to the* Fifth Reader *in 1857. Grimké died in 1834, so that one can only guess where his loyalties would have rested when his home state of South Carolina seceded from the Union. However, the continued use of this respected Southern speaker's plea for union in the editions before and during the war was certainly a calculated move by the publishers.*

party spirit. Let the American orator labor then, with all the solemnity of a religious duty, with all the intensity of filial love, to convince his countrymen that the danger to liberty in this country is to be traced to those sources. Let the European tremble for his institutions, in the presence of military power and for the warrior's ambition.

7. Let the American dread, as the arch-enemy of republican institutions, the shock of exasperated parties, and the implacable revenge of demagogues. The discipline of standing armies, is the terror of freedom in Europe; but the tactics of parties, the standing armies of America, are still more formidable to liberty with us.

8. Let the American orator frown, then, on that ambition, which, pursuing its own aggrandizement and gratification, perils the harmony and integrity of the union, and counts the grief, anxiety, and expostulations of millions, as the small dust of the balance. Let him remember that ambition, like the Amruta cup of Indian fable, gives to the virtuous an immortality of glory and happiness, but to the corrupt an immortality of ruin, shame and misery.

9. Let not the American orator, in the great questions on which he is to speak or write, appeal to the mean and groveling qualities of human nature. Let him love the people, and respect himself too much to dishonor them, and degrade himself by an appeal to selfishness and prejudice, to jealousy, fear, and contempt. The greater the interests, and the more sacred the rights which may be at stake, the more resolutely should he appeal to the generous feelings, the noble sentiments, the calm considerate wisdom, which become a free, educated, peaceful Christian people. Even if he battle against criminal ambition and base intrigue, let his weapons be a logic, manly, intrepid, honorable, and an eloquence magnanimous, disinterested, and spotless.

10. What a contrast between his duties and those of Athenian eloquence! where the prince of orators was but the prince of demagogues. How could it be otherwise! with a religion that commanded no virtue, and prohibited no vice; with deities, the model of every crime and folly, which deform and pollute even man; with a social system, in which refinement, benevolence, forbearance, found no place. How could it be otherwise! with a political system, in which war was the chief element of power and honor in the individual, and of strength, security, and glory in the state; while the ambition or resentment of rulers found a cheerful response in the love of **conquest, plunder, or revenge on the part of the people.**

11. How could it be otherwise! with such domestic relations between the republics as made it the duty of the ancient orator to aggrandize his own at the expense of all the rest, to set state against state, to foment jealousies and bickerings among them, to deceive and weaken the strong, to oppress and seize on the feeble. How could it be otherwise! when such were the domestic and foreign relations, viewed as a whole, that the duty of the ancient orator was to cultivate the union of the states, not as a matter of deep and lasting importance at home, not as the very life of peace and harmony there, but only as an expedient against foreign invasion, while partial and hostile combinations, headed by Athens, or Thebes, or Sparta, were the current events of their domestic policy.

12. Compared to such duties and such scenes, who can turn to the obligations and field of American eloquence, without a thrill of spirit-stirring admiration and gratitude? His office in our union, how full of benignity and peace, of justice, majesty, and truth! Where, except in the Christian pulpit, shall we find its parallel? And why do we find it there? but that the Christian ministry are, like him, the advocates of purity, forbearance and love. How delightful, how honorable the task, to calm the angry passions, to dissipate error, to reconcile prejudice, to banish jealousy, and silence the voice of selfishness!

13. But American eloquence must likewise cultivate a fixed, unalterable devotion to the union, a frank, generous, ardent attachment of section to section, of state to state: and in the citizen, liberal sentiments towards his rulers, and cordial love for his countrymen. Nor is this all. Let the American orator comprehend, and live up to the grand conception, that the union is the property of the world, no less than of ourselves; that it is a part of the divine scheme for the moral government of the earth, as the solar system is a part of the mechanism of the heavens; that it is destined, whilst traveling from the Atlantic to the Pacific, like the ascending sun, to shed its glorious influence backward on the states of Europe, and forward on the empires of Asia.

14. Let him comprehend its sublime relations to time and eternity; to God and man; to the most precious hopes, the most solemn obligations, and the highest happiness of human kind. And what an eloquence must that be whose source of power and wisdom are God himself, the objects of whose influence are all the nations of the earth; whose sphere of duty is co-extensive with all that is sublime in

This passage is one of the few clear articulations in the McGuffeys of what later came to be called "Manifest Destiny": a belief in the inevitability of the United States' continued territorial expansion as "part of the divine scheme." The phrase became the slogan for expansionists and many politicians from the mid-1840's until the Spanish-American War.

The questions following the lessons were designed as an important part of the Readers, as McGuffey's Preface to a number of the early Readers emphasizes:

All he [the student] knows, and, not unfrequently, more than he knows, will be put in requisition by the questions appended to the lessons. It is deliberately intended to lead the mind of the pupil, as often as practicable, beyond the pages of the book in his hands. Let him not think this unfair. . . .

It may even happen, that some of the questions cannot at once be intelligently answered by the instructor. And what then? Is a teacher never to admit that there are some things which he does not know? The teacher who never dares to say "I do not know" . . . must be conscious of extreme ignorance. . . . Still, there is nothing to be met with, in the following pages, but what an intelligent teacher of a "common school" might be expected to know, or might, at least, easily acquire. Nothing is so well taught, as that which the teacher has most recently acquired. This book is intended to aid and stimulate the teacher, as well as the pupil.

religion, beautiful in morals, commanding in intellect, and touching in humanity. How comprehensive, and therefore how wise and benevolent, must then be the genius of American eloquence, compared to the narrow-minded, narrow-hearted, and therefore selfish, eloquence of Greece and Rome.

15. How striking is the contrast, between the universal social spirit of the former, and the individual, exclusive character of the latter. The boundary of this is the horizon of a plain ; the circle of that the horizon of a mountain summit. Be it then the duty of American eloquence to speak, to write, to act, in the cause of Christianity, patriotism, and literature ; in the cause of justice, humanity, virtue, and truth ; in the cause of the people, of the union, of the whole human race, and of the unborn of every clime and age. Then shall American eloquence, the personification of truth, beauty, and love,

> "———walk the earth, that she may hear her name
> Still hymn'd and honor'd by the grateful voice
> Of human kind, and in her fame rejoice."

QUESTION.—1. How shall the orator be regarded who attempts to dissolve the union ? 2. Suppose he believe a separation desirable, what shall he do with his opinion ? 3. Why is freedom of speech and the press allowed both to bad and good ? 4. What feeling towards the union must be cherished in every American bosom ? 5. How should the American regard party spirit, and the arts of demagogues ? 6. To what sentiments of the human mind should he always appeal, and to what others never ? 7. Contrast the American with the Athenian orator, 10–13. 8. While the orator cherishes union of state to state, of section to section, how shall he regard the country in respect to the world ? 9. To time—eternity ? 10. Sum up the contrast contained in the close of this lesson, between what ancient eloquence was, and what American eloquence ought to be.

ERRORS.—gib-bet-ed ought to be pronounced jib-bet-ted ; 'lus-tra-ous for il-lus-tri-ous ; mon-er-ment for mon-u-ment ; ir-re-vo'-ca-ble for ir-rev'-o-ca-ble ; for-got for for-got-ten ; zas-per-ate for ex-as-per-ate.

SPELL AND DEFINE.—1. disinterested ; 2. gibbeted, independent, dissolution ; 3. monarchist, aristocrat, confederacy ; 4. irrevocable ; 5. indissoluble, dissimulation ; 10. demagogues ; 11. combinations ; 14. comprehend.

LESSON XCIV

RULE.—Be careful to give the vowels their proper sound.

The Patriotism of Western Literature.
DR. DRAKE.

1. Our literature cannot fail to be patriotic, and its patriotism will be American—composed of a love of country, mingled with an admiration for our political institutions.

2. The slave, whose very mind has passed under the yoke, and the senseless ox, whom he goads onward in the furrow, are attached to the spot of their animal companionship, and may even fight for the cabin and the field where they came into existence; but this affection, considered as an ingredient of patriotism, although the most universal, is the lowest; and to rise into a virtue it must be discriminating and comprehensive, involving a varied association of ideas, and embracing the beautiful of the natural and moral world, as they appear around us.

3. To feel in his heart, and infuse into his writings, the inspiration of such a patriotism, the scholar must feast his taste on the delicacies of our scenery, and dwell with enthusiasm on the genius of our constitution and laws. Thus sanctified in its character, this sentiment becomes a principle of moral and intellectual dignity—an element of fire, purifying and subliming the mass in which it glows.

4. As a guiding star to the will, its light is inferior only to that of Christianity. Heroic in its philanthropy, untiring in its enterprises, and sublime in the martyrdoms it willingly suffers, it justly occupies a high place among the virtues which ennoble the human character. A literature, animated with this patriotism, is a national blessing, and such will be the literature of the West.

5. The literature of the whole Union must be richly endowed with this spirit; but a double portion will be the lot of the interior, because the foreign influences, which dilute and vitiate this virtue in the extremities, cannot reach the heart of the continent, where all that lives and moves is American.

6. Hence a native of the West may be confided in as his country's hope. Compare him with the native of a great maritime city, on the verge of the nation,—his birth-place

THE EARLY EDITIONS OF THE McGUFFEY READERS WERE HEAVILY promoted as the textbooks of the West, and this lesson serves as a good example of such regional pride—free from "foreign influences." It was part of the first edition of the Fourth Reader *and remained in use until the 1857 edition. One reason for its departure from the series at that time might have been its use of the word "slave" in the second paragraph; that was a word normally avoided in the McGuffeys. A more probable explanation for its removal, however, is that by 1857 the* McGuffeys *already dominated in the West and were trying harder to be recognized as a* national *textbook.*

Dr. Daniel Drake (1785–1852) was a prominent physician, educator, and civic leader in Cincinnati. He founded the Ohio Medical College in 1819 and was an active member of the "Teachers' College," along with both William and Alexander McGuffey; Lyman Beecher and his daughters Catherine and Harriet; Calvin Stowe; Alexander Campbell (founder of the Disciples of Christ); and Thomas Grimké.

A number of Drake's ideas regarding education (such as the teaching of anatomy in the public schools and compulsory education of all children) were dismissed at the time as terribly impractical, but he was generally accepted as a valuable member of society. Drake's voice would probably have deserved a place within the McGuffey Readers even if he hadn't just selected William Holmes McGuffey as President of the new Cincinnati College. That venture didn't turn out too well, since the College went bankrupt in 1839; but the friendship between the McGuffeys and Drake continued. In 1839 Alexander McGuffey married Drake's daughter, Elizabeth.

the fourth story of a house, hemmed in by surrounding edifices, his play-ground a pavement, the scene of his juvenile rambles an arcade of shops, his young eyes feasted on the flags of a hundred alien governments, the streets in which he wanders crowded with foreigners, and the ocean, common to all nations, forever expanding to his view.

7. Estimate *his* love of country, as far as it depends on local and early attachments, and then contrast him with the young backwoodsman, born and reared amidst objects, scenes, and events, which you can all bring to mind;—the jutting rocks in the great road, half alive with organic remains, or sparkling with crystals; the quiet old walnut tree, dropping its nuts upon the yellow leaves, as the morning sun melts the October frost; the grape-vine swing; the chase after the cowardly black snake, till it creeps under the rotten log; the sitting down to rest upon the crumbling trunk, and an idle examination of the mushrooms and mosses which grow from its ruins.

8. Then the wading in the shallow stream, and upturning of the flat stones, to find bait with which to fish in the deeper waters; next the plunder of a bird's nest, to make necklaces of the speckled eggs, for her who has plundered him of his young heart; then the beech tree with its smooth body, on which he cuts the initials of her name interlocked with his own; finally, the great hollow stump, by the path that leads up the valley to the log school-house, its dry bark peeled off, and the stately polk-weed growing from its center, and bending with crimson berries: which invite him to sit down and write upon its polished wood, how much pleasanter it is to extract ground squirrels from beneath its roots, than to extract the square root, under that labor-saving machine, the ferule of a teacher!

9. The affections of one who is blest with such reminiscences, like the branches of our beautiful trumpet flower, strike their roots into every surrounding object, and derive support from all which stand within their reach. The love of country is with him a constitutional and governing principle. If he be a mechanic, the wood and iron which he moulds into form, are dear to his heart, because they remind him of his own hills and forests; if a husbandman, he holds companionship with growing corn, as the offspring of his native soil; if a legislator, his dreams are filled with sights of national prosperity to flow from his beneficent enactments; if a scholar, devoted to the interests of literature, in his lone and excited hours of midnight study, while the winds are hushed and all animated nature sleeps, when the silence is

U

so profound, that the stroke of his own pen grates, loud and harsh, upon his ear, and fancy, from the great deep of his luminous intellect, draws up new forms of smiling beauty and solemn grandeur; the genius of his country hovers nigh, and sheds over its pages an essence of patriotism, sweeter than the honey-dew which the summer night distils upon the leaves of our forest trees.

———

QUESTIONS.—1. What is American patriotism? 2. Where is this kind of patriotism most likely to be found? in the cities of the sea-shore, or in the West? 3. What are the causes which make it greater in the West?

ERRORS.—*cum-po-sed* for com-po-sed; *com-pra-hen-sive* for com-pre-hen-sive; *dil-ute* for di-lute; *na-tyve* for na-tive.

SPELL AND DEFINE.—1. patriotism; 2. discriminating; 3. intellectual; 6. arcade; 7. backwoods; 8. initials; 9. reminiscences, constitutional.

———

LESSON XCV.

RULE.—In poetry that does not rhyme, no pause need be made at the end of such lines as terminate with unimportant words, except when the sense requires it.

Rome.—BYRON.

1. Oh Rome! my country! city of the soul!
   The orphans of the heart must turn to thee,
   Lone mother of dead empires! and control
   In their shut breasts their petty misery.
   What are our woes and sufferance? Come and see
   The cypress, hear the owl, and plod your way
   O'er steps of broken thrones, and temples, ye!
   Whose agonies are evils of a day—
   A world is at our feet, as fragile as our clay.

2. The Niobe of nations! there she stands,
   Childless, and crownless, in her voiceless woe;
   An empty urn within her withered hands,
   Whose holy dust was scattered long ago;
   The Scipios' tomb contains no ashes now;
   The very sepulchers are tenantless
   Of their heroic dwellers; dost thou flow,
   Old Tiber! through a marble wilderness?
   Rise, with thy yellow waves, and mantle her distress!

In another lesson, "Natural Ties Among Western States" (which appeared only in the 1837 Reader), Dr. Drake was much more specific in his call for regional pride:

In short, we should foster western genius, encourage western publishers, augment the number of western readers, and create a western heart. . . . When these great objects shall come seriously to occupy our minds, the union will be secure; for its center will be sound. . . .

This is one of the lessons which McGuffey (and nearly all his competitors) "borrowed" from the famous children's tales of Maria Edgeworth. It has appeared in every edition of the McGuffeys since 1841—never once carrying any acknowledgement of authorship. British authors were gleefully pirated at will by American publishers who paid no royalties, and often— especially if they were women—these authors were not even credited by name. This selection (originally retitled by McGuffey as "Careful Ben and the Whip-Cord") was used in the Second Reader until 1857, when it was elevated to the Fourth.

LESSON XVI.

2. Ex-am′ine; *v.* to look at carefully.

6. Sig′ni-fies; *v.* to be important.

22. Prize; *n.* a reward for excellence.

30. Ev-er-last′ing; *adj.* lasting always.

WASTE NOT, WANT NOT.

Utter distinctly each consonant in such words as the following: *parcels, exactly, string, yours, three, excellent, afterward, arrows, marksman, settled, pronounced, rules, trial, prudently.* See Ex. IV, page 15.

1. *Mr. Jones.* Boys, if you have nothing to do, will you unpack these †parcels for me′?

2. The two parcels were †exactly alike, both of them well tied up with good whip-cord. Ben took his parcel to the table, and began to examine the knot, and then to †untie it.

3. John took the other parcel, and tried first at one corner, and then at the other, to *pull* off the string. But the cord had been too well secured, and he only drew the knots †*tighter.*

4. *John.* I wish these people would not tie up their parcels so tight, as if they were never to be †undone. Why, Ben, how did you get *yours* undone? What is in your parcel? I wonder what is in mine! I wish I could get the string off. I will *cut* it.

5. *Ben.* O no, do not *cut* it, John′! Look, what a nice cord this is, and yours is the same. It is a *pity* to *cut* it.

6. *John.* Pooh! what signifies a bit of †packthread?

7. *Ben.* It is †whip-cord.

8. *John.* Well, *whip-cord* then! what signifies a bit of whip-cord? You can get a piece of whip-cord twice as long as that for three cents; and who cares for three cents? Not I, for one. So, here it goes.

9. So he took out his knife, and cut it in several places.

10. *Mr. Jones.* Well, my boys, have you undone the parcels for me?

11. *John.* Yes, sir; here is the parcel.

12. *Ben.* And here is my parcel, father, and here is also the string.

13. *Mr. Jones.* You may *keep* the string, Ben.

14. *Ben.* Thank you, sir. What †excellent whip-cord it is!

15. *Mr. Jones.* And you, John, may keep your string, too, if it will be of any use to you.

16. *John.* It will be of *no* use to me, thank you, sir.

17. *Mr. Jones.* No, I am afraid not, if *this* is it.

18. A few weeks after this, Mr. Jones gave each of his sons a new top.

19. *John.* How is this, Ben? These tops have no strings. What shall we do for strings?

20. *Ben.* I have a string that will do very well for *mine.* And he pulled it out of his pocket.

21. *John.* Why, if that is not the whip-cord! I wish I had saved *mine.*

22. A few days afterward, there was a †shooting-match, with bows and †arrows, among the lads. The prize was a fine bow and arrows, to be given to the best †marksman. "Come, come," said Master Sharp. "I am within one inch of the mark. I should like to see who will go nearer."

23. John drew his bow, and shot. The arrow struck within a quarter of an inch of Master Sharp's. "Shoot away," said Sharp; "but you must understand

Maria Edgeworth (1767–1849) was born in England, but spent much of her life in Ireland, where she helped her father manage the family estate of Edgeworthstown. Her first publication, Letters to Literary Ladies *(1795) pleaded for better education of women, and her novel* Castle Rackrent *(1800) established her reputation as a writer. She then turned her attention to children's education and produced a series of children's books popular in both England and America. Most of these were collections of short stories with clear didactic objectives, as some of the titles indicate:* Moral Tales; Early Lessons; Popular Tales; *and* The Parent's Assistant *(in which this story first appeared).*

"Waste Not, Want Not, or Two Strings to Your Bow" was over ten times longer in Edgeworth's unabridged version and contained several demonstrations of the whipcord's utility which McGuffey cut. The man in her story is named Mr. Gresham, and the boys (his nephews, not his sons) are named Hal and Ben. Thrifty Ben is the only one whose name survives in the McGuffey text—probably because McGuffey was swayed by a footnote in Edgeworth's original text: "Benjamin, so called from Dr. Benjamin Franklin."

Maria Edgeworth might not have appreciated the presumptuous treatment McGuffey offered her text, but she would probably have been proud of the lesson's impact. In at least one respect, "Waste Not, Want Not" became among the most influential literary works of its time—responsible in large part for several generations of American string savers.

the rules. We settled them before you came. You are to have three shots with your own arrows. Nobody is to †borrow or lend. So shoot away."

24. John †seized his second arrow; "If I have any luck," said he;—but just as he †pronounced the word "*luck*," the string broke, and the arrow fell from his hands.

25. *Master Sharp.* There! It is all over with you.

26. *Ben.* Here is my bow for him, and welcome.

27. *Master Sharp.* No, no, sir; that is not fair. Did you not hear the rules? There is to be no lending.

28. It was now Ben's turn to make his †trial. His first arrow missed the mark; the *second* was exactly as near as John's *first*. Before †venturing the last arrow, Ben very prudently examined the string of his bow; and, as he pulled it to try its strength, it *snapped*.

29. Master Sharp clapped his hands and danced for joy. But his dancing suddenly ceased, when careful Ben drew out of his pocket an excellent piece of cord, and began to tie it to the bow.

30. "The everlasting whip-cord, I declare!" cried John. "Yes," said Ben; "I put it in my pocket to-day, because I thought I might want it."

31. Ben's last arrow won the prize; and when the bow and arrows were handed to him, John said, "How †valuable that whip-cord has been to you, Ben. I'll take care how I waste any thing, hereafter."

EXERCISES.—What is this lesson designed to teach? Which of the boys preserved his whip-cord? What good did it do him? What did the other boy do with his? What was the consequence? What did he learn from it?

In the thirtieth paragraph, what two *nouns* are there? In what number are they both? What is number? See Pinneo's Primary Grammar, page 45, Art. 77.

LESSON XXXIII.

4. Case′ment; *n.* the outside part of a window. 6. Chrys′a-lis; *n.* that from which the butterfly comes.

WHAT IS DEATH?

Pronounce correctly and distinctly. Do not say *laughin* for laugh-ing; *casemunt* for case-ment; *chryslis* for chrys-*a*-lis; *some thin* for some-thing; *wonderin* for won-der-ing; *dyin* for dy-ing.

Child. 1. Mother, how still the baby lies!
  I can not hear his breath;
  I can not see his laughing eyes;
  They tell me this is death.

 2. My little work I thought to bring,
  And sit down by his bed,
  And †pleasantly I tried to sing;
  They †hushed me: he is dead!

 3. They say that he again will rise,
  More †beautiful than now;
  That God will bless him in the skies;
  O mother, tell me how!

Mother. 4. †Daughter, do you remember, dear,
  The cold, dark thing you brought,
  And laid upon the casement here?
  A †withered worm, you thought.

 5. I told you, that †Almighty power
  Could break that withered shell;
  And show you, in a future hour,
  Something would please you well.

The earliest McGuffey readers *were saturated with the subject of death in both verse and prose. In the prose selections death is usually treated more directly than in the verse, but nowhere do the* McGuffeys *mask the fact that death exists and must be faced by all. In contrast, many of today's elementary school books completely avoid mention of death, leaving children to wrestle with this unknown on their own.*

The chrysalis and the lily, which appears in other lessons, are two traditional Christian symbols for death that derive from natural analogies. And death in the McGuffeys is nearly always—as here—treated well within the Christian tradition, with no reservations or questions invited regarding life hereafter.

6. Look at that chrysalis, my love;
    An empty shell it lies;
Now raise your †wondering glance above,
    To where yon †insect flies!

Child. 7. O yes, mamma! how very gay
    Its wings of starry gold!
And see! it lightly flies away
    Beyond my gentle hold.

8. O mother! now I know full well,
    If God that worm can change,
And draw it from this broken †cell,
    On golden wings to range;

9. How beautiful will brother be
    When God shall give him wings,
Above this dying world to flee,
    And live with †heavenly things!

---

10. Our life is like a summer's day,
    It seems so quickly past:
Youth is the morning, bright and gay,
And if 't is spent in wisdom's way,
We meet old age without dismay,
    And death is sweet at last.

EXERCISES.—What is this piece of poetry about? What was this little girl going to do? What did her mother tell her? Will little children be raised from the dead? From what book do we learn this?

ARTICULATION.

Cht.	Broachd,	screechd,	poachd,	coachd,	peachd.
Sht.	Plashd,	slashd,	clashd,	fishd,	fleshd.
Shr.	Shroud,	shrink,	shrunk,	shrewd,	shrivel.

154

LESSON XXXIV.

1. **Va′grant**; *n.* one who strolls from place to place.
2. **E-gyp′tians**, *n.* those who live in Egypt.
2. **De-scend′ants**; *n.* offspring.
2. **Con′quer-ors**; *n.* those who subdue.
6. **At-trac′tion**; *n.* power of drawing.
8. **Em′i-nence**; *n.* distinction.

THE STOLEN CHILD AND THE GYPSIES.

1. +Gypsies are a class of people who have no settled place to live in, but +wander about from spot to spot, and sleep at night in tents or in barns. We have no gypsies in our country,* for here every person can find +employment of some kind, and there is no excuse for idlers and vagrants.

2. But in many parts of Europe the gypsies are very +numerous; and they are often wicked and +troublesome. It is said that they are descendants of the Egyptians,* and have lived a wandering life ever since the year 1517, at which time they refused to submit to the Turks, who were the conquerors of Egypt.

3. Well; I have a short story to tell you about these gypsies. Many years ago, as a boat was putting off, a boy ran along the side of the canal, and desired to be taken in. The master of the boat, however, refused to take him, because he had not quite money enough to pay the usual fare.

* Gypsies are said to have come originally from India. They entered Europe in the 14th or 15th century, and are now scattered over Turkey, Russia, Hungary, Spain, England, etc. They live by theft, fortune-telling, horse-jockeying, tinkering, and the like. There are a very few gypsies in this country.

ONE OF McGUFFEY'S ORIGINAL INCLUSIONS IN THE SECOND READER *(where it was entitled "The* Lost *Child and the Gipseys"), this selection remained in the series through the 1866 edition. It must have generated considerable editorial debate, however, as the spelling of* gypsies *changes in nearly every edition (from* gipseys *to* gipsys *to* gipsies *to* gypsies *and back again).*

The exaggerated claim of full employment in the United States is modified slightly by the footnote in the 1866 edition (reprinted here), but is typical of the emphasis on work throughout the McGuffeys.

The "discovery" of a long-lost child was such a standard plot technique in eighteenth-century romances and novels (see Fielding's Joseph Andrews *and* Tom Jones) *that it was often parodied. Here, however, it is incorporated into an adventure story with a didactic twist: if the merchant had not exercised charity, he would have lost his son forever. Naturally Albert "rose to eminence" in later life, which closes out this lesson most neatly.*

4. A rich merchant being pleased with the looks of the boy, whom I shall call Albert, and being touched with +compassion toward him, paid the money for him, and +ordered him to be taken on board. The little fellow thanked the merchant for his kindness, and jumped into the boat.

5. Upon talking with him afterward, the merchant found that Albert could readily speak in three or four different +languages. He also learned that the boy had been stolen away, when a child, by a gypsy, and had +rambled ever since, with a gang of these +strollers, up and down several parts of Europe.

6. It +happened that the merchant, whose heart seems to have inclined toward the boy by a secret kind of attraction, had himself lost a child some years before. The parents, after a long search for him, had +concluded that he had been +drowned in one of the canals, with which the country abounds; and the mother was so afflicted at the loss of her son, that she died of grief for him.

7. Upon +comparing all the facts, and +examining the marks by which the child was described when he was first missing, Albert proved to be the long-lost son of the merchant. The lad was well pleased to find a father who was so kind and +generous; while the father was not a little delighted to see a son return to him, whom he had given up for lost.

8. Albert +possessed a quick +understanding, and in time he rose to eminence, and was much +respected for his talents and +knowledge. He is said to have visited, as a public minister, several countries, in which he formerly wandered as a gypsy.

EXERCISES.—What is this lesson about? What are gypsies? Have we gypsies? What feelings did the merchant have toward little Albert? Whom did he prove to be? To whom should they have been grateful for being thus brought together?

In the last sentence, which is the pronoun? The verb? The preposition? What does the word *preposition* mean? Why is it so called? What does it govern? See Pinneo's Primary Grammar, Rule 4, page 127.

———— •◦• ————

LESSON XXXVI.

———

4. STAT′URE; *n.* the size of any one.

8. LEV′EL-*ED*; *v.* threw down.

8. STREW′*ED*; *v.* (*pro.* strū́ed or strṓde), scattered.

10. AB-HOR′; *v.* to dislike much.

———

THE CHILD'S INQUIRY.

REMARK.—Remember that in reading poetry, there is always danger of forgetting the sense in the rhyme, and therefore of reading, not as if you were expressing some thought or feeling to another mind, but as if you were chanting something to please the ear.

UTTER each sound distinctly. Do not say *hunred* for hundred; *hans* for hands; *chile* for child; *wy* for why.

1. †ALEXANDER lived many hundred years ago. He was king of Macedon, one of the states of Greece. His life was spent in war. He first conquered the other Grecian states, and then Persia, and India, and other †countries one by one, till the whole known world was conquered by him.

2. It is said that he wept, because there were no more worlds for him to conquer. He died, at the age of thirty-three, from drinking too much wine. In †consequence of his great success in war, he was called, "Alexander the *Great.*"

3. *Son.* How big was Alexander, Pa,
    That people call him great?
    Was he, like old Goliah, tall?
    His spear a hundred weight?

4th Rd. 10.

THIS WAS ONE OF MCGUFFEY'S ORIGINAL SELECTIONS, APPEARING IN the Third Reader *from 1837 to 1857, and then in the* Fourth Reader *until its deletion in 1879. The highly selective biographical lead-in to the poem was omitted in the earliest editions, but only because the entire preceding lesson was given over to Alexander's moral weaknesses. The title for the lesson remained unchanged (although first spelled "Enquiry"), but the poem itself is much better known by its famous first line.*

No authorial attribution for the poem is ever provided in the McGuffeys. It is today usually credited to Elijah Jones, about whom little else is known.

Was he so large that he could stand
    Like some tall steeple high;
And while his feet were on the ground,
    His hands could touch the sky?

4. *Fath.* O no, my child: about as large
    As I or uncle James.
'T was not his *stature* made him great,
    But greatness of his *name*.

5. *Son.* His *name* so great? I know 't is *long*,
    But easy quite to spell;
And more than half a year ago,
    I knew it very well.

6. *Fath.* I mean, my child, his +*actions* were
    So great, he got a name,
That every body speaks with praise,
    That tells about his fame.

7. *Son.* Well, what great actions did he do?
    I want to know it all.

8. *Fath.* Why, he it was that +conquered Tyre,
    And leveled down her wall,
And thousands of her people slew;
    And then to Persia went,
And fire and sword, on every side,
    Through many a region sent.
A hundred conquered +cities shone
    With midnight burnings réd;
And strewed o'er many a battle ground,
    A thousand soldiers bled.

9. *Son.* Did *killing people* make him great?
    Then why was Abdel Young,
Who killed his neighbor, tráining-day,
    Put into jail and hung?
I never heard them call him great.

10. *Fath.* Why, no, 't was not in war;
    And him that kills a single **man**,
    His neighbors all abhor.

11. *Son.* Well, then, if I should kill **a man**,
    I'd kill a hundred more;
    I should be GREAT, and not get hung,
    Like Abdel Young, before.

12. *Fath.* Not so, my child, 't will never do:
    The Gospel bids be kind.

13. *Son.* Then they that *kill* and they that *praise*,
    The Gospel do not mind.

14. *Fath.* You know, my child, the Bible says
    That you must always do
    To other people, as you wish
    To have them do to you.

15. *Son.* But, Pa´, did Alexander wish
    That some strong man would come,
    And burn his house, and kill him, too,
    And do as he had done´?
    And every body calls him GREAT,
    For killing people so`!
    Well, now, what *right* he had to kill,
    I should be glad to know`.
    If one should burn the †buildings here,
    And kill the folks within´,
    Would any body call him great´,
    For such a wicked thing´?

EXERCISES.—What was the child's inquiry about Alexander?
Who was Alexander? What did he do? How did he die? In
what respect was he different from a common murderer?

Which are the emphatic words in this lesson? What words in
the last paragraph have the rising inflection? What the falling?

*The lesson here is reproduced from the 1866 edition,
where it follows "Things by Their Right Names"—also a
father-son dialogue, but in prose. In that lesson the father
agrees to tell his son a story of "a bloody murder," which the
son eventually realizes is actually a description of warfare.
As the father admits, "I do not know of any murders half so
bloody." The exercises following the present selection invite
a comparison with that previous lesson and a continuation
of its discussion. Both lessons are representative of the
Readers' consistent anti-war posture, one which appears to
reflect McGuffey's firm personal position.*

LESSON XLII.

2. Toil'ed; *v.* labored hard.
3. Grat'i-tude; *n.* thankfulness.
8. Re-quite'; *v.* to reward.

3. Heath; *n.* a place full of shrubs.
5. Grudge; *v.* to envy.
6. Range; *v.* to rove about.

THE OLD HORSE.

Utter each consonant distinctly in the following words: *children, strong, protect, gratitude, merits, play-ground, comfort, shortest, across, best.*

1. No, children, he shall not be sold`;
   Go, lead him home, and dry your tears`;
'T is true, he 's blind, and lame, and old´,
   But he has served us twenty years`.

2. Well has he served us; gentle, strong,
   And willing, through life's varied stage;
And having toiled for us so long,
   We will protect him in his age.

3. Our debt of gratitude to pay´,
   His faithful merits to requite,
His play-ground be the heath by day´,
   A shed shall shelter him at night`.

4. In comfort he shall end his days`;
   And when I must to market go´,
I 'll cut across the shortest ways,
   And set out earlier home, you know.

5. A life of labor was his lot;
   He always tried to do his best;
Poor fellow, now we 'll grudge thee not
   A little liberty and rest.

This anonymous selection appeared in the McGuffeys from 1844 to 1879—first in the Second, then in the Fourth Reader. Inculcating moral virtues that are familiar in a number of McGuffey selections—especially the importance of gratitude—this was one of the earliest lessons to project the sentimentality that became so strong in the later editions.

6. Go‵, then, old friend´; thy future fate
    To range the heath, from harness free,
And just below the cottage-gate,
    I 'll go and build a shed for thee.

7. And there we 'll feed and tend thee well,
    And with these comforts we 'll engage,
No other horse shall ever tell,
    Of a more happy, green old age‵.

EXERCISES.—What did the father say to his children about the horse? What did he promise them he would do for him in his old age? Where are rising inflections in the lesson? Where falling inflections?

ARTICULATION.

NOTE.—Combinations composed of *two* elementary sounds having been thus far given for practice, the following exercises will contain principally combinations of *three, four,* and *five* elements. This progressive plan has been adopted, because in this way the development of the organs will be better secured, and the habit of distinct articulation more easily acquired.

OBSERVE that *e* in blabb*ed*, gabbl*es*, &c., is omitted.

Bz,	bst.	Blabs,	blabst:	throbs,	throbst.
Bd,	bdst.	Blabbd,	blabbdst:	throbbd,	throbbst.
Blz,	blst.	Gabbls,	gabblst:	quibbls,	quibblst.
Bld,	bldst.	Gabbld,	gabbldst:	quibbld,	quibbldst.

EXERCISES ON THE VOCALS.

Pronounce each word distinctly; then give a clear enunciation of the sounds of the italicised letters.

a, as in fat.—The camel *ha*s traveled o'er the s*a*nds. The m*a*dm*a*n h*a*d a pl*ai*d h*a*t. He b*a*de him st*a*nd by the c*a*nnon. I f*a*ncy the b*a*t h*a*d fl*a*pped his wings.

a, as in far.—The f*a*r-off st*a*r gives h*ea*rt to the gu*a*rd. No al*a*rm h*au*nts the f*a*ther's h*ea*rth. Nothing d*au*nted, his *au*nt ch*a*rged into the h*au*nted house.

Although the first four Readers are relatively free of humor, the articulation exercises must have provided some compensation. It is hard to imagine even the sternest teacher preventing some smiles or snickers among the students listening to their peers attempt these sounds. At the same time, of course, students were learning how to pronounce words clearly, a practice too little emphasized today—indeed, perhaps a lost art.

LESSON LII.

1. Em-u-la'tion; *n.* rivalry; contest.	2. Ri'vals; *n.* those who pursue the same thing.
1. Com-pe-ti'tion; *n.* rivalry.	3. An'ec-dote; *n.* a short story.
2. Ex-cel'led; *v.* surpassed; exceeded in good qualities.	8. Tu-i'tion; *n.* payment for teaching.

EMULATION.

PRONOUNCE correctly. Do not say *speakin* for speak-ing; *recollec* for rec-ol-lect; *evinin* for e-ven-ing; *frienship* for friendship; *widder* for wid-ow; *gain* for gained; *seein* for see-ing. See Ex. V, pages 24–28.

1. FRANK'S father was speaking to a friend, one day, on the subject of competition at school. He said that he could answer for it, that envy is not always connected with it.

2. He had been excelled by many, but did not recollect ever having felt envious of his successful rivals; "nor did my †winning many a prize from my friend Birch," said he, "ever †lessen his friendship for me."

3. In †support of the truth of this, a friend who was present, †related an anecdote which had fallen under his own †notice, in a school in his †neighborhood.

4. At this school, the sons of several wealthy †farmers, and others, who were poorer, †received †instruction. Frank †listened with great attention, while the gentleman gave the following account of the two rivals.

5. It happened that the son of a rich farmer, and of a poor widow, came in competition for the head

---

THIS IS ANOTHER OF McGUFFEY'S ORIGINAL SELECTIONS THAT survived all editions from 1836 to the present. The author is never mentioned and may have been McGuffey himself; he supposedly wrote some of the early lessons, but which ones have never been identified. This particular lesson, which is more concise than most samples of McGuffey's personal style, started out in the Second Reader and was shifted to the Fourth Reader for the 1857 and subsequent editions.

of their class. They were so nearly equal, that the teacher could scarcely decide between them; some days one, and some days the other, †gained the head of the class. It was †determined, by seeing who should be at the head of the class for the greater number of days in the week.

6. The widow's son, by the last day's trial, gained the victory, and kept his place the following week, till the school was dismissed for the holidays.

7. When they met again, the widow's son did not appear, and the farmer's son being next to him, might now have been at the head of his class. Instead of †seizing the vacant place, however, he went to the widow's house, to inquire what could be the cause of her son's †absence.

8. †Poverty was the cause; she found that she was not able, with her utmost †efforts, to continue to pay for his tuition and books, and the poor boy had returned to labor for her support.

9. The farmer's son, out of the †allowance of pocket-money, which his father gave him, bought all the necessary books, and paid for the tuition of his rival. He also permitted him to be brought back again to the head of his class, where he continued for some time, at the expense of his generous rival.

EXERCISES.—What is the subject of this lesson? What do you mean by emulation? What is envy? What story is told about the two rivals? Is it right to envy a classmate who has learned his lessons better than yourself?

ARTICULATION.

Nd,	ndz,	ndst.	Str$\overset{2}{a}$nd,	str$\overset{2}{a}$nds,	str$\overset{2}{a}$ndst.
Ndl,	ndlz,	ndlst.	Dw$\overset{2}{i}$ndl,	dw$\overset{2}{i}$ndls,	dw$\overset{2}{i}$ndlst.
Ndld,	ndldst.		Dw$\overset{2}{i}$ndld,	dw$\overset{2}{i}$ndldst:	f$\overset{2}{o}$ndldst.
Nks,	nkst.		Th$\overset{2}{a}$nks,	th$\overset{2}{a}$nkst:	pl$\overset{2}{a}$nkst.
Nkd,	nkdst.		Th$\overset{2}{a}$nkd,	th$\overset{2}{a}$nkdst:	pl$\overset{2}{a}$nkdst.

In addition to providing a representative lesson on the evils of envy and the benefits of charity and gratitude, this selection also offers some insight into the classroom practices of the early nineteenth century. There were weekly contests to determine who would garner the privileges that came with being the "head of the class." Correspondingly, there were also identifiable dunces, as was illustrated so well by the drone in "The Idle Schoolboy" (pages 30–31).

LESSON LV.

2. DIS-CHARG'ING; *v.* performing.	10. CHIEF'TAIN; *n.* the chief.
4. UN-CON'SCIOUS; *adj.* not know-ing.	11. BOOM'ING; *adj.* roaring.
	13. WREATH'ING; *adj.* curling.
4. RE-POS'ED; *v.* put; placed.	15. PEN'NON; *n.* a small flag.

CASABIANCA.

UTTER distinctly each consonant: *terrible, thunders, brave, distant, progress, trust, mangled, burning, bright.* See Exercise IV, page 15.

1. THERE was a little boy, about thirteen years old, whose name was Casabianca. His father was the †commander of a ship-of-war. The little boy went with his father to the seas. His ship was once in a †terrible battle off the mouth of the Nile.

2. In the midst of the thunders of the battle, while the shot were flying thickly around, and flooding the decks with blood, this brave boy stood by the side of his father, †faithfully discharging the duties which were †assigned to him.

3. At last his father placed him in a certain part of the ship, to perform some †service, and told him to remain at his post till he should call him away. As the father went to some distant part of the ship, to notice the †progress of the battle, a ball from the †enemy's vessel laid him dead upon the deck.

4. But the son, unconscious of his father's death, and faithful to the trust reposed in him, remained at his post, waiting for his father's orders. The battle raged †dreadfully around him. The blood of the slain flowed at his feet. The ship took fire, and the †threatening flames drew nearer and nearer.

5. Still, this noble-hearted boy would not †disobey his father. In the face of blood, and balls, and fire, he stood firm and †obedient. The sailors began to desert the burning and sinking ship, and the boy cried out, "Father, may I go?"

6. But no voice of †permission could come from the mangled body of his lifeless father; and the boy, not knowing that he was dead, would rather die than disobey. And there that boy stood, at his post, till every man had deserted the ship; he stood and perished in the flames. His death has been described in the following beautiful lines.

7. The boy stood on the burning deck,
    Whence all but him had fled,
The flame that lit the battle's †wreck,
    Shone round him o'er the dead.

8. Yet beautiful and bright he stood,
    As born to rule the storm;
A creature of heroic blood,
    A proud, though child-like form.

9. The flames rolled on; he would not go,
    Without his father's word;
That father, faint in death below,
    His voice no longer heard.

10. He called aloud, "Say, father, say,
    If yet my task is done?"
He knew not that the chieftain lay
    Unconscious of his son.

11. "Speak, father," once again he cried,
    "If I may yet be gone;
And"—but the booming shot replied,
    And fast the flames rolled on.

The author of this famous poem was Mrs. Felicia Dorothea Hemans (1793–1835), although her name was never attributed in any of the many reprintings of this verse in the McGuffeys. Among the most popular poets of her time in both England and America, Mrs. Hemans was widely praised for the lofty intentions and moral purity of her verse. "Casabianca" (1829) was her most famous poem, though not her best.

With its focus on moral obedience and death, "Casabianca" *was a natural selection for inclusion in the* McGuffeys. *It was one of McGuffey's earliest choices, appearing in the Second Reader from the first edition (1836) until 1857 when it was shifted to the* Fourth. *It was deleted from the series in 1879, however—perhaps because it was too well known; perhaps because of numerous schoolboy parodies, such as "The boy stood on the burning deck, eating peanuts by the peck . . . ."*

12. Upon his brow he felt their breath,
    And in his waving hair;
And looked from that lone post of death,
    In still, yet brave, despair;

13. And shouted but once more aloud,
    "My father, must I stay?"
While o'er him fast, through sail and shroud,
    The wreathing fires made way.

14. They ⁺wrapped the ship in splendor wild,
    They caught the flag on high,
And streamed above the gallant child,
    Like ⁺banners in the sky.

15. Then came a burst of thunder-sound:
    The boy—oh! where was he?
Ask of the winds, that far around
    With ⁺fragments ⁺strewed the sea.

16. With mast, and helm, and pennon fair,
    That well had borne their part:
But the noblest thing that ⁺perished there,
    Was that young faithful heart.

EXERCISES.—What is this story about? Who was Casabianca? By whose side did he stand in the midst of battle? What happened to his father? What took fire? What did the sailors begin to do? What did the little boy do? Why did he stand there amid so much danger? What became of him?

ARTICULATION.

Nz,	nst.	Opens,	openst:	sickens,	sickenst.
Nt,	nts.	Rant,	rants:	plant	plants.
Nch,	ncht.	Clinch,	clinchd:	quench,	quenchd.

S. Poh, poh! That is just one of Tim's large stories. I do assure you, it was not, at first, bigger than my thumb-nail, and I am certain it has not grown any since.

D. At least, however, let her have something she will eat, since she refuses hay.

S. She did, indeed, refuse hay this morning; but the only reason was that she was crammed full of oats. You have nothing to fear, neighbor; the mare is in perfect trim; and she will skim you over the ground like a bird. I wish you a good journey and a profit-able job.

EXERCISES.—Relate the facts of this dialogue. What is a dialogue? What do you think of the honesty of such men as Scrapewell? Why did he, at last, accommodate Mr. Derby? Was his conduct the result of kindness or selfishness? Are those who do kind acts through selfish motives entitled to praise? Why not?

LESSON LXXV.

1. LU′RID; *adj.* dismal; gloomy.
1. PHAN′TA-SY; *n.* specter-like appearance.
1. BLENT; *v.* mingled together.
2. TI′DINGS; *n.* news.
5. AN′GUISH; *n.* deep distress.
5. RE-PRESS′ED; *v.* kept back.
7. GREET; *v.* welcome.
8. PAR′DON; *n.* forgiveness.
8. EN-TWINE′; *v.* clasp together.

THE DYING SOLDIERS.

1. A WASTE of land, a †sodden plain,
   A lurid sunset sky,
   With clouds that fled and faded fast
   In †ghostly phantasy;
   A field upturned by trampling feet,
   A field uppiled with slain,
   With horse and rider blent in death
   Upon the battle-plain.

THIS IS ONE OF THE FEW LESSONS INTRODUCED INTO THE READERS IN 1866 in response to the just-ended Civil War. It was retained in all subsequent editions.

"The Dying Soldiers" is usually anthologized under the title of "The Blue and The Gray," although (because there are so many poems with that title) it has also appeared as "Death, the Peacemaker." It is, as far as can be determined, the only surviving poem of Ellen H. Flagg.

2. The dying and the dead lie low;
    For them, no more shall rise
The evening moon, nor midnight stars,
    Nor daylight's soft +surprise:
They will not wake to tenderest call,
    Nor see again each home,
Where waiting hearts shall throb, and break.
    When this day's tidings come.

3. Two soldiers, lying as they fell
    Upon the reddened clay—
In daytime, foes; at night, in peace
    Breathing their lives away!
Brave hearts had stirred each manly breast;
    Fate only, made them foes;
And lying, dying, side by side,
    A softened feeling rose.

4. "Our time is short," one faint voice said;
    "To-day we 've done our best
On different sides: what matters now?
    To-morrow we shall rest!
Life lies behind.   I might not care
    For only my own sake;
But far away are other hearts,
    That this day's work will break.

5. "Among New Hampshire's snowy hills,
    There pray for me to-night
A woman, and a little girl
    With hair like golden light;"
And at the thought, broke forth, at last,
    The cry of anguish wild,
That would not longer be repressed—
    "O God! my wife, my child!"

6. "And," said the other dying man,
    "Across the Georgia plain,
There watch and wait for me loved ones
    I ne'er shall see again:
A little girl, with dark, bright eyes,
    Each day waits at the door;
Her father's step, her father's kiss,
    Will never greet her more.

7. "To-day we sought each other's lives:
    Death levels all that now;
For soon before God's mercy-seat
    Together we shall bow.
Forgive each other while we may;
    Life's but a weary game,
And, right or wrong, the morning sun
    Will find us, dead, the same."

8. The dying lips the pardon breathe;
    The dying hands entwine;
The last ray fades, and over all
    The stars from heaven shine;
And the little girl with golden hair,
    And one with dark eyes bright,
On Hampshire's hills, and Georgia's plain,
    Were fatherless that night!

EXERCISES.—What do the first two stanzas describe? What does the third? What did one soldier say to the other? Where was his home? What friends had he there? Where was the home of the other soldier? Who waited for him? Did they forgive each other? Repeat the last stanza.

EXERCISES ON THE VOCALS.

LONG VOWEL SOUNDS.—*Pay* the *evil* and *idle* b*oa*ster the *usu*ry of t*oi*l. An *A*pril *e*vening f*i*nds the s*o*ldier *ou*t at *u*seful t*oi*l. *O'*er the pl*ai*n the *ea*gle, fl*y*ing, scr*ea*ms al*ou*d. *A, e, i, o,* and *u* are vowels.

Most of the verse generated by the Civil War was sentimental, often bathetic. This, although perhaps more truly moving than many, is representative of the Civil War entries in the McGuffey Readers, *which were calculated to sell in Atlanta and Charleston as well as Cincinnati and New York.*

LESSON LXXVI.

1. A-GREE'A-BLE; *a.* pleasing; welcome.
2. AF-FIRM'ED; *v.* said; declared.
4. SE-DATE'; *adj.* calm; quiet.
6. SO'CIA-BLY; *adv.* in a friendly way.
13. RE-SEM'BLANCE; *n.* that which is like, or similar.
14. DIL'I-GENT; *a.* carefully attentive; industrious.
14. VIS'AGE; *n.* the face or look of a person, or of other animals.
15. CAR'PEN-TER; *n.* a workman in timber; a builder of houses or ships.

HUGH IDLE AND MR. TOIL.

1. HUGH IDLE loved to do only what was agreeable, and took no delight in labor of any kind. But while Hugh was yet a little boy, he was sent away from home, and put under the care of a very strict school-master, who went by the name of Mr. Toil.

2. Those who knew him best, affirmed that Mr. Toil was a very worthy character, and that he had done more good, both to children and grown people, than any body else in the world. He had, however, a severe and ugly countenance; his voice was harsh; and all his ways and customs were †disagreeable to our young friend, Hugh Idle.

3. The whole day long this terrible old school-master †stalked about among his scholars, with a big cane in his hand; and unless a lad chose to attend constantly and quietly to his book, he had no chance of enjoying a single quiet moment. "This will never do for me," thought Hugh; "I'll run off, and try to find my way home."

4. So the very next morning off he started, with only some bread and cheese for his breakfast, and very little pocket-money to pay his expenses. He had gone but

WHEN THIS TALE FIRST APPEARED (IN THE 1866 EDITION OF THE FOURTH **Reader,** *reprinted here), it carried no attribution. In subsequent editions, however, it is attributed to Nathaniel Hawthorne. It is rather freely adapted from Hawthorne's story of "Little Daffydowndilly."*

a short distance, when he overtook a man of grave and sedate appearance †trudging, at a †moderate pace, along the road.

5. "Good morning, my fine lad!" said the stranger; and his voice seemed hard and severe, yet had a sort of kindness in it; "whence do you come so early, and whither are you going?"

6. Now Hugh was a boy of very frank disposition, and had never been known to tell a lie in all his life. Nor did he tell one now, but confessed that he had run away from school on account of his great dislike to Mr. Toil. "O, very well, my little friend!" answered the stranger; "then we will go together; for I likewise have had a good deal to do with Mr. Toil, and should be glad to find some place where he was never heard of." So they walked on very sociably side by side.

7. By and by their road led them past a field, where some hay-makers were at work. Hugh could not help thinking how much pleasanter it must be to make hay in the sunshine, under the blue sky, than to learn lessons all day long, shut up in a †dismal school-room, continually watched by Mr. Toil.

8. But in the midst of these thoughts, while he was stopping to peep over the stone-wall, he started back and caught hold of his companion's hand. "Quick, quick!" cried he; "let us run away, or he will catch us!"

9. "Who will catch us?" asked the stranger.

10. "Mr. Toil, the old school-master," answered Hugh; "don't you see him among the hay-makers?" and Hugh pointed to an elderly man, who seemed to be the owner of the field.

11. He was busily at work in his shirt sleeves. The drops of sweat stood upon his brow; and he kept constantly crying out to his work-people to make hay while the sun shone. Strange to say, the †features of the old farmer were precisely the same as those of

Nathaniel Hawthorne (1804–1864) is, of course, now recognized as one of America's greatest literary figures, but his recognition came relatively late in life. Known today primarily for his novels—especially The Scarlet Letter *(1850)* and The House of the Seven Gables *(1851)—Hawthorne's fame in the mid-nineteenth century derived mainly from his moral allegories as published first in the gift annuals of the time, especially* The Token. *They were later collected in book form as* Twice-Told Tales *(1837),* Mosses From an Old Manse *(1846), and others. He also wrote a number of books expressly for children, including* Grandfather's Chair *(1841);* Liberty Tree *(1841);* A Wonder Book *(1852); and* Tanglewood Tales *(1853).*

Mr. Toil, who at that very moment must have been just entering the school-room.

12. "Do n't be afraid," said the stranger; "this is not Mr. Toil, the school-master, but a brother of his, who was bred a farmer. He won't trouble you, unless you become a laborer on his farm."

13. Hugh believed what his companion said, but was glad when they were out of sight of the old farmer, who bore such a singular resemblance to Mr. Toil. The two travelers came to a spot where some carpenters were building a house. Hugh begged his companion to stop awhile, for it was a pretty sight to see how neatly the carpenters did their work with their saws, planes, and hammers; and he was beginning to think he too should like to use the saw, and the plane, and the hammer, and be a carpenter himself. But †suddenly he caught sight of something that made him seize his friend's hand, in a great fright.

14. "Make haste! quick, quick!" cried he; "there's old Mr. Toil again." The stranger cast his eyes where Hugh pointed his finger, and saw an elderly man, who seemed to be overseeing the carpenters, as he went to and fro about the unfinished house, marking out the work to be done, and urging the men to be diligent; and wherever he turned his hard and wrinkled visage, they sawed and hammered, as if for dear life.

15. "O, no! this is not Mr. Toil, the school-master," said the stranger; "it is another brother of his, who follows the trade of carpenter."

16. "I am very glad to hear it," quoth Hugh; "but if you please, sir, I should like to get out of his way as soon as possible."

EXERCISES.—To whose school was Hugh Idle sent? What was the character of the school-master? Why did Hugh leave the school? What did the stranger propose to Hugh? Give Hugh's adventure with the hay-makers. With the carpenters.

LESSON LXXVII.

1. Gay′ly; *adv.* finely; splendidly.

1. Vent′ure; *v.* to dare; to risk.

3. Dis-may′; *n.* fright; terror.

4. En-list′; *v.* to put one's name on a roll; to join.

5. Com-pos′ed-ly; *adv.* calmly; quietly.

6. Re-sum′ed; *v.* recommenced.

8. Dex-ter′i-ty; *n.* skill; quickness.

10. Ob-serv′ed; *v.* remarked.

12. Dis-guise′; *n.* something put on to conceal one's real self.

15. Com-pan′ion; *n.* comrade.

16. Ap-pro-ba′tion; *n.* regarding with pleasure.

HUGH IDLE AND MR. TOIL—CONCLUDED.

1. Now Hugh and the stranger had not gone much further, when they met a company of soldiers, gayly dressed, with feathers in their caps, and glittering muskets on their shoulders. In front marched the drummers and fifers, making such merry music, that Hugh would gladly have followed them to the end of the world. If he were only a soldier, he said to himself, old Mr. Toil would never venture to look him in the face.

2. "Quick step! forward! march!" shouted a †gruff voice.

3. Little Hugh started in great dismay; for this voice sounded precisely like that which he had heard every day in Mr. Toil's school-room. And turning his eyes to the captain of the company, what should he see but the very image of old Mr. Toil himself, in an officer's dress, to be sure, but looking as ugly and disagreeable as ever.

4. "This is certainly old Mr. Toil," said Hugh, in a trembling voice. "Let us away, for fear he should make us enlist in his company."

The importance of work is constantly stressed in the McGuffeys, but Hawthorne's tale here would strike most readers today—even those with no prejudice against allegory—as too openly didactic. The ubiquitous Mr. Toil looks far more palatable, however, when compared with the didacticism of such earlier lessons as "The Truant" (quoted here from the 1836 Second Reader):

Who is he that sleeps till a late hour, and when he wakes, yawns and wishes for the return of night . . .? He is the idle and worthless truant. He comes forth clothed in the garments of slovenliness. In his step is the heaviness of stupid sloth . . . .

Wretched are the parents of such a son!—Grief and shame is theirs. His name shall be stamped with the mark of infamy when their broken hearts shall moulder in the grave!

5. "You are mistaken again, my little friend," replied the stranger very composedly. "This is only a brother of Mr. Toil's, who has served in the army all his life. You and I need not be afraid of him."

6. "Well, well," said Hugh, "if you please, sir, I don't want to see the soldiers any more." So the child and the stranger resumed their journey; and, after awhile, they came to a house by the roadside, where a number of young men and rosy-cheeked girls, with smiles on their faces, were dancing to the sound of a fiddle.

7. "O, let us stop here," cried Hugh; "Mr. Toil will never dare to show his face where there is a fiddler, and where people are dancing and making merry."

8. But the words had scarcely died away on the little boy's tongue, when, happening to cast his eyes on the fiddler, whom should he behold again but the likeness of Mr. Toil, armed with a fiddle-bow this time, and flourishing it with as much ease and dexterity, as if he had been a fiddler all his life.

9. "O, dear me!" whispered he, turning pale; "it seems as if there were nobody but Mr. Toil in the world."

10. "This is not your old school-master," observed the stranger, "but another brother of his, who has learned to be a fiddler. He is ashamed of his family, and generally calls himself Master Pleasure; but his real name is Toil, and those who know him best, think him still more disagreeable than his brothers."

11. "Pray, let us go on," said Hugh.

12. Well, thus the two went wandering along the highway, and in shady lanes, and through pleasant villages, and wherever they went, behold! there was the image of old Mr. Toil. If they entered a house, he sat in the parlor; if they peeped into the kitchen,

4th Rd. 20.

he was there! He made himself at home in every cottage, and stole, under one disguise or another, into the most splendid mansions. Every-where they stumbled on some of the old school-master's †innumerable brothers.

13. At length, little Hugh found himself completely worn out with running away from Mr. Toil. "Take me back! take me back!" cried the poor fellow, bursting into tears. "If there is nothing but Toil all the world over, I may just as well go back to the school-house."

14. "Yonder it is; there is the school-house!" said the stranger; for though he and little Hugh had taken a great many steps, they had traveled in a circle instead of a straight line. "Come, we will go back to the school together."

15. There was something in his companion's voice that little Hugh now remembered; and it is strange that he had not remembered it sooner. Looking up into his face, behold! there again was the likeness of old Mr. Toil, so that the poor child had been in company with Toil all day, even while he had been doing his best to run away from him.

16. Little Hugh Idle, however, had learned a good lesson, and from that time forward, was diligent at his task, because he now knew that diligence is not a whit more toilsome than sport or idleness. And when he became better acquainted with Mr. Toil, he began to think his ways were not so disagreeable, and that the old school-master's smile of approbation made his face sometimes appear almost as pleasant as even that of Hugh's mother.

EXERCISES.—Whom did Hugh see with the soldiers? What is said of the fiddler? Give, in your own language, the further adventures of Hugh and the stranger. What lesson is taught by this story?

LXXII. THE OLD OAKEN BUCKET.

By **Samuel Woodworth**, who was born in Massachusetts in 1785. He was both author and editor. This is his best known poem.

1. How dear to this heart are the scenes of my childhood,
   When fond recollection presents them to view!
   The orchard, the meadow, the deep tangled wild-wood,
   And every loved spot which my infancy knew;

ORIGINALLY PICKED BY MCGUFFEY AS ONE OF THE SELECTIONS IN THE first edition of the Third Reader, this famous poem has appeared in each of the subsequent editions (since 1857 as part of the Fourth Reader). Woodworth's first title for it was simply "The Bucket" (1826), but that was altered to "The Moss Covered Bucket" in the early editions of the McGuffeys, and finally to the title shown here. Set to music by Frederick Smith, it quickly became one of the century's most popular songs.

The wide-spreading pond, and the mill that stood by it:
　The bridge and the rock where the cataract fell:
The cot of my father, the dairy-house nigh it,
　And e'en the rude bucket which hung in the well:
The old oaken bucket, the iron-bound bucket,
　The moss-covered bucket which hung in the well.

2. That moss-covered vessel I hail as a treasure;
　For often, at noon, when returned from the field,
I found it the source of an exquisite pleasure,
　The purest and sweetest that nature can yield.
How ardent I seized it, with hands that were glowing,
　And quick to the white-pebbled bottom it fell;
Then soon, with the emblem of truth overflowing,
　And dripping with coolness, it rose from the well:
The old oaken bucket, the iron-bound bucket,
　The moss-covered bucket arose from the well.

3. How sweet from the green mossy brim to receive it,
　As poised on the curb, it inclined to my lips!
Not a full blushing goblet could tempt me to leave it,
　Though filled with the nectar which Jupiter sips;
And now, far removed from thy loved situation,
　The tear of regret will intrusively swell,
As fancy reverts to my father's plantation,
　And sighs for the bucket which hangs in the well:
The old oaken bucket, the iron-bound bucket,
　The moss-covered bucket, which hangs in the well.

DEFINITIONS.—1. Căt′a-răct, *a great fall of water.* 2. O-ver-flōw′ing, *running over.* Ex′qui-ṣĭte, *exceeding, extreme.* 3. Poiṣed′, *balanced.* Gŏb′let, *a kind of cup or drinking vessel.* Nĕc′tar, *the drink of the gods.* In-trụ′ṣĭve-ly, *without right or welcome.* Re-vĕrts′, *returns.*

EXERCISES. — Who was the author of "The Old Oaken Bucket?" What is said of this piece? What does the poem describe? and what feeling does it express?

Samuel Woodworth (1785–1842) was born and raised in Scituate, Massachusetts, where school was taught only during the three winter months each year. According to Woodworth's memoirs, the teacher for that school was chosen primarily on the basis of how little remuneration he was willing to work for, so that the schoolmaster was often as ignorant as his pupils. Later Woodworth became a journalist in New York City, editing the New York Mirror *and writing poems and plays. The latter included* LaFayette *(1824) and* The Forest Rose *(1825).*

This light piece by an unknown author is one of the most pleasant—and more memorable—of the moral verses in the McGuffeys. Much too frivolous in approach for inclusion in the earliest editions, it appeared in the Readers first in 1857 and has been retained in all editions since.

VII. LAZY NED.

1. " 'T is royal fun," cried lazy Ned,
   "To coast upon my fine, new sled,
   And beat the other boys;
   But then, I can not bear to climb
   The tiresome hill, for every time
   It more and more annoys."

2. So, while his schoolmates glided by,
   And gladly tugged uphill, to try
   Another merry race,
   Too indolent to share their plays,
   Ned was compelled to stand and gaze,
   While shivering in his place.

3. Thus, he would never take the pains
   To seek the prize that labor gains,
   Until the time had passed;
   For, all his life, he dreaded still
   The silly bugbear of *uphill,*
   And died a dunce at last.

DEFINITIONS.—1. Roy'al, *excellent, noble.* Cōast, *to slide.* Annoys', *troubles.* 2. In'do-lent, *lazy.* 3. Prīze, *a reward.* Bŭg'beàr, *something frightful.* Dŭnçe, *a silly fellow.*

EXERCISES.—What did Ned like? What did he not like?

IX. MEDDLESOME MATTY.

1. OH, how one ugly trick has spoiled
    The sweetest and the best!
  Matilda, though a pleasant child,
    One grievous fault possessed,
  Which, like a cloud before the skies,
  Hid all her better qualities.

2. Sometimes, she'd lift the teapot lid
    To peep at what was in it;
  Or tilt the kettle, if you did
    But turn your back a minute.
  In vain you told her not to touch,
  Her trick of meddling grew so much.

3. Her grandmamma went out one day,
    And, by mistake, she laid
  Her spectacles and snuffbox gay,
    Too near the little maid;
  "Ah! well," thought she, "I'll try them on,
  As soon as grandmamma is gone."

4. Forthwith, she placed upon her nose
    The glasses large and wide;
  And looking round, as I suppose,
    The snuffbox, too, she spied.
  "Oh, what a pretty box is this!
  I'll open it," said little miss.

5. "I know that grandmamma would say,
    'Don't meddle with it, dear;'
  But then she's far enough away,
    And no one else is near;

THIS POPULAR SELECTION ENTERED THE McGUFFEY SECOND READERS IN 1844 and has been part of the Fourth Reader *since 1857. Although no authorial attribution is ever given in the McGuffeys, the verse belongs to England's Ann Taylor (1782–1866). The daughter of one minister and widow of another, she collaborated with her sister Jane to produce such books as* Rhymes for the Nursery *(1806),* Hymns for Infant Minds *(1808), and* Original Hymns *for Sunday-Schools (1820). Together they have been called the inventors of the "awful warning" school of poetry.*

Beside, what can there be amiss
In opening such a box as this?"

6. So, thumb and finger went to work
    To move the stubborn lid;
And, presently, a mighty jerk
    The mighty mischief did;
For all at once, ah! woeful case!
The snuff came puffing in her face.

7. Poor eyes, and nose, and mouth, and chin
    A dismal sight presented;
And as the snuff got further in,
    Sincerely she repented.
In vain she ran about for ease,
She could do nothing else but sneeze.

8. She dashed the spectacles away,
    To wipe her tingling eyes;
And, as in twenty bits they lay,
    Her grandmamma she spies.
"Heyday! and what's the matter now?"
Cried grandmamma, with angry brow.

9. Matilda, smarting with the pain,
    And tingling still, and sore,
Made many a promise to refrain
    From meddling evermore;
And 't is a fact, as I have heard,
She ever since has kept her word.

DEFINITIONS.—1. Qual'i-ties, *traits of character.* 2. Mĕd'-dling, *interfering without right.* 4. Fŏrth-wĭth', *at once.* Spīed, *saw.* 5. A-mĭss', *wrong, faulty.* 6. Wōe'fụl, *sad, sorrowful.* 8. Tĭn'gling, *smarting.* 9. Re-frāin', *to keep from.*

EXERCISES.—What did Matilda do? How was she punished? What effect did it have on her?

"Thou shalt not meddle with other's property"—an important McGuffey commandment. Matilda is just one of many who learn—usually with both pain and chagrin—that property is important and that "meddling" (a favorite McGuffey word) is nearly as bad as stealing.

XII. WHERE THERE IS A WILL THERE IS A WAY.

1. HENRY BOND was about ten years old when his father died. His mother found it difficult to provide for the support of a large family, thus left entirely in her care. By good management, however, she contrived to do so, and also to send Henry, the oldest, to school, and to supply him, for the most part, with such books as he needed.

2. At one time, however, Henry wanted a grammar, in order to join a class in that study, and his mother could not furnish him with the money to buy it. He was very much troubled about it, and went to bed with a heavy heart, thinking what could be done.

3. On waking in the morning, he found that a deep snow had fallen, and the cold wind was blowing furiously. "Ah," said he, "it is an ill wind that blows nobody good."

4. He rose, ran to the house of a neighbor, and offered his service to clear a path around his premises. The offer was accepted. Having completed this work, and received his pay, he went to another place for the same purpose, and then to another, until he had earned enough to buy a grammar.

5. When school commenced, Henry was in his seat, the happiest boy there, ready to begin the lesson in his new book.

6. From that time, Henry was always the first in all his classes. He knew no such word as fail, but always succeeded in all he attempted. Having the will, he always found the way.

DEFINITIONS.—1. Măn′aġe-ment, *manner of directing things.* 2. Fûr′nish, *to supply.* 3. Fū′ri-oŭs-ly, *violently.* 4. Sĕrv′Içe, *labor.* Prĕm′i-seṣ, *grounds around a house.*

THIS LESSON DID NOT ENTER THE SERIES UNTIL 1857, BUT HAS REMAINED in the Fourth Reader *since then. Henry's problem in finding the necessary cash to purchase a textbook was a common one, however, throughout the century. Students were expected to furnish their own texts, which were then usually passed down from one member of the family to the next. Many old copies now in libraries are marked with a single surname— and as many as six or seven given names, both boys and girls.*

Prices advertised in an 1844 Reader *offer some insight into Henry's problem. McGuffey's Speller and First Reader were listed at twelve-and-a-half cents each. The* Second Reader *was priced at twenty-five cents, the* Third *at fifty cents, and the* Fourth *at seventy-five cents. If these prices sound cheap, however, we should remember that the daily wage for the average laborer in 1840 was fifty cents.*

XIX. TWO WAYS OF TELLING A STORY.

By Henry K. Oliver.

1. In one of the most populous cities of New England, a few years ago, a party of lads, all members of the same school, got up a grand sleigh ride. The sleigh was a very large one, drawn by six gray horses.

2. On the following day, as the teacher entered the schoolroom, he found his pupils in high glee, as they chattered about the fun and frolic of their excursion. In answer to some inquiries, one of the lads gave him an account of their trip and its various incidents.

3. As he drew near the end of his story, he exclaimed: "Oh, sir! there was one thing I had almost forgotten. As we were coming home, we saw ahead

of us a queer looking affair in the road. It proved
to be a rusty old sleigh, fastened behind a covered
wagon, proceeding at a very slow rate, and taking up
the whole road.

4. "Finding that the owner was not disposed to
turn out, we determined upon a volley of snowballs
and a good hurrah. They produced the right effect,
for the crazy machine turned out into the deep snow,
and the skinny old pony started on a full trot.

5. "As we passed, some one gave the horse a good
crack, which made him run faster than he ever did
before, I'll warrant.

6. "With that, an old fellow in the wagon, who was
buried up under an old hat, bawled out, 'Why do you
frighten my horse?' 'Why don't you turn out,
then?' says the driver. So we gave him three rous-
ing cheers more. His horse was frightened again, and
ran up against a loaded wagon, and, I believe, almost
capsized the old creature—and so we left him."

7. "Well, boys," replied the teacher, "take your
seats, and I will tell you a story, and all about a
sleigh ride, too. Yesterday afternoon a very venerable
old clergyman was on his way from Boston to Salem,
to pass the rest of the winter at the house of his son.
That he might be prepared for journeying in the
following spring he took with him his wagon, and for
the winter his sleigh, which he fastened behind the
wagon.

8. "His sight and hearing were somewhat blunted
by age, and he was proceeding very slowly; for his
horse was old and feeble, like his owner. He was
suddenly disturbed by loud hurrahs from behind, and
by a furious pelting of balls of snow and ice upon the
top of his wagon.

9. "In his alarm he dropped his reins, and his horse began to run away. In the midst of the old man's trouble, there rushed by him, with loud shouts, a large party of boys, in a sleigh drawn by six horses. 'Turn out! turn out, old fellow!' 'Give us the road!' 'What will you take for your pony?' 'What's the price of oats, old man?' were the various cries that met his ears.

10. "'Pray, do not frighten my horse!' exclaimed the infirm driver. 'Turn out, then! turn out!' was the answer, which was followed by repeated cracks and blows from the long whip of the 'grand sleigh,' with showers of snowballs, and three tremendous hurrahs from the boys.

11. "The terror of the old man and his horse was increased, and the latter ran away with him, to the great danger of his life. He contrived, however, to stop his horse just in season to prevent his being dashed against a loaded wagon. A short distance brought him to the house of his son. That son, boys, is your instructor, and that 'old fellow,' was your teacher's father!"

12. When the boys perceived how rude and unkind their conduct appeared from another point of view, they were very much ashamed of their thoughtlessness, and most of them had the manliness to apologize to their teacher for what they had done.

DEFINITIONS.—1. Pŏp'u-loŭs, *full of inhabitants.* 2. Ex-cûr'-sion, *a pleasure trip.* In'çi-dents, *things that happen, events.* 5. Wạr'rant, *to declare with assurance.* 6. Cap-sīzed', *upset.* 7. Vĕn'-er-a-ble, *deserving of honor and respect.* 8. Blŭnt'ed, *dulled.*

EXERCISES.—Repeat the boys' story of the sleigh ride. The teacher's story. Were the boys ill-natured or only thoughtless? Is thoughtlessness any excuse for rudeness or unkindness?

The McGuffey *world is one of such firm moral absolutes that it is refreshing to find an occasional lesson like this, which dulcifies its didacticism with a little relativity.*

XXVIII. THE VOICE OF THE GRASS.

By Sarah Roberts.

1. Here I come, creeping, creeping, everywhere;
    By the dusty roadside,
    On the sunny hillside,
    Close by the noisy brook,
    In every shady nook,
  I come creeping, creeping, everywhere.

2. Here I come, creeping, creeping everywhere;
    All round the open door,
    Where sit the aged poor,
    Here where the children play,
    In the bright and merry May,
  I come creeping, creeping, everywhere.

3. Here I come, creeping, creeping, everywhere;
    You can not see me coming,
    Nor hear my low, sweet humming,
    For in the starry night,
    And the glad morning light,
  I come, quietly creeping, everywhere.

4. Here I come, creeping, creeping, everywhere;
    More welcome than the flowers,
    In summer's pleasant hours;
    The gentle cow is glad,
    And the merry birds not sad,
  To see me creeping, creeping, everywhere.

SARAH ROBERTS WAS BORN IN PORTSMOUTH IN 1812 AND DIED IN 1869. Beyond that there is little known about her, other than what one can conjecture from her titles. In addition to "The Voice of the Grass" she published My Childhood *(1852) and* My Step-Mother *(1857).*

5. Here I come, creeping, creeping, everywhere;
When you're numbered with the dead,
In your still and narrow bed,
In the happy spring I'll come,
And deck your narrow home,
Creeping, silently creeping, everywhere.

6. Here I come, creeping, creeping, everywhere;
My humble song of praise,
Most gratefully I raise,
To Him at whose command
I beautify the land,
Creeping, silently creeping, everywhere.

XXIX. THE EAGLE.

1. THE eagle seems to enjoy a kind of supremacy over the rest of the inhabitants of the air. Such is the loftiness of his flight, that he often soars in the sky beyond the reach of the naked eye, and such is his strength that he has been known to carry away children in his talons. But many of the noble qualities imputed to him are rather fanciful than true.

2. He has been described as showing a lofty independence, which makes him disdain to feed on anything that is not slain by his own strength. But Alexander Wilson, the great naturalist, says that he has seen an eagle. feasting on the carcass of a horse. The eagle lives to a great age. One at Vienna is stated to have died after a confinement of one hundred and four years.

ALTHOUGH A NUMBER OF NATURAL HISTORY LESSONS IN THE READERS were deleted in the later 1800's, this lesson remained; it has been part of the series since 1843. The authority cited here is Alexander Wilson (1766–1813), the Scottish-born ornithologist and poet who came to America in 1794. His major work was the nine-volume American Ornithology *(1808–1814).*

3. There are several species of the eagle. The golden eagle, which is one of the largest, is nearly four feet from the point of the beak to the end of the tail. He is found in most parts of Europe, and is also met with in America. High rocks and ruined and lonely towers are the places which he chooses for his abode. His nest is composed of sticks and rushes. The tail feathers are highly valued as ornaments by the American Indians.

4. The most interesting species is the bald eagle, as this is an American bird, and the adopted emblem of our country. He lives chiefly upon fish, and is found in the neighborhood of the sea, and along the shores and cliffs of our large lakes and rivers.

5. According to the description given by Wilson, he depends, in procuring his food, chiefly upon the labors of others. He watches the fishhawk as he dives into the sea for his prey, and darting down upon him as he rises, forces him to relinquish his victim, and then seizes it before it again reaches the water.

6. One of the most notable species is the harpy eagle. This is said to be bold and strong, and to attack beasts, and even man himself. He is fierce, quarrelsome, and sullen, living alone in the deepest forests. He is found chiefly in South America.

DEFINITIONS.—1. Su-prĕm′a-çy, *highest authority.* Sōarṣ, *flies aloft.* Im-pūt′ed, *ascribed to.* 2. Lŏft′y, *haughty, dignified.* Diṣ-dāin′, *to scorn.* Cär′cass, *the dead body of an animal.* 3. Spē′-ciēṣ, *classes.* 4. In′ter-ĕst-ing, *engaging the attention.* A-dŏpt′ed, *selected, chosen.* Em′blem, *that which is supposed to resemble some other thing in certain qualities, and is used to represent it.* 5. Re-lĭn′quish, *to give up.* 6. Nŏt′a-ble, ***worthy of notice.*** Sŭl′len, *gloomily angry and silent.*

While one purpose of this lesson is clearly to debunk some of the myths about the eagle (such as its lofty independence), it is doubtful if that motive accounts for the close juxtaposition here of the bald eagle as "emblem of our country" with its description as depending "chiefly upon the labors of others." That's the problem with symbols examined too closely. (The irony here is almost certainly unintentional.)

This lesson and its companion piece, "The Advantages of Industry" (the next selection reprinted here) were the products of Jacob Abbott (1803–1879), whose lesson "On Speaking the Truth" appeared earlier (pages 75–77). Author of over 200 volumes (many of them translated into French and German), Abbott's works were highly regarded in the nineteenth century as models of the best writing for young readers—in both description and simplicity of statement.

XXXIX. CONSEQUENCES OF IDLENESS.

1. Many young persons seem to think it of not much consequence if they do not improve their time well in youth, vainly expecting that they can make it up by diligence when they are older. They also think it is disgraceful for men and women to be idle, but that there can be no harm for persons who are young to spend their time in any manner they please.

2. George Jones thought so. When he was twelve years old, he went to an academy to prepare to enter college. His father was at great expense in obtaining books for him, clothing him, and paying his tuition. But George was idle. The preceptor of the academy would often tell him that if he did not study diligently when young he would never succeed well.

3. But George thought of nothing but present pleasure. He would often go to school without having made any preparation for his morning lesson; and, when called to recite with his class, he would stammer and make such blunders that the rest of the class could not help laughing at him. He was one of the poorest scholars in the school, because he was one of the most idle.

4. When recess came, and all the boys ran out of the academy upon the playground, idle George would come moping along. Instead of studying diligently while in school, he was indolent and half asleep. When the proper time for play came, he had no relish for it. I recollect very well, that, when "tossing up" for a game of ball, we used to choose everybody on the playground before we chose George;

and if there were enough without him we used to leave him out. Thus he was unhappy in school and out of school.

5. There is nothing which makes a person enjoy play so well as to study hard. When recess was over, and the rest of the boys returned, fresh and vigorous, to their studies, George might be seen lagging and moping along to his seat. Sometimes he would be asleep in school; sometimes he would pass his time in catching flies, and penning them up in little holes, which he cut in his seat; and sometimes, when the preceptor's back was turned, he would throw a paper ball across the room.

6. When the class was called up to recite, George would come drowsily along, looking as mean and ashamed as though he were going to be whipped. The rest of the class stepped up to the recitation with alacrity, and appeared happy and contented. When it came George's turn to recite, he would be so long in doing it, and make such blunders, that all most heartily wished him out of the class.

7. At last, George went with his class to enter college. Though he passed a very poor examination, he was admitted with the rest; for those who examined him thought it was possible that the reason why he did not answer questions better was because he was frightened. Now came hard times for poor George. In college there is not much mercy shown to bad scholars; and George had neglected his studies so long that he could not now keep up with his class, let him try ever so hard.

8. He could, without much difficulty, get along in the academy, where there were only two or three boys of his own class to laugh at him. But now he had

Although there are no girls mentioned here, Abbott was not as isolated from them as William Holmes McGuffey. In fact, in 1829 Abbott started the Mount Vernon School in Boston— a girl's school soon recognized as one of the first in the country to give girls an education equal to that available to boys. And he shocked many educators by making the school largely self-governing, with the girls establishing the rules, judging infractions, and setting penalties for minor misdeeds. Although it produced no immediate effect on classroom procedures elsewhere, Abbott's liberal approach evidently worked quite effectively.

to go into a large recitation room, filled with students from all parts of the country. In the presence of all these, he must rise and recite to a professor. Poor fellow! He paid dearly for his idleness.

9. You would have pitied him if you could have seen him trembling in his seat, every moment expecting to be called upon to recite. And when he was called upon, he would stand up and take what the class called a "dead set;" that is, he could not recite at all. Sometimes he would make such ludicrous blunders that the whole class would burst into a laugh. Such are the applauses an idler gets. He was wretched, of course. He had been idle so long that he hardly knew how to apply his mind to study. All the good scholars avoided him; they were ashamed to be seen in his company. He became discouraged, and gradually grew dissipated.

10. The officers of the college were soon compelled to suspend him. He returned in a few months, but did no better; and his father was then advised to take him from college. He left college, despised by everyone. A few months ago, I met him, a poor wanderer, without money and without friends. Such are the wages of idleness. I hope every reader will, from this history, take warning, and "stamp improvement on the wings of time."

DEFINITIONS. — 1. Cŏn′se-quençe, *importance, influence.* 2. A-căd′e-my, *a school of high order.* Cŏl′leġe, *a seminary of learning of the highest order.* Pre-çĕp′tor, *a teacher.* 3. Prĕp-a-rā′tion, *a making ready.* 5. Vĭḡ′or-oŭs, *full of activity and strength.* 6. A-lăc′ri-ty, *cheerfulness, sprightliness.* 8. Pro-fĕss′or, *a teacher in a college.* 9. Lŭ′di-croŭs, *adapted to raise laughter.* Ap-plaus′eș, *praises.* Dĭs′-si-pā-ted, *given up to bad habits.* 10. Im-prove′ment, *increase of knowledge.*

Abbott is clearly more mellow in this lesson than in the pulpit oratory of his "On Speaking the Truth," partly because of editorial revisions later in the century. The 1837 version of this lesson, for instance, stated pointedly: "Every child who would be a Christian, and have a house in heaven, must guard against this sin."

XL. ADVANTAGES OF INDUSTRY.

1. I GAVE you, in the last lesson, the history of George Jones, an idle boy, and showed you the consequences of his idleness. I shall now give you the history of Charles Bullard, a classmate of George. Charles was about the same age as George, and did not possess superior talents. Indeed, I doubt whether he was equal to him in natural powers of mind.

2. But Charles was a hard student. When quite young, he was always careful and diligent in school. Sometimes, when there was a very hard lesson, instead of going out to play during recess, he would stay in to study. He had resolved that his first object should be to get his lessons well, and then he could play with a good conscience. He loved play as well as anybody, and was one of the best players on the ground. I hardly ever saw any boy catch a ball better than he could. When playing any game, everyone was glad to get Charles on his side.

3. I have said that Charles would sometimes stay in at recess. This, however, was very seldom; it was only when the lessons were very hard indeed. Generally, he was among the first on the playground, and he was also among the first to go into school when called. Hard study gave him a relish for play, and play again gave him a relish for hard study; so he was happy both in school and out. The preceptor could not help liking him, for he always had his lessons well committed, and never gave him any trouble.

4. When he went to enter college, the preceptor gave him a good recommendation. He was able to

(4.—8.)

In the McGuffeys *it seems almost inevitable that the negative example of a George Jones would be countered by a positive one. Consequently, these two lessons remained paired—from the first edition of the* Third Reader *in 1837, to the present edition (having been elevated to the* Fourth Reader *in 1857).*

answer all the questions which were put to him when he was examined. He had studied so well when he was in the academy, and was so thoroughly prepared for college, that he found it very easy to keep up with his class, and had much time for reading interesting books.

5. But he would always get his lesson well before he did anything else, and would review it just before recitation. When called upon to recite, he rose tranquil and happy, and very seldom made mistakes. The officers of the college had a high opinion of him, and he was respected by all the students.

6. There was, in the college, a society made up of all the best scholars. Charles was chosen a member of that society. It was the custom to choose some one of the society to deliver a public address every year. This honor was conferred on Charles; and he had studied so diligently, and read so much, that he delivered an address which was very interesting to all who heard it.

7. At last he graduated, as it is called; that is, he finished his collegiate course, and received his degree. It was known by all that he was a good scholar, and by all that he was respected. His father and mother, brothers and sisters, came on the commencement day to hear him speak.

8. They all felt gratified, and loved Charles more than ever. Many situations of usefulness and profit were opened to him; for Charles was now an intelligent man, and universally respected. He is still a useful and a happy man. He has a cheerful home, and is esteemed by all who know him.

9. Such are the rewards of industry. How strange it is that any person should be willing to live in idle-

The theme of moral industry is often, as here, associated with a pupil's duty to his or her parents who have sacrificed to make the schooling possible. In the early editions of the Second Reader, *for instance, "The Diligent Scholar" is described in large part through his parents: "Happy the parents of such a son! Gladness and triumph are theirs. His name shall be crowned with honor by the virtuous . . ." etc. Here, Charles must content himself with being only "loved more than ever" and "universally respected."*

ness, when it will certainly make him unhappy! The idle boy is almost invariably poor and miserable; the industrious boy is happy and prosperous.

10. But perhaps some child who reads this, asks, "Does God notice little children in school?" He certainly does. And if you are not diligent in the improvement of your time, it is one of the surest evidences that your heart is not right with God. You are placed in this world to improve your time. In youth you must be preparing for future usefulness. And if you do not improve the advantages you enjoy, you sin against your Maker.

> With books, or work, or healthful play,
>   Let your first years be passed;
> That you may give, for every day,
>   Some good account, at last.

DEFINITIONS.—1. His'to-ry, *a description or a narration of events.* 2. Cŏn'science, *our own knowledge of right and wrong.* Gāme, *play, sport.* 3. Com-mĭt'ted, *fixed in mind.* 4. Rĕc-om-men-dā'tion, *what is said in praise of anyone.* 5. Re-view', *to examine again.* Trăn'quil, *quiet, calm.* 6. Con-fērred', *given to or bestowed upon anyone.* 7. Grăd'u-ā-ted, *received a degree from a college.* Com-mĕnçe'ment, *the day when students receive their degree.* 8. U-ni-vēr'sal-ly, *by all, without exception.* 9. In-vā'ri-a-bly, *always, uniformly.* 10. Ev'i-den-çes, *proofs.* Ad-vàn'ta-ġes, *opportunities for improvement.*

EXERCISES.—What was the character of George Jones? Of Charles Bullard? How did George appear in the class at school? How did he behave at recess? How did Charles differ from him in these respects? Relate what happened when George went to college. What became of him? Did Charles succeed at college? Which of them do you think more worthy of imitation? What is said of the idle? What is said of the industrious? Who watches all our actions wherever we may be? For what are we placed in this world? Should you not then be diligent in your studies?

In this 1879 version of the dual lessons the ethic remains pragmatic and secular—without religious reinforcement—until the final paragraph. Although that paragraph reflects what is often labeled the "Protestant Work Ethic," it is worth noting that at this point the ethic is almost totally subordinated to elements of religious instruction. The study questions below reinforce the shift in emphasis.

THIS SELECTION FIRST APPEARED IN THE 1866 EDITION, ACCOMPANIED *by the Twenty-Third Psalm in full. It stands alone in later editions: one of the few surviving verses of James Thomas Fields, who was much better known in his time as a publisher and editor. For years he headed the prominent Boston publishing firm of Ticknor, Reed & Fields, and—from 1861 to 1871—he edited the* Atlantic Monthly. *Fields retired from both positions in the early seventies to devote more time to writing and lecturing. His successor as editor of the* Atlantic *was his former assistant, William Dean Howells.*

XLV. THE TEMPEST.

By **James T. Fields** (born 1817, died 1881), who was born at **Portsmouth, N. H.** He was a poet, and the author, also, of some well known prose works. Of these, his "Yesterdays with Authors" is the most noted.

1. WE were crowded in the cabin;
    Not a soul would dare to sleep:
   It was midnight on the waters,
    And a storm was on the deep.

2. 'Tis a fearful thing in winter
    To be shattered by the blast,
   And to hear the rattling trumpet
    Thunder, "Cut away the mast!"

3. So we shuddered there in silence,
    For the stoutest held his breath,
   While the hungry sea was roaring,
    And the breakers threatened death.

4. And as thus we sat in darkness,
    Each one busy in his prayers,
   "We are lost!" the captain shouted,
    As he staggered down the stairs.

5. But his little daughter whispered,
    As she took his icy hand,
   "Isn't God upon the ocean,
    Just the same as on the land?"

6. Then we kissed the little maiden,
    And we spoke in better cheer;
   And we anchored safe in harbor
    When the morn was shining clear.

DEFINITIONS.—1. Deep, *the ocean.* 2. Blàst, *tempest.* 3. Breăk'-ers, *waves of the sea broken by rocks.* 6. Cheer, *state of mind.*

LV. SOMEBODY'S DARLING.

1. Into a ward of the whitewashed halls,
       Where the dead and dying lay,
   Wounded by bayonets, shells, and balls,
       Somebody's darling was borne one day;

2. Somebody's darling, so young and brave,
       Wearing yet on his pale, sweet face,
   Soon to be hid by the dust of the grave,
       The lingering light of his boyhood's grace.

3. Matted and damp are the curls of gold,
       Kissing the snow of that fair young brow;
   Pale are the lips of delicate mold—
       Somebody's darling is dying now.

4. Back from his beautiful, blue-veined brow,
       Brush all the wandering waves of gold;
   Cross his hands on his bosom now;
       Somebody's darling is still and cold.

5. Kiss him once for somebody's sake,
       Murmur a prayer soft and low;
   One bright curl from its fair mates take;
       They were somebody's pride, you know;

6. Somebody's hand has rested there;
       Was it a mother's, soft and white?
   And have the lips of a sister fair
       Been baptized in the waves of light?

The 1866 revision of the Fourth Reader *retained all the 1857 edition, with the same pagination, and added ten new lessons at the end. The announced intent was to produce a better text, but one which could be used in conjunction with older editions (a practical and considerate policy that contrasts strikingly with the planned obsolescence of current textbooks). The 1866 Preface announced: "This present edition is considerably enlarged, the additional selections being all new, and several of them relating to recent historical events, of enduring interest to all Americans." The recent event most in mind, of course, was the Civil War, but only three of the ten new lessons dealt with the war. This lesson, written by Marie Ravenel LaConte (or LaCoste), was one of them and has appeared in all editions of the* Fourth Reader *since then.*

7. God knows best! he was somebody's love:
   Somebody's heart enshrined him there;
Somebody wafted his name above,
   Night and morn, on the wings of **prayer.**

8. Somebody wept when he marched away,
   Looking so handsome, brave, and **grand;**
Somebody's kiss on his forehead lay;
   Somebody clung to his parting hand.

9. Somebody's watching and waiting for him,
   Yearning to hold him again to her heart;
And there he lies, with his blue eyes dim,
   And the smiling, childlike lips apart.

10. Tenderly bury the fair young dead,
    Pausing to drop on his grave a tear;
Carve on the wooden slab at his head,
    "Somebody's darling slumbers here."

DEFINITIONS.—1. Bāy′o-net, *a short, pointed iron weapon, fitted to the muzzle of a gun.* Där′ling, *one dearly loved.* 2. Lĭn′ḡer-ing, *protracted.* 3. Măt′ted, *twisted together.* Dĕl′i-cate, *soft and fair.* Mōld, *shape.* 4. Wạn′der-ing, *straying.* 7. En-shrīned′, *cherished.* Wȧft′ed, *caused to float.* 9. Yèarn′ing, *being eager, longing.* 10. Tĕn′der-ly, *gently, kindly.*

LVI. KNOWLEDGE IS POWER.

1. "WHAT an excellent thing is knowledge," said a sharp-looking, bustling little man, to one who was much older than himself. "Knowledge is an excellent thing," repeated he. "My boys know more at six and seven years old than I did at twelve. They can read

paths of sin. If a mother can feel so much, what must be the feelings of our Father in heaven for those who have strayed from his love? If man can feel so deep a sympathy, what must be the emotions which glow in the bosom of angels?

DEFINITIONS.—1. Sĕp′a-rāt-ed, *parted.* 2. Dis-trăct′ed, *made crazy.* Sus-pēnse′, *doubt, uncertainty.* 3. Trăv′ersed, *passed over and examined.* 5. As-çer-tāined′, *made certain.* 6. Sy̆m′pa-thīzed, *felt for.* De-clĭv′i-ty, *descent of land.* 7. Cŏn-sul-tā′tion, *a meeting of persons to advise together.* 8. Lănd′scāpe, *a portion of territory which the eye can see in a single view.* 10. Pro-clāimed′, *made known publicly.* 11. Pro-çĕs′sion, *a train of persons walking or riding.* 13. Rĕp-re-ṣen-tā′tion, *the act of describing or showing.*

LXII. WHICH?

BY MRS. E. L. BEERS.

1. WHICH shall it be? Which shall it be?
   I looked at John—John looked at me;
   Dear, patient John, who loves me yet
   As well as though my locks were jet.
   And when I found that I must speak,
   My voice seemed strangely low and weak:
   "Tell me again what Robert said!"
   And then I, listening, bent my head.
   "This is his letter:"

2.   "'I will give
   A house and land while you shall live,
   If, in return, from out your seven,
   One child to me for aye is given.'"
   I looked at John's old garments worn,
   I thought of all that John had borne

MRS. ETHELINDA BEERS (1827-1879) WAS AN AMERICAN POET WHO started contributing verse to the periodicals when she was quite young, signing them "Ethel Lynn." After her marriage to William H. Beers, her works usually appeared under the name of Mrs. Ethel Lynn Beers. Her reputation during her life rested chiefly on her popular Civil War poem "The Picket Guard" (see page 319 in this collection), but "Which Shall It Be?" (as it is often titled) is probably her best known verse today. Her only book, All Quiet Along the Potomac and Other Poems *was published on October 10, 1879—the day she died.*

Of poverty, and work, and care,
Which I, though willing, could not share;
I thought of seven mouths to feed,
Of seven little children's néed,
And then of this.

3.   "Come, John," said I,
"We'll choose among them as they lie
Asleep;" so, walking hand in hand,
Dear John and I surveyed our band.
First to the cradle light we stepped,
Where Lilian the baby slept,
A glory 'gainst the pillow white.

Softly the father stooped to lay
His rough hand down in loving way,
When dream or whisper made her stir,
And huskily he said: "Not her!"

4. We stooped beside the trundle-bed,
And one long ray of lamplight shed
Athwart the boyish faces there,
In sleep so pitiful and fair;
I saw on Jamie's rough, red cheek,
A tear undried. Ere John could speak,
"He's but a baby, too," said I,
And kissed him as we hurried by.

5. Pale, patient Robbie's angel face
Still in his sleep bore suffering's trace:
"No, for a thousand crowns, not him,"
He whispered, while our eyes were dim.

Mrs. Beers's "Which" appears only in the 1879 and 1920 editions of the Readers. *Its dramatic form incorporates the soft, occasionally sticky-sweet sentimentality that appears increasingly in the later editions of the* McGuffeys.

6. Poor Dick! bad Dick! our wayward son,
   Turbulent, reckless, idle one—
   Could he be spared? "Nay, He who gave,
   Bade us befriend him to the grave;
   Only a mother's heart can be
   Patient enough for such as he;
   And so," said John, "I would not dare
   To send him from her bedside prayer."

7. Then stole we softly up above
   And knelt by Mary, child of love.
   "Perhaps for her 't would better be,"
   I said to John. Quite silently
   He lifted up a curl that lay
   Across her cheek in willful way,
   And shook his head. "Nay, love, not thee,"
   The while my heart beat audibly.

8. Only one more, our eldest lad,
   Trusty and truthful, good and glad—
   So like his father. "No, John, no—
   I can not, will not let him go."

9. And so we wrote in courteous way,
   We could not drive one child away.
   And afterward, toil lighter seemed,
   Thinking of that of which we dreamed;
   Happy, in truth, that not one face
   We missed from its accustomed place;
   Thankful to work for all the seven,
   Trusting the rest to One in heaven!

DEFINITIONS.—2. Aye, *always.* 3. Sur-veyed', *took a view of.* 5. Crown, *an English silver coin worth about* $1.20. 6. Wāy'-ward, *willful.* Tûr'bu-lent, *disposed to disorder.* 9. Coûr'te-oŭs, *polite.* Ac-cŭs'tomed, *usual.*

LXXVIII. LIVING ON A FARM.

1. How brightly through the mist of years,
My quiet country home appears!
My father busy all the day
In plowing corn or raking hay;
My mother moving with delight
Among the milk pans, silver-bright;
We children, just from school set free,
Filling the garden with our glee.
The blood of life was flowing warm
When I was living on a farm.

2. I hear the sweet churchgoing bell,
As o'er the fields its music fell,
I see the country neighbors round
Gathering beneath the pleasant sound;
They stop awhile beside the door,
To talk their homely matters o'er—
The springing corn, the ripening grain,
And "how we need a little rain;"
"A little sun would do no harm,
We want good weather for the farm."

3. When autumn came, what joy to see
The gathering of the husking bee,
To hear the voices keeping tune,
Of girls and boys beneath the moon,
To mark the golden corn ears bright,
More golden in the yellow light!
Since I have learned the ways of men,
I often turn to these again,
And feel life wore its highest charm
When I was living on the farm.

THIS ANONYMOUS SELECTION IS REPRESENTATIVE OF MANY OF THE lessons added in the 1879 edition—and of countless lessons appearing in competing textbooks at the end of the century: a yearning for the simple past as seen through the mist of sentimentality. To a large degree this particular lesson is reflecting the nostalgia of many who participated in the urban migration in the later nineteenth century. In its echoing of Goldsmith's "Deserted Village," however, as well as in its anticipation of our contemporary craze for nostalgia, it is also reflective of western man's fin de siècle *reassessment of "progress."*

evil spirits. Knĕll (*pro.* nĕl), *the stroke of a bell rung at a funeral or at the death of a person.*

NOTES.—The above poem was written at Bristol, England, in 1802, and recounts an old tradition.

2. *The Inchcape Rock* is at the entrance of the Frith of Tay, Scotland, about fifteen miles from shore.

———

LXXXIX. MY MOTHER'S GRAVE.

1. IT was thirteen years since my mother's death, when, after a long absence from my native village, I stood beside the sacred mound beneath which I had seen her buried. Since that mournful period, a great change had come over me. My childish years had passed away, and with them my youthful character. The world was altered, too; and as I stood at my mother's grave, I could hardly realize that I was the same thoughtless, happy creature, whose cheeks she so often kissed in an excess of tenderness.

2. But the varied events of thirteen years had not effaced the remembrance of that mother's smile. It seemed as if I had seen her but yesterday — as if the blessed sound of her well-remembered voice was in my ear. The gay dreams of my infancy and childhood were brought back so distinctly to my mind that, had it not been for one bitter recollection, the tears I shed would have been gentle and refreshing.

3. The circumstance may seem a trifling one, but the thought of it now pains my heart; and I relate it, that those children who have parents to love them may learn to value them as they ought. My mother had been ill a long time, and I had become so accus-

INTRODUCED IN THE 1866 FOURTH READER *AND RETAINED AT THAT level in subsequent editions, "My Mother's Grave" is a good example of the type of lesson selected by the publisher's editors to replace or supplement McGuffey's original selections. The element of death is a constant, as is the general emphasis on the commandment to "Honor thy Father and thy Mother." But these are now treated sentimentally, and—as becomes increasingly common in the later nineteenth century—the focus is on the mother.*

tomed to her pale face and weak voice, that I was not frightened at them, as children usually are. At first, it is true, I sobbed violently; but when, day after day, I returned from school, and found her the same, I began to believe she would always be spared to me; but they told me she would die.

4. One day when I had lost my place in the class, I came home discouraged and fretful. I went to my mother's chamber. She was paler than usual, but she met me with the same affectionate smile that always welcomed my return. Alas! when I look back through the lapse of thirteen years, I think my heart must have been stone not to have been melted by it. She requested me to go downstairs and bring her a glass of water. I pettishly asked her why she did not call a domestic to do it. With a look of mild reproach, which I shall never forget if I live to be a hundred years old, she said, "Will not my daughter bring a glass of water for her poor, sick mother?"

5. I went and brought her the water, but I did not do it kindly. Instead of smiling, and kissing her as I had been wont to do, I set the glass down very quickly, and left the room. After playing a short time, I went to bed without bidding my mother good night; but when alone in my room, in darkness and silence, I remembered how pale she looked, and how her voice trembled when she said, "Will not my daughter bring a glass of water for her poor, sick mother?" I could not sleep. I stole into her chamber to ask forgiveness. She had sunk into an easy slumber, and they told me I must not waken her.

6. I did not tell anyone what troubled me, but stole back to my bed, resolved to rise early in the morning and tell her how sorry I was for my con-

duct. The sun was shining brightly when I awoke, and, hurrying on my clothes, I hastened to my mother's chamber. She was dead! She never spoke more— never smiled upon me again; and when I touched the hand that used to rest upon my head in blessing, it was so cold that it made me start.

7. I bowed down by her side, and sobbed in the bitterness of my heart. I then wished that I might die, and be buried with her; and, old as I now am, I would give worlds, were they mine to give, could my mother but have lived to tell me she forgave my childish ingratitude. But I can not call her back; and when I stand by her grave, and whenever I think of her manifold kindness, the memory of that reproachful look she gave me will bite like a serpent and sting like an adder.

DEFINITIONS.—1. Mōurn′fụl, *full of sorrow.* Rḗ′al-īze, *to cause to seem real.* Ex-çĕss′, *that which goes beyond what is usual.* 2. Vȧ′ried, *different.* Ef-fāçed′, *worn away.* Pĕt′tish-ly, *in an ill-tempered way.* 6. Re-sŏlved′, *determined.* 7. In-g̅răt′i-tūde, *unthankfulness.* Măn′i-fōld, *various, multiplied.*

XC. A MOTHER'S GIFT—THE BIBLE.

1. REMEMBER, love, who gave thee this,
    When other days shall come,
    When she who had thine earliest kiss,
    Sleeps in her narrow home.
    Remember! 'twas a mother gave
    The gift to one she'd die to save!

Both this lesson and "A Mother's Gift" which follows below are presented without attribution to any author. In the 1879 and 1920 editions the policy appears to have been to credit authors, particularly if they were well known. But in the earlier editions (perhaps to avoid royalty payments) no credit is provided. As the Preface to the 1866 edition explains: "The Reading Lessons are drawn from a great variety of sources. Many of them are translations. They have been extensively remodeled, and some of them re-written. The names of the authors, from whom they are derived, are therefore omitted, they not being responsible for them in their present form."

2. That mother sought a pledge of love,
   The holiest for her son,
And from the gifts of God above,
   She chose a goodly one;
She chose for her belovèd boy,
The source of light, and life, and joy.

3. She bade him keep the gift, that, when
   The parting hour should come,
They might have hope to meet again
   In an eternal home.
She said his faith in this would be
Sweet incense to her memory.

4. And should the scoffer, in his pride,
   Laugh that fond faith to scorn,
And bid him cast the pledge aside,
   That he from youth had borne,
She bade him pause, and ask his breast
If SHE or HE had loved him best.

5. A parent's blessing on her son
   Goes with this holy thing;
The love that would retain the one,
   Must to the other cling.
Remember! 'tis no idle toy:
A mother's gift! remember, boy.

DEFINITIONS.—2. Plĕdġe, *proof, evidence.* 3. In'çĕnse, *something offered in honor of anyone.* Fāith, *belief.* 4. Scŏff'er, *one who laughs at what is good.*

"A MOTHER'S GIFT" FIRST APPEARED IN THE 1843 THIRD READER, but was shifted to the Fourth Reader *in 1857 and all subsequent editions. Some of the editions list the author as anonymous, some—as here—remain silent on the matter, and a few credit the poem to a W. Ferguson. It is in many respects a typical McGuffey lesson—essentially moral, associated with death treated sentimentally, and thoroughly religious at base.*

Fifth Reader

LESSON XLVIII.

THE MISERIES OF IMPRISONMENT.

BESHREW the sombre pencil'! said I vauntingly'—I envy not its powers', which paint the evils of life with so hard and deadly a coloring'. The mind *herself'* sits terrified at the objects' which she herself has magnified and blackened': reduce them to their proper light and hue', she overlooks' them. 'Tis true', said I', correcting the proposition—the Bastile * is an evil' not to be despised'; but strip it of its towers'; fill up the foss'; unbarricade the doors'; call it simply a confinement', and suppose it is some tyrant of a *distemper'*—not a *man'*—which holds' you in it; *half'* the evil vanishes', and you bear the *other'* half, without complaint'.

I was interrupted in the hey-day of this soliloquy', with a voice, which I took to be that of a child', which complained', "it could not get out'." I looked up' and down' the passage, and seeing neither man, woman, nor child', I went out, without farther attention'. In my return back through the passage', I heard the same words repeated twice over'; and, looking up', I saw it was a starling', hung in a little cage': "*I can't get out'!—I can't get out'!*" said the starling'.

I stood looking at the bird'; and to every person who came

---

* A strong castle in Paris, for a long time used as a place of confinement for state prisoners.

through the passage', it ran fluttering to the side towards which
they approached' it, with the same lamentations of its captivity';
"*I can't get out*'," said the starling'. "God help' thee !" said
I', "but I will *let* thee out, cost what it may'." So I turned
about the cage', to get at the door'. It was twisted and double-
twisted so fast with wire', there was no getting it open without
pulling the cage to pieces'. I took both hands' to it. The bird
flew to the place where I was attempting his deliverance', and
thrusting his head through the trellis', pressed his breast against
it as impatient'. "I fear, poor creature'!" said I', "that I cannot
set thee at liberty':" "No'," said the starling', "*I can't get out*',
I can't get out'!" said the starling.

I never had my affections more tenderly awakened'; nor do I
remember an incident in my life', where the dissipated spirits to
which my reason had been a bubble', were so suddenly called
home'. Mechanical as the notes were', yet so true in tune to
nature were, they chanted', that in one moment they overthrew
all my systematic reasonings upon the Bastile'; and I heavily
walked up stairs', unsaying every word I had said going down'
them.

Disguise thyself as thou wilt', yet, still, oppression, thou art a
bitter draught'! and though thousands in all ages have been made
to drink' of thee, thou art no less bitter on *that*' account. 'Tis
thou', Liberty'! thrice sweet and gracious goddess'! whom all in
public or private worship', whose taste is grateful', and ever will'
be so, till nature herself shall change'. No tint of words can
spot thy snowy mantle', or chimic power turn thy scepter into
iron'. With thee, to smile upon him, as he eats his crust', the
swain is happier than his monarch, from whose courts thou art
exiled'. Gracious Heaven'! Grant me but health', thou Great
Bestower' of it, and give me but this fair goddess as my companion', and shower down thy honors', if it seem good unto thy
divine Providence', upon those heads which are aching' for them.

The bird in his cage pursued me into my room'. I sat down
close by my table', and leaning my head upon my hand', I began to figure to myself the the miseries of confinement'. I was
in a right frame' for it, so I gave full scope to my imagination'.
I was going to begin with the millions of my fellow creatures',
born to no inheritance but misery'; but finding, however affecting
the picture was', that I could not bring it near' me, and that the
multitude of sad groups in it, did but distract' me, I took a single captive', and having first shut him up in his dungeon', I then
looked through the twilight of his grated door', to take his picture'.
I beheld his body half wasted away with long expectation and
confinement', and felt what kind of sickness of the heart it is',
which arises from hope deferred'. Upon looking nearer', I saw

*There are a number of alterations made to Sterne's text
in this adaptation, most of them relatively minor changes in
style and punctuation. Some of the modifications, however, are
significant, most specifically the replacement of the word
slavery wherever it appears with such substitutes as oppression
and misery. Regional tensions were ominously present
throughout the 1840's, and clearly a deliberate decision had
been made to avoid phrases such as "the millions of my
fellow creatures, born to no inheritance but slavery."*

Evidently, even with the word slavery *removed, this lesson was still considered too inflammatory. So, in a hastily revised printing of that first edition (still in 1837) it was yanked from the series, the only lesson so treated in that edition. One other selection touching on the subject managed to slip through, however. Entitled "Character of Wilberforce," it praised that man as one of the best members of the British Parliament: "The man whose labors abolished the Slave Trade, at one blow struck away the barbarism of a hundred nations, and elevated myriads of human beings, degraded to the brute, into all the dignified capacities of civilized man." Surprisingly, this selection survived the hasty purge of 1837, lasting until 1844 when the second edition appeared.*

him pale and feverish'; in thirty years', the western breeze had not once fanned his blood'; he had seen no sun', no moon', in all that time'; nor had the voice of friend or kinsman' breathed through his lattice'; his children'—but here my heart began to bleed'—and I was forced to go on with another part of the portrait'.

He was sitting upon the ground upon a little straw', in the farthest corner of his dungeon', which was alternately his chair and bed'. A little calendar of small sticks was laid at the head', notched all over with the dismal days and nights he had passed' there. He had one of these little sticks in his hand, and with a rusty nail' he was etching *another* day of misery to add to the heap'. As I darkened the little light he had', he lifted up a hopeless eye towards the door', cast it down', shook his head', and went on with his work of affliction'. I heard his chains upon his legs', as he turned his body', to lay his little stick upon the bundle'; he gave a deep sigh'; I saw the iron enter into his soul'; I burst into tears'—I could not sustain the picture of confinement' which my fancy had drawn'.—STERNE.

LESSON XLIX.

THE PRISONER FOR DEBT.

Look' on him : through his dungeon-grate',
    Feebly and cold, the morning light
Comes stealing round' him. dim and late',
    As if it loathed the sight'.
Reclining on his strawy bed',
His hand upholds his drooping head';
His bloodless cheek' is scan'd and hard';
Unshorn his gray, neglected beard';
And o'er his bony fingers flow'
His long, dishevel'd locks of snow'.

No grateful fire before him glows',
    And yet the winter's breath is chill :
And o'er his half-clad person goes'
    The frequent ague-thrill'.
Silent', save ever and anon',
A sound, half-murmur and half-groan,
Forces apart the painful grip'
Of the old sufferer's bearded lip'.
O, sad and crushing is the fate'
Of old age chain'd and desolate .

Just GOD'! why lies that old man there'?
    A murderer shares his prison-bed',

pursuits. To fail for want of knowing what education would have taught him, would be great disgrace ; but to fail when conscious of talents exerted, and carefulness ever active, will take away from the man's own mind, and from the opinion of by-standers, all that is disgraceful. He may even gain honor, by the exertions made to prevent, or by the disposition shown during the deep adversity. The lessons of education may be as useful to him in this case as in the other. All that he has learned will help him in some shape, and the labor once endured, will, even in his sorrowing moments, yield him assistance, satisfaction, and perhaps tranquillity, peace, and joy.

If the object of education is then so important, if the effects of it are so strong, so enduring, is it not worth all the labor and privation which it can ever occasion ?—TAYLOR.

LESSON LXXXVIII.

THE AMBITIOUS YOUTH.

THE incident described in this lesson is said to have occurred, some years since, at the Natural Bridge, in Virginia. This bridge is an immense mass of rock, thrown by the hand of nature over a considerable stream of water, thus forming a natural passage over the stream.

THERE are three or four lads standing in the channel below the natural bridge, looking up with awe to that vast arch of unhewn rocks, which the Almighty bridged over these everlasting abutments, ' when the morning stars sang together.' The little piece of sky spanning those measureless piers, is full of stars, although it is mid-day. It is almost five hundred feet from where they stand, up those perpendicular bulwarks of limestone, to the key-rock of that vast arch, which appears to them only the size of a man's hand. The silence of death is rendered more impressive by the little stream that falls from rock to rock down the channel. The sun is darkened, and the boys have unconsciously uncovered their heads, as if standing in the presence-chamber of the Majesty of the whole earth.

At last, this feeling begins to wear away ; they begin to look around them. They see the names of hundreds cut in the limestone abutments. A new feeling comes over their young hearts, and their knives are in their hands, in an instant. ' What man has done, man can do,' is their watchword, as they draw themselves up and carve their names a foot above those of a hundred full grown men who had been there before them. They are all satisfied with this feat of physical exertion except one, whose example illustrates perfectly the forgotten truth, that there is no royal road to intellectual eminence. This ambi-

THIS LESSON CONTAINS ELEMENTS OF ADVENTURE AND SUSPENSE THAT are all too rare in the McGuffey Readers. It also, of course, contains a pointed moral application, as the title signals clearly. The title itself deliberately understates the drama of this lesson—in contrast with the flashier titles used for the same selection by McGuffey's competitors. The National Fourth Reader, for instance, bills the lesson as "Terrific Scene at the Natural Bridge."

The Fifth Reader *(or McGuffey's Rhetorical Guide, as it was originally entitled) was the editorial product of Alexander Hamilton McGuffey, the younger brother of William. Originally intended for use at the high school and even college level, it had a dual purpose that differed from the first four* Readers.

It was to be both a collection of the best literature in the language and *a rhetorical and oratorical guide. That difference in purpose helps in part to account for the unique flavor of the* Fifth Reader, *but there is a different personality behind it, too. Alexander Hamilton McGuffey was much more widely read in English and American literature than his older brother. He also had a keener sense of humor and a deeper appreciation for both the ironic and the truly poetic.*

tious youth sees a name just above his reach, a name that will be green in the memory of the world, when those of Alexander, Cesar, and Bonaparte shall rot in oblivion. It was the name of Washington. Before he marched with Braddock to that fatal field, he had been there and left his name a foot above all his predecessors.

It was a glorious thought of the boy, to write his name, side by side with that of the great father of his country. He grasps his knife with a firmer hand; and, clinging to a little jutting crag, he cuts again into the limestone, about a foot above where he stands; he then reaches up and cuts another place for his hands. It is a dangerous adventure; but as he puts his feet and hands into those notches, and draws himself up carefully to his full length, he finds himself a foot above every name chronicled in that mighty wall. While his companions are regarding him with concern and admiration, he cuts his name in rude capitals, large and deep, into that flinty album. His knife is still in his hand, and strength in his sinews, and a new created aspiration in his heart. Again he cuts another niche, and again he carves his name in large capitals.

This is not enough. Heedless of the entreaties of his companions, he cuts and climbs again. The graduations of his ascending scale grow wider apart. He measures his length at every gain he cuts. The voices of his friends wax weaker and weaker, till their words are finally lost on his ear. He now, for the first time, casts a look beneath him. Had that glance lasted a moment, that moment would have been his last. He clings with a convulsive shudder to his little niche in the rock. An awful abyss awaits his almost certain fall. He is faint with severe exertion, and trembling from the sudden view of the dreadful destruction to which he is exposed. His knife is worn halfway to the haft. He can hear the voices, but not the words, of his terror-stricken companions below. What a moment! What a meager chance to escape destruction! There was no retracing his steps. It is impossible to put his hands into the same niche with his feet, and retain his slender hold a moment.

His companions instantly perceive this new and fearful dilemma, and await his fall with emotions that "freeze their young blood." He is too high, too faint, to ask for his father and mother, his brothers and sisters, to come and witness or avert his destruction. But one of his companions anticipates his desire. Swift as the wind, he bounds down the channel, and the situation of the fated boy is told upon his father's hearth-stone.

Minutes of almost eternal length roll on; and there are hundreds standing in that rocky channel, and hundreds on the bridge above, all holding their breath, and awaiting the fearful catastrophe. The poor boy hears the hum of new and numerous voices both above and below. He can just distinguish the tones of his father, who is shouting with all the energy of despair, "*William! William! don't look down! Your mother, and Henry, and Harriet, are all here praying for you! Don't look down! Keep your eye towards the top!*" The boy didn't look *down.* His eye is fixed like a flint towards Heaven, and his young heart on him who reigns there.

He grasps again his knife. He cuts another niche, and another foot is added to the hundreds that remove him from the reach of human help from below. How carefully he uses his wasting blade! How anxiously he selects the softest places in that vast pier! How he avoids every flinty grain! How he economizes his physical powers, resting a moment at each gain he cuts. How every motion is watched from below. There stand his father, mother, brother, and sister, on the very spot, where, if he falls, he will not fall alone.

The sun is now half way down the west. The lad has made fifty additional niches in that mighty wall, and now finds himself directly under the middle of that vast arch of rocks, earth, and trees. He must cut his way in a new direction, to get from under this overhanging mountain. The inspiration of hope is dying in his bosom; its vital heat is fed by the increased shouts of hundreds perched upon cliffs and trees, and others, who stand with ropes in their hands on the bridge above, or with ladders below. Fifty gains more must be cut, before the longest rope can reach him. His wasting blade strikes again into the limestone. The boy is emerging painfully, foot by foot, from under that lofty arch.

Spliced ropes are ready in the hands of those who are leaning over the outer edge of the bridge. Two minutes more and all will be over. That blade is worn to the last half inch. The boy's head reels; his eyes are starting from their sockets. His last hope is dying in his heart; his life must hang upon the next gain he cuts. That niche is his last. At the last faint gash he makes, his knife, his faithful knife, falls from his nerveless hand, and ringing along the precipice, falls at his mother's feet. An involuntary groan of despair runs like a death-knell through the channel below, and all is still as the grave.

At the height of nearly three hundred feet, the devoted boy lifts his hopeless heart and closing eyes to commend his soul to God. 'Tis but a moment—there!—one foot swings off!—he is reeling—trembling—toppling over into eternity! Hark! a shout falls on his ear from above! The man who is lying with half his length over the bridge, has caught a glimpse of the boy's head and shoulders. Quick as thought, the noosed rope is with-

The author of "The Ambitious Youth" was Elihu Burritt (1811-1879), a New Englander known as the "Learned Blacksmith." Largely self-educated (he taught himself not only most European languages, but many Oriental languages as well), Burritt became one of the leading reformers of his time. Initially his voice was heard through the weekly Christian Citizen, in which he strongly advocated anti-slavery, pacifism, temperance, and self-cultivation. Later, as one of America's first real internationalists, he helped to organize a series of world peace congresses and founded, in 1847, the League of Universal Brotherhood in London.

in reach of the sinking youth. No one breathes. With a faint, convulsive effort, the swooning boy drops his arms into the noose. Darkness comes over him, and with the words, God! and mother! whispered on his lips just loud enough to be heard in heaven, the tightening rope lifts him out of his last shallow niche. Not a lip moves while he is dangling over that fearful abyss: but when a sturdy Virginian reaches down and draws up the lad, and holds him up in his arms before the tearful, breathless multitude, such shouting, such leaping and weeping for joy, never greeted the ear of human being so recovered from the yawning gulf of eternity.—E. BURRITT.

LESSON LXXXIX.

INCENTIVES TO YOUTHFUL DEVOTION.

I EARNESTLY wish that I could induce all young persons to divest religion of every gloomy and repulsive association; to feel that it does not consist,—as some would fain represent it,—in solemn looks and a sanctified demeanor, or in an affected fondness for long sermons or long prayers; but that, properly understood, it is—and especially for the young—a cheerful and lightsome spirit, reposing with affectionate confidence in an Almighty Father, unalloyed with fear, unshaken by distrust.

Would you have within your bosoms, that peace which the world can neither give, nor take away? Would you possess a source of the purest and sweetest pleasures? Would you have that highest of all blessings—a disposition to relish, in their highest perfection, all the innocent and rational enjoyments of life? Then, let me conjure you to cherish a spirit of devotion; a simple-hearted, fervent, and affectionate piety. Accustom yourselves to conceive of God, as a merciful and gracious parent, continually looking down upon you, with the tenderest concern, and inviting you to be good, only that you may become everlastingly happy. Consider yourselves as placed upon earth, for the express purpose of doing the will of God; and remember, if this be your constant object, whatever trials, disappointments, and sorrows, you may be doomed to experience, you will be sustained under them all, by the noblest consolations.

With a view of keeping up a perpetual sense of your dependence upon God, never omit to seek him habitually in prayer, and to connect the thought of him with all that is affecting or impressive, in the events of your lives; with all that is stupendous, and vast, and beautiful, in the productions of his creative power and skill. Whatever excites you; whatever, in the world of nature, or the world of man, strikes you as new and extraordinary;

18

LESSON CCXXVIII.

WESTMINSTER ABBEY.

WHEN I am in a serious humor, I very often walk by myself in Westminster Abbey, where the gloominess of the place, and the use to which it is applied, with the solemnity of the building, and the condition of the people who lie in it, are apt to fill the mind with a kind of melancholy, or rather thoughtfulness, that is not disagreeable. I yesterday passed the whole afternoon in the church-yard, the cloisters, and the church, amusing myself with the tomb-stones and inscriptions that I met with in those several regions of the dead. Most of them recorded nothing else of the buried person, but that he was born upon one day, and died upon another; the whole history of his life being comprehended in those two circumstances, that are common to all mankind. I could not but look upon these registers of existence, whether of brass or marble, as a kind of satire upon the departed persons, who had left no other memorial of them, but that they were born, and that they died.

Upon my going into the church, I entertained myself with the digging of a grave, and saw in every shovelfull of it that was thrown up, the fragment of a bone or skull, intermixed with a kind of fresh, moldering earth, that, sometime or other, had a place in the composition of a human body. Upon this, I began to consider with myself, what innumerable multitudes of people lay confused together under the pavement of that ancient cathedral; how men and women, friends and enemies, priests and soldiers, monks and prebendaries, were crumbled among one another, and blended together in the same common mass; how beauty, strength, and youth, with old age, weakness, and deformity, lay undistinguished in the same promiscuous heap of matter.

After having thus surveyed this magazine of mortality, as it were in the lump, I examined it more particularly, by the accounts which I found on several of the monuments, which are raised in every quarter of that ancient fabric. Some of them were covered with such extravagant epitaphs, that if it were possible for the dead person to be acquainted with them, he would blush at the praises which his friends have bestowed upon him. There are others so excessively modest, that they deliver the character of the person departed, in Greek or Hebrew, and, by that means, are not understood once in a twelvemonth. In the poetical quarter, I found there were poets who had no monuments, and monuments which had no poets. I observed, indeed, that the present war had filled the church with many of those uninhabited monuments, which had been erected to the memory of per-

THE AUTHOR OF THIS FAMOUS PASSAGE WAS JOSEPH ADDISON (1672-1719), *who joined with Sir Richard Steele to entertain England in the early eighteenth century with periodical essays in* The Tatler *(1709–1711), and the* Spectator *(1711–1712). Addison was, during his lifetime, highly praised for his tragedy* Cato *(1713), but his fame today rests primarily on his earlier essays—particularly those in the* Spectator, *of which this is one.*

Dr. Samuel Johnson wrote in his Lives of the Poets, *"He who would form a good style should give his days and his nights to the study of Addison." American textbook compilers in the nineteenth century evidently agreed wholeheartedly; Addison's work appears with great regularity throughout the century. This particular passage was selected by William for the first edition of the* Fourth Reader, *then appropriated by Alexander for the first edition of the* Fifth, *where it remained in use until 1879.*

sons, whose bodies were, perhaps, buried in the plains of Blenheim, or in the bosom of the ocean.

I know, that entertainments of this nature are apt to raise dark and dismal thoughts in timorous minds and gloomy imaginations; but, for my own part, though I am always serious, I do not know what it is to be melancholy; and can, therefore, take a view of nature in her deep and solemn scenes, with the same pleasure, as in her most gay and delightful ones. By this means, I can improve myself with those objects, which others consider with terror. When I look upon the tombs of the great, every emotion of envy dies in me; when I read the epitaphs of the beautiful, every inordinate desire goes out; when I meet with the grief of parents upon a tombstone, my heart melts with compassion; when I see the tomb of the parents themselves, I consider the vanity of grieving for them, whom we must quickly follow; when I see kings lying by those who deposed them, when I see rival wits lying side by side, or holy men that divided the world by their contests and disputes, I reflect, with sorrow and astonishment, on the little competitions, factions, and debates of mankind. When I read the several dates of the tombs, of some that died yesterday, some, six hundred years ago, I consider that great day when we shall all of us be contemporaries, and make our appearance together.—ADDISON.

LESSON CCXXIX.

THE THREE WARNINGS.

THE tree of deepest root is found
Least willing still to quit the ground;
'T was therefore said, by ancient sages,
  That love of life increased with years,
So much, that in our latter stages,
When pains grow sharp and sickness rages,
  The greatest love of life appears.
This great affection to believe,
Which all confess, but few perceive,
If old assertions can't prevail,
Be pleased to hear a modern tale.

When sports went round, and all were gay,
On neighbor Dobson's wedding-day;
Death called aside the jocund groom
With him into another room;
And looking grave, "You must" says he,
"Quit your sweet bride, and come with me."

Addison's admission that he rather enjoyed melancholy thoughts—indeed that he cultivated them by going to places like Westminster Abbey—is rather unusual to hear from a refined speaker in the age of Queen Anne. He does provide a rationale for cultivating such thoughts, but in many respects he anticipates not only the "graveyard school" of poets and Gothic novelists of the mid- and late eighteenth century, but also the Romantic poets of the early nineteenth century.

LESSON XV.

THE HOUR OF PRAYER.

1. Child', amid the flowers at play',
   While the red light fades away';
   Mother', with thine earnest eye',
   Ever following silently';
   Father', by the breeze at eve'
   Call'd thy harvest-work to leave';
   Pray'! Ere yet the dark hours be',
   Lift the heart, and bend the knee'.

2. Traveler', in the stranger's land',
   Far from thine own household band';
   Mourner', haunted by the tone
   Of a voice from this world gone';
   Captive', in whose narrow cell
   Sunshine hath not leave to dwell';
   Sailor', on the darkening sea';
   Lift the heart, and bend the knee'.

3. Warrior', that from battle won',
   Breathest now at set of sun';
   Woman', o'er the lowly slain',
   Weeping on his burial plain';
   Ye that triumph', ye that sigh',
   Kindred by one holy tie';
   Heaven's first star alike ye see',
   Lift the heart', and bend the knee'.

MRS. HEMANS.

LESSON XVI.

PROSPECTS OF THE CHEROKEES.

In this lesson, the inflections belonging to interrogative sentences may be noticed.

1. WHITHER are the Cherokees to go'? What are the benefits' of the change? What system has been matured for their security'? What laws for their government'? These questions are answered' only by gilded promises in general terms'; they are to become enlightened and civilized husbandmen'. They now live by the cultivation of the soil' and the mechanical arts'. It is proposed to send them from their cotton fields', their farms and their gardens', to a distant and unsubdued wilderness'; to make them tillers of the earth'; to remove them from their looms', their work-shops', their printing-press', their schools and churches', near the white settlements', to frowning forests', surrounded with naked savages', that they may become enlightened' and civilized'!

2. We have pledged to them our protection'; and, instead of

THIS IS ANOTHER VERSE FROM THE PEN OF MRS. FELICIA DOROTHEA Hemans, author of "Casabianca" (see pages 165–66). It experienced a curious history in the McGuffeys: initially used in the first edition of the Fifth Reader in 1844, it was then made part of the first edition of the Sixth Reader in 1857, and finally demoted back to the Fifth in the 1879 and 1920 editions.

THIS SPEECH WAS PROBABLY WRITTEN IN THE 1830'S AFTER THE CHEROkees had unsuccessfully appealed to the United States Supreme Court for an injunction to restrain the State of Georgia from interfering with the Cherokees or imposing their laws on the tribe. The background involved a United States treaty with the Cherokees in 1791 guaranteeing them the remainder of their property, but it also involved a federal promise to the State of Georgia in 1802 that all Indians were to be removed from the state limits as soon as it could be done peacefully and reasonably. When Georgians started to move into the disputed territory in the late 1820's, the Cherokees appealed to President Jackson without results, turning finally to the Supreme Court. But Georgia refused to defend the suit and the majority opinion of the Court was that the Cherokees were neither citizens of the United States nor a foreign nation and thus could not be recognized before the Supreme Court.

This particular passage may have been selected by Alexander because its oratorical nature suited well the intent of the Fifth Reader *in which it first appeared (1844). But the inhumane treatment of the Indians was clearly a concern of both McGuffey brothers, and there is less hyperbole in this passage than might appear. The Age of Jackson accounted for a staggering number of Indian graves.*

shielding them where they now are, within our reach, under our own arm', we send these natives of a southern clime' to northern' regions, among fierce and warlike barbarians'. And what security do we propose' to them ? A new guaranty'! Who can look an Indian in the face', and say' to him, We and our fathers, for more than forty years', have made to you the most solemn promises'; we now violate and trample upon them all'; but offer you in their stead'—another' guaranty !

3. Will they be in no danger of attack from the primitive inhabitants of the regions to which they emigrate' ? How can it be otherwise' ? The official documents show us the fact', that some of the few who have already gone', were involved in conflict with the native tribes, and compelled to a second' removal.

4. How are they to subsist' ? Has not that country now as great an Indian population as it can sustain' ? What has become of the original' occupants? Have we not already caused accession to their numbers', and been compressing them more and more' ? Is not the consequence inevitable', that some must be stinted in the means of subsistence' ? Here too we have the light of experience'. By an official communication from Governor Clark, the superintendent of Indian affairs', we learn that the most powerful tribes, west of the Mississippi', are, every year, so distressed by famine, that many die for want of food'. The scenes of their suffering' are hardly exceeded by the sieges of Jerusalem and Samaria'. There', might be seen the miserable mother, in all the tortures which hunger could inflict, giving her last morsel for the sustenance of her child', and then fainting', sinking', and actually dying' of starvation ! And the orphan' ! no one can spare *it*' food': it is put alive' into the grave of the parent, which thus closes over the quick' and the dead'. And this is not a solitary' instance only', " The living child' is often' buried with the dead mother."

5. I know, sir', to what I expose' myself. To feel any solicitude for the fate of the Indians', may be ridiculed as false philanthropy' and morbid sensibility'. Others may boldly say', "Their blood be upon us';" and sneer at scruples', as weakness unbecoming the stern character of a politician'. If, sir, in order to become a politician', it be necessary to divest the mind of the principles of good faith and moral obligation', and harden the heart against every touch of humanity', I confess that I am not—and by the blessing of heaven', will never' be—a politician.

6. Sir', we cannot wholly silence the monitor within'. It may not be heard amid the clashing of the arena , in the tempest and convulsions of political contentions'; but its still small voice will speak' to us, when we meditate alone at even-tide'; in the silent

watches of the night'; when we lie down' and when we rise up from a solitary pillow ; and in that dread hour', when,—"not what we have done for *ourselves'*, but what we have done for *others*'," will be our joy and strength'; when, to have secured, even to a poor and despised *Indian*', a spot of earth upon which to rest his aching head'; to have given him but a cup of cold *water*' in charity', will be a greater treasure, than to have been the conquerors of kingdoms', and lived in luxury upon the spoils'.

SPRAGUE.

REMARK. It will be observed that the words "Indian" and "water" in the last paragraph, receive the falling inflection as a mark of emphasis, since there is no other reason why they should not have the rising inflection. There is also, in the same paragraph, an example of the inflections belonging to a series of members, and also to antithesis, which subjects will be more particularly noticed hereafter.

EXERCISES ON INFLECTION—CONTINUED.

THE *rising inflection* is generally used,
1. Where the sense is incomplete. Rule IV.
2. At the last pause but one in a sentence. Rule VI.
3. After the nominative addressed. Rule IV.
4. In negative sentences. Rule V.
5. In interrogative sentences which *can* be answered by "yes" or "*no.*" Rule VII.
6. After an exclamation, when used interrogatively, or as an echo of the thought. Rule VIII.
7. At one of the members of an antithesis. Rule IX.
8. At the first member of a sentence, the parts of which are united by a disjunctive conjunction. Rule X.
9. At the last member of a commencing series. Rule XI.
10. At the last member but one of a concluding series. Rule XI.
11. At the close of a parenthesis, when it is preceded by the rising inflection. Rule XII.

The *falling inflection* is generally used,
1. Where the sense is complete. Rule I.
2. In emphatic expressions, such as imperative mood, passionate exclamations, emphatic repetition, &c. Rule II.
3. In interrogative sentences, which *cannot* be answered by "yes" or "*no.*" Rule III.
4. At one of the members of an antithesis (generally the last.) Rule IX.
5. At the last member of a sentence, the parts of which are united disjunctively. Rule X.
6. At all the members of a commencing series, except the last. Rule XI.
7. At all the members of a concluding series, except the last but one. Rule XI.

Charles Sprague (1791–1875) was a Boston businessman, banker, orator, and poet. Although he wrote relatively little of either verse or prose, he held a sound reputation as a writer and speaker during his lifetime. His most famous poem is entitled "Curiosity," which he delivered in 1829 to the Phi Beta Kappa society in Cambridge, Massachusetts. His collected **Prose and Poetical Writings** *was published in 1850.*

All of the early editions of the **Fifth Reader** *included special instructions and exercises in articulation and inflections, often occupying as many as sixty pages before the first lesson appeared. The 1857 edition carried the following announcement and chart of symbols: "The INFLECTIONS marked are in accordance with the best authorities, both American and English, among whom may be mentioned SHERIDAN KNOWLES as a leading and standard author on this subject."*

The subjoined characters are used in the following pages:

THE RISING INFLECTION IS DENOTED BY	(´)
THE FALLING INFLECTION ″ ″	(`)
THE RISING CIRCUMFLEX ″ ″	(˘)
THE FALLING CIRCUMFLEX ″ ″	(˄)
THE MONOTONE, BY A LINE PLACED OVER THE VOWEL . .	(−)
EMPHATIC WORDS ARE DENOTED BY ITALICS OR CAPITALS.	
THE EMPHATIC PAUSE, BY A LINE BEFORE OR AFTER THE WORD	(—)
THE CESURA IS DENOTED BY	(‖)
THE DEMI-CESURA ″ ″	(│)
A HIGH TONE ″ ″	(h)
A HIGHER TONE ″ ″	(hh)
A LOW TONE ″ ″	(l)
A LOWER TONE ″ ″	(ll)

lay it by for a thief'. The *prudent men'* are the men that live beyond their means'. Happen what may', *they* are safe'. *They'* have taken time by the forelock'. *They'* have anticipated fortune'. "The wealthy fool', with gold in store'," has only denied himself so much enjoyment', which another will seize at his expense'. Look at these people in a *panic'*. See who are the fools *then'*. You know them by their long faces'. You may say, as one of them goes by', in an agony of apprehension', "There is a stupid fellow' who fancied himself rich, because he had fifty thousand dollars in bank'." The history of the last ten years has taught the moral, "spend, and regale'." Whatever is laid up beyond the *present hour'*, is put in jeopardy'. There is no certainty but in instant enjoyment'. Look at school-boys sharing a plum-cake'. The knowing ones' eat, as for a race'; but a *stupid'* fellow *saves his* portion; just nibbles a bit', and "keeps the rest for another time'." Most provident blockhead'! The others', when they have gobbled up *their'* shares, set upon *him'*, plunder' him, and thresh him for crying out'.

7. Before the terms "depreciation'," "suspension'," and "going into liquidation'," were heard, there might have been some reason in the practice of "laying up';" but *now'* it denotes the darkest blindness'. The *prudent men* of the present time', are the men in debt'. The tendency being to sacrifice creditors to debtors', and the debtor party acquiring daily new strength', every one is in haste to get into the favored class'. In any case, the *debtor'* is safe'. He has put his enjoyments *behind'* him; they are safe'; no turns of fortune can disturb' them. The substance he has eaten up, is irrecoverable'. The future' cannot trouble his past'. He has nothing to apprehend'. He has anticipated' more than fortune would ever have granted' him. He has *tricked'* fortune; and his creditors'—bah'! who feels for creditors'? What *are'* creditors? Landlords'; a pitiless and unpitiable tribe'; all griping extortioners'! What would become of the world of debtors', if it did not steal a march upon this rapacious class'?

ANON.

LESSON XLVIII.

THE BROKEN HEART.

[This sketch, from the pen of a favorite American author, is inserted here as a better specimen of truly pathetic eloquence, than the lesson in former editions for which it is substituted. Where the books of the pupils disagree, it can be omitted.]

1. EVERY one must recollect the tragical story of young Emmet', the Irish patriot'; it was too touching to be soon for-

"THE BROKEN HEART" WAS THE LESSON CHOSEN TO REPLACE STERNE'S "Miseries of Imprisonment" and its uncomfortable suggestions about slavery. The "favorite American author" here is Washington Irving, and his "truly pathetic eloquence" is safely distanced from the issue of slavery—or nearly any other issue of substance.

gotten'. His fate made a deep impression on public sympathy'. During the troubles in Ireland' he was tried, condemned, and executed, on a charge of treason'. He was so young', so intelligent', so generous', so brave', so every' thing that we are apt to like in a young man'. His conduct under trial, too, was so lofty' and intrepid'. The noble indignation with which he repelled the charge of treason against his country', the eloquent vindication of his name', and his pathetic appeal to posterity', in the hopeless hour of condemnation', all these entered deeply into every generous bosom', and even his enemies' lamented the stern policy' that dictated his execution'.

2. But there was *one'* heart', whose anguish it would be impossible to describe. In happier days and fairer fortunes', he had won the affections of a beautiful and interesting girl', the daughter of a late celebrated Irish barrister'. She loved him with the disinterested fervor of a woman's first and early love'. When every worldly maxim arrayed itself against him'; when blasted in fortune', and disgrace and danger darkened around his name', she loved him the more ardently for his very sufferings. If, then, his fate could awaken the sympathy even of his foes', what must have been the agony of her' whose whole soul was occupied by his image! Let *those* tell who have had the portals of the tomb suddenly closed between them and the being they most loved on earth', who have sat at its threshold, as one shut out in a cold and lonely world', whence all that was most lovely and loving had departed'.

3. But then the horrors of such' a grave! so frightful', so dishonored'! there was nothing for memory to dwell on that could soothe the pangs of separation', none of those tender though· melancholy circumstances, which endear the parting scene', nothing to melt sorrow into those blessed tears', sent like the dews of heaven to revive the heart in the parting hour of anguish'.

4. To render her widowed situation more desolate', she had incurred her father's displeasure by her unfortunate attachment', and was an exile from the paternal roof'. But could the sympathy and kind offices of friends have reached a spirit so shocked and driven in by horror', she would have experienced no want of consolation', for the Irish are a people of quick and generous sensibilities'. The most delicate and cherishing attentions were paid her by families of wealth and distinction'. She was led into society, and they tried by all kinds of occupation and amusement to dissipate her grief', and wean her from the tragical story of her love.

5. But it was all in vain'. There are some strokes of calamity which scathe and scorch the soul', which penetrate to the vital

Love as anything but a praiseworthy abstract term is seldom seen in the McGuffeys, and physical love is totally taboo. Only in narratives dealing with romantic love were careful exceptions made, since in most of these cases—as here— death intervened to heighten the pathos (often bathos) and to terminate any suggestions of a physical relationship.

seat of happiness', and blast it, never again to put forth bud or blossom'. She never objected to frequent the haunts of pleasure', but was as much alone there as in the depths of solitude'; walking about in a sad reverie', apparently unconscious of the world around her'. She carried with her an inward woe that mocked at all the blandishments of friendship', and "heeded not the song of the charmer', charm he never so wisely'."

6. The person who told me her story had seen her at a masquerade'. There can be no exhibition of far-gone wretchedness more striking and painful' than to meet it in such' a scene. To find it wandering like a specter lone and joyless', where all around is gay', to see it dressed out in the trappings of mirth, and looking so wan and woe-begone', as if it had tried in vain to cheat the poor heart into a momentary forgetfulness of sorrow'. After strolling through the splendid rooms and giddy crowd with an air of utter abstraction', she sat herself down on the steps of an orchestra', and, looking about for some time with a vacant air, that showed her insensibility to the garish scene', she began with the capriciousness of a sickly heart, to warble a little plaintive air'. She had an exquisite voice; but on this occasion it was so simple', so touching', it breathed forth such a soul of wretchedness', that she drew a crowd mute and silent around her', and melted every one into tears'.

7. The story of one so true and tender', could not but excite great interest in a country remarkable for enthusiasm'. It completely won the heart of a brave officer', who paid his addresses to her', and thought that one so true to the dead could not but prove affectionate to the living. She declined his attentions', for her thoughts were irrevocably engrossed by the memory of her former lover'. He, however, persisted in his suit'. He solicited not her tenderness', but her esteem'. He was assisted by her conviction of his worth', and her sense of her own destitute and dependent situation', for she was existing on the kindness of friends. In a word, he at length succeeded in gaining her hand', though with the solemn assurance that her heart was unalterably another's'.

8. He took her with him to Sicily', hoping that a change of scene' might wear out the remembrance of her early woes'. She was an amiable and exemplary wife', and made an effort to be a happy' one; but nothing could cure the silent and devouring melancholy that had entered into her very soul'. She wasted away in a slow but hopeless decline', and, at length, sunk into the grave,' the victim of a broken heart'.

W. Irving.

It is quite possible that the decision to replace the passage from Sterne with this sentimental gushing was made by the publishers of the McGuffeys, *not by Alexander Hamilton McGuffey. His literary taste was nearly always better than this, but the publishers were fairly well attuned to what the public wanted (more sentiment) and what they didn't want (discussion of slavery).*

LESSON XCV.

THE WELL OF ST. KEYNE.

St. Keyne was a Welch princess, who lived and died near the well which was named after her. It was popularly believed, that she laid upon this well the spell described in this ballad.

1. A WELL there is in the West Country,
    And a clearer one never was seen;
    There is not a wife in the West Country,
    But has heard of the well of St. Keyne.

2. An oak and an elm tree stand beside,
    And behind does an ash tree grow,
    And a willow from the bank above,
    Droops to the water below.

3. A traveler came to the well of St. Keyne;
    Joyfully he drew nigh,
    For from cock-crow he had been traveling,
    And there was not a cloud in the sky.

4. He drank of the water, so cool and clear,
    For thirsty and hot was he;
    And he sat down upon the bank,
    Under the willow tree.

5. There came a man from the neighboring town,
    At the well to fill his pail;
    On the well-side he rested it,
    And he bade the stranger hail.

6. "Now art thou a bachelor, stranger?" quoth he;
    "For an * thou hast a wife,
    The happiest draught thou hast drunk this day,
    That ever thou didst in thy life.

7. "Or has thy good woman, if one thou hast,
    Ever here, in Cornwall been?
    For an * she have, I'll venture my life,
    She has drunk of the well of St. Keyne."

8. "I have left a good woman, who never was here,
    The stranger he made reply;
    "But that my draught should be better for that,
    I pray you, answer me why."

9. "St. Keyne," quoth the Cornish-man, "many a time
    Drank of this crystal well,
    And before the angel summoned her,
    She laid on the water a spell.

10. "If the husband, of this gifted well
    Shall drink before his wife,
    A happy man thenceforth is he,
    For he shall be master for life.

---

* *An* is here an obsolete word signifying *if.*

BOTH THIS LESSON AND THE GOLDSMITH POEM THAT FOLLOWS ARE good indications that the selections for the Fifth Reader *were made by Alexander, rather than by William McGuffey. To begin with, William might well have disapproved of this poem because of its references to a saint and to magical (or blessed) "spells." (He always considered poetry a "minor avocation" anyway, according to family records.) But the basic quality these poems share is their comic view of life—a quality that Alexander evidently appreciated more than William was ever able to do.*

Robert Southey (1774–1843) was England's Poet Laureate from 1813 to 1843. A man of considerable energy, he published an immense amount of both prose and verse, including a number of long poems (much admired at the time); some long histories and ecclesiastical books; and biographies of such diverse figures as Wesley, Cowper, and Admiral Nelson. His longer poems and prose are now largely forgotten, but such shorter poems as "The Inchcape Rock" and "The Battle of Blenheim" (see pages 274–76) are still anthologized. Poems like "The Well of St. Keyne" and "The Devil's Thoughts" suggest that perhaps his greatest skill lay in a lighter style.

11. " But if the wife should drink of it first,
      God help the husband, then !"
    The stranger stooped to the well of St. Keyne,
      And drank of the water again.

12. " *You* drank of the well, I warrant, betimes !"
      He to the Cornish-man said :
    But the Cornish-man smiled, as the stranger spake,
      And sheepishly shook his head.

13. " I hastened, as soon as the wedding was done,
      And left my wife in the porch ;
    But, i' faith ! she had been wiser than I,
      For *she* took a bottle to church."
                                    SOUTHEY.

LESSON XCVI.

ELEGY ON MADAM BLAIZE.

1. GOOD people all, with one accord,
     Lament for Madam Blaize ;
   Who never wanted a good word—
     From those who spoke her praise.

2. The needy seldom passed her door,
     And always found her kind ;
   She freely lent to all the poor—
     Who left a pledge behind.

3. She strove the neighborhood to please,
     With manner wondrous winning ;
   She never followed wicked ways—
     Unless when she was sinning.

4. At church, in silks and satins new,
     With hoop of monstrous size,
   She never slumbered in her pew—
     But when she shut her eyes.

5. Her love was sought, I do aver,
     By twenty beaux, or more ;
   The king himself has followed her—
     When she has walked before.

6. But now, her wealth and finery fled,
     Her hangers-on cut short all,
   Her doctors found, when she was dead—
     Her last disorder mortal.

7. Let us lament, in sorrow sore ;
     For Kent-street well may say,
   That, had she lived a twelvemonth more—
     She had not died to-day.
                                    GOLDSMITH.

OLIVER GOLDSMITH (1730?–1774) WAS A FRIEND OF DR. JOHNSON AND one of the original members of "The Club." His description in Boswell's Life of Johnson *is generally unflattering, representing him as vain, ridiculous, and petty—although a simple, good-natured man. That rendering has been too influential in shaping Goldsmith's reputation today and needs to be reassessed. Perhaps what should be remembered first is that Goldsmith's many writings include the most popular play of his day (*She Stoops to Conquer, *1773), one of the era's most popular poems (*The Deserted Village, *1770), and one of the most popular novels of the century (*The Vicar of Wakefield, 1766). And, in addition to their popularity, they are all works of substantial literary merit—no mean accomplishment for a poor Irish boy.*

LESSON XLI.

1. ARCH'-I-TECTS; *n.* (pro. *ark'-e-tects*), builders, makers.
1. DES'-TI-NIES; *n.* ultimate fate, appointed condition.
2. ME-DI-OC'-RI-TY; *n.* a middle state, or degree of talents.
2. ME'-DI-O-CRE; *n.* (pro. *me'-di-o-ker*), a man of moderate talents.
4. FI'-AT; *n.* decree.

5. CON'-DOR; *n.* a large bird.
5. EM-PYR'-E-AL; *adj.* relating to the highest and purest region of the heavens.
6. CA-REER'-ING; *adj.* moving rapidly.
6. PROW'-ESS; *n.* bravery, boldness.
6. A-CHIEVE'-MENTS; *n.* something accomplished by exertion.

NO EXCELLENCE WITHOUT LABOR.

UTTER each sound distinctly. Do not say *ch'rac-ter* for char-ac-ter; *dif'-rent* for dif-fer-ent; *op'-site* for op-po-site; *em'-nunce* for em-i-nence; *in-vig'-ra-ted* for in-vig-o-rated; *vig'-rous* for vig-or-ous.

1. THE †education, moral and †intellectual, of every individual, must be, chiefly, his own work. Rely upon it, that the ancients were right; both in morals and intellect, we give the final shape to our characters, and thus become, †emphatically, the architects of our own fortune. How else could it happen, that young men, who have had †precisely the same opportunities, should be continually presenting us with such different results, and rushing to such opposite destinies?

2. Difference of talent will not solve it, because that difference is very often in favor of the disappointed candidate. You will see issuing from the walls of the same college, nay, sometimes from the bosom of the same family, two young men, of whom one will be admitted to be a genius of high order, the other scarcely above the point of mediocrity; yet you will see the genius sinking and perishing in poverty, †obscurity, and wretchedness; while, on the other hand, you will observe the mediocre plodding his slow but sure way up the hill of life, gaining steadfast footing at every step,

THE AUTHOR OF THIS LESSON WAS WILLIAM WIRT (1722–1834), A MARY-land-born lawyer who served as United States Attorney General from 1817 to 1829. A devout Presbyterian and president of the Maryland Bible Society, Wirt also did some serious writing. Of this the most interesting is his Life of Patrick Henry (1817), *which served its subject (to a lesser degree) as Parson Weems had served Washington: Wirt recreated many of Henry's speeches from partial notes and oral tradition. In 1832 Wirt was the presidential candidate of the Anti-Masonic party, but he carried only the state of Vermont.*

"There is no excellence without great labor"—a point stressed in many of the McGuffey lessons, but stated here so forcefully that this short piece became a standard entry in declamation contests for the rest of the century. One of W. H. McGuffey's first selections, it has appeared in every edition of the Readers—in the Fourth Reader from 1837 to 1857, thereafter in the Fifth.

and mounting, at length, to †eminence and distinction, an ornament to his family, a blessing to his country.

3. Now, whose work is this? †Manifestly their own. They are the architects of their respective fortunes. The best seminary of learning that can open its portals to you, can do no more than to afford you the †opportunity of instruction: but it must depend, at last, on yourselves, whether you will be instructed or not, or to what point you will push your †instruction.

4. And of this be assured, I speak from †observation a certain truth: THERE IS NO EXCELLENCE WITHOUT GREAT LABOR. It is the fiat of fate, from which no power of genius can absolve you.

5. Genius, unexerted, is like the poor moth that flutters around a candle, till it scorches itself to death. If genius be desirable at all´, it is only of that great and †magnanimous kind, which, like the condor of South America, pitches from the summit of †Chimborazo, above the clouds, and sustains itself at pleasure, in that empyreal region, with an energy rather †invigorated than weakened by the effort .

6. It is this capacity for high and long-continued exertion`, this †vigorous power of profound and searching †investigation`, this careering and wide-spreading †comprehension of mind`, and these long †reaches of thought, that

> "Pluck bright honor from the pale-faced moon,
> Or dive into the bottom of the deep,
> And drag up drowned honor by the locks´;"

this is the prowess`, and these the hardy achievements, which are to enroll your names among the great men of the earth.

QUESTIONS.—Whose work is the education of every man? What did the ancients say upon this point? By what reasoning does the writer prove this to be the case? What, then, is required to secure excellence?

Explain the inflections marked in this lesson.

226

LESSON XLII.

1. IN-EX'-O-RA-BLE; *adj.* that can not be made to bend.
1. DES'-POT-ISM; *n.* absolute, uncontrolled power.
1. PER-PE-TU'-I-TY; *n.* continued, uninterrupted existence.
3. A-LOOF'; *adv.* at a distance.
3. VOR'-TEX; *n.* a whirling motion of water, a whirlpool.
4. SUF'-FRAGE; *n.* vote given in choosing men for office.
5. FORE-BO'-DING; *n.* a foretelling.
5. FOUND'-ER-ING; *n.* being filled with water and sinking.

6. HAR'-BIN-GER; *n.* that which precedes and gives notice beforehand of any thing.
7. RE-VERSE'; *v.* to turn to the contrary.
7. A-NAL'-O-GY; *n.* resemblance between things.
8. IM'-MI-NENCE; *n.* a hanging over.
10. SPASMS; *n.* } violent
10. CON-VUL'-SIONS; *n.* } and irregular contraction of the muscles of the body.
10. EX-TORT'; *v.* to wring or force out of.

NECESSITY OF EDUCATION.

PRONOUNCE correctly. Do not say *ed-dy-cate* nor *ej-ju-cate* for ed-*u*-cate; *spiles* for spoils; *vic-ter-y* for vic-to-ry; *pop-py-la-tion* for pop-*u*-la-tion; *man-y-fac-ters* for man-*u*-fact-ures; *ag-ri-cul-ter* nor *ag-ri-cul-tshure* for ag-ri-cult-*ure*; *prov-i-dunce* for prov-i-dence; *ub-an-don* for *a*-ban-don; *prov-er-ca-tion* for prov-o-ca-tion; *spas-ums* for spa*sms*.

1. WE must ⁺educate ! We must educate ! or we must perish by our own prosperity . If we do not ´, short will be our race from the cradle to the grave. If, in our haste to be rich and mighty ´, we outrun our literary and religious institutions, they will never overtake us, or only come up after the battle of liberty is fought and lost, as spoils to ⁺grace the victory, and as ⁺resources of inexorable despotism for the perpetuity of our bondage.

2. But what will become of the West, if her prosperity rushes up to such a majesty of power, while those great ⁺institutions linger which are necessary to form the mind, and the ⁺conscience, and the heart of the vast

AMONG THE MORE IMPORTANT ELEMENTS OF THE EARLY READERS were the exercises in pronunciation, particularly the brief sections on how NOT to pronounce words. Some of these raise smiles today, of course, but they played a vital role in standardizing American pronunciation. One can only conjecture on this point, but it seems quite likely that without such exercises there would be much more variance in American regional pronunciations today. One should also remember that the McGuffey Readers for years were the major texts for the teaching of English as a foreign language to the "huddled masses" of immigrants who entered the United States in the nineteenth century. In many respects the McGuffeys helped to provide the common base for standard pronunciation then, that national radio and television provide today.

This lesson was the product of Lyman Beecher (1795–1863), the famous American clergyman who moved to the Cincinnati area in 1832 to become president of the new Lane Theological Seminary. He and several of his children soon became active members of the intellectual circle which included the McGuffey brothers. It was, in fact, his daughter Catherine (then conducting a seminary for girls near Cincinnati), who turned down a publisher's request to compile a series of Western readers, but suggested that the publishers ask William Holmes McGuffey.

Lyman Beecher was one of the most popular and influential clergymen of his time. He was in the front ranks of nearly all the reform movements of the era, including the anti-dueling, temperance, and anti-slavery campaigns. Not the least of his accomplishments, however, was his raising of a large family. Beecher (who was married three times) was the father of 13 children, most famous of whom were Henry Ward Beecher and Harriet Beecher Stowe. Nearly all of his children, however, were leaders in various nineteenth-century reform movements, and together they achieved enough prominence that a disgruntled opponent once opined that the human race consisted of "men, women, and Beechers."

world? It must not be permitted. And yet what is done must be done quickly, for population will not wait´, and †commerce will not cast anchor´, and manufactures will not shut off the steam´, nor shut down the gate, and agriculture, pushed by millions of freemen on their fertile soil, will not withhold her corrupting abundance`.

3. And let no man at the East quiet himself, and dream of liberty, whatever may become of the West. Our †alliance of blood, and " political institutions, and common interests, is such, that we can not stand aloof in the hour of her calamity, should it ever come. *Her´* destiny is *our`* destiny; and the day that her gallant ship goes down, our little boat sinks in the vortex!

4. The great experiment is now making, and from its extent and rapid filling up. is making in the West, whether the perpetuity of our republican institutions can be †reconciled with universal suffrage. Without the education of the *head`* and *heart`* of the nation, they can not be; and the question to be decided is, can the nation, or the vast balance power of it, be so imbued with intelligence and virtue as to bring out, in laws and their administration, a perpetual self-preserving energy. We know that the work is a vast one, and of great difficulty; and yet we believe it can be done.

5. I am aware that our ablest patriots are looking out on the deep, vexed with storms, with great forebodings and failings of heart, for fear of the things that are coming upon us; and I perceive a spirit of †impatience rising, and distrust in respect to the perpetuity of our republic; and I am sure that these fears are well founded, and am glad that they exist. It is the star of hope in our dark †horizon. Fear is what we need, as the ship needs wind on a rocking sea, after a storm, to prevent foundering. But when our fear and our efforts shall †correspond with our danger, the danger is past.

6. For it is not the impossibility of self-preservation which threatens´ us; nor is it the unwillingness of the nation to pay the price of the *preservation´*, as she has

paid the price of the *purchase* of our liberties. It is *inattention* and *inconsideration*, protracted till the crisis is past, and the things which belong to our peace are hid from our eyes. And blessed be God, that the tokens of a national waking up, the harbinger of God's mercy, are multiplying upon us!

7. We did not, in the darkest hour, believe that God had brought our fathers to this goodly land to lay the foundation of religious liberty, and wrought such wonders in their preservation, and raised their descendants to such hights of civil and religious liberty, only to reverse the analogy of his †providence, and abandon his work.

8. And though there now be clouds, and the sea roaring, and men's hearts failing, we believe there is light behind the cloud, and that the imminence of our danger is intended, under the guidance of Heaven, to call forth and apply a holy, †fraternal fellowship between the East and the West, which shall secure our preservation, and make the †prosperity of our nation durable as time, and as abundant as the waves of the sea.

9. I would add, as a motive to immediate action, that, if we do fail in our great †experiment of self-government, our destruction will be as signal as the birthright abandoned, the mercies abused, and the †provocation offered to beneficent Heaven. The descent of desolation will correspond with the past elevation.

10. No punishments of Heaven are so severe as those for mercies abused`; and no instrumentality employed in their infliction is so dreadful as the wrath of man`. No spasms are like the spasms of expiring liberty, and no †wailing such as her convulsions extort.

11. It took Rome three hundred years to die`; and our death, if we perish, will be as much more terrific, as our intelligence and free institutions have given us more bone, sinew, and vitality. May God hide from me the day when the dying agonies of my country shall begin`! Oh thou beloved land´, bound together by the ties of

This is merely one of a number of lessons in the early McGuffeys stressing the importance of education. Another is Samuel Lewis' 1836 speech to the Ohio Assembly, "A Plan for Common Schools," which appears only in the 1837 edition of the Fourth Reader (and, because of its length, is not included in this collection). Like Beecher, Lewis argues with historical analogies, suggesting that the anarchy that overtook the French Revolution was due to the failure to educate the masses, thus forcing the educated few to turn to Napoleon— "the most galling tyranny"—to save themselves from the "ignorant mob." But Lewis also reminds the legislators of the many promises of free education used by Ohio promoters to lure immigrants from the East, and he warns them: "These children about your streets, some of whom cannot even speak your language, are your future sovereigns. Is it not important that they should be well educated?"

This was one of the early selections promoting the West, chosen by W. H. McGuffey in 1837 for the Fourth Reader. *Its import goes beyond mere regionalism, however, and it has remained in the series in every edition—moving up to the* Fifth Reader *in 1857 and then to the* Sixth *in 1879. The regional tensions and talk about the disruption of the Union were threats even in the 1830's—as this lesson reflects quite clearly—but the ultimate solution, it is argued here, is more social than political.*

brotherhood´, and common interest´, and perils´! live forever—one and undivided`!

QUESTIONS.—Why is education so necessary in this country? Can the nation continue free, without the influence of education and religion? Why should we regard the prospects of this nation with fear? What can be the advantage of a spirit of fear? Why may we trust that God will not abandon our nation to ruin? What will insure her destruction? What is said of the greatness of such a destruction? What are the most dreadful punishments that heaven can inflict upon a nation? How would our destruction compare with that of Rome?

Give the reasons for the inflections marked in the 2d paragraph. (The principle of negative sentences prevails in this sentence.)

In what mode, tense, number, and person, is must educate," in the first sentence? In the 3d paragragh, for what noun does the pronoun "*her*" stand? Parse the last word in the lesson.

LESSON XLIII.

2. O'-NYX; *n.* a gem partly transparent.
2. SAP'-PHIRE; *n.* (pro. *saf'-fer*), a precious stone, blue, red, violet, &c.
2. CRYS'-TAL; *n.* a regular solid of any mineral.
2. COR'-AL; *n.* a kind of animal and its shell. [lowish color.
2. TO'-PAZ; *n.* a gem of a yel-
5. AD-JUST'-ED; *v.* settled, reduced to a right standard.
5. PRE-SCRI'BED; *v.* laid down as rules.

TRUE WISDOM.

PRONOUNCE correctly. Do not say *pur-chis'd* for pur-chas'd; *jules* for jew-els; *co-rul* for cor-al; *dis-truc-tion* for de-struc-tion.

1. WHERE shall ✝wisdom be found`?
And where is the place of ✝understanding`?
Man knoweth not the price thereof;
Nor can it be found in the land of the living.

2. The deep saith´, It is not with me`;
And the sea saith´, It is not with me`.
It can not be gotten for gold,
Nor shall silver be weighed out as the price thereof.
It can not be ✝purchased with the gold of Ophir,

LESSON XLVIII.

1. TROW; *v.* suppose, think.
1. TRAP'-PINGS; *n.* ornaments.
2. IM'-BE-CILE; *n.* (pro. *im'-be-cil*) a sick person.
3. IN-TER-VE'NED; *v.* situated between.
4. TINT'-INGS; *n.* colorings.
5. STI'-FLED; *v.* suppressed.

IT SNOWS.

REMARK.—Avoid reading in a faint and low tone. This is a very common fault and should be carefully guarded against.

PRONOUNCE correctly. Do not say *trou* for trow (pro. tro); *geth-uz* for gath-ers; *to-ward'* for to'-ward; *un-heerd* for un-heard (pro. un-herd).

1. "IT snows!" cries the School-boy, "Hurrah!" and his shout
   Is ringing through parlor and hall,
While swift as the wing of a swallow, he's out,
   And his playmates have answered his call;
It makes the heart leap but to witness their joy,
   Proud wealth has no pleasures, I trow,
Like the †rapture that throbs in the pulse of the boy,
   As he gathers his †treasures of snow;
Then lay not the trappings of gold on thine heirs,
While health, and the riches of nature, are theirs.

2. "It snows!" sighs the Imbecile, "Ah!" and his breath
   Comes heavy, as †clogged with a weight;
While, from the pale †aspect of nature in death,
   He turns to the blaze of his grate;
And nearer and nearer, his soft-cushioned chair
   Is wheeled toward the life-giving flame;
He dreads a chill puff of the snow-burdened air,
   Lest it wither his †delicate frame;
Oh! small is the pleasure †existence can give,
When the fear we shall die only proves that we live!

3. "It snows!" cries the Traveler, "Ho!" and the word
   Has quickened his steed's †lagging pace;

THIS POEM WAS WRITTEN BY MRS. SARAH JOSEPHA HALE (1788-1879), ONE *of the most interesting of the authors included in the McGuffeys. Left a widow with five children when her husband died in 1822, she turned to writing and—despite the odds—managed to support her family. In 1828 she became editor of* Ladies' Magazine *in Boston, the first periodical in America to be published for women. And in 1837, when her magazine was consolidated with the famous* Godey's Lady's Book, *she moved to Philadelphia to edit it for the next forty years.*

Mrs. Hale's early novel Northwood *(1827) is still remembered by some today as the work in which it was first proposed that Thanksgiving "like the Fourth of July . . . be considered a national festival and observed by all our people." But it was in a series of editorials she wrote for* Godey's Lady's Book *that she began in earnest her fight for a common Thanksgiving Day. For the next seventeen years she waged her editorial*

campaign, eventually gaining enough support to lead President
Lincoln to issue such a proclamation in 1863. Similar annual proclamations were made by subsequent presidents until
1941, when Thanksgiving officially became a national holiday.

An early champion of women's rights, Mrs. Hale compiled an anthology of English and American female poets, The
Ladies' Wreath, and also wrote the popular Woman's Record,
or Sketches of All Distinguished Women from the Creation to the Present Day (1853, with later revisions and updates).
The selection here, "It Snows," demonstrates that she was a
poet of more depth than many of her more celebrated contemporaries, but her reputation today unfortunately rests all
too heavily on her earlier verse: "Mary's Lamb"' ("Mary
had a little lamb"—see pages 14–15).

The wind rushes by, but its howl is unheard,
　　Unfelt the sharp drift in his face;
For bright through the tempest his own home appeared,
　　Ay, though leagues intervened, he can see:
There's the clear, glowing hearth, and the table prepared,
　　And his wife with her babes at her knee;
Blest thought! how it lightens the grief-laden hour,
That those we love dearest are safe from its power!

4. "It snows!" cries the Belle, "Dear, how lucky!" and
　　　turned
From her mirror to watch the flakes fall,
Like the first rose of summer, her †dimpled cheek burns,
　　While musing on sleigh-ride and ball:
There are visions of conquests, of †splendor, and mirth,
　　Floating over each drear winter's day;
But the tintings of Hope, on this storm-beaten earth,
　　Will melt like the snowflakes away:
Turn, turn thee to Heaven, fair maiden, for bliss;
That world has a pure †fount ne'er opened in this.

5. "It snows!" cries the Widow, "Oh, God!" and her
　　　sighs
Have stifled the voice of her prayer;
Its burden ye'll read in her tear-swollen eyes,
　　On her cheek sunk with fasting and care.
'T is night, and her fatherless ask her for bread;
　　But "He gives the young ravens their food,"
And she trusts, till her dark hearth adds †horror to
　　dread,
　　And she lays on her last chip of wood.
Poor †sufferer! that sorrow thy God only knows;
'T is a most bitter lot to be poor, when it snows!

QUESTIONS.—Why does the school-boy rejoice when it snows?
What feelings are excited in the sick man by the snow storm? What
effect does it have upon the traveler, and what does he think about?
Why does the belle congratulate herself, and of what are her dreams?
What are the poor widow's troubles in a time like this?

dead faces shall express what their spirits were, and are to be, by a lingering smile of memory and hope.

16. Drink, then, and be refreshed! The water is as pure and cold as when it slaked the thirst of the red hunter, and flowed beneath the aged bough, though now this gem of the wilderness is treasured under these hot stones, where no shadow falls, but from the brick buildings. But, still is this †fountain the source of health, peace, and happiness, and I behold with certainty and joy, the approach of the period, when the virtues of cold water, too little valued since our father's days, will be fully †appreciated and †recognized by all.

QUESTIONS.—Describe the various characters who are supposed to approach the pump for a drink, and the pump's remarks to them.

LESSON LIX.

Ex-ACT'; v. to compel to pay.	NOM'-I-NA-TED; v. named.
FOR'-FEIT; n. that to which the right is lost by breach of contract.	PEN'-AL-TY; n. the suffering or loss to which one is subjected by not fulfilling certain conditions.
CAR'-RI-ON; adj. putrid.	
DUC'-AT; n. a piece of money worth from one to two dollars.	CON'-FIS-CATE; adj. taken away and devoted to the public use.
HU'-MOR; n. disposition, fancy.	AL'-IEN, (pro. ale'-yen); n. one who is not entitled to the privilege of a citizen.
BANED; v. poisoned.	
GAP'-ING; adj. open mouthed.	
STRAIN'-ED; v. forced.	COF'-FER; n. treasury.
EX-PO-SI'-TION; n. explanation.	TEN'-OR; n. meaning.

SHYLOCK, OR THE POUND OF FLESH.

REMARK.—Let the pupil stand at a distance from the teacher, and try to read so loud and distinctly, that the teacher may hear each syllable.

ARTICULATE distinctly. Do not say pen'lt-y for pen-al-ty; qual'ty for qual-i-ty; per-j'ry for per-ju-ry; law-f'ly for law-ful-ly; ex-p'si-tion for ex-po-si-tion; prin-c'p'l for prin-ci-pal; in-d'rect for in-di-rect.

Judge. WHAT! is Antonio here?
Antonio. Ready, so please your grace.

PERHAPS IT WAS ASSUMED THAT EVERYONE KNEW THE AUTHOR OF THIS selection, but it is somewhat surprising nonetheless that William Shakespeare's name is not even noted. The play from which the lesson is adapted is, of course, The Merchant of Venice—*but that too goes unmentioned. First appearing in the 1844* Fourth Reader, *the selection was transferred to the* Fifth Reader *for the 1857 and 1866 editions, and was then quietly retired from the* McGuffey *stage.*

The text of this play as it appears here has been drastically abridged, with many lines cut or "rearranged," some characters eliminated, and others combined (the Duke and the disguised Portia, for instance, are combined here into the Judge).

Most of the line deletions damage the poetry immeasurably, but appear to have been motivated by a desire to reduce the scene to its basic plot line and to eliminate passages that might confuse with archaic words or images. In one case, however, the excision of lines was determined by other, more sinister motives—that being the cut of Shylock's response to the Judge's (the Duke's) question: "How shalt thou hope for mercy, rendering none?"

Shylock: *What judgment shall I dread, doing no wrong?*
You have among you many a purchased slave,
Which, like your asses and your dogs and mules,
You use in abject and in slavish parts,
Because you bought them: shall I say to you,
Let them be free, marry them to your heirs?
Why sweat they under burthens? let their beds
Be made as soft as yours and let their palates
Be season'd with such viands? You will answer
'The slaves are ours': so do I answer you. . . .

There were some things not even Shakespeare could say in the 1840's and 1850's.

Ju. I am sorry for thee; thou art come to answer
A stony ⁺adversary, an inhuman wretch,
⁺Incapable of pity.

Ant. I am armed to suffer.

(*Enter Shylock.*)

Ju. Dost thou now exact the penalty,
Which is a pound of this poor merchant's flesh?

Shy. By our holy Sabbath, I have sworn,
To have the due and forfeit of my bond.

Ju. This is no answer, thou unfeeling man,
To excuse the ⁺current of thy ⁺cruelty.

Shy. I am not bound to please thee with my answer.
You 'll ask me why I rather choose to have
A weight of carrion flesh, than to receive
Three thousand ducats.   I 'll not answer that:
But say it is my humor.   Is it answered?
What if my house be troubled with a rat,
And I be pleased to give ten thousand ducats
To have it baned?   What, are you answered yet?
Some men there are, love not a gaping pig;
Some, that are mad, if they behold a cat;
As there is no firm reason to be ⁺rendered,
Why one can not abide a gaping pig;
Another, a harmless, ⁺necessary cat;
So can I give no reason, and I will not,
More than a lodged hate, and a certain loathing
I bear Antonio, that I follow thus
A losing suit against him.

Ju. Do all men kill the things they do not love?

Shy. Hates any man the thing he would not kill?

Ant. For thy three thousand ducats, here are six.

Shy. If every ducat in six thousand ducats
Were in six parts, and every part a ducat,
I would not draw them; I would have my bond.

Ju. How shalt thou hope for mercy, ⁺rendering none?

Shy. The pound of flesh which I demand of him,
Is dearly bought; is mine; and I will have it:
If you deny me, fy upon your law!

I stand for †judgment; answer; shall I have it?

Ju.   Antonio, do you confess the bond?

Ant.   I do.

Ju.   Then must the Jew be merciful.

Shy. On what †compulsion *must* I? tell me *that.*

Ju.   The quality of mercy is not †strained;
It droppeth as the gentle rain from heaven
Upon the place beneath; it is twice blessed;
It blesseth him that gives, and him that takes.

Shy. My deed's upon my head!   I †crave the law,
The penalty and forfeit of my bond.

Ju.   Is he not able to discharge the money?

Ant.   Yes, here I tender it to him in the court;
Yea, twice and thrice the sum.

Shy. I'll have my bond, I will not take thy offer.

Ju.   There is no power in Venice
Can alter a †decree †established.

Shy. Oh wise, wise Judge, how do I honor thee!

Ju.   I pray you let me look upon the bond.

                         (*Gives it to the Judge.*)

Shy. Here 't is, most †reverend doctor,* here it is.

Ju.   Shylock, there's thrice thy money offered thee.

Shy. An oath, an oath, I have in Heaven:
Shall I lay perjury upon my soul?
No, not for Venice.

Ju.   Why, this bond is forfeit:
And lawfully by this the Jew may claim
A pound of flesh, to be by him cut off
Nearest the merchant's heart; be merciful;
Take thrice the money; bid me tear the bond.

Shy. When it is paid according to the tenor.
You know the law, your †exposition
Hath been most sound.
There is no power in the tongue of man
To alter me: I stand here on my bond.

---

* This word here means a learned man.

By this point in Shakespeare's version the "Judge" was no longer the Duke, but Portia in disguise. Her famous set speech on the "quality of mercy" is reduced here by more than half, but it evidently still had an impact on American readers. Perhaps the best indication of this is shown in an anecdote related in W. W. Livengood's Our Heritage *(a brief history of the American Book Company, 1947):*

The story is told that a Georgia defense lawyer quoted Portia's plea for mercy in behalf of his client. The Judge broke in to inquire the source of the quotation. The lawyer answered, 'Shakespeare.' Thereupon the prosecutor leaped to his feet and shouted, 'The defense is wrong in this, as in all else in this trial. That quotation is from McGuffey's Readers!' The Judge beamed knowingly, nodded his head: 'The correction is sustained. The clerk will please set down 'McGuffey'—not 'Shakespeare.'

Passages from Shakespeare are not as prevalent in the McGuffeys as selections from the Bible (or even, more surprisingly, from Washington Irving), but there are a good number of lessons taken from Shakespeare. Many of them are set speeches or passages describing the character of some historical personage, and none of them are placed in context. This, in fact, has been one of the most valid criticisms of the McGuffeys' use of Shakespeare, that is, that villains like Iago really do seem to be "honest" in the short excerpts given, and that other similar misleading fragments are used. It is true that the Readers did turn some of Shakespeare into clichés while ignoring more important passages, but at least a partial defense can be offered. The McGuffey Readers were often the only contact many Americans ever had with classics of English or American literature, and—whatever their weaknesses—they did expose passages of Shakespeare and other great writers to large numbers of people, some of whom were probably inspired to read further in these works.

Ant. Most heartily do I beseech the court
To give the judgment.

Ju. Why, then, thus it is.
You must prepare your bosom for his knife.

Shy. Oh noble Judge!

Ju. For the intent and purpose of the law
Hath full relation to the penalty,
Which here appeareth due unto the bond.

Shy. 'T is very true: Oh wise and upright Judge!

Ju. Therefore, lay bare your bosom.   (*To Antonio.*)

Shy. Ay, his breast:
So says the bond; does it not, noble Judge?
Nearest his heart, those are the very words.

Ju. It is so.   Are there balance here, to weigh
The flesh?

Shy. I have them ready.

Ju. Have by some surgeon, Shylock, on your charge.
To stop his wounds, lest he do bleed to death.

Shy. Is it so *nominated* in the bond?

Ju. It is not so *expressed;* but what of *that?*
'T were good you do so much in *charity.*

Shy. I can not find it; 't is not in the bond.

Ju. Come, merchant, have you any thing to say?

Ant. But little; I am armed and well prepared.

Ju. Shylock! A pound of that same merchant's flesh is
thine!
The court awards it, and the law doth give it.

Shy. Most rightful Judge!

Ju. And you must cut the flesh from off his breast;
The law allows it, and the court awards it.

Shy. Most learned Judge!   A sentence: come, prepare.

Ju. Tarry a little; there is something else.
This bond doth give thee here no jot of blood;
The words expressly are, a pound of flesh:
But, in the cutting it, if thou dost shed
One drop of Christian blood, thy lands and goods

     Are, by the law of Venice, confiscate
     Unto the State of Venice.

Shy. Is that the law?

Ju. Thyself shalt see the act;
     For, as thou urgest justice, be †assured
     Thou shalt have justice, more than thou desirest.

Shy. I take his offer, then; pay the bond thrice,
     And let the Christian go.

Ju. The Jew shall have all justice; soft! no haste!
     He shall have nothing but the penalty.
     Therefore prepare thee to cut off the flesh.
     Shed thou not blood; nor cut thou less nor more,
     Than just one pound; be it but so much
     As makes it light or heavy, in the substance,
     Or the division of the twentieth part
     Of one poor †scruple; nay, if the scale do turn
     But in the †estimation of a hair,
     Thou diest, and all thy goods are confiscate.
     Why doth the Jew pause? take thy †forfeiture.

Shy. Give me my †principal, and let me go.

Ju. Thou hast refused it in the open court;
     Thou shalt have merely justice, and the bond.

Shy. Shall I not barely have my †principal?

Ju. Thou shalt have nothing but the forfeiture,
     To be so taken at thy peril, Jew.

Shy. Why, then, the devil give him good of it!
     I'll stay no longer question.

Ju. Tarry, Jew:
     The law hath yet another hold on you.
     It is enacted in the laws of Venice,
     If it be proved against an alien,
     That by direct or indirect †attempts,
     He seeks the life of any citizen,
     The party 'gainst the which he doth †contrive,
     Shall seize one half his goods; and the other half
     Comes to the privy coffer of the State,
     And the offender's life lies in the mercy
     Of the court only.

Much of the anti-Semitism of Shakespeare's text is retained here, but some of it is muted or—as with Antonio's requirement that Shylock convert to Christianity—silently eliminated. A good deal remains, of course, but it should be noted that it is one of only a few lessons in the McGuffeys reflecting anti-Jewish sentiments. An earlier lesson on "The Bible" by S. H. Tyng (in the 1837 and 1838 Third Reader) speaks of the Jews as among "the bitterest enemies of the Christian name," but grudgingly gives them some credit for preserving the Old Testament: "It was their own sacred volume, which contained the most extraordinary predictions concerning the infidelity of their nation, and the rise, progress, and extensive prevalence of Christianity." But that lesson disappeared quickly, and the Jews receive fairly unbiased treatment from that time on, in the very few lessons where they appear.

Shy. Take my life, then, and all, and pardon not that.
You take my house, when you do take the prop
That doth sustain my house; you take my life,
When you do take the means by which I live.

Ju. The court in mercy spares thy life,
But the forfeiture of thy estate,
Comes not within our power to +remedy;
The law is strict in its demands of justice.
Are you +contented, Jew? What dost thou say?

Shy. I pray you, give me leave to go from hence;
I am not well; Oh give me leave to go
Where I may die in peace:
Since what I hold dearer than my life,
Is taken from me.

Ju. The court has mercy on your life;
Go, repent, and live,
And with a softer heart, remember mercy too.

QUESTIONS.—Why did Shylock choose the pound of flesh rather than the payment of his debt? What does he mean by saying "my deeds upon my head?" In whose favor does the judge decide? How does he eventually relieve Antonio from his danger? How is Shylock punished? Was his punishment just? Why?

In the last three lines, which are the verbs? Which of them is in the indicative mode? Which are in the imperative mode? What does the word *indicative* mean? Why is this mode so called? What does the word *imperative* mean? See Pinneo's Analytical Grammar, page 68, Art. 163.

EXERCISE XXVII.

When similar sounds come at the end of one word, and at the beginning of the next, they must not be blended.

He sinks sorrowing to the tomb. Man loves society. Time flies swiftly. The birds sing. Man never dies. The heart turns away. The lip pants. The dim mournful light tries vainly to enter. The quick creak comes grating. Give vantage ground.

Even more liberties were taken with Shakespeare's text at the end of this version than earlier. Here, to terminate the lesson more neatly, new lines were written and the Bard "improved." The changes also helped, of course, to point out the moral more clearly than Shakespeare had been able to manage in the original.

LESSON LXVI.

Can'-ni-bals; *n.* men who eat human flesh.   [vaders.
Ag-gres'-sors; *n.* the first in-
Ven'-i-son; *n.* (pro. *ven'-e-z'n* or
ven'z'n) the flesh of deer.

Col'-o-ny; *n.* a company of persons removing to a new country, but remaining subject to
the parent country.
Reg'-i-ment; *n.* a body of troops.

CHARLES II. AND WILLIAM PENN.

Pronounce correctly. Do not say *sav-ij-is* for sav-*a*-ges; *kit-tle*
for ket-tle; *idee* for i-de-*a*; *reg-i-munt* for reg-i-ment; *musk-its* for
musk-ets; *con-tra'-ry* for con'-tra-ry; *sub-jics* for sub-jects;
weap'n for weap-on.

King Charles. WELL`, friend William´! I have sold
you a noble province in North America; but still, I suppose you have no thoughts of going thither *yourself.*

Penn. Yes, I have, I ⁺assure thee, friend Charles; and
I am just come to bid thee farewell.

K. C. What`! venture yourself among the ⁺savages
of North America´! Why`, man´, what ⁺security have
you that you will not be in their war kettle in two hours
after setting foot on their shores?

P. The best security in the world.

K. C. I doubt that, friend William; I have no idea of
any security, against those cannibals, but in a ⁺regi-
ment of good soldiers, with their muskets and ⁺bayonets.
And mind`, I tell you beforehand´, that, with all my
good will for you and your family, to whom I am under
⁺obligations, I will not send a *single soldier* with you.

P. I want none of thy soldiers, Charles: I depend on
something better than thy soldiers.

K. C. Ah´! what may *that*` be?

P. Why, I depend upon *themselves*`; on the working
of their *own hearts*`; on their notions of *justice*`; on
their *moral sense.*

*HERE AGAIN IS THE WORK OF THE COLORFUL PARSON WEEMS, WHOSE
"George and the Hatchet" appeared earlier (see pages 44–45).
In this selection Weems is doing to (for?) William Penn what
he had done earlier with Washington: fabricating a myth,
making a hero.*

In this passage Weems provides Penn with such a simplistic and exaggerated description of the Indians that the implied skepticism of King Charles is somewhat justified. But the essence of the description is consistent with the McGuffeys' treatment of Indians throughout the series.

K. C. A fine thing, this same *moral sense*, no doubt; but I fear you will not find *much* of it among the Indians of North America.

P. And why not among *them*, as well as *others?*

K. C. Because if they had possessed any, they would not have treated my ⁺subjects so ⁺barbarously as they have done.

P. That is no ⁺proof of the ⁺contrary, friend Charles. Thy subjects were the *aggressors.* When thy subjects first went to North America, they found these poor people the *fondest* and *kindest creatures* in the world. *Every day*, they would *watch* for them to come ashore, and hasten to *meet* them, and feast them on the best fish, and venison, and corn, which were all they had. In return for this hospitality of the *savages*, as we call them, thy subjects, termed *Christians*, seized on their country and rich hunting grounds, for farms for themselves. Now, is it to be wondered at, that these much injured people should have been driven to ⁺desperation by such ⁺injustice; and that, burning with ⁺revenge, they should have committed some ⁺excesses?

K. C. Well, then, I hope you will not complain when they come to treat you in the same manner.

P. I am not afraid of it.

K. C. Ah! how will you avoid it? You mean to get their hunting grounds too, I suppose?

P. Yes, but not by driving these poor people away from them.

K. C. No, indeed? How then will you get their lands?

P. I mean to *buy* their lands of them.

K. C. Buy their lands of *them?* Why, man, you have already bought them of *me.*

P. Yes, I know I have, and at a dear rate, too: but I did it only to get thy good will, not that I thought thou hadst any right to their lands.

K. C. How, man? *no right* to their lands?

P. No, friend Charles, *no right, no right* at all: *what* right hast thou to their lands?

K. C. Why`, the right of ⁺*discovery*`, to be sure; the right which the Pope and all Christian kings have agreed to give one another.

P. The right of *discovery?* A strange kind of right, indeed. Now, suppose, friend Charles, that some ⁺canoe load of these Indians, crossing the sea, and ⁺discovering this island of Great Britain, were to claim it as their own, and set it up for sale over thy head, what wouldst thou think of it?

K. C. Why—why—why—I must confess, I should think it a piece of great ⁺*impudence*` in them.

P. Well, then, how canst *thou,* a *Christian,* and a *Christian prince* too, do *that* which thou so utterly condemnest in *these people,* whom thou callest *savages?* Yes, friend Charles; and suppose, again, that these Indians, on thy refusal to give up thy island of Great Britain, were to *make war* on thee, and, having weapons more ⁺destructive than thine, were to destroy many of thy subjects, and drive the rest away,—wouldst thou not think it ⁺horribly cruel?

K. C. I must say, friend William, that I should; how can I say otherwise?

P. Well, then, how can I, who call myself a *Christian,* do what I should ⁺abhor even in the *heathen?* No. I will not do it. But I will buy the right of the proper owners, even of the Indians themselves. By doing this, I shall ⁺imitate God himself, in his ⁺justice and mercy, and thereby insure his blessing on my colony, if I should ever live to plant one in North America.

QUESTIONS.—What part of the United States was purchased and settled by William Penn? Upon what was the king's right founded? In whom was the real right? Why? What did Penn say to convince the king that America did not belong to him? What plan did Penn propose to adopt, to secure the good will of the Indians? Explain the inflections marked.

In the last sentence, which are the personal pronouns of the first person? Which of the third person? Which are the verbs? Which of them is in the participal mode? Which are in the future tense, indicative mode?

The description of the righteous Penn standing up to an English king and addressing him with such fearless logic is one that was calculated to appeal to American audiences. It also, of course, helped to certify William Penn as one of the few American heroes promoted by the McGuffey Readers as worthy of emulation. The only others who get repeated and unreserved praise in the Readers are Washington and Lafayette. Curiously, there is no mention of Western stars—not only are such folk heroes as Daniel Boone, Davy Crockett, and Mike Fink missing, but virtually no references are made to men like Andrew Jackson or Abraham Lincoln. The mythologizing of Lincoln occurred later in the century, of course, but even by 1879 it was well underway. Lincoln could have provided the McGuffeys with a splendid illustration of the self-made man climbing from the log cabin to the White House, etc. Such a portrait would probably not have sold well, however, in the South; and perhaps for that reason the Lincoln myth had to develop without the aid of the McGuffey Readers.

LESSON LXVII.

1. Dis-so-lu′-tion; *n.* death, separation of the soul and body.
5. In-ad′-e-quate; *adj.* partial, not equal to the reality.
5. Rav′-a-ges; *n.* destruction, ruin.
7. Ex-trem′-i-ties; *n.* utmost distress: *last extremities* here means *death.*
8. Pro-lon-ga′-tion; *n.* the act of lengthening.
8. Ve′-hi-cles; *n.* carriages of any kind.
8. Re-cep′-ta-cles; *n.* places in which to receive any thing.
9. As-si-du′-i-ties; *n.* services rendered with zeal and kindness.
10. Con-ta′-gion; *n.* pestilence, sickness spreading from the touch.
12. De-ci′-pher'd; *v.* explained.

HORRORS OF WAR.

Pronounce correctly. Do not say *hull* for whole; *dis-sy-lu-tion* for dis-so-lu-tion; *at-tact* for at-tack; *mod-er-it* for mod-er-ate; *cli-mits* for cli-mates; *rav-ij-is* for rav-a-ges; hea-ven, pro. *heav'n.*

1. Though the whole race of man is doomed to dissolution, and we are hastening to our long home; yet, at each †successive moment, life and death seem to divide between them the †dominion of mankind, and life to have the larger share. It is otherwise in war; death reigns there without a rival, and without †control.

2. War is the work, the element, or rather the sport and triumph of death, who here glories not only in the extent of his conquests, but in the richness of his spoil. In the other methods of attack, in the other forms which death †assumes, the feeble and the aged, who at best can live but a short time, are usually the victims; here they are the †vigorous and the strong.

3. It is remarked by the most ancient of poets, that in *peace, children* bury their *parents´;* in *war, parents* bury their *children`,* nor is the difference small. *Children* lament their *parents,* sincerely, indeed, but with that moderate and †tranquil sorrow, which it is natural for those to feel who are conscious of retaining many tender ties, many animating prospects.

"Horrors of War" was part of a longer work entitled Reflections on War *(1802) written by Robert Hall (1764–1831), an English Baptist clergyman (not to be confused with Robert Bernard Hall [1812–1868], an American Episcopalian clergyman active in the anti-slavery movement). Among the foremost British pulpit orators of his time, Hall was also noted for his fluid prose style. His best known works include the study from which this lesson is taken, and* Modern Infidelity Considered with Respect to its Influence on Society *(1800).*

4. *Parents* mourn for their *children* with the bitterness of despair; the aged parent, the widowed mother, loses, when she is deprived of her children, every thing but the capacity of suffering; her heart, withered and †desolate, admits no other object, †cherishes no other hope. It is Rachel, weeping for her children, and refusing to be comforted, because they are not.

5. But, to confine our attention to the number of the slain, would give us a very inadequate idea of the ravages of the sword. The lot of those who perish †instantaneously may be considered, apart from religious prospects, as †comparatively happy, since they are exempt from those lingering diseases and slow torments to which others are so liable.

6. We can not see an individual †expire, though a stranger or an enemy, without being sensibly moved and prompted by compassion to lend him every †assistance in our power. Every trace of †resentment vanishes in a moment; every other emotion gives way to pity and terror.

7. In the last extremities, we remember nothing but the respect and tenderness due to our common nature. What a scene, then, must a field of battle present, where thousands are left without assistance, and without pity, with their wounds exposed to the †piercing air, while the blood, freezing as it flows, binds them to the earth, amid the †trampling of horses, and the insults of an †enraged foe!

8. If they are spared by the humanity of the enemy, and carried from the field, it is but a prolongation of †torment. Conveyed in uneasy vehicles, often to a remote distance, through roads almost impassable, they are lodged in ill-prepared receptacles for the wounded and sick, where the †variety of distress baffles all the efforts of †humanity and skill, and renders it impossible to give to each the attention he demands.

9. Far from their native home, no tender assiduities of friendship, no well-known voice, no wife, or mother, or sister, are near to soothe their sorrows, relieve their

From the start the McGuffey Readers *were most consistent in opposing war, this being but one of many lessons attesting to that fact. In contrast with most competing textbooks (which often included some anti-war oratory cancelled out by lots of lessons describing brave soldiers and military heroes), the* McGuffeys *paid more than lip service to their position on this subject—especially in the earlier editions which most clearly show the McGuffey brothers' personal involvement. This particular selection appeared in the* Fourth Reader *from 1837 to 1857, and then in the* Fifth Reader *until 1879, when it was removed—perhaps because of its oratorical excesses, but more likely because it served too well as a reminder of the Civil War horrors the country was trying hard to forget.*

Although this passage was written in 1802, it had special relevance in the 1866 edition, when the wounded nation was counting its casualties. The Civil War was the costliest war America has ever known, with over 618,000 service deaths. And over two-thirds of these were non-battle casualties—with all of the causes listed here by Hall playing their deadly roles. Of these, the greatest killer—on both sides—was typhoid.

thirst, or close their eyes in death! Unhappy man! and must you be swept into the grave †unnoticed and †unnumbered, and no friendly tear be shed for your sufferings, or mingled with your dust?

10. We must remember, however, that as a very small proportion of †military life is spent in actual †combat, so it is a very small part of its miseries which must be ascribed to this source. More are consumed by the rust of †inactivity than by the edge of the sword; confined to a scanty or †unwholesome diet, exposed in sickly climates, harassed with tiresome marches and †perpetual alarms; their life is a continual scene of hardships and danger. They grow †familiar with hunger, cold, and watchfulness. Crowded into hospitals and prisons, contagion spreads among their ranks, till the ravages of disease exceed those of the enemy.

11. We have hitherto only †adverted to the sufferings of those who are engaged in the profession of arms, without taking into our account the situation of the countries which are the scenes of hostilities. How dreadful to hold every thing at the mercy of an enemy, and to receive life itself as a boon dependent on the sword!

12. How boundless the fears which such a situation must inspire, where the †issues of life and death are determined by no known laws, principles, or customs, and no †conjecture can be formed of our destiny, except so far as it is dimly deciphered in characters of blood, in the †dictates of revenge, and the caprices of power!

13. Conceive, but for a moment, the consternation which the approach of an †invading army would impress on the peaceful villages in our own neighborhood. When you have placed yourselves in that situation, you will learn to †sympathize with those unhappy countries which have sustained the ravages of arms. But how is it possible to give you an idea of these horrors!

14. Here, you behold rich harvests, the bounty of heaven, and the reward of industry, consumed in a moment, or trampled under foot, while famine and

†pestilence follow the steps of †desolation. There, the cottages of peasants given up to the flames, mothers expiring through fear, not for themselves, but their infants; the inhabitants flying with their helpless babes in all directions, miserable fugitives on their native soil!

15. In another place, you witness †opulent cities taken by storm; the streets, where no sounds were heard but those of peaceful industry, filled on a sudden with slaughter and blood, resounding with the cries of the pursuing and the pursued; the palaces of nobles demolished, the houses of the rich pillaged, and every age, sex, and rank, mingled in †promiscuous massacre and ruin!

LESSON LXVIII.

1. Rev'-el-ry; *n.* noisy feasting and gayety.	4. Squad'-ron; *n.* a body of troops.
1. Chiv'-al-ry; *n.* knighthood, a body of knights or brave men.	5. Ar'-dennes; *n.* (pro. *Ar'-dens*) a forest near Waterloo.
1. Vo-lup'-tu-ous; *adj.* exciting animal pleasure.	6. Mar'-shal-ing; *n.* arranging in order.
	6. Blent; *v.* mixed, united.

BATTLE OF WATERLOO.*

In reading the following extract, much variety of expression is required. The description of the ball should be read in a lively, animated manner; that of the distant alarm in low, hurried tones, as if intently listening and deeply anxious; the haste of preparation and departure requires life; and the third and last two stanzas should be read in a mournful and plaintive style.

1. There was a sound of revelry by night,
   And Belgium's †capital had gathered then

---

* This battle was fought on June 18th, 1815, between the French army on one side, commanded by Napoleon Bonaparte, and the English army and allies on the other side, commanded by the Duke of Wellington. At the commencement of the battle, some of the officers were at a ball at Brussels, a short distance from Waterloo, and being notified of the approaching contest by the cannonade, left the ballroom for the field of battle. This was the last of Napoleon's battles. He was here completely overthrown.

WRITTEN BY WILLIAM ELLERY CHANNING (BUT NOT ATTRIBUTED TO him until the later editions), this selection has been a part of the McGuffeys since their beginning. Appearing first in the 1837 Fourth Reader, it has since 1857 been located in the Fifth Reader.

Channing (1780–1842) was one of the most prominent New England clergymen and orators of the early 1800's. A Harvard graduate at the age of eighteen, he was installed as pastor of the Federal Street Church in Boston in 1803, a charge he held until his death. Known primarily for his liberal theological views, Channing articulated in 1819 what eventually became the creed of the Unitarians, and helped to found the group which in 1825 became the American Unitarian Association.

In addition to his work toward theological reform, Channing was also active in social reform. He opposed slavery and drunkenness, though he also opposed the violent methods of many abolitionists and temperance fanatics. Other issues received his ardent support as well, including prison reform, labor problems, and the need for improved public education.

LESSON LXXXVIII.

1. REC-OG-NI′-TION; *n.* acknowledgment.
2. FAB′-RIC, *n.* any system composed of connected parts.
2. E-RA′SED; *v.* blotted out.
3. PER′-PE-TRA-TOR, *n.* one that commits a crime.
3. EX-TINC′-TION; *n.* a putting an end to
4. FER′-TIL-IZE; *v.* to make fruitful.
4. A′-THE-ISM; *n.* disbelief in God.
4. SENS-U-AL′-I-TY: *n.* indulgence in animal pleasure.

RELIGION, THE ONLY BASIS OF SOCIETY.

ARTICULATE clearly *all* the consonants in the following and similar words in this lesson: stability, prosperity, interested, principles, friend, suspect, comprehends, fabric, concerns, itself, improvements, perpetrator, extinction, describe, unprotected, trample, restraints.

1. RELIGION is a social concern; for it operates powerfully on society, †contributing, in various ways to its stability and prosperity. Religion is not merely a private affair; the †community is deeply interested in its †diffusion; for it is the best support of the virtues and principles, on which the social order rests. Pure and undefiled religion is, to do good; and it follows, very plainly, that, if God be the Author and Friend of society, then, the recognition of him must enforce all social duty, and enlightened piety must give its whole strength to public order.

2. Few men suspect, perhaps no man †comprehends, the extent of the support given by religion to every virtue. No man, perhaps, is aware, how much our moral and †social sentiments are fed from this fountain; how †powerless conscience would become without the belief of a God; how palsied would be human benevolence, were there not the sense of a higher benevolence to quicken and sustain it; how suddenly the whole social fabric would quake, and with what a fearful crash it would sink into hopeless ruin, were the ideas of a supreme Being, of †accountableness and of a future life, to be utterly erased from every mind.

3. And, let men thoroughly believe that they are the work and sport of chance; that no superior †intelligence concerns itself with human affairs; that all their improvements perish forever at death; that the weak have no †guardian, and the injured no †avenger; that there is no †recompense for sacrifices to uprightness and the public good; that an oath is unheard in heaven; that secret crimes have no witness but the perpetrator; that human existence has no purpose, and human virtue no unfailing friend; that this brief life is every thing to us, and death is total, †everlasting extinction; once let them *thoroughly* †abandon religion, and who can conceive or describe the extent of the desolation which would follow?

4. We hope, perhaps, that human laws and natural sympathy would hold society together. As reasonably might we believe, that were the sun quenched in the heavens, *our* torches would †illuminate, and *our* fires quicken and fertilize the creation. What is there in human nature to awaken respect and tenderness, if man is the †unprotected insect of a day? And what is he more, if atheism be true?

5. Erase all thought and fear of God from a community, and selfishness and sensuality would absorb the whole man. Appetite, knowing no restraint, and suffering, having no solace or hope, would trample in scorn on the restraints of human laws. Virtue, duty, principle, would be mocked and spurned as unmeaning sounds. A †sordid self-interest would †supplant every feeling; and man would become, in fact, what the theory in atheism declares him to be,—*a companion for brutes.*

QUESTIONS.—What is the operation of religion upon society? What would be the effect of the removal of religion, upon the whole fabric of virtue? Why would not human laws and sympathies hold society together?

Channing's liberal humanitarian views were a major influence on the intellectual and philosophical movement of New England transcendentalism. For the most part, however, his influence in the West was minimal. There the religious orthodoxy, such as that embodied by the views of William Holmes McGuffey, continued to reign. And if Westerners did send their brightest sons back East to school, it was to Yale or to the properly Presbyterian Princeton—not to the liberal heretics at Harvard and nearby Boston.

LESSON XCV.

2. AD-VENT'-UR-ERS; *n.* those who attempt difficult enterprises.
2. SUM'-MA-RY; *adj.* short, brief.
2. OUT'-RAGE; *n.* violence.

3. SIG'-NAL-IZED; *v.* made remarkable.
3. DE-TACH'-MENT; *n.* a party sent off from the main body.

SPEECH OF LOGAN, CHIEF OF THE MINGOES.

REMARK.—Let every pupil notice, as each one reads, when the final consonant of any word is joined to the vowel of the next word.

ARTICULATE distinctly. Do not say *who lof*, for whole of; *an dindeed*, for and indeed; *eminen torators*, for eminent orators; *talen tsin*, for talents in; *celebraty din pea san dwar*, for celebrated in peace and war.

1. I MAY ⁺challenge the whole of the orations of Demosthenes and Cicero, and indeed, of any more eminent orators, if Europe or the world, has furnished more eminent, to produce a single passage superior to the speech of Logan, a Mingo chief, delivered to Lord Dunmore, when governor of Virginia. As a ⁺testimony of Indian talents in this line, I beg leave to introduce it, by first stating the ⁺incidents necessary for understanding it.

2. In the spring of the year 1774, a robbery was committed by some Indians, upon certain land adventurers on the Ohio river. The whites in that quarter, according to their custom, undertook to punish this outrage in a summary way. Captain Michael Cresap and one Daniel Greathouse, leading on these parties, surprised, at different times, traveling and hunting parties of the Indians, who had their women and children with them, and murdered many. Among these, were ⁺unfortunately the family of Logan, a chief celebrated in peace and war, and long ⁺distinguished as the friend of the whites.

3. This unworthy return provoked his ⁺vengeance. He accordingly signalized himself in the war which ensued. In the autumn of the same year, a ⁺decisive

THIS FAMOUS SPEECH WAS FIRST PUBLISHED IN THOMAS JEFFERSON'S Notes on Virginia, *but its authenticity has been frequently questioned. Its presence in the McGuffeys (from 1837 until 1879) is accounted for partially by its embodiment of the "Noble Savage" concept, and partially by the attractiveness of the alleged oratory.*

battle was fought at the mouth of the Great Kanawha, between the collected forces of the Shawnees, the Mingoes, and the Delawares, and a detachment of the Virginia militia. The Indians were defeated, and sued for peace. Logan, however, †disdained to be seen among the †suppliants: but, lest the †sincerity of a treaty, from which so distinguished a chief absented himself, should be distrusted, he sent, by a messenger, the following speech to be delivered to Lord Dunmore.

4. "I appeal to any white man to say, if ever he entered Logan's cabin hungry, and he gave him not meat; if ever he came cold and naked, and he clothed him not. During the course of the last long and bloody war, Logan remained idle in his cabin, an †advocate for peace. Such was my love for the whites, that my countrymen pointed as they passed, and said 'Logan is the friend of the white men.' I had even thought to live with you, but for the injuries of one man. Colonel Cresap, last spring, in cold blood, and †unprovoked, murdered all the †relatives of Logan, not sparing even my women and children. There runs not a drop of my blood in the veins of any living creature. This called on me for revenge. I have sought it. I have killed many. I have fully †glutted my †vengeance. For my country, I rejoice at the beams of peace: but do not †harbor a thought that mine is the joy of fear. Logan never felt fear. He will not turn on his heel to save his life. Who is there to mourn for Logan? Not one."

QUESTIONS. — Who was Demosthenes? Cicero? Who undertook to punish the Indians? Whose family were killed? Where was a decisive battle fought? Where does the Kanawha rise? Why did not Logan appear among the suppliants?

In the sentence, 'Logan never felt fear,' which is the subject? Which the attribute? See Pinneo's Analytical Grammar.

Logan was the English name of the Indian Chief Tah-gah-jute (c. 1725–1780). He adopted his English name from that of James Logan (1674–1751), Provincial Secretary of Pennsylvania and a noted friend of the Indians. Early in his life Chief Logan was famous primarily for his striking personal appearance, his pleasant personality, and his friendship for whites. But after he moved his family to the banks of the Ohio in 1770, he started having serious personal problems—mainly excessive drinking. The massacre of his family in 1774—with which Cresap probably had no connection—did lead him to instigate the war here described; and Logan did refuse to sue for peace; but the authenticity of the speech itself is doubtful. Logan's death, when it actually occurred, left him even fewer mourners than he had anticipated: in a state of intoxication he attacked a party of his friends, and was killed by his relative Tod-had-dohs, acting in self-defense.

The unidentified author of this verse is John Moultrie (1799–1874), a British clergyman and poetaster, one-time rector at Rugby. The titles of some of his books appear to be accurate indications of his thematic concerns. They include My Brother's Grave and Other Poems (1837); The Dream of Life (1843); and Altar's Hearth and Graves (1854). *This particular poem was selected for only the 1857 and 1866 editions of the* McGuffeys.

LESSON LXXXIX.

2. Fer'-ven-cy; *n.* warmth.	5. Re-veal'-ing; *v.* making known.
3. Mim'-ics; *v.* imitates.	7. Ser'-aph; *n.* an angel.

THE THREE SONS.

1 I have a son, a little son, a boy just five years old,
With eyes of thoughtful †earnestness, and mind of gentle
    mold.
They tell me that unusual grace in all his ways appears;
That my child is grave and wise of heart beyond his childish
    years.

2 I can not say how this may be; I know his face is fair,
And yet his sweetest †comeliness is his sweet and serious air;
I know his heart is kind and fond, I know he loveth me,
But loveth yet his mother more, with grateful fervency.
But that which others most admire is the thought which fills
    his mind;
The food for grave, inquiring speech he every where doth find.

3. Strange questions doth he ask of me, when we together walk;
He scarcely thinks as children think, or talks as children talk.
Nor cares he much for childish sports, dotes not on bat or ball,
But looks on manhood's ways and works, and aptly mimics all.
His little heart is busy still, and oftentimes perplexed
With thoughts about this world of ours, and thoughts about
    the next.

4. He kneels at his dear mother's knee, she teaches him to pray;
And strange, and sweet, and solemn, then, are the words which
    he will say.
O, should my gentle child be spared to manhood's years like
    me,
A holier and a wiser man I trust that he will be;
And when I look into his eyes, and press his thoughtful brow,
I dare not think what I should feel, were I to lose him now.

5. I have a son, a second son, a simple child of three;
I'll not declare how bright and fair his little features be,
How silver sweet those tones of his when he †prattles on my
knee:
I do not think his light-blue eye is, like his brother's, keen,
Nor his brow so full of childish thought as his has ever been;
But his little heart's a †fountain, pure, of kind and tender
feeling;
And his every look's a gleam of light, rich depths of love
revealing.
When he walks with me, the country folks, who pass us in the
street,
Will shout for joy, and bless my boy, he looks so mild and
sweet.

6. A playfellow is he to all, and yet with cheerful tone
Will sing his little song of love, when left to sport alone.
His presence is like sunshine sent, to †gladden home and
hearth,
To comfort us in all our griefs, and sweeten all our mirth.
Should he grow up to riper years, God grant his heart may
prove
As sweet at home for heavenly grace as now for earthly love;
And if, beside his grave, the tears our aching eyes must dim,
God comfort us for all the love that we shall lose in him.

7. I have a son, a third sweet son; his age I can not tell,
For they reckon not by years and months where he is gone to
dwell.
To us for fourteen †anxious months his infant smiles were given,
And then he bid farewell to earth, and went to live in heaven.
I can not tell what form his is, what looks he weareth now,
Nor guess how bright a glory crowns his shining seraph brow;
The thoughts that fill his sinless soul, the †bliss which he doth
feel,
Are numbered with the secret things which God will not †reveal.

8. But I know (for God hath told me this) that he is now at rest,
Where other blessed infants be, on their Savior's loving breast:
I know his spirit feels no more this weary load of flesh,
But his sleep is blessed with endless dreams of joy forever
fresh.

A nineteenth-century critic once described Moultrie as a "poet of elegant mind and of considerable pathetic power. Many of his lyrics overflow with sentiment and feeling." A more modern view would be that Moultrie's "overflow" too often becomes an uncontrolled flood. See, for instance, his lyrics "Forget Thee?" and "Dear Little Violets."

I know the angels fold him close beneath their glittering wings,
And soothe him with a song that breathes of heaven's ⁺divin-
est things.
I know that we shall meet our babe (his mother dear and I)
Where God for aye shall wipe away all tears from every eye.
Whate'er befalls his brethren twain, his bliss can never cease;
Their lot may here be grief and fear, but his is certain peace.

9. It may be that the tempter's wiles their souls from bliss may
sever,
But, if our own poor faith fail not, he must be ours forever.
When we think of what our darling is, and what we still
must be;
When we muse on that world's perfect bliss, and this world's
misery;
When we groan beneath this load of sin, and feel this grief
and pain,
O, we'd rather lose our other two, than have him here again.

QUESTIONS.—How many sons are spoken of? What is said of the
first? Of the second? Of the third?

LESSON XC.

1. GEN'-IAL; *adj.* cheerful.	4. UR'-CHIN; *n.* a child.
2. EN-AM'-ELED; *v.* made hard and smooth.	5. VAR'-LET; *n.* scoundrel.
3. REV'-EL-RY; *n.* merriment.	6. VO-LUPT'-U-A-RY; *n.* pleasure seeker. [to the stomach.
4. EC'-STA-SY; *n.* rapture.	7. GAS-TRO-NOM'-IC; *adj.* relating

---

THE BOBLINK.

ARTICULATE distinctly. Do not say *happies* for hap-pi-es*t*; *potse*
for poets; *fulles* for full-es*t*; *tinklin* for tink-lin*g*; *feel'n* for feel-
in*g*; *buds* for bir*ds.*

1. THE happiest bird of our spring, however, and one
that rivals the European lark in my estimation, is the
boblincon, or boblink, as he is commonly called. He
arrives at that choice portion of our year, which, in this
latitude, answers to the description of the month of May
so often given by the poets. With us it begins about the
middle of May, and lasts until nearly the middle of

*"THE BOBLINK" DID NOT ENTER THE READER UNTIL 1857. BUT IT HAS AP-
peared in every edition of the Fifth Reader since then: an ideal
combination of a lesson based on nature that also inculcates
a clear moral.*

June. Earlier than this, winter is apt to return on its traces, and to blight the opening beauties of the year; and later than this, begin the parching, and panting, and †dissolving heats of summer. But in this genial interval, Nature is in all her freshness and †fragrance: "the rains are over and gone, the flowers appear upon the earth, the time of the singing of birds is come, and the voice of the turtle is heard in the land."

2. The trees are now in their fullest †foliage and brightest verdure; the woods are gay with the clustered flowers of the laurel; the air is perfumed with the sweet-brier and the wild rose; the meadows are enameled with clover blossoms; while the young apple, peach, and the plum begin to swell, and the cherry to glow among the green leaves.

3. This is the chosen season of revelry of the boblink. He comes amid the pomp and fragrance of the season; his life seems all †sensibility and enjoyment, all song and sunshine. He is to be found in the soft bosoms of the freshest and sweetest meadows, and is most in song when the clover is in blossom. He †perches on the topmost twig of a tree, or on some long, †flaunting weed, and as he rises and sinks with the breeze, pours forth a †succession of rich, tinkling notes, crowding one upon another, like the outpouring melody of the sky-lark, and possessing the same †rapturous character.

4. Sometimes, he pitches from the summit of a tree, begins his song as soon as he gets upon the wing, and flutters †tremulously down to the earth, as if overcome with ecstasy at his own music. Sometimes he is in pursuit of his mate; always in full song, as if he would win her by his †melody; and always with the same appearance of †intoxication and delight. Of all the birds of our groves and meadows, the boblink was the envy of my boyhood. He crossed my path in the sweetest weather, and the sweetest season of the year, when all nature called to the fields, and the rural feeling throbbed in every bosom; but when I, luckless urchin! was doomed to be mewed up, during the livelong day, in a school room.

Excerpted from a longer work entitled Birds of Spring, *this selection is another from the prose work of Washington Irving (1783–1859). Like so many of his writings, this piece combines some careful observations of nature with personal anecdotes, blended together with moralizing, seasoned with gentle humor, and served with a fluid and inviting style (garnished just a bit too heavily).*

The Logan here referred to is John Logan (1748–1788), a Scottish poet whose authorship of "Ode to the Cuckoo" is still contested (the other claimant being Michael Bruce). Until 1786 Logan was a Presbyterian clergyman, but his authorship of a play (Runnamede) and his intemperate habits combined to give offence to his dour flock—and he spent the rest of his short life as a Grub-Street writer in London. His best known work is "The Braes of Yarrow."

5. It seemed as if the little varlet mocked at me, as he flew by in full song, and sought to ⁺taunt me with his happier lot. O, how I envied him! No lessons, no task, no school; nothing but holiday, frolic, green fields, and fine weather. Had I been then more versed in poetry I might have addressed him in the words of Logan to the cuckoo:—

"Sweet bird, thy bower is ever green,
    Thy sky is ever clear;
Thou hast no sorrow in thy song,
    No winter in thy year.

"O, could I fly, I'd fly with thee;
    We'd make, on joyful wing,
Our annual visit round the globe,
    Companions of the spring."

6. Further observation and experience have given me a different idea of this feathered voluptuary, which I will venture to ⁺impart, for the benefit of my young readers, who may regard him with the same unqualified envy and admiration which I once indulged. I have shown him only as I saw him at first, in what I may call the poetical part of his career, when he, in a manner, devoted himself to elegant pursuits and enjoyments, and was a bird of music, and song, and taste, and sensibility, and ⁺refinement. While this lasted he was sacred from injury; the very schoolboy would not fling a stone at him, and the merest ⁺rustic would pause to listen to his strain.

7. But mark the difference. As the year advances, as the clover blossoms disappear, and the spring fades into summer, he gradually gives up his elegant tastes and habits, doffs his poetical suit of black, assumes a ⁺russet, dusty garb, and sinks to the gross enjoyment of common, vulgar birds. His notes no longer ⁺vibrate on the ear; he is stuffing himself with the seeds of the tall weeds on which he lately swung and chanted so melodiously. He has become a " bon vivant," a "gourmand:" with him now there is nothing like the "joys of the table." In a little while, he grows tired of plain, homely fare, and is off on a gastronomic tour in quest of foreign luxuries.

8. We next hear of him, with myriads of his kind, †banqueting among the reeds of the Delaware, and grown †corpulent with good feeding. He has changed his name in traveling. Boblincon no more, he is the reed-bird now, the much-sought-for †titbit of Pennsylvania †epicures, the rival in unlucky fame of the ortolan! Wherever he goes, pop! pop! pop! every rusty firelock in the country is blazing away. He sees his companions falling by thousands around him. Does he take warning and reform? Alas! not he. Again he wings his flight. The rice swamps of the south invite him. He gorges himself among them almost to bursting; he can scarcely fly for †corpulency. He has once more changed his name, and is now the famous rice-bird of the Carolinas. Last stage of his career: behold him spitted, with dozens of his corpulent companions, and served up, a vaunted dish, on some southern table.

9. Such is the story of the boblink; once spiritual, musical, admired, the joy of the meadows, and the favorite bird of spring; finally, a gross little †sensualist, who †expiates his sensuality in the †larder. His story contains a moral, worthy the attention of all little birds and little boys; warning them to keep to those refined and intellectual pursuits, which raised him to so high a pitch of popularity during the early part of his career, but to †eschew all tendency to that gross and dissipated indulgence, which brought this mistaken little bird to an untimely end.

QUESTIONS.—When does the boblink come? How does he appear? What does he do? As the year advances what change occurs in him? What does he become at last?

EXERCISE XXXIX.

Mind, minds, mindst; find, finds, findst; yield, yields, yieldst; length'n, length'ns, length'nst, length'nd, length'ndst; bright'n, brighnt'ns, bright'nst, bright'nd, bright'nd'st.

5th R.—27

By now the lesson's moral is all too clear, and the poor boblink—weighed down with didactic trappings—is doomed to death for his gluttony! But Irving explains the moral in detail anyway, for those who might have been feeling sorry for this "gross little sensualist," and then brings his entertaining piece to its timely end.

THE UNIDENTIFIED AUTHOR OF THIS VERSE IS JOHN GREENLEAF Whittier (1807–1892), the New England Quaker who was clearly among the most highly esteemed American poets in the latter half of the nineteenth century. His initial publications were either heavily romantic (he particularly admired the poetry of Burns) or strongly didactic (he worked for years with William Lloyd Garrison, the leading Abolitionist), but in his later verse he turns more to the countryside as his subject. "Maud Miller" appeared in 1856 in The Panorama and Other Poems, along with another well-known Whittier poem: "The Barefoot Boy." Whittier's most famous poem is "Snow Bound" (1866), which—with a few other selected ballads and narratives—is still sometimes anthologized, but his reputation has declined significantly in the twentieth century.

LESSON LXXXIV.

1. WROUGHT; *v.* labored.
1. ECH'O-ED; *v.* repeated; sounded back.   [certain.
2. VAGUE; *adj.* indefinite; un-
4. QUAFF'ED; *v.* drank eagerly.
5. SUR-PRISE'; *n.* wonder; astonishment.   [color.
5. HA'ZEL; *adj.* a light brown
9. HAR'VEST-ER; *n.* one who gathers a harvest.
11. DOW'ER; *n.* the property which a wife brings her husband.
12. GAR'NISH-ED; *adj.* adorned; beautified.
14. SPIN'ET; *n.* a musical instrument.
14. AS'TRAL; *n.* an ornamental lamp.
14. LUG; *n.* the fire-place.
14. DŌZ'ING; *adj.* half-asleep; drowsy.
15. RE-PIN'ER; *n.* a complainer.
15. DRUDGE; *n.* an unwilling laborer.

MAUD MULLER.

1. MAUD MULLER, on a summer's day,
Raked the meadow sweet with hay.
Beneath her torn hat glowed the wealth
Of simple beauty and rustic health.
Singing, she wrought, and her merry glee
The mock-bird echoed from his tree.

2. But, when she glanced to the far-off town,
White from its hill-slope looking down,
The sweet song died, and a vague unrest,
And a nameless longing filled her breast;
A wish, that she hardly dared to own,
For something better than she had known.

3. The Judge rode slowly down the lane,
Smoothing his horse's chestnut mane:
He drew his bridle in the shade
Of the apple-trees to greet the maid;
And ask a draught from the spring that flowed,
Through the meadow, across the road.

4. She stooped where the cool spring bubbled up,
And filled for him her small tin cup,

And blushed as she gave it, looking down
On her feet so bare, and her tattered gown.
"Thanks!" said the Judge, "a sweeter draught
From a fairer hand was never quaffed."

5. He spoke of the grass, and flowers, and trees,
Of the singing birds and the humming bees;
Then talked of the haying, and wondered whether
The cloud in the west would bring foul weather.
And Maud forgot her brier-torn gown,
And her graceful ankles bare and brown,
And listened, while a pleased surprise
Looked from her long-lashed hazel eyes.

6. At last, like one who for delay
Seeks a vain excuse, he rode away.
Maud Muller looked and sighed: "Ah, me!
That I the Judge's bride might be!
He would dress me up in silks so fine,
And praise and toast me at his wine.

7. "My father should wear a broadcloth coat;
My brother should sail a painted boat;
I'd dress my mother so grand and gay,
And the baby should have a new toy each day;
And I'd feed the hungry and clothe the poor,
And all should bless me who left our door."

8. The Judge looked back as he climbed the hill,
And saw Maud Muller standing still.
"A form more fair, a face more sweet,
Ne'er has it been my lot to meet;
And her modest answer and graceful air
Show her wise and good as she is fair.

9. "Would she were mine, and I to-day,
Like her, a harvester of hay:
No doubtful balance of rights and wrongs,
Nor weary lawyers with endless tongues;
But low of cattle, and song of birds,
And health, and quiet, and loving words."

5th Rd. 25

10. But he thought of his sisters, proud and cold,
And his mother, vain of her rank and gold;
So, closing his heart, the Judge rode on,
And Maud was left in the field alone:
But the lawyers smiled that afternoon,
When he hummed in court an old love-tune;
And the young girl mused beside the well,
Till the rain on the unraked clover fell.

11. He wedded a wife of richest dower,
Who lived for fashion, as he for power;
Yet oft, in his marble hearth's bright glow,
He watched a picture come and go;
And sweet Maud Muller's hazel eyes,
Looked out in their innocent surprise.

12. Oft, when the wine in his glass was red,
He longed for the wayside well instead;
And closed his eyes on his garnished rooms,
To dream of meadows and clover-blooms.
And the proud man sighed, with secret pain,
"Ah, that I were free again!
Free as when I rode that day,
Where the barefoot maiden raked her hay."

13. She wedded a man unlearned and poor,
And many children played round her door;
But care and sorrow and wasting pain
Left their traces on heart and brain.
And oft, when the summer sun shone hot,
On the new-mown hay in the meadow lot,
And she heard the little spring brook fall
Over the roadside, through the wall,
In the shade of the apple-tree again,
She saw a rider draw his rein,
And gazing down with timid grace,
She felt his pleased eyes read her face.

14. Sometimes her narrow kitchen walls
Stretched away into stately halls;
The weary wheel to a spinet turned;
The tallow candle an astral burned;

"Maud Miller" was a popular poem in the nineteenth century with its sad narrative of a love that might have been; yet it appeared only in the 1866 Fifth Reader. Why it was deleted in following editions is now impossible to determine, but there may be a clue in the fact that—as vague and innocuous as the poem appears to twentieth-century readers—this love story is more suggestive of physical attractions between the sexes than any other passage in the McGuffeys.

And for him who sat by the chimney lug,
Dozing and grumbling o'er pipe and mug,
A manly form at her side she saw,
And joy was duty, and love was law:
Then she took up her burden of life again,
Saying only, "It might have been!"

15. Alas for maiden, alas for Judge,
For rich repiner and household drudge!
God pity them both! and pity us all,
Who vainly the dreams of youth recall;
For of all sad words of tongue or pen,
The saddest are these: "It might have been!"
Ah, well! for us all some sweet hope lies
Deeply buried from human eyes;
And in the hereafter, angels may
Roll the stone from its grave away!

ROCK ME TO SLEEP.

1. Backward, turn backward, O Time, in your flight!
Make me a child again, just for to-night!
Mother, come back from the echoless shore;
Take me again to your arms as of yore;
Kiss from my forehead the furrows of care;
Smooth the few silver threads out of my hair;
Over my slumbers your loving watch keep;
Rock me to sleep, mother, rock me to sleep!

2. Backward, flow backward, O tide of years!
I am so weary of toils and of tears;
Toils without recompense, tears all in vain;
Take them, and give me my childhood again!
I have grown weary of dust and decay,
Weary of flinging my soul-wealth away;
Weary of sowing for others to reap;
Rock me to sleep, mother, rock me to sleep!

3. Tired of the hollow, the base, the untrue;
Mother, O mother, my heart calls for you!

"Rock Me to Sleep" was written by a woman known usually as Elizabeth Akers Allen (1832–1911). Her maiden name was Chase, but most of her early verse was published under the pseudonym of Florence Percy. Her first marriage, to a man named Taylor, ended shortly after in divorce; her next marriage (to the sculptor Benjamin Paul Akers) lasted only a year before he died. Several years later, when she was still under thirty, she married E. M. Allen, a New York merchant.

When "Rock Me to Sleep" first appeared in an 1860 Saturday Evening Post, it gained such instant popularity that within a very short time there were five different people attempting to claim authorship. The dispute lasted several years, but our Elizabeth of many names emerged triumphant—with all the facts established in the May 27, 1867, New York Times. The poem appeared in her second volume, entitled simply Poems, in 1866—the same year that it first entered the McGuffeys. Its popularity continued throughout the century: it was set to music more than thirty times and included in all subsequent editions of the McGuffeys.

Among Mrs. Allen's later volumes of verse are The Silver Bridge (1866); The High Top Sweeting (1891); and The Sunset Song and Other Verses (1902). Although much of her verse—as here—suffers from an overdose of schmaltz, she must have been a fascinating person. Later in life, she offered the following views:

I believe in labor as a saving grace, in equal rights and equal morals for men and women, in the right of women to decline marriage without being killed or ridiculed for it, in the abolition of wife-beating, drunkenness, political corruption, gambling, and custom-houses, and in the prevention of cruelty to all creatures, dumb and otherwise.

Many a summer the grass has grown green,
Blossomed and faded, our faces between;
Yet with strong yearnings and passionate pain,
Long I to-night for your presence again;
Come from the silence so long and so deep!
Rock me to sleep, mother, rock me to sleep!

4. Over my heart in the days that are flown,
No love like a mother's love ever has shone
No other worship abides and endures,
Faithful, unselfish, and patient like yours:
None like a mother can charm away pain
From the sick soul, and the world-weary brain;
Slumber's soft calm o'er my heavy lids creep;
Rock me to sleep, mother, rock me to sleep!

5. Come, let your brown hair, just lighted with gold,
Fall on your shoulders again, as of old;
Let it fall over my forehead to-night,
Shielding my faint eyes away from the light;
For with its sunny-edged shadows once more,
Haply will throng the sweet visions of yore:
Lovingly, softly, its bright billows sweep;
Rock me to sleep, mother, rock me to sleep!

6. Mother, dear mother! the years have been long
Since I last hushed to your lullaby song;
Sing, then, and unto my soul it shall seem
Womanhood's years have been but a dream;
Clapsed to your arms in a loving embrace,
With your long lashes just sweeping my face,
Never hereafter to wake or to weep;
Rock me to sleep, mother, rock me to sleep!

EXERCISES.—Who was Maud Muller? What did the Judge say as he drank the cool spring water? Why did Maud wish to be the Judge's bride? What were the Judge's thoughts as he climbed the hill? Are the hopes of youth often realized in after life? What is the moral of this poem?

Repeat the first stanza of the second poem. Why did the poet wish to be a child again? What does the poem say of a mother's love? Repeat the last stanza.

LESSON XCIII.

1. LE′GION; *n.* division of an army.
2. CORSE; *n.* a dead body.
2. HOARD; *n.* what is laid up.
5. CO′QUET-RY; *n.* trifling in love.
5. CHO′RUS; *n.* music in which all join.
6. YORE; *adv.* old times.

The word BINGEN is pronounced *Bing′en*; not *Bin′gen*, or *Bin′jen*.

THE SOLDIER OF THE RHINE.

1. A SOLDIER of the Legion lay dying in Algiers,
There was lack of woman's nursing, there was †dearth of woman's tears,
But a comrade stood beside him, while the life-blood ebbed away,
And bent with pitying glances to hear what he might say.
The dying soldier faltered, as he took that comrade's hand,
And he said: "I never more shall see my own, my native land!
Take a message and a token to some distant friends of mine,
For I was born at BINGEN, at Bingen on the Rhine!

2. "Tell my brothers and companions, when they meet and crowd around,
To hear my mournful story, in the pleasant †vineyard ground,
That we fought the battle bravely, and when the day was done,
Full many a corse lay ghastly pale, beneath the setting sun;
And 'mid the dead and dying, were some grown old in wars,
The death-wound on their gallant breasts, the last of many scars!
But some were young, and suddenly beheld Life's morn decline,
And *one* had come from Bingen, fair Bingen on the Rhine!

3. "Tell my mother that her other sons shall comfort her old age,
For I was aye a truant bird, that thought his home a cage;
For my father was a soldier, and, even when a child,
My heart leaped forth to hear him tell of struggles fierce and wild;
And when he died, and left us to divide his †scanty hoard,
I let them take whate'er they would, but kept my father's sword!
And with boyish love I hung it where the bright light used to shine,
On the cottage wall at Bingen, calm Bingen on the Rhine!

THIS IS THE POEM RECALLED BY A CHARACTER IN STEPHEN CRANE'S famous short story "The Open Boat" (1897), in which four ship-wrecked men face the likelihood of their deaths:

To chime the notes of his emotion, a verse mysteriously entered the correspondent's head. He had even forgotten that he had forgotten this verse, but it suddenly was in his mind. . . . In his childhood the correspondent had been made acquainted with the fact that a soldier of the Legion lay dying in Algiers, but he had never regarded the fact as important. Myriads of his schoolfellows had informed him of the soldier's plight, but the dinning had naturally ended by making him perfectly indifferent. He had never considered it his affair that a soldier of the Legion lay dying in Algiers, nor had it appeared to him as a matter of sorrow. It was less to him than the breaking of a pencil's point.

Now, however, it quaintly came to him as a human, living thing. It was no longer merely a picture of a few throes in the breast of a poet, meanwhile drinking tea and warming his feet at the grate; it was an actuality—stern, mournful, and fine.

The correspondent . . . was moved by a profound and perfectly impersonal comprehension. He was sorry for the soldier of the Legion who lay dying in Algiers.

The author of this popular verse was Caroline Elizabeth Sarah Sheridan Norton (1808–1877), English poet and novelist, granddaughter of the dramatist Richard Brinsley Sheridan. Married to George Chapple Norton when she was only fifteen, she gained a divorce after his 1836 lawsuit against the Viscount Melbourne (charging the Viscount of criminal correspondence with Caroline). This famous lawsuit, in which she was totally vindicated, served as Charles Dickens' model for "Bardell vs. Pickwick" in The Pickwick Papers.

Of Mrs. Norton's many books (including verse, fiction, and works advocating social reform), her most influential was English Laws for English Women of the Nineteenth Century. Generated by her own experiences in the break with Norton (who claimed not only custody of the children, but also the income from her writings!), the pamphlet eventually led to some changes in British women's legal rights. But her most popular poem continued to be "The Soldier of the Rhine," which has been included in the Fifth Reader since 1857.

4. "Tell my sister not to weep for me, and sob with drooping head,
When the troops come marching home again, with glad and
⁺gallant tread;
But to look upon them proudly, with a calm and steadfast eye,
For her brother was a soldier, too, and not afraid to die!
And if a comrade seek her love, I ask her in my name
To listen to him kindly, without ⁺regret or shame;
And to hang the old sword in its place, (my father's sword and
mine,)
For the honor of old Bingen, dear Bingen on the Rhine!

5. "There's another, not a sister; in happy days gone by,
You'd have known her by the ⁺merriment that sparkled in
her eye;
Too innocent for coquetry, too fond for idle ⁺scorning,
O! friend, I fear the lightest heart makes sometimes heaviest
mourning!
Tell her the last night of my life—(for, ere the moon be risen,
My body will be out of pain, my soul be out of prison),
I dreamed I stood with her, and saw the yellow sunlight shine
On the vine-clad hills of Bingen, fair Bingen on the Rhine!

6. "I saw the blue Rhine sweep along: I heard, or seemed to hear,
The German songs we used to sing, in chorus sweet and clear;
And down the pleasant river, and up the slanting hill,
The ⁺echoing chorus sounded, through the evening calm and
still;
And her glad blue eyes were on me, as we passed with friendly
talk,
Down many a path beloved of yore, and well-remembered walk;
And her little hand lay lightly, ⁺confidingly in mine;
But we'll meet no more at Bingen, loved Bingen on the Rhine!"

7. His voice grew faint and hoarser, his grasp was childish weak,
His eyes put on a dying look, he sighed and ceased to speak;
His comrade bent to lift him, but the spark of life had fled,
The soldier of the Legion, in a foreign land, was dead!
And the soft moon rose up slowly, and calmly she looked down
On the red sand of the battle-field, with bloody corpses strewn!
Yes, calmly on that dreadful scene, her pale light seemed to
shine,
As it shone on distant Bingen, fair Bingen on the Rhine.

I. THE GOOD READER.

1. It is told of Frederick the Great, King of Prussia, that, as he was seated one day in his private room, a written petition was brought to him with the request that it should be immediately read. The King had just re-

(39)

stressed in the McGuffeys, *often—as here—in fictionalized form depicting the problems of those who cannot read. In an earlier* Reader, *for instance, the plight of a man is described who took the wrong turn at a crossroads and subjected himself to pain and inconvenience—all because he could not read. Here the page boys illustrate a number of the errors in articulation and delivery that the* McGuffeys— *particularly the* Fifth *and* Sixth Readers—*sought to eliminate. However, earlier lessons like "On Elocution and Reading" (first used in the 1837* Fourth Reader*) emphasize the need for reading skills on more practical grounds. Arguing that reading should "occupy* three-fold more time *than it does," that lesson states pointedly: "We would rather have a child, even of the other sex,* return to us from school a first-rate reader, than a first-rate performer on the pianoforte [italics added]."*

---

turned from hunting, and the glare of the sun, or some other cause, had so dazzled his eyes that he found it difficult to make out a single word of the writing.

2. His private secretary happened to be absent; and the soldier who brought the petition could not read. There was a page, or favorite boy servant, waiting in the hall, and upon him the King called. The page was a son of one of the noblemen of the court, but proved to be a very poor reader.

3. In the first place, he did not articulate distinctly. He huddled his words together in the utterance, as if they were syllables of one long word, which he must get through with as speedily as possible. His pronunciation was bad, and he did not modulate his voice so as to bring out the meaning of what he read. Every sentence was uttered with a dismal monotony of voice, as if it did not differ in any respect from that which preceded it.

4. "Stop!" said the King, impatiently. "Is it an auctioneer's list of goods to be sold that you are hurrying over? Send your companion to me." Another page who stood at the door now entered, and to him the King gave the petition. The second page began by hemming and clearing his throat in such an affected manner that the King jokingly asked him whether he had not slept in the public garden, with the gate open, the night before.

5. The second page had a good share of self-conceit, however, and so was not greatly confused by the King's jest. He determined that he would avoid the mistake which his comrade had made. So he commenced reading the petition slowly and with great formality, emphasizing every word, and prolonging the articulation of every syllable. But his manner was so tedious that the King cried out, "Stop! are you reciting a lesson in the elementary sounds? Out of the room! But no: stay! Send me that little girl who is sitting there by the fountain."

6. The girl thus pointed out by the King was a daughter

of one of the laborers employed by the royal gardener; and she had come to help her father weed the flower beds. It chanced that, like many of the poor people in Prussia, she had received a good education. She was somewhat alarmed when she found herself in the King's presence, but took courage when the King told her that he only wanted her to read for him, as his eyes were weak.

7. Now, Ernestine (for this was the name of the little girl) was fond of reading aloud, and often many of the neighbors would assemble at her father's house to hear her; those who could not read themselves would come to her, also, with their letters from distant friends or children, and she thus formed the habit of reading various sorts of handwriting promptly and well.

8. The King gave her the petition, and she rapidly glanced through the opening lines to get some idea of what it was about. As she read, her eyes began to glisten, and her breast to heave. "What is the matter?" asked the King; "don't you know how to read?" "Oh, yes! sire," she replied, addressing him with the title usually applied to him: "I will now read it, if you please."

9. The two pages were about to leave the room. "Remain," said the King. The little girl began to read the petition. It was from a poor widow, whose only son had been drafted to serve in the army, although his health was delicate and his pursuits had been such as to unfit him for military life. His father had been killed in battle, and the son had a strong desire to become a portrait painter.

10. The writer told her story in a simple, concise manner, that carried to the heart a belief of its truth; and Ernestine read it with so much feeling, and with an articulation so just, in tones so pure and distinct, that when she had finished, the King, into whose eyes the tears had started, exclaimed, "Oh! now I understand what it is all about; but I might never have known, certainly I never should have felt, its meaning had I trusted to these young

The inclusion of the more sentimental subplot (the widow's plight) marks this as a later arrival into the McGuffeys (a part of the Fifth Reader only since 1857). Ernestine's instant and magnificent reward, however, is very much in keeping with the pattern established in earlier selections made by McGuffey himself. Perhaps the chief difference between this lesson and those of the earliest editions is seen in the subsequent rise to distinction by the errant pages; William Holmes McGuffey would almost certainly have eliminated any second chance, and might well have described them as doomed to disgrace for their incompetence.

gentlemen, whom I now dismiss from my service for one year, advising them to occupy their time in learning to read."

11. "As for you, my young lady," continued the King, "I know you will ask no better reward for your trouble than the pleasure of carrying to this poor widow my order for her son's immediate discharge. Let me see whether you can write as well as you can read. Take this pen, and write as I dictate." He then dictated an order, which Ernestine wrote, and he signed. Calling one of his guards, he bade him go with the girl and see that the order was obeyed.

12. How much happiness was Ernestine the means of bestowing through her good elocution, united to the happy circumstance that brought it to the knowledge of the King! First, there were her poor neighbors, to whom she could give instruction and entertainment. Then, there was the poor widow who sent the petition, and who not only regained her son, but received through Ernestine an order for him to paint the King's likeness; so that the poor boy soon rose to great distinction, and had more orders than he could attend to. Words could not express his gratitude, and that of his mother, to the little girl.

13. And Ernestine had, moreover, the satisfaction of aiding her father to rise in the world, so that he became the King's chief gardener. The King did not forget her, but had her well educated at his own expense. As for the two pages, she was indirectly the means of doing them good, also; for, ashamed of their bad reading, they commenced studying in earnest, till they overcame the faults that had offended the King. Both finally rose to distinction, one as a lawyer, and the other as a statesman; and they owed their advancement in life chiefly to their good elocution.

DEFINITIONS.—1. Pe-ti′tion, *a formal request.* 3. Ar-tĭe′u-lāte, *to utter the elementary sounds.* Mŏd′u-lāte, *to vary or inflect.* Mo-nŏt′o-ny, *lack of variety.* 4. Af-fēet′ed, *unnatural and silly.*

IV. THE GRANDFATHER.

Charles G. Eastman (*b.* 1816, *d.* 1861) was born in Maine, but removed at an early age to Vermont, where he was connected with the press at Burlington, Woodstock, and Montpelier. He published a volume of poems in 1848, written in a happy lyric and ballad style, and faithfully portraying rural life in New England.

1. The farmer sat in his easy-chair
   Smoking his pipe of clay,
While his hale old wife with busy care,
   Was clearing the dinner away;
A sweet little girl with fine blue eyes,
On her grandfather's knee, was catching flies.

2. The old man laid his hand on her head,
   With a tear on his wrinkled face,
He thought how often her mother, dead,
   Had sat in the selfsame place;
As the tear stole down from his half-shut eye,
"Don't smoke!" said the child, "how it makes you cry!"

3. The house dog lay stretched out on the floor,
   Where the shade, afternoons, used to steal;
The busy old wife by the open door
   Was turning the spinning wheel,
And the old brass clock on the manteltree
Had plodded along to almost three.

4. Still the farmer sat in his easy-chair,
   While close to his heaving breast
The moistened brow and the cheek so fair
   Of his sweet grandchild were pressed;
His head bent down, on her soft hair lay;
Fast asleep were they both on that summer day.

DEFINITIONS. — 1. Hāle, *healthy.* 3. Măn′tel-tree, *shelf over a fireplace.* Plŏd′ded, *went slowly.* 4. Hēav′ing, *rising and falling.*
(5.—4.)

SOMETIMES DESCRIBED BY HIS CONTEMPORARIES AS THE "BURNS OF the Green Mountains," Charles Eastman's single volume contained a number of verses that were popular in the mid- and late 1800's. In addition to "The Grandfather," the most successful were "The Pauper's Burial" and "Come, Sing Me the Song That You Sang Years Ago." His other major contribution to the times was his zealous but unsuccessful attempt to build up the Democratic Party in Vermont, but such information was—not surprisingly—not included in the **McGuffey** *note. "The Grandfather" first appeared in the 1857* **Fifth Reader** *and has occupied a slot at that level ever since, although no authorial attribution appeared until 1879.*

THE AUTHOR'S NOTE FURNISHED (IN THIS REPRODUCTION FROM THE 1920 edition) was left unchanged from the 1879 edition, despite the fact that it fails to mention any of Warner's later works or even his death in 1900. An editor of Harper's Magazine *from 1884 until shortly before his death, Warner led an active literary career, publishing several novels, many travel books, and biographies of Captain John Smith and Washington Irving—plus several collections of essays in addition to those mentioned in the note here.*

His name is remembered today chiefly because he collaborated with his friend Mark Twain (Samuel Clemens) in writing a novel The Gilded Age *(1873). The book itself is seldom read now, but the title has survived to become a label often used to describe the whole era. (Mark Twain, incidentally, was never included in the* McGuffeys, *although he was definitely well known enough to suggest that the omission was a conscious one.)*

V. A BOY ON A FARM.

Charles Dudley Warner (*b.* 1829, ———) was born at Plainfield, Mass. In 1851 he graduated at Hamilton College, and in 1856 was admitted to the bar at Philadelphia, but moved to Chicago to practice his profession. There he remained until 1860, when he became connected with the press at Hartford, Conn., and has ever since devoted himself to literature. "My Summer in a Garden," "Saunterings," and "Backlog Studies" are his best known works. The following extract is from "Being a Boy."

1. SAY what you will about the general usefulness of boys, it is my impression that a farm without a boy would very soon come to grief. What the boy does is the life of the farm. He is the factotum, always in demand, always expected to do the thousand indispensable things that nobody else will do. Upon him fall all the odds and ends, the most difficult things.

2. After everybody else is through, he has to finish up. His work is like a woman's,—perpetually waiting on others. Everybody knows how much easier it is to eat a good dinner than it is to wash the dishes afterwards. Consider what a boy on a farm is required to do,—things that must be done, or life would actually stop.

3. It is understood, in the first place, that he is to do all the errands, to go to the store, to the post office, and to carry all sorts of messages. If he had as many legs as a centiped, they would tire before night. His two short limbs seem to him entirely inadequate to the task. He would like to have as many legs as a wheel has spokes, and rotate about in the same way.

4. This he sometimes tries to do; and the people who have seen him "turning cart wheels" along the side of the road, have supposed that he was amusing himself and idling his time; he was only trying to invent a new mode of locomotion, so that he could economize his legs, and do his errands with greater dispatch.

5. He practices standing on his head, in order to accustom himself to any position. Leapfrog is one of his

methods of getting over the ground quickly. He would willingly go an errand any distance if he could leapfrog it with a few other boys.

6. He has a natural genius for combining pleasure with business. This is the reason why, when he is sent to the spring for a pitcher of water, he is absent so long; for he stops to poke the frog that sits on the stone, or, if there is a penstock, to put his hand over the spout, and squirt the water a little while.

7. He is the one who spreads the grass when the men have cut it; he mows it away in the barn; he rides the horse, to cultivate the corn, up and down the hot, weary rows; he picks up the potatoes when they are dug; he drives the cows night and morning; he brings wood and water, and splits kindling; he gets up the horse, and puts out the horse; whether he is in the house or out of it, there is always something for him to do.

8. Just before the school in winter he shovels paths; in summer he turns the grindstone. He knows where there are lots of wintergreens and sweet flags, but instead of going for them, he is to stay indoors and pare apples, and stone raisins, and pound something in a mortar. And yet, with his mind full of schemes of what he would like to do, and his hands full of occupations, he is an idle boy, who has nothing to busy himself with but school and chores!

9. He would gladly do all the work if somebody else would do the chores, he thinks; and yet I doubt if any boy ever amounted to anything in the world, or was of much use as a man, who did not enjoy the advantages of a liberal education in the way of chores.

DEFINITIONS. — 1. Fac-tō'tum, *a person employed to do all kinds of work.* In-dis-pĕn'sa-ble, *absolutely necessary.* 2. Per-pĕt'u-al-ly, *continually.* 3. Cĕn'ti-pĕd, *an insect with a great number of feet.* 4. E-cŏn'o-mīze, *to save.* Dis-pătch', *diligence, haste.* 6. Pĕn'-stŏck, *a wooden tube for conducting water.* 8. Chōreș, *the light work of the household either within or without doors.*

The London Spectator *characterized Warner's work as follows: "Banter and paradox, always handled with cleverness and subtlety; an active fancy that sometimes rises into imagination or pathos, irony that is never bitter, and sarcasm that is never savage: these, and with them what we might call scorn—if scorn were not most ungentle—of all that is uncultured, of shoddy aristocrats,* nouveux riches *and the like." Add to that a tendency toward nostalgia, such as that displayed in this lesson, but it is largely redeemed here by a humorous tone. The emphasis on the importance of chores made this an almost automatic selection for the McGuffeys, and it has been part of both the 1879 and 1920 editions.*

VIII. WORK.

Eliza Cook (*b.* 1817, *d.* 1889) was born at London. In 1837 she commenced contributing to periodicals. In 1840 the first collection of her poems was made. In 1849 she became editor of "Eliza Cook's Journal."

1. WORK, work, my boy, be not afraid;
    Look labor boldly in the face;
   Take up the hammer or the spade,
    And blush not for your humble place.

2. There's glory in the shuttle's song;
    There's triumph in the anvil's stroke;
   There's merit in the brave and strong
    Who dig the mine or fell the oak.

3. The wind disturbs the sleeping lake,
    And bids it ripple pure and fresh;
   It moves the green boughs till they make
    Grand music in their leafy mesh.

4. And so the active breath of life
    Should stir our dull and sluggard wills;
   For are we not created rife
    With health, that stagnant torpor kills?

5. I doubt if he who lolls his head
    Where idleness and plenty meet,
   Enjoys his pillow or his bread
    As those who earn the meals they eat.

6. And man is never half so blest
    As when the busy day is spent
   So as to make his evening rest
    A holiday of glad content.

DEFINITIONS.—3. Měsh, *network.* 4. Rīfe, *abounding.* Stăg′nant, *inactive.* Tôr′por, *laziness, stupidity.* 5. Lŏlls, *reclines, leans.*

VERSIFIED HOMILIES SUCH AS THIS APPEAR WITH REGULARITY throughout the Readers, *especially in the lower levels. Among the better known examples not included in this collection are T. H. Palmer's "Try, Try Again" and a single verse from Isaac Watt's "How doth the little busy bee/Improve each shining hour," which originally appeared in the* Primer, *but by 1879 had graduated to the* Second Reader.

XIII. RESPECT FOR THE SABBATH REWARDED.

1. In the city of Bath, not many years since, lived a barber who made a practice of following his ordinary occupation on the Lord's day. As he was on the way to his morning's employment, he happened to look into some place of worship just as the minister was giving out his text — "Remember the Sabbath day, to keep it holy." He listened long enough to be convinced that he was constantly breaking the laws of God and man by shaving and dressing his customers on the Lord's day. He became uneasy, and went with a heavy heart to his Sabbath task.

2. At length he took courage, and opened his mind to his minister, who advised him to give up Sabbath work, and worship God. He replied that beggary would be the consequence. He had a flourishing trade, but it would almost all be lost. At length, after many a sleepless night spent in weeping and praying, he was determined to cast all his care upon God, as the more he reflected, the more his duty became apparent.

3. He discontinued his Sabbath work, went constantly and early to the public services of religion, and soon enjoyed that satisfaction of mind which is one of the rewards of doing our duty, and that peace which the world can neither give nor take away. The consequences he foresaw actually followed. His genteel customers left him, and he was nicknamed " Puritan " or " Methodist." He was obliged to give up his fashionable shop, and, in the course of years, became so reduced as to take a cellar under the old market house and shave the poorer people.

4. One Saturday evening, between light and dark, a stranger from one of the coaches, asking for a barber, was directed by the hostler to the cellar opposite. Coming in hastily, he requested to be shaved quickly, while they changed horses, as he did not like to violate the Sabbath.

THIS SELECTION, ATTRIBUTED ONLY TO "EDINBURGH PAPER" WHEN IT *first appeared in the 1844* Fourth Reader, *has been located in the* Fifth Reader *in all editions since 1857. No specific attribution was ever given, and eventually even the vague indication of its source went unmentioned.*

Although this religious exemplum is supposedly based on fact, it has an aura of wishful romance and contains such incredible coincidences as to raise reasonable doubts. Even if it is totally fictionalized, however, the tale fits well into the rags-to-riches formula of many early McGuffey lessons—yet another anticipation of the tales of Horatio Alger, Jr.

This was touching the barber on a tender chord. He burst into tears; asked the stranger to lend him a half-penny to buy a candle, as it was not light enough to shave him with safety. He did so, revolving in his mind the extreme poverty to which the poor man must be reduced.

5. When shaved, he said, "There must be something extraordinary in your history, which I have not now time to hear. Here is half a crown for you. When I return, I will call and investigate your case. What is your name?" "William Reed," said the astonished barber. "William Reed?" echoed the stranger: "William Reed? by your dialect you are from the West." "Yes, sir, from Kingston, near Taunton." "William Reed from Kingston, near Taunton? What was your father's name?" "Thomas." "Had he any brother?" "Yes, sir, one, after whom I was named; but he went to the Indies, and, as we never heard from him, we supposed him to be dead."

6. "Come along, follow me," said the stranger, "I am going to see a person who says his name is William Reed, of Kingston, near Taunton. Come and confront him. If you prove to be indeed he who you say you are, I have glorious news for you. Your uncle is dead, and has left an immense fortune, which I will put you in possession of when all legal doubts are removed."

7. They went by the coach; saw the pretended William Reed, and proved him to be an impostor. The stranger, who was a pious attorney, was soon legally satisfied of the barber's identity, and told him that he had advertised him in vain. Providence had now thrown him in his way in a most extraordinary manner, and he had great pleasure in transferring a great many thousand pounds to a worthy man, the rightful heir of the property. Thus was man's extremity God's opportunity. Had the poor barber possessed one half-penny, or even had credit for a candle, he might have remained unknown for years; but he trusted God, who never said, "Seek ye my face," in vain.

XIX. HOW TO TELL BAD NEWS.

Mr. H. and the Steward.

Mr. H. HA! Steward, how are you, my old boy? How do things go on at home?

Steward. Bad enough, your honor; the magpie's dead.

H. Poor Mag! So he's gone. How came he to die?

S. Overeat himself, sir.

H. Did he? A greedy dog; why, what did he get he liked so well?

S. Horseflesh, sir; he died of eating horseflesh.

H. How came he to get so much horseflesh?

S. All your father's horses, sir.

H. What! are they dead, too?

S. Ay, sir; they died of overwork.

H. And why were they overworked, pray?

S. To carry water, sir.

H. To carry water! and what were they carrying water for?

S. Sure, sir, to put out the fire.

H. Fire! what fire?

S. O, sir, your father's house is burned to the ground.

H. My father's house burned down! and how came it set on fire?

S. I think, sir, it must have been the torches.

H. Torches! what torches?

S. At your mother's funeral.

H. My mother dead!

S. Ah, poor lady! she never looked up, after it.

H. After what?

S. The loss of your father.

H. My father gone, too?

S. Yes, poor gentleman! he took to his bed as soon as he heard of it.

(5.—6.)

FARCE HAS BEEN AROUND A LONG TIME, ALTHOUGH ITS GENEALOGY has been less carefully recorded than those of tragedy and high comedy. Certainly elements of farce were very much a part of frontier humor, but even if William Holmes McGuffey had appreciated such comedy (and all indications argue the contrary), he definitely did not think they belonged in his Readers. *"How to Tell Bad News" is one of the funniest passages in the* McGuffeys, *but it has been included only since 1879.*

H. Heard of what?

S. The bad news, sir, and please your honor.

H. What! more miseries! more bad news!

S. Yes, sir; your bank has failed, and your credit is lost, and you are not worth a shilling in the world. I made bold, sir, to wait on you about it, for I thought you would like to hear the news.

XX. THE BATTLE OF BLENHEIM.

Robert Southey (*b.* 1774, *d.* 1843) was born in Bristol, England. He entered Balliol College, Oxford, in 1793. In 1804 he established himself permanently at Greta Hall, near Keswick, Cumberland, in the "Lake Country," where he enjoyed the friendship and society of Wordsworth and Coleridge, other poets of the "Lake School." He was appointed poet laureate in 1813, and received a pension of £300 a year from the government in 1835. Mr. Southey was a voluminous writer in both prose and verse. As a poet, he can not be placed in the first rank, although some of his minor poems are very happy in thought and expression. Among his most noted poetical works are "Joan of Arc," "Thalaba the Destroyer," "Madoc," "Roderick," and the "Curse of Kehama."

1. It was a summer evening,
   Old Kaspar's work was done,
   And he, before his cottage door,
   Was sitting in the sun;
   And by him sported on the green,
   His little grandchild Wilhelmine.

2. She saw her brother Peterkin
   Roll something large and round,
   Which he beside the rivulet,
   In playing there, had found;
   He came to ask what he had found,
   That was so large, and smooth, and round.

The practice of furnishing biographical notes on authors was not introduced in the Readers until 1879. Prior to that, many lessons were casually or even perhaps deliberately (because of copyright infringements) allowed to stand unattributed. One reason for the change in policy was that the new Appleton Readers were doing it—and they were offering the strongest competition the McGuffey Readers had faced in years. Another reason, however, was that the teachers apparently wanted such notes. They provided some good, tough facts for objective testing. Moreover, such notes (like this) were sometimes gossipy in tone and thereby provided a comfortable escape from dealing with the poem itself. In fact, the graphic placement of the biographical material before the literary selection too often came to represent the emphasis each received. In time this led to the "New Critics," who called for decreased emphasis on the biographies of authors and a closer, almost exclusive attention to the works of literature.

3. Old Kaspar took it from the boy,
    Who stood expectant by;
And then the old man shook his head,
    And, with a natural sigh,
"'T is some poor fellow's skull," said he,
"Who fell in the great victory.

4. "I find them in the garden,
    For there's many hereabout;
And often when I go to plow,
    The plowshare turns them out;
For many thousand men," said he,
"Were slain in that great victory."

5. "Now tell us what 't was all about,"
    Young Peterkin he cries;
While little Wilhelmine looks up
    With wonder-waiting eyes;
"Now tell us all about the war,
And what they killed each other for."

6. "It was the English," Kaspar cried,
    "Who put the French to rout,
But what they killed each other for,
    I could not well make out;
But everybody said," quoth he,
"That 't was a famous victory:

7. "My father lived at Blenheim then,
    Yon little stream, hard by;
They burnt his dwelling to the ground,
    And he was forced to fly;
So, with his wife and child he fled,
Nor had he where to rest his head.

Southey's "Battle of Blenheim" was such a popular poem in the nineteenth century that it probably would have been included in the McGuffeys even if it hadn't illustrated so memorably the futility of war. That, however, insured its inclusion: first in the 1844 Fifth Reader, *then in the 1857 and 1866 editions of the* Sixth, *and finally back to the* Fifth Reader *for both the 1879 and 1920 editions.*

Such descriptions as the "many thousand bodies . . .
rotting in the sun" are seldom part of the happier world pictured
in the typical textbooks of the early and mid-twentieth
century. Southey's poem is quite mild, however, compared
with some anti-war selections in earlier McGuffey Readers.
One such selection, "The Field of Waterloo" by Lady Morgan,
appeared in the 1837 Fourth Reader with the following
macabre description:

I could mark with my eye, the spots where the most
desperate carnage had been. The bodies had been
heaped together, and scarcely more than covered: and so
enriched is the soil, that, in these spots, the grain never
ripens. It grows rank and green to the end of harvest.

8. "With fire and sword, the country round
    Was wasted, far and wide;
And many a nursing mother then,
    And newborn baby died;
But things like that, you know, must be
At every famous victory.

9. "They say it was a shocking sight
    After the field was won;
For many thousand bodies here
    Lay rotting in the sun:
But things like that, you know, must be
After a famous victory.

10. "Great praise the Duke of Marlboro' won,
    And our young prince, Eugene."
"Why, 't was a very wicked thing!"
    Said little Wilhelmine.
"Nay, nay, my little girl!" quoth he,
"It was a famous victory.

11. "And everybody praised the Duke
    Who this great fight did win."
"But what good came of it at last?"
    Quoth little Peterkin.
"Why, that I can not tell," said he,
"But 't was a glorious victory."

NOTES. — The Battle of Blenheim, in the "War of the Spanish
Succession," was fought August 13, 1704, near Blenheim, in
Bavaria, between the French and Bavarians, on one side, and
an allied army under the great English general, the Duke of
Marlborough, and Eugene, Prince of Savoy, on the other. The
latter won a decisive victory: 10,000 of the defeated army were
killed and wounded, and 13,000 were taken prisoners.

XXI. "I PITY THEM."

1. A POOR man once undertook to emigrate from Castine, Me., to Illinois. When he was attempting to cross a river in New York, his horse broke through the rotten timbers of the bridge, and was drowned. He had but this one animal to convey all his property and his family to his new home.

2. His wife and children were almost miraculously saved from sharing the fate of the horse; but the loss of this poor animal was enough. By its aid the family, it may be said, had lived and moved; now they were left helpless in a land of strangers, without the ability to go on or return, without money or a single friend to whom to appeal. The case was a hard one.

3. There were a great many who "passed by on the other side." Some even laughed at the predicament in which the man was placed; but by degrees a group of people began to collect, all of whom pitied him.

4. Some pitied him a great deal, and some did not pity him very much, because, they said, he might have known better than to try to cross an unsafe bridge, and should have made his horse swim the river. Pity, however, seemed rather to predominate. Some pitied the man, and some the horse; all pitied the poor, sick mother and her six helpless children.

5. Among this pitying party was a rough son of the West, who knew what it was to migrate some hundreds of miles over new roads to locate a destitute family on a prairie. Seeing the man's forlorn situation, and looking around on the bystanders, he said, "All of you seem to pity these poor people very much, but I would beg leave to ask each of you how much."

6. "There, stranger," continued he, holding up a ten-dollar bill, "there is the amount of my pity; and if others

NEARLY ALL LESSONS PROJECTING ANY SUGGESTIONS OF REGIONAL prejudice were removed after the Civil War, largely because by then the McGuffey Readers were truly national in distribution. Occasionally, however, some mark of regional pride would slip back in, as it does here, with the "rough son of the West" teaching charity to the upstate New Yorkers. This lesson appears only in the 1879 and 1920 editions.

will do as I do, you may soon get another pony. God bless you." It is needless to state the effect that this active charity produced. In a short time the happy emigrant arrived at his destination, and he is now a thriving farmer, and a neighbor to him who was his "friend in need, and a friend indeed."

DEFINITIONS. — 1. Em′i-g̅rāte, *to remove from one country or state to another for the purpose of residence, to migrate.* 2. Mĭ-răc′u-loŭs-ly, *as if by miracle, wonderfully.* A-bĭl′i-ty, *power, capability.* 3. Pre-dĭc′a-ment, *condition, plight.* 4. Pre-dŏm′i-nāte, *to prevail, to rule.* 5. Lō′cāte, *to place.* Dĕs′ti-tūte, *needy, poor.* 6. Dĕs-ti-nā′tion, *end of a journey.* Thrĭv′ing, *prosperous through industry, economy, and good management.*

278

XXIX. THE TOWN PUMP.

Nathaniel Hawthorne (*b*. 1804, *d*. 1864) was born in Salem, Mass. He graduated at Bowdoin College in 1825. His earliest literary productions, written for periodicals, were published in two volumes — the first in 1837, the second in 1842 — under the title of "Twice-Told Tales." "Mosses from an Old Manse," another series of tales and sketches, was published in 1845. From 1846 to 1850 he was surveyor of the port of Salem. In 1852 he was appointed United States consul for Liverpool. After holding this office four years, he traveled for some time on the continent. His most popular works are "The Scarlet Letter," a work showing a deep knowledge of human nature, "The House of the Seven Gables," "The Blithedale Romance," and "The Marble Faun," an Italian romance, which is regarded by many as the best of his works. Being of a modest and retiring disposition, Mr. Hawthorne avoided publicity. Most of his works are highly imaginative. As a prose writer he has no superior among American authors. He died at Plymouth, N. H., while on a visit to the White Mountains for his health.

[SCENE. — *The corner of two principal streets. The Town Pump talking through its nose.*]

1. NOON, by the north clock! Noon, by the east! High noon, too, by those hot sunbeams which fall, scarcely aslope, upon my head, and almost make the water bubble and smoke in the trough under my nose. Truly, we public characters have a tough time of it! And among all the town officers, chosen at the yearly meeting, where is he that sustains, for a single year, the burden of such manifold duties as are imposed, in perpetuity, upon the Town Pump?

2. The title of town treasurer is rightfully mine, as guardian of the best treasure the town has. The overseers of the poor ought to make me their chairman, since I provide bountifully for the pauper, without expense to him that pays taxes. I am at the head of the fire department, and one of the physicians of the board of health. As a keeper of the peace, all water drinkers confess me equal to the constable. I perform some of the duties of the town clerk, by promulgating public notices, when they are pasted on my front.

THIS ALLEGORICAL TEMPERANCE LESSON ENTERED THE McGUFFEYS *IN the 1844* **Fourth Reader** *but has been located in the* **Fifth Reader** *since 1857. Although the biographical note was not furnished until later editions, the lesson itself was one of the earliest to carry a brief attribution and has always been acknowledged by the* **McGuffeys** *as Hawthorne's.*

3. To speak within bounds, I am chief person of the municipality, and exhibit, moreover, an admirable pattern to my brother officers by the cool, steady, upright, downright, and impartial discharge of my business, and the constancy with which I stand to my post. Summer or winter, nobody seeks me in vain; for all day long I am seen at the busiest corner, just above the market, stretching out my arms to rich and poor alike; and at night I hold a lantern over my head, to show where I am, and to keep people out of the gutters.

4. At this sultry noontide, I am cupbearer to the parched populace, for whose benefit an iron goblet is chained to my waist. Like a dramseller on the public square, on a muster day, I cry aloud to all and sundry, in my plainest accents, and at the very tiptop of my voice. "Here it is, gentlemen! Here is the good liquor! Walk up, walk up, gentlemen, walk up, walk up! Here is the superior stuff! Here is the unadulterated ale of father Adam! better than Cognac, Hollands, Jamaica, strong beer, or wine of any price; here it is, by the hogshead or the single glass, and not a cent to pay. Walk up, gentlemen, walk up and help yourselves!"

5. It were a pity if all this outcry should draw no customers. Here they come. A hot day, gentlemen. Quaff and away again, so as to keep yourselves in a nice, cool sweat. You, my friend, will need another cupful to wash the dust out of your throat, if it be as thick there as it is on your cowhide shoes. I see that you have trudged half a score of miles to-day, and, like a wise man, have passed by the taverns, and stopped at the running brooks and well curbs. Otherwise, betwixt heat without and fire within, you would have been burnt to a cinder, or melted down to nothing at all — in the fashion of a jellyfish.

6. Drink, and make room for that other fellow, who seeks my aid to quench the fiery fever of last night's potations, which he drained from no cup of mine. Welcome, most

rubicund sir! You and I have been strangers hitherto; nor, to confess the truth, will my nose be anxious for a closer intimacy, till the fumes of your breath be a little less potent.

The massive editorial revision of 1879 was prompted largely by the new Appleton Readers, *which contained many fine illustrations. The publishers of the* McGuffeys *followed suit— commissioning work for their new edition from the best-known artists and engravers of the time. Among those selected was the young Howard Pyle (1853–1911), whose work was already establishing a solid reputation. He contributed this illustration and one other for the new* Fifth Reader, *and a single one for the* Sixth.

Pyle combined writing with illustrating, doing both in such original works as Pepper and Salt, or Seasoning for Young Folks *(1885),* The Wonder Clock *(1887), and* A Modern Aladdin *(1891). Even more popular were his illustrated versions of* The Merry Adventures of Robin Hood *and* King Arthur and His Knights. *He became the most successful magazine illustrator of his time and is recognized today as one of America's most important and influential illustrators.*

By this point the governing intent of the tale is quite clearly in league with many of the vociferously anti-drinking lessons in the McGuffeys. It is, however, more humorously presented (at times the voice sounds forth like the nasal blare of W. C. Fields), and Hawthorne's general approach is clearly less evangelistic than the earlier temperance lessons with their dire threats. The 1836 First Reader, for instance, contained two temperance lessons. The first, "Don't Take Strong Drink," cited religious authority, as follows: "And oh, how dreadful to die a drunkard. The Bible says that no drunkard shall inherit the kingdom of heaven." The other, "The Whisky Boy," presented the horrifying object lesson of a lad whose father let him taste sugared whisky: "Before John was eight years old, he was a dreadful object . . . His eyes were red, and his face was red, and full of blisters. He was found drunk one day in the street, and carried to the poor house, where he died in two weeks."

7. Mercy on you, man! The water absolutely hisses down your red-hot gullet, and is converted quite into steam in the miniature Tophet, which you mistake for a stomach. Fill again, and tell me, on the word of an honest toper, did you ever, in cellar, tavern, or any other kind of dramshop, spend the price of your children's food for a swig half so delicious? Now, for the first time these ten years, you know the flavor of cold water. Good-by; and whenever you are thirsty, recollect that I keep a constant supply at the old stand.

8. Who next? Oh, my little friend, you are just let loose from school, and come hither to scrub your blooming face, and drown the memory of certain taps of the ferule, and other schoolboy troubles, in a draught from the Town Pump. Take it, pure as the current of your young life; take it, and may your heart and tongue never be scorched with a fiercer thirst than now.

9. There, my dear child, put down the cup, and yield your place to this elderly gentleman, who treads so tenderly over the paving stones that I suspect he is afraid of breaking them. What! he limps by without so much as thanking me, as if my hospitable offers were meant only for people who have no wine cellars.

10. Well, well, sir, no harm done, I hope! Go, draw the cork, tip the decanter; but when your great toe shall set you a-roaring, it will be no affair of mine. If gentlemen love the pleasant titillation of the gout, it is all one to the Town Pump. This thirsty dog, with his red tongue lolling out, does not scorn my hospitality, but stands on his hind legs, and laps eagerly out of the trough. See how lightly he capers away again! Jowler, did your worship ever have the gout?

11. Your pardon, good people! I must interrupt my stream of eloquence, and spout forth a stream of water to replenish the trough for this teamster and his two yoke of oxen, who have come all the way from Staunton, or

somewhere along that way. No part of my business gives me more pleasure than the watering of cattle. Look! how rapidly they lower the watermark on the sides of the trough, till their capacious stomachs are moistened with a gallon or two apiece, and they can afford time to breathe, with sighs of calm enjoyment! Now they roll their quiet eyes around the brim of their monstrous drinking vessel. An ox is your true toper.

12. I hold myself the grand reformer of the age. From my spout, and such spouts as mine, must flow the stream that shall cleanse our earth of a vast portion of its crime and anguish, which have gushed from the fiery fountains of the still. In this mighty enterprise, the cow shall be my great confederate. Milk and water!

13. Ahem! Dry work this speechifying, especially to all unpracticed orators. I never conceived till now what toil the temperance lecturers undergo for my sake. Do, some kind Christian, pump a stroke or two, just to wet my whistle. Thank you, sir. But to proceed.

14. The Town Pump and the Cow! Such is the glorious partnership that shall finally monopolize the whole business of quenching thirst. Blessed consummation! Then Poverty shall pass away from the land, finding no hovel so wretched where her squalid form may shelter itself. Then Disease, for lack of other victims, shall gnaw his own heart and die. Then Sin, if she do not die, shall lose half her strength.

15. Then there will be no war of households. The husband and the wife, drinking deep of peaceful joy, a calm bliss of temperate affections, shall pass hand in hand through life, and lie down, not reluctantly, at its protracted close. To them the past will be no turmoil of mad dreams, nor the future an eternity of such moments as follow the delirium of a drunkard. Their dead faces shall express what their spirits were, and are to be, by a lingering smile of memory and hope.

These hyperbolic flourishes in oratorical delivery almost suggest that Hawthorne is offering a parody of the temperance movement's projection of an alcohol-free society—with all problems under control. This is surely not intended ironically, however; such visions of the future were confidently held by many of the leading reformers. And when neither of the two major political parties would adopt a temperance platform that could help achieve the envisioned society, the temperance reformers established their own: The Prohibition Party. Founded in 1869, this party has nominated candidates for every presidential election since then, reaching their peak of popular support in 1892 with over 270,000 votes.

16. Drink, then, and be refreshed! The water is as pure and cold as when it slaked the thirst of the red hunter, and flowed beneath the aged bough, though now this gem of the wilderness is treasured under these hot stones, where no shadow falls, but from the brick buildings. But, still is this fountain the source of health, peace, and happiness, and I behold, with certainty and joy, the approach of the period when the virtues of cold water, too little valued since our father's days, will be fully appreciated and recognized by all.

DEFINITIONS. — 1. Pĕr-pe-tū'i-ty, *endless duration.* 2. Pro-mŭl'-ḡāt-ing, *announcing.* 3. Mu-nĭc-i-păl'i-ty, *a division of a country or of a city.* 4. Mŭs'ter dāy, *parade day.* Sŭn'dry, *several.* Un-a-dŭl'ter-āt-ed, *pure, unmixed.* Co'gnae (*pro.* Kōn'yak), *a French brandy.* 6. Po-tā'tionṣ, *drinkings.* Rụ'bi-cund, *inclining to redness.* 7. Tŏ'phet, *the infernal regions.* 10. Tĭt-il-lā'tion, *tickling.* 11. Re-plĕn'ish, *to fill again.* 14. Mo-nŏp'o-līze, *to obtain the whole.* Cŏn-sum-mā'tion, *completion, termination.* Squaṛ'd, *filthy.* 15. Pro-trăct'ed, *delayed.* 16. Slāked, *quenched.*

XXX. GOOD NIGHT.

Samuel Griswold Goodrich (*b.* 1793, *d.* 1860) was born in Ridgefield, Conn. Mr. Goodrich is best known as "Peter Parley," under which assumed name he commenced the publication of a series of juvenile works about 1827. He edited "Parley's Magazine" from 1841 to 1854. He was appointed United States consul for Paris in 1848, and held that office four years. He was a voluminous writer, and his works are interesting and popular. His "Recollections of a Lifetime" was published in 1857, and "Peter Parley's Own Story" the year after his death.

1. THE sun has sunk behind the hills,
    The shadows o'er the landscape creep;
A drowsy sound the woodland fills,
    As nature folds her arms to sleep:
            Good night — good night.

XLIII. THE GENEROUS RUSSIAN PEASANT.

1. LET Vergil sing the praises of Augustus, genius celebrate merit, and flattery extol the talents of the great. "The short and simple annals of the poor" engross my pen; and while I record the history of Flor Silin's virtues, though I speak of a poor peasant, I shall describe a noble man. I ask no eloquence to assist me in the task; modest worth rejects the aid of ornament to set it off.

2. It is impossible, even at this distant period, to reflect without horror on the miseries of that year known in Lower Volga by the name of the "Famine Year." I remember the summer, whose scorching heats had dried up all the fields, and the drought had no relief but from the tears of the ruined farmer.

3. I remember the cold, comfortless autumn, and the despairing rustics, crowding round their empty barns, with folded arms and sorrowful countenances, pondering on their misery, instead of rejoicing, as usual, at the golden harvest. I remember the winter which succeeded, and I reflect with agony on the miseries it brought with it. Whole families left their homes to become beggars on the highway.

4. At night the canopy of heaven served them as their only shelter from the piercing winds and bitter frost. To describe these scenes would be to harm the feelings of my readers; therefore, to my tale. In those days I lived on an estate not far from Simbirsk; and, though but a child, I have not forgotten the impression made on my mind by the general calamity.

5. In a village adjoining lived Flor Silin, a poor, laboring peasant,—a man remarkable for his assiduity and the skill and judgment with which he cultivated his lands. He was blessed with abundant crops; and his means being

AS THE McGUFFEYS *PROGRESSED THROUGH THEIR VARIOUS nineteenth-century editions, among the lessons slowly being discarded were many of those that focused primarily on a single foreign country. This lesson, however, stands as a major exception to that trend. It was one of W. H. McGuffey's original 1837 selections for the* Third Reader, *and (though moved to Alexander's* Fifth Reader *in 1857) its tale has been told in every edition.*

larger than his wants, his granaries, even at this time, were full of corn. The dry year coming on had beggared all the village except himself. Here was an opportunity to grow rich. Mark how Flor Silin acted. Having called the poorest of his neighbors about him, he addressed them in the following manner:

6. "My friends, you want corn for your subsistence. God has blessed me with abundance. Assist in thrashing out a quantity, and each of you take what he wants for his family." The peasants were amazed at this unexampled generosity; for sordid propensities exist in the village as well as in the populous city.

7. The fame of Flor Silin's benevolence having reached other villages, the famished inhabitants presented themselves before him, and begged for corn. This good creature received them as brothers; and, while his store remained, afforded all relief. At length, his wife, seeing no end to the generosity of his noble spirit, reminded him how necessary it would be to think of their own wants, and hold his lavish hand before it was too late. "It is written in the Scripture," said he, "'Give, and it shall be given unto you.'"

8. The following year Providence listened to the prayers of the poor, and the harvest was abundant. The peasants who had been saved from starving by Flor Silin now gathered around him.

9. "Behold," said they, "the corn you lent us. You saved our wives and children. We should have been famished but for you; may God reward you; he only can; all we have to give is our corn and grateful thanks." "I want no corn at present, my good neighbors," said he; "my harvest has exceeded all my expectations; for the rest, thank heaven: I have been but an humble instrument."

10. They urged him in vain. "No," said he, "I shall not accept your corn. If you have superfluities, share them

among your poor neighbors, who, being unable to sow their fields last autumn, are still in want; let us assist them, my dear friends; the Almighty will bless us for it." "Yes," replied the grateful peasants, "our poor neighbors shall have this corn. They shall know it is to you that they owe this timely succor, and join to teach their children the debt of gratitude due to your benevolent heart." Silin raised his tearful eyes to heaven. An angel might have envied him his feelings.

— *Nikolai Karamzin.*

DEFINITIONS. — 1. Ex-tŏl', *to elevate by praise.* An'nals, *history of events.* En-g̅rōss', *to occupy wholly.* El'o-quençe, *the power of speaking well.* 2. Drought (*pro.* drout), *want of rain or water.* 4. Es-tāte', *property in land.* 5. Grăn'a-ry, *a storehouse for grain.* 6. Sub-sist'ençe, *means of support.* Pro-pĕn'si-ties, *bent of mind, inclination.* 10. Sū-per-flū'i-ties, *greater quantities than are wanted.* Sūc'eor, *aid, help.*

NOTES. — 1. *Vergil* was the greatest of Roman poets. He was born in the year 70 B.C., and died 19 B.C.

Augustus Cæsar was emperor of Rome in the latter portion of Vergil's life, and received many compliments in the verses of his friend the poet.

2. *Lower Volga* is a district in eastern Russia, bordering on the Caspian Sea, and takes its name from the river Volga.

4. *Simbirsk* is a town of eastern Russia, on the Volga.

XLIV. FORTY YEARS AGO.

1. I'VE wandered to the village, Tom,
    I've sat beneath the tree,
   Upon the schoolhouse playground,
    That sheltered you and me;
   But none were left to greet me, Tom,
    And few were left to know,
   Who played with me upon the green,
    Just forty years ago.

Nikolai Mikhailovich Karamzin (1766–1826) was the Russian author of the novels Poor Liza *(1792) and* Natalia, the Boyar's Daughter *(1793). He wrote in Russian at a time when many Russian authors wrote only in French; and his writings helped to establish both a new reading audience and a sentimental trend in Russian literature.*

"FORTY YEARS AGO" APPEARS ONLY IN THE 1879 AND 1920 EDI-
tions of the Readers. *It is an oft-anthologized, sentimental
favorite that has long outlived the fame of both writers who
claimed authorship: Francis Huston and Dill Armor Smith.*

2. The grass was just as green, Tom,
    Barefooted boys at play
Were sporting, just as we did then,
    With spirits just as gay.
But the master sleeps upon the hill,
    Which, coated o'er with snow,
Afforded us a sliding place,
    Some forty years ago.

3. The old schoolhouse is altered some;
    The benches are replaced
By new ones very like the same
    Our jackknives had defaced.
But the same old bricks are in the wall,
    The bell swings to and fro;
Its music's just the same, dear Tom,
    'T was forty years ago.

4. The spring that bubbled 'neath the hill,
   Close by the spreading beech,
   Is very low; 't was once so high
   That we could almost reach;
   And kneeling down to take a drink,
   Dear Tom, I started so,
   To think how very much I've changed
   Since forty years ago.

5. Near by that spring, upon an elm,
   You know, I cut your name,
   Your sweetheart's just beneath it, Tom;
   And you did mine the same.
   Some heartless wretch has peeled the bark;
   'T was dying sure, but slow,
   Just as that one whose name you cut
   Died forty years ago.

6. My lids have long been dry, Tom,
   But tears came in my eyes:
   I thought of her I loved so well,
   Those early broken ties.
   I visited the old churchyard,
   And took some flowers to strew
   Upon the graves of those we loved
   Just forty years ago.

7. Some are in the churchyard laid,
   Some sleep beneath the sea;
   And none are left of our old class
   Excepting you and me.
   And when our time shall come, Tom,
   And we are called to go,
   I hope we'll meet with those we loved
   Some forty years ago.

The nostalgia of this selection touches on many of the themes that appear in late edtions of the McGuffeys: time, death, romantic love, and the good old school days—all seen through a sentimental haze.

HIGHLY ESTEEMED DURING THE NINETEENTH CENTURY AS ONE OF the famous New England triumvirate of poets (along with Longfellow and Oliver Wendell Holmes), Lowell is read and praised much less frequently today. The reputations of his friends have also suffered; and the American poets of Lowell's era now most acclaimed are Walt Whitman and Emily Dickinson (neither of whom was ever included in the McGuffeys). Most of Lowell's best poems and essays were written before he was thirty years old, but he did important editing work later—as the first editor of the Atlantic Monthly, *and then as a co-editor of the* North American Review.

LXX. THE HERITAGE.

James Russell Lowell (*b.* 1819, *d.* 1891) was born in Cambridge, Mass., and was graduated from Harvard College. He entered the profession of law; but, in 1843, turned aside to publish "The Pioneer, a Literary and Critical Magazine." In 1855 he was appointed professor of Belles-lettres in Harvard College. From 1877 to 1885 he was U.S. Minister, first to Spain, afterwards to Great Britain. Lowell's powers as a writer were very versatile, and his poems range from the most dreamy and imaginative to the most trenchant and witty. Among his most noted poetical works are "The Biglow Papers," "A Fable for Critics," "The Vision of Sir Launfal," "The Cathedral," and "The Legend of Brittany;" while "Conversations on some of the Old Poets," "Among my Books," and "My Study Windows," place him in the front rank as an essayist.

1. THE rich man's son inherits lands,
  And piles of brick, and stone, and gold,
 And he inherits soft white hands,
  And tender flesh that fears the cold,
  Nor dares to wear a garment old;
 A heritage, it seems to me,
 One scarce would wish to hold in fee.

2. The rich man's son inherits cares;
  The bank may break, the factory burn,
 A breath may burst his bubble shares,
  And soft white hands could hardly earn
  A living that would serve his turn;
 A heritage, it seems to me,
 One scarce would wish to hold in fee.

3. The rich man's son inherits wants,
  His stomach craves for dainty fare;
 With sated heart, he hears the pants
  Of toiling hinds with brown arms bare,
  And wearies in his easy-chair;
 A heritage, it seems to me,
 One scarce would wish to hold in fee.

4. What doth the poor man's son inherit?
    Stout muscles and a sinewy heart,
A hardy frame, a hardier spirit;
    King of two hands, he does his part
    In every useful toil and art;
A heritage, it seems to me,
A king might wish to hold in fee.

5. What doth the poor man's son inherit?
    Wishes o'erjoyed with humble things,
A rank adjudged by toil-won merit,
    Content that from employment springs,
    A heart that in his labor sings;
A heritage, it seems to me,
A king might wish to hold in fee.

6. What doth the poor man's son inherit?
    A patience learned of being poor,
Courage, if sorrow come, to bear it,
    A fellow-feeling that is sure
    To make the outcast bless his door;
A heritage, it seems to me,
A king might wish to hold in fee.

7. O rich man's son! there is a toil
    That with all others level stands:
Large charity doth never soil,
    But only whiten soft, white hands. —
    This is the best crop from thy lands;
A heritage, it seems to me,
Worth being rich to hold in fee.

8. O poor man's son! scorn not thy state;
    There is worse weariness than thine
In merely being rich and great:

Lowell may not have been exactly a "rich man's son," but he was relatively affluent and clearly proud of his heritage. So it is ironic—and perhaps even hypocritical—when he speaks so freely of "wishes o'erjoyed with humble things." If one can forget the author and his position, however, the poem may perhaps be better enjoyed—as a splendid example of the platitudinous declamations so popular at that time.

An *1892 assessment of Lowell in the* National Cyclopedia of American Biography *says it all:*

It is not strange that, planted in such a soil, and fed by such influences, his inherited genius flowered out to be the finest expression of purely American thought and culture that has been seen in this century. He does not sound the organ notes of Whittier, nor sing the household songs of Longfellow, nor has he the seerlike vision of Emerson, but more fully than all these does he embody the critical thought, virile strength, and soaring imagination of America today. He has laid his ear to the great heart of time, and has echoed its pulsations in words that are the heartbeats of more than sixty millions.

> Toil only gives the soul to shine,
> And makes rest fragrant and benign;
> A heritage, it seems to me,
> Worth being poor to hold in fee.

9. Both, heirs to some six feet of sod,
> Are equal in the earth at last;
> Both, children of the same dear God,
> Prove title to your heirship vast
> By record of a well-filled past;
> A heritage, it seems to me,
> Well worth a life to hold in fee.

DEFINITIONS. — 1. Hĕr'it-aġe, *that which is inherited, or taken by descent, from an ancestor.* 3. Săt'ed, *surfeited, glutted.* Hindṣ, *peasants, countrymen.* 5. Ad-jŭdġed', *decided, determined.* 8. Be-nīgn' (*pro.* be-nīn'), *having healthful qualities, wholesome.*

NOTES. — 1. *To hold in fee,* means to have as an inheritance.
9. *Prove title.* That is, to prove the right of ownership.

Sixth Reader

CHARLES DICKENS (1812–1870) ESTABLISHED HIS REPUTATION IN America almost as quickly as he had in his homeland. Many of his novels appeared first in serialized periodicals, and often an unauthorized American reprinting would begin in a magazine here shortly after the mail arrived with the British periodical carrying the first installment. The "Death of Little Nell" is excerpted from The Old Curiosity Shop (1841) and was a popular fixture in many American texts, although some textbooks—evidently wanting to be somewhat different— selected instead the death scene of Paul Dombey in Dombey and Son (1848). Dickens' popularity in America was further enhanced—despite his rancid comments about much in the United States—when he visited here in 1842 and 1867–68, giving public readings.

X. — DEATH OF LITTLE NELL.

FROM DICKENS.

CHARLES DICKENS of England, is one of the most popular writers of the day, and is admired as a graphic delineator of human character. He has published numerous interesting works, and is, at present, conductor of the periodical "Household Words."

1. SHE wās dēad. No sleep so beautiful and calm´, so free from trace of pain´, so fair to look` upon. She seemed a creature fresh from the hand of God, and waiting for the breath of life`; not one who had lived´, and suffered death`. Her couch was dressed with here and there some winter berries and green leaves, gathered in a spot she had been used to favor. "When I die´, put near me something that has loved the light, and had .the sky above it always`." Those were her words.

2. She wās dēad. Dear, gentle, patient, noble Nell was dead`. Her little bird, a poor slight thing the pressure of a finger would have crushed, was stirring nimbly in its cage´, and the strong heart of its child-mistress was mute and motionless forever`! Where were the traces of her early cares, her sufferings, and fatigues`? All gone`. Sorrow was dead, indeed, in her; but peace and perfect happiness were born, imaged, in her tranquil beauty and profound repose.

3. And still her former self lay there, unaltered in this change. Yes`! the old fireside had smiled upon that same sweet face`; it had passed, like a dream´, through the haunts of misery and care`; at the door of the poor schoolmaster on the summer evening`, before the furnace-fire upon the cold wet night`, at the still bedside of the dying boy´, there had been the same mild and lovely look. So shall we know the angels, in their majesty, after death.

4. The old man held one languid arm in his, and the small tight hand folded to his breast for warmth. It was the hand she had stretched out to him with her last smile`; the hand that had led him on through all their wanderings`. Ever and anon he pressed it to his lips; then hugged it to his breast again, murmuring that it was warmer now, and, as he said it, he looked in agony to those who stood around, as if imploring them to help her.

5. She was dead, and past all help, or need of help. The ancient rooms she had seemed to fill with life, even while her own was waning fast´, the garden she had tended´, the eyes she had gladdened´, the noiseless haunts of many a thoughtless hour´, the paths she had trodden, as it were, but yesterday, could know her no more`.

6. "It is not," said the schoolmaster, as he bent down to kiss her on the cheek, and gave his tears free vent, "it is not in *this* world that Heaven's justice ends. Think what it is, compared with the world to which her young spirit has winged its early flight, and say, if one deliberate wish, expressed in solemn tones above this bed, could call her back to life´, which of us would utter` it?"

7. She had been dead two days. They were all about her at the time, knowing that the end was drawing on. She died soon after daybreak. They had read and talked to her in the earlier portion of the night; but, as the hours crept on, she sank to sleep. They could tell by what she faintly uttered in her dreams, that they were of her journeyings with the old man; they were of no painful scenes, but of those who had helped them, and used them kindly; for she often said "God bless you!" with great fervor.

8. Waking, she never wandered in her mind but once, and that was at beautiful music, which, she said, was in the air. God knows. It may have been. Opening her eyes, at last, from a very quiet sleep, she begged that they would kiss her once again. That done, she turned to the old man, with a lovely smile upon her face, such, they said, as they had never seen, and could never forget, and clung, with both her arms, about his neck. She had never murmured or complained; but, with a quiet mind, and manner quite unaltered, save that she every day became more earnest and more grateful to them, faded like the light upon the summer's evening.

9. The child who had been her little friend, came there, almost as soon as it was day, with an offering of dried flowers, which he begged them to lay upon her breast. He told them of his dream again, and that it was of her being restored to them, just as she used to be. He begged hard to see her: saying, that he would be very quiet, and that they need not fear his being alarmed for he had sat alone by his younger

The schoolmaster's short message is one that permeates the Readers—softly here, but heavily in the pointed religious instruction of the earlier editions. The death of the innocent and the surer promises of Heaven to those pure ones were familiar reassurances provided to school children, most of whom had lost brothers and sisters to death—not in some distant hospital, but at home and often in their presence.

During both of Dickens' visits to the United States he spoke ardently, but unsuccessfully, in support of an international copyright law. The United States had taken—and continued to hold until 1952—an embarrassing position on this subject, refusing to participate with other civilized countries in providing even the minimum of protection to foreign authors. In fact, until late in the 1800's, the works of foreign authors (and especially British authors) were freely pirated by American publishers. As an ironic byproduct of Dickens' speeches in America, for instance, more of his writings began to appear in the textbooks here, with no royalties paid. The "Death of Little Nell" was just one of several selections from Dickens in the McGuffeys, appearing in the Sixth Reader from 1857 to the present.

brother all day long when he was dead, and he had felt glad to be so near him. They let him have his wish; and, indeed, he kept his word, and was, in his childish way, a lesson to them all.

10. Up to that time, the old man had not spoken once, except to her, or stirred from the bedside. But, when he saw her little favorite, he was moved as they had not seen him yet, and made as though he would have him come nearer. Then, pointing to the bed, he burst into tears for the first time, and they who stood by, knowing that the sight of this child had done him good, left them alone together.

11. Soothing him with his artless talk of her, the child persuaded him to take some rest, to walk abroad, to do almost as he desired him. And, when the day came, on which they must remove her, in her earthly shape, from earthly eyes forever, he led him away, that he might not know when she was taken from him. They were to gather fresh leaves and berries for her bed.

12. And now the bell, the bell she had so often heard by night and day, and listened to with solemn pleasure, almost as a living voice, rung its remorseless toll for her, so young, so beautiful, so good. Decrepit age, and vigorous life, and blooming youth, and helpless infancy, on crutches, in the pride of health and strength, in the full blush of promise, in the mere dawn of life, gathered round her. Old men were there, whose eyes were dim and senses failing, grandmothers, who might have died ten years ago, and still been old, the deaf, the blind, the lame, the palsied, the living dead, in many shapes and forms, to see the closing of that early grave.

13. Along the crowded path they bore her now, pure as the newly fallen snow that covered it, whose day on earth had been as fleeting. Under that porch where she had sat, when Heaven, in its mercy, brought her to that peaceful spot, she passed again, and the old church received her in its quiet shade.

XII. — THE LONE INDIAN.

MOHAWKS; a tribe of Indians who formerly lived in the state of New York.

1. FOR many a returning autumn, a lone Indian was seen standing at the consecrated spot we have mentioned; but, just thirty years after the death of Soonseetah, he was noticed for the last time. His step was then firm, and his figure erect, though he seemed old and way-worn. Age had not dimmed the fire of his eye, but an expression of deep melancholy had settled on his wrinkled brow. It was Powontonamo`; he who had once been the eagle of the Mohawks. He came to lie down and die beneath the broad oak, which shadowed the grave of Sunny-eye.

2. Alas! the white man's ax` had been there. The tree that he had planted was dead`; and the vine, which had leaped so vigorously from branch to branch, now yellow and withering, was falling to the ground. A deep groan burst from the soul of the savage. For thirty wearisome years, he had watched that oak, with its twining tendrils. They were the only things left in the wide world for him to love`, and they were gone.

3. He looked abroad. The hunting-land of his tribe was changed, like its chieftain. No light canoe now shot down the river, like a bird upon the wing. The laden boat of the white man alone broke its smooth surface. The Englishman's road wound like a serpent around the banks of the Mohawk`; and iron hoofs had so beaten down the war-path, that a hawk's eye could not discover an Indian track. The last wigwam was destroyed`; and the sun looked boldly down

THE FIRST FOUR READERS WERE ORIGINALLY PREPARED BY WILLIAM Holmes McGuffey and published in 1837 and 1838. The Fifth Reader, which followed in 1844, was primarily the work of Alexander Hamilton McGuffey. But the Sixth Reader— which first appeared in 1857—was the result of collaboration between Alexander McGuffey, Dr. Timothy S. Pinneo (author of Pinneo's Grammars) and Mr. Obed J. Wilson (a member of the publishing firm). It was at this time that all the Readers were extensively revised, with many lessons being moved to higher-level Readers. The new Sixth Reader included some new material, but most of it consisted of lessons used previously in either the Fourth or Fifth Readers.

"The Lone Indian" (attributed in the 1844 Fifth Reader to a "Miss Francis") was one of the lessons elevated to the first edition of the Sixth Reader. It was retained in the 1866 version, but dropped from the series in 1879.

upon spots he had only visited by stealth´, during thousands and thousands of moons.

4. The few remaining trees, clothed in the fantastic mourning of autumn´; the long line of heavy clouds melting away before the evening sun´; and the distant mountain, seen through the blue mist of departing twilight´, alone remained as he had seen them in his boyhood. All things spoke a sad language to the heart of the desolate Indian. "Yes`," said he, "the young oak and the vine are like the Eagle and the Sunny-eye. They are cut down`, torn´ and trampled` on. The leaves are falling, and the clouds are scattering like my people. I wish I could once more see the trees standing thick, as they did when my mother held me to her bosom, and sung the warlike deeds of the Mohawks."

5. A mingled expression of grief and anger passed over his face, as he watched a loaded boat in its passage across the stream. "The white man carries food to his wife and children, and he finds them in his home`," said he; "where are the squaw and pappoose of the red` man? They are here`!" As he spoke, he fixed his eye thoughtfully on the grave. After a gloomy silence, he again looked round upon the fair scene, with a wandering and troubled gaze. "The pale` face may like it," murmured he; "but an Indian´ can not die here in peace`." So saying´, he broke his bow-string`, snapped his arrows`, threw them on the burial-place of his fathers´, and departed forever`.

REMARK.—The words "down," "torn," and "trampled," in the last paragraph but one, and "string," "arrows," "fathers," and "forever," in the last paragraph, are examples of inflection which may, perhaps, more appropriately come under the head of "series;" but, by examining them, it will be found, that the rule which gives them the falling inflection wherever the sense is complete, and that which requires the last but one to be the rising inflection, are applicable in these cases. Indeed, the rule for series is substantially the combination of these two principles, with that of emphasis, as laid down in Rule II.

XXII. — A POLITICAL PAUSE.

FROM THE SPEECHES OF FOX.

Fox was a celebrated English statesman. This is an extract from a speech delivered during a truce in the war between England and France.

In this lesson, the influence of a *negative* in determining the rising inflection, is particularly noticeable.

1. "BUT we must pause`," says the honorable gentleman, What`! must the bowels of Great Britain be torn out´, her best blood spilt´, her treasures wasted´, that you may make an experiment´? Put yourselves`,—O! that you *would* put yourselves on the field of battle´, and learn to judge of the sort of horrors you excite`. In former´ wars, a man might, at least, have some` feeling, some` interest, that served to balance in his mind the impressions which a scene of carnage and death must inflict`.

2. But if a man were present now at the field of slaughter, and were to inquire for what they were fighting´,—"Fighting´!"* would be the answer´; "they are not *fighting*´; they are *pausing*`." "Why is that man expiring`? Why is that other writhing with agony`? What means this implacable fury`?" The answer must be, "You are quite wrong, sir, you *deceive*` yourself,—they are not *fighting*´,—do not disturb´ them,—they are merely pausing`! This man is not expiring with agony´,—that man is not dead´,—he is only pausing`! Bless you, sir, they are not *angry*´ with one another; they have now no cause of quarrel; but their country thinks that there should be a *pause*`. All that you see is nothing like fighting´,—there is no harm´, nor cruelty´, nor bloodshed´ in it; it is nothing more than a political *pause*`! It is merely to try an experiment—to see whether Bonaparte will not behave himself better` than heretofore; and in the mean time, we have agreed to a *pause*`, in pure friendship!"

3. And is this the way that you are to show yourselves the advocates of order´? You take up a system calculated to uncivilize the world`, to destroy order`, to trample on

---

*Rule VIII.

THE *1879 VERSION OF THIS BRIEF AUTHOR'S NOTE WAS MUCH ENLARGED,* providing not only additional facts, but also some gratuitous value judgments and some irrelevant moral instruction. Here is a portion of that note:

Charles James Fox, 1749–1806, a famous English orator and statesman, was the son of Hon. Henry Fox, afterward Lord Holland; he was also a lineal descendant of Charles II of England and of Henry IV of France. He received his education at Westminster, Eton, and Oxford, but left the University without graduating. He was first elected to the Parliament before he was twenty years old . . . . In his later years, Mr. Fox was as remarkable for carelessness in dress and personal appearance, as he had been for the opposite in his youth. He possessed many pleasing traits of character, but his morals were not commendable; he was a gambler and a spendthrift. Yet he exercised a powerful influence on the politics of his times . . . .

Long before Orwell and others in the twentieth century bemoaned the corruption of the language by political and military euphemisms, here was Fox offering a strong rebuff to those who twisted the meanings of words. Fox's speech is particularly unusual in the McGuffeys, in that he relies heavily on verbal irony—a device which was evidently considered suspect by McGuffey and/or his publishers.

THIS LESSON IS A TYPICAL McGUFFEY SELECTION FROM SHAKESPEARE: a set speech with excellent potential for recitation and declamation. The lesson is taken from The Life of Henry the Fifth *(Act III, Scene 1), but as is customary in the* McGuffeys, *no context is provided.*

religion˅, to stifle in the heart, not merely the generosity of noble sentiment˴, but the affections of social nature; and in the prosecution of this system, you spread terror and devastation all around˅ you.

REMARK.—The words "pause" and "pausing" may, perhaps, with equal propriety, receive the falling circumflex.

XLIII. — HENRY V. TO HIS TROOPS.

FROM SHAKSPEARE.

[THIS lesson requires a high key.]

1. ONCE more unto the breach, dear friends˴, once more ;
   Or close the wall up with our English dead.
   In *peace˴*, there's nothing so becomes a man
   As modest stillness and humility ;
   But when the blast of *war* blows in our ears,
   Then˴, imitate the action of the tiger˅;
   Stiffen the sinews˅, summon up the blood˅;
   Disguise fair nature with hard-favor'd rage :
   Then˴, lend the eye a terrible aspect ;
   Let it pry through the portage of the head,
   Like the brass cannon ; let the brow o'erwhelm it,
   As fearfully as doth a galled rock
   O'erhang and jutty his confounded base,
   Swill'd with the wild and wasteful ocean.

2. Now *set* the *teeth˅*, and *stretch* the *nostril wide*,
   Hold hard the *breath˅*, and *bend˅* up every *spirit*
   To its full hight !   *On˅, on˅*, you noble English˴ !
   Whose blood is set from fathers of war-proof ;
   Fathers, that, like so many Alexanders,
   Have, in these parts, from morn till even, fought,
   And sheath'd their swords for lack of argument ;
   Be copy now to men of grosser blood,
   And teach them how to war!

3.   And *you*, good yeomen˴,
   Whose limbs were made in England, show˅ us here
   The mettle of your pasture ; let us swear
   That you are worth your breeding˅, which I doubt not ;
   For there is none of you so mean and base,
   That hath not noble luster in your eyes.
   I see you stand like grayhounds in the slips,
   Straining upon the start.   The game's afoot˅;
   Follow your spirit˅: and, upon this charge,
   Cry—*God* for *Harry! England!* and *St. George!*

LXXVII. — A PSALM OF LIFE.

FROM LONGFELLOW.

1. TELL me not in mournful numbers,
    Life is but an empty dream!
   For the soul is dead that slumbers,
    And things are not what they seem.

2. Life is real! Life is earnest!
    And the grave is not its ⁺goal;
   Dust thou art, to dust returnest,
    Was not written of the soul.

3. Not enjoyment, and not sorrow,
    Is our ⁺destin'd end and way,
   But to act, that each to-morrow
    Find us farther than to-day.

4. Art is long, and time is fleeting,
    And our hearts, though stout and brave,
   Still, like ⁺muffled drums, are beating
    Funeral marches to the grave.

5. In the world's broad field of battle,
    In the ⁺bivouac of life,
   Be not like dumb, driven cattle!
    Be a hero in the strife!

6. Trust no future, howe'er pleasant,
    Let the dead Past bury its dead!
   Act!—act in the living Present!
    Heart within, and God o'er head.

7. Lives of great men all remind us,
    We can make our lives ⁺sublime,
   And, departing, leave behind us,
    Footprints on the sands of time.

8. Footprints, that perhaps another,
    Sailing o'er life's solemn ⁺main,
   A forlorn and shipwreck'd brother,
    Seeing, shall take heart again.

9. Let us, then, be up and doing,
    With a heart for any fate;
   Still ⁺achieving, still pursuing,
    Learn to labor and to wait.

HENRY WADSWORTH LONGFELLOW (1807-1882) GRADUATED FROM Bowdoin in 1825 (a classmate of Nathanial Hawthorne), but his first book of poems, Voices of the Night, *did not appear until 1839. It was from those pages that "A Psalm of Life" was chosen by Alexander McGuffey for the first edition of the* Fifth Reader *in 1844. The poem was then transferred to the new* Sixth Reader *in 1857, where it has remained in all subsequent editions.*

During his lifetime Longfellow became one of the most popular and most honored of American poets, and after his death he was the first American to be distinguished with a bust in Westminster Abbey's famous Poets' Corner. To twentieth-century readers, however, most of Longfellow's poetry suffers from excessive romanticism, symbolism, and didacticism (especially in such early poems as this and another McGuffey *favorite, "The Village Blacksmith"). Like his contemporaries Lowell, Holmes, and Whittier, Longfellow's reputation has declined significantly in recent years.*

CXLVII. — IMPEACHMENT OF WARREN HASTINGS.

WARREN HASTINGS was a Governor of the British possessions in India, and was impeached for †maladministration.

EDMUND BURKE, who, as attorney-general for the crown, conducted the prosecution of Warren Hastings, was born in 1730. As an orator, politician, and author, he stood high among his cotemporaries. He died in 1797.

1. THE place in which the †impeachment of Warren Hastings was conducted, was worthy of such a trial. It was the great hall of William Rufus; the hall, which had resounded with †acclamations, at the inauguration of thirty kings; the hall, which had witnessed the just sentence of Bacon, and the just †absolution of Somers; the hall, where the eloquence of Stafford had for a moment awed and melted a victorious party inflamed with just resentment; the hall, where Charles had †confronted the High Court of Justice, with the placid courage which half redeemed his fame.

2. Neither military nor civil pomp was wanting. The avenues were lined with grenadiers. The streets were kept clear by cavalry. The peers, robed in gold and ermine, were marshaled by heralds. The judges, in their †vestments of state, attended to give advice on points of law. The long galleries were crowded by such an audience as has rarely excited the fears or emulation of an orator. There, were gathered together, from all points of a great, free, enlightened, and prosperous realm, grace and female loveliness, wit and learning, the representatives of every science and every art.

3. There, were seated around the queen, the fair-haired, young daughters of the house of Brunswick. There, the †embassadors of great kings and commonwealths gazed with admiration on a spectacle which no other country in the world could present. There, Siddons,* in the pride of her majestic beauty, looked with emotion on a scene †surpassing all the imitations of the stage. There, Gibbon, the historian of the Roman Empire, thought of the days when Cicero pleaded the cause of Sicily against Verres: and when, before a senate which had some show of freedom, Tacitus thundered against

---

*A celebrated actress.

the oppressor of Africa; and there too, were seen, side by side, the greatest painter and the greatest scholar of the age; for the spectacle had †allured Reynolds from his easel, and Parr, from his study.

4. The †sergeants made †proclamation. Hastings advanced to the bar, and bent his knee. The culprit was indeed not unworthy of that great presence. He had ruled an extensive and populous country; had made laws and treaties; had sent forth armies; had set up, and pulled down princes; and in his high place he had so borne himself, that all had feared him, that most had loved him, and that hatred itself could deny him no title to glory, except virtue. A person, small and †emaciated, yet deriving dignity from a carriage which, while it indicated †deference to the court, indicated, also, habitual self-possession and self-respect; a high and intellectual forehead; a brow, pensive, but not gloomy; a mouth of †inflexible decision; a face, pale and worn, but on which a great and well-balanced mind was legibly written: such formed the aspect with which the great pro-consul presented himself to his judges.

5. The charges, and the answers of Hastings, were first read. This †ceremony occupied two whole days. On the third, Burke rose. Four sittings of the court were occupied by his opening speech, which was intended to be a general introduction to all the charges. With an †exuberance of thought and a splendor of diction, which more than satisfied the highly-raised expectations of the audience, he described the character and institutions of the natives of India; recounted the circumstances in which the Asiatic Empire of Britain had originated; and set forth the Constitution of the Company and of the English Presidencies.

6. Having thus attempted to communicate to his hearers an idea of eastern society, as vivid as that which existed in his own mind, he proceeded to †arraign the administration of Hastings, as systematically conducted in defiance of morality and public law. The energy and pathos of the great orator †extorted expressions of unwonted admiration from all; and, for a moment, seemed to pierce even the resolute heart of the defendant. The ladies in the galleries, unaccustomed to such displays of eloquence, excited by the solemnity of the occa-

The "culprit," as Macaulay calls him, was Warren Hastings (1732–1818), an English colonial administrator and first governor-general of British India. Unlike many British administrators in India, Hastings appears not to have used his position to acquire personal wealth (Macaulay himself later spent only four years in India and returned with an alleged fortune of over £30,000!), and the expenses of the impeachment exhausted all of Hastings' money. The trial, which extended from 1788 to 1795, occupying 148 days of testimony and defense, was in large part instigated by Whig politicians attacking the system, not the man. And it ended in a manner one could hardly have expected from reading only this fragment of Macaulay's version: Hastings was acquitted by a large majority on each separate count of the impeachment.

sion, and perhaps not unwilling to display their taste and sensibility, were in a state of incontrollable emotion. Handkerchiefs were pulled out; smelling-bottles were handed round; †hysterical sobs and screams were heard, and some were even carried out in fits.

7. At length, the orator concluded. Raising his voice, till the old arches of Irish oak resounded—"Therefore," said he, "hath it in all confidence been ordered by the Commons of Great Britain, that I †impeach Warren Hastings of high crimes and misdemeanors. I impeach him in the name of the Commons House of Parliament, whose trust he has betrayed. I impeach him in the name of the English nation, whose ancient honor he has sullied. I impeach him in the name of the people of India, whose rights he has trodden under foot, and whose country he has turned into a desert. Lastly, in the name of human nature itself, in the name of both sexes, in the name of every age, in the name of every rank, I impeach the common enemy and oppressor of all."

LXXX.—AMBITION.

From Willis.

1. What is ambition? 'T is a glorious cheat!
It seeks the chamber of the gifted boy,
And lifts his humble window, and comes in;
The narrow walls †expand, and spread away
Into a kingly palace, and the roof
Lifts to the sky, and unseen fingers work
The ceilings with rich †blazonry, and write
His name in burning letters over all.
And ever, as he shuts his wildered eyes,
The †phantom comes and lays upon his lids
A spell that murders sleep, and in his ear
Whispers a deathless word, and on his brain
Breathes a fierce thirst no waters will allay.

2. He is its slave henceforth. His days are spent
In chaining down his heart, and watching where
To rise by human weaknesses. His nights
Bring him no rest in all their blessèd hours.
His kindred are forgotten or †estranged;
Unhealthful fires burn constant in his eye.

PART OF THE McGUFFEY *JUGGLING ACT INVOLVED BALANCING THOSE lessons which implied that success would bless hard work and sound morals, with its counterpointing group of lessons deprecating ambition and advocating a humble, contented acceptance of one's station in life. This poem, obviously in the counterpoint, is an inferior rephrasing of the "vanity of human wishes" theme. Present in the first two editions of the* Sixth Reader, *it was omitted in the 1879 revision.*

N[athaniel] P[arker] Willis (1806–1867) was an American writer and editor widely acclaimed in the nineteenth century, but relatively unknown today. His presentation of himself as an aesthete (and his reputation for rakish escapades) prompted Oliver Wendell Holmes to describe Willis as "something of a remembrance of Count D'Orsay and an anticipation of Oscar Wilde." But as co-editor of the New York Mirror *and author of many books of verse, fiction, and travel sketches, Willis acquired sufficient fame that his pallbearers included Longfellow, Lowell, and Holmes.*

His lip grows restless, and its smile is curled
Half into scorn; till the bright, fiery boy,
That 't was a daily blessing but to see,
His spirit was so bird-like and so pure,
Is frozen, in the very flush of youth,
Into a cold, †care-fretted, heartless *man*.

3. And what is its reward? At best, a name!
Praise—when the ear has grown too dull to hear;
Gold—when the senses it should please are dead;
Wreaths—when the hair they cover has grown gray :
Fame—when the heart it should have †thrilled is numb;
All things but *love*—when *love* is all we want;
And close behind comes Death, and ere we know,
That even these †unavailing gifts are ours,
He sends us, stripped and naked, to the grave.

LXXXI.—LAMENT FOR THE DEAD.
From Ossian.

1. *Reyno.* THE wind and rain are over; calm is the noon of day. The clouds are divided in heaven; over the green hill flies the inconstant sun; red, through the stony vale, comes down the stream of the hill. Sweet are thy †murmurs, O stream! But more sweet is the voice I hear. It is the voice of Alpin, the son of song, mourning for the dead. Bent is his head of age, and red his tearful eye. Alpin, thou son of song, why alone on the silent hill? Why complainest thou as a blast in the wood, as a wave on the lonely shore?

2. *Alpin.* My tears, O Reyno! are for the dead; my voice for the †inhabitants of the grave. Tall thou art on the hill; fair among the sons of the slain. But thou shalt fall like Morar; and the mourners shall sit on thy tomb. The hills shall know thee no more, thy bow shall lie in the halls, unstrung.

3. Thou wert swift, O Morar! as a roe on the hill; terrible as a †meteor of fire. Thy wrath was as the storm; thy sword in battle, as lightning in the field. Thy voice was like a stream after rain; like thunder on distant hills. Many fell by thy arm; they were consumed in the flames of thy wrath. But when thou didst return from war, how peaceful was thy brow! Thy face was like the sun, after rain; like the moon,

Ossian (or, more traditionally, oisin) was a legendary Gaelic warrior and bard who supposedly lived in the third century. Although some brief fragments attributed to him have survived from later times, he owes his reputation mainly to the eighteenth-century forgeries of the Scot, James Macpherson (1736–1796). Macpherson's Ossian *poems (especially the epic* Fingal, 1762) *were vastly admired at the time for their romantic spirit and as "evidence" of the Noble Savage in British genealogy. Their authenticity was pointedly questioned by Dr. Johnson and a few others, but Macpherson managed to maintain the pretext of Ossian's authorship during his own lifetime. Subsequent scholars have upheld Johnson's objections (linguistic analysis alone, for instance, destroys most of Macpherson's claims), and the poems are now viewed chiefly as interesting relics of a classic hoax. Macpherson possessed enough creative ability to suggest that he might have established a significant name for himself as a poet, but he insisted the poems were authentic (while refusing to produce the originals), and his name is remembered today only for this literary fraud.*

This selection was picked by Alexander McGuffey for his 1844 Fifth Reader, *probably more for its declamatory potential than for its pathetic treatment of death. It was transferred to the* Sixth Reader *in 1857, but omitted from the series in 1879.*

in the silence of night; calm as the breast of the lake, when the loud wind is hushed into repose. Narrow is thy dwelling, now: dark the place of thine abode. With three steps, I †compass thy grave, O thou, who wast so great before! Four stones, with their heads of moss, are the only †memorial of thee. A tree with scarce a leaf, long grass whistling in the wind, mark to the hunter's eye, the grave of mighty Morar.

4. Morar! thou art low indeed; thou hast no mother to mourn thee; no maid with her tears of love. Dead is she that brought thee forth; fallen is the daughter of Morglan. Who, on his staff, is this? Who this, whose head is white with age, whose eyes are †galled with tears, who quakes at every step? It is thy father, O Morar! the father of no son but thee. Weep, thou father of Morar, weep; but thy son heareth thee not. Deep is the sleep of the dead, low their pillow of dust. No more shall he hear thy voice, no more awake at thy call. When shall it be morn in the grave, to bid the slumberer awake? Farewell, thou bravest of men; thou conqueror of the field; but the field shall see thee no more, nor the gloomy wood be lightened by the splendor of thy steel. Thou hast left no son,—but the song shall preserve thy name.

LXXXII.—THE CHURCH-YARD.
FROM KARAMISIN.
[THE two Voices from the Grave.]

First Voice.
How frightful the grave! how deserted and drear!
With the howls of the storm-wind, the †creaks of the bier,
  And the white bones all †clattering together!

Second Voice.
How peaceful the grave: its quiet how deep!
Its †zephyrs breathe calmly, and soft is its sleep,
  And flow'rets perfume it with ether.

First Voice.
There †riots the †blood-crested worm on the dead,
And the yellow scull serves the foul toad for a bed,
  And snakes in the nettle-weeds hiss.

XCIII.—THE PHILOSOPHER'S SCALES.

FROM JANE TAYLOR.

1. A MONK, when his rites †sacerdotal were o'er,
In the depth of his cell with his stone-covered floor,
Resigning to thought his †chimerical brain,
Once formed the contrivance we now shall explain;
But whether by magic's or †alchemy's powers,
We know not; indeed, 't is no business of ours.

2. Perhaps it was only by patience and care,
At last, that he brought his invention to bear;
In youth 't was †projected, but years stole away,
And ere 't was complete, he was wrinkled and gray;
But success is secure, unless energy fails;
And, at length, he produced the philosopher's scales.

3. "What were they?" you ask. You shall presently see;
These scales were not made to weigh sugar and tea;
O no; for such †properties wondrous had they,
That qualities, feelings, and thoughts, they could weigh;
Together with articles small or immense,
From mountains or planets, to †atoms of sense.

4 Naught was there so bulky, but there it would lay,
And naught so †ethereal, but there it would stay,
And naught so †reluctant, but in it must go:
All which some examples more clearly will show.

5 The first thing he weighed was the head of Voltaire,
Which retained all the wit that had ever been there;
As a weight he threw in a torn scrap of a leaf,
Containing the prayer of the †penitent thief;
When the skull rose aloft with so sudden a spell,
That it bounced like a ball on the roof of the cell.

6 One time, he put in Alexander the Great,
With a garment that Dorcas had made, for a weight,
And, though †clad in armor from †sandals to crown,
The hero rose up, and the garment went down.

7 A long row of alms-houses, amply †endowed
By a well-esteemed †Pharisee, busy and proud,
Next loaded one scale; while the other was prest
By those mites the poor widow dropped into the chest,
Up flew the †endowment, not weighing an ounce,
And down, down the farthing-worth came with a bounce.

21

JANE TAYLOR (1783-1824) SELDOM RECEIVES CREDIT FOR WHAT IS perhaps her greatest achievement: her composition of the long-popular children's verse beginning "Twinkle, twinkle, little star." The daughter of the British minister Isaac Taylor, she collaborated with her sister Ann (see page 179) in writing a number of juvenile works, including Hymns for Infant Minds *(1808) and* Essays in Rhyme on Morals and Manners *(1816).*

This selection (which appeared first in the Fifth, and then the Sixth Reader *until 1879) embodies the anti-intellectual flavor present in a number of the McGuffey lessons. It is perhaps most visible in the fifth stanza, where all the wit of Voltaire is outweighed by the "prayer of a penitent thief," but it permeates the entire piece. Common sense and the proper moral values, the McGuffey Readers regularly emphasize, are worth far more than the things the world values, including intellectual eminence.*

8. By further +experiments, (no matter how,)
   He found that ten chariots weighed less than one plow;
   A sword with gilt trapping rose up in the scale,
   Though balanced by only a ten-penny nail;
   A shield and a helmet, a buckler and spear,
   Weighed less than a widow's +uncrystalized tear.

9. A lord and a lady went up at full sail,
   When a bee chanced to light on the opposite scale;
   Ten doctors, ten lawyers, two courtiers, one earl,
   Ten counselors' wigs, full of powder and curl,
   All heaped in one balance and swinging from thence,
   Weighed less than a few grains of +candor and sense;

10. A first water +diamond, with +brilliants begirt,
    Than one good potato, just washed from the dirt;
    Yet not mountains of silver and gold could suffice,
    One pearl to outweigh, 't was the pearl of great price.

11. Last of all, the whole world was bowled in at the grate,
    With the soul of a beggar to serve for a weight,
    When the former sprang up with so strong a +rebuff,
    That it made a vast rent and escaped at the roof;
    When, balanced in air, it ascended on high,
    And sailed up aloft, a balloon in the sky;
    While the scale with the soul in 't so mightily fell,
    That it jerked the +philosopher out of his cell.

XCIV.—ORIGIN OF PROPERTY.

FROM BLACKSTONE.

1. In the beginning of the world, we are informed by Holy Writ, the all-bountiful Creator gave to man "dominion over all the earth, and over the fishes of the sea, and over the fowl of the air, and over every living thing that moved upon the earth." This is the only true and solid foundation of man's dominion over external things, whatever airy, +metaphysical notions may have been started by fanciful writers on this subject. The earth, therefore, and all things therein, are the general property of mankind, +exclusive of other beings, from the immediate gift of the Creator. And while the earth continued bare of inhabitants, it is reasonable to

CXI.—NORTH AMERICAN INDIANS.

FROM SPRAGUE.

1. NOT many generations ago, where you now sit, +encircled with all that exalts and +embellishes civilized life, the rank thistle nodded in the wind, and the wild fox dug his hole unscared. Here, lived and loved another race of beings. Beneath the same sun that rolls over your head, the Indian hunter pursued the panting deer; gazing on the same moon that smiles for you, the Indian lover wooed his +dusky mate. Here, the wigwam blaze beamed on the tender and helpless, and the council-fire glared on the wise and daring. Now, they dipped their noble limbs in your +sedgy lakes, and now, they paddled the light canoe along your rocky shores. Here, they warred; the echoing +whoop, the bloody +grapple, the defying death-song, all were here; and when the tiger-strife was over, here, curled the smoke of peace.

2. Here, too, they worshiped; and from many a dark bosom went up a fervent prayer to the Great Spirit. He had not written his laws for them on tables of stone, but he had traced them on the tables of their hearts. The poor child of nature knew not the God of Revelation, but the God of the +universe he acknowledged in every thing around. He beheld him in the star that sank in beauty behind his lonely dwelling; in the sacred orb that flamed on him from his midday throne; in the flower that snapped in the morning breeze; in the lofty pine that defied a thousand whirlwinds; in the timid +warbler that never left its native grove; in the fearless eagle, whose untired +pinion was wet in clouds; in the worm that crawled at his feet; and in his own +matchless form, glowing with a spark of that light, to whose mysterious source he bent in humble, though blind adoration.

3. And all this has passed away. Across the ocean came a +pilgrim bark, bearing the seeds of life and death. The former were sown for you; the latter sprang up in the path of the simple native. Two hundred years have changed the character of a great continent, and blotted forever from its face, a whole, peculiar people. Art has +usurped the bowers of nature, and the anointed children of education have been too powerful for the tribes of the ignorant. Here and there, a

24

CHARLES SPRAGUE (1791–1875) WAS THE AUTHOR OF THE EARLIER selection entitled "Prospects of the Cherokees" (see pages 217–19). In that piece he was speaking more directly to a specific historical event, whereas here he romanticizes in a general vein. Stressing the theistic element of pantheism, he paints an attractive portrait of the Noble Savage as he supposedly once lived—and then bemoans the inevitable extinction of the Indian race.

McGuffey *selections on the American Indians were neither as common as the lessons collected here might suggest, nor as exclusively complimentary. There were, for instance, descriptions of an Indian massacre or two, along with portraits of some Indians which showed less flattering characteristics.*

But for the most part, the McGuffeys *remain consistent in treating the Indians as unfortunate victims of the white man; and lessons such as this (employed in the* Readers *from 1844 to the present) were the ones retained when revisions forced others out of the series.*

stricken few remain; but how unlike their bold, untamable †progenitors. The Indian of †falcon glance and lion bearing, the †theme of the touching ballad, the hero of the pathetic tale, is gone! and his degraded †offspring crawls upon the soil where *he* walked in majesty, to remind *us* how miserable is man, when the foot of the conqueror is on his neck.

4. As a race, they have withered from the land. Their arrows are broken, their springs are dried up, their cabins are in the dust. Their †council-fire has long since gone out on the shore, and their war-cry is fast fading to the untrodden west. Slowly and sadly they climb the distant mountains, and read their doom in the setting sun. They are shrinking before the mighty tide which is pressing them away; they must soon hear the roar of the last wave, which will settle over them forever. Ages hence, the †inquisitive white man, as he stands by some growing city, will ponder on the †structure of their disturbed remains, and wonder to what manner of persons they belonged. They will live only in the songs and †chronicles of their †exterminators. Let these be faithful to their rude virtues, as men, and pay due tribute to their unhappy fate, as a people.

CXII.—RED JACKET, THE INDIAN CHIEF.

FROM HALLECK.

FITZ GREENE HALLECK, a native of Connecticut; he has written little, but ranks high among American poets.

ROB ROY and ROBIN HOOD; celebrated outlaws, the one of Scotland, the other of England. UPAS; a poisonous tree which grows in India.

1. THOU wert a monarch born. Tradition's pages
   Tell not the planting of thy parent tree,
   But that the forest tribe have bent for ages,
   To thee, and to thy sires, the subject knee.

2. Thy name is princely, though no poet's †magic
   Could make Red Jacket grace an English rhyme,
   Unless he had a genius for the tragic,
   And introduced it into †pantomime.

3. Yet it is music in the language spoken
   Of thine own land; and on her herald roll,

It led me to the port of peace.
Now, safely moored, my perils o'er,
I'll sing, first in night's *diadem,
Forever and for evermore,
The Star, the Star of Bethlehem.

CXXXI.—THE BEST KIND OF REVENGE.

1. SOME years ago, a *warehouseman in Manchester, England, published a *scurrilous pamphlet, in which he endeavored to hold up the house of Grant Brothers to ridicule. William Grant remarked upon the occurrence, that the man would live to repent of what he had done; and this was conveyed by some tale-bearer to the libeler, who said, "O, I suppose he thinks I shall some time or other be in his debt; but I will take good care of that." It happens, however, that a man in business can not always choose who shall be his *creditors. The pamphleteer became a *bankrupt, and the brothers held an *acceptance of his, which had been *indorsed to them by the drawer, who had also become a bankrupt.

2. The wantonly-libeled men had thus become creditors of the libeler! They now had it in their power to make him repent of his audacity. He could not obtain his certificate without their signature, and without it he could not enter into business again. He had obtained the number of signatures required by the bankrupt law, except one. It seemed folly to hope that the firm of "the brothers" would supply the *deficiency. What! they, who had cruelly been made the laughing-stock of the public, forget the wrong and favor the wrong-doer? He despaired. But the claims of a wife and children forced him at last to make the application. Humbled by misery, he presented himself at the counting-house of the wronged.

3. Mr. William Grant was there alone, and his first words to the *delinquent were, "Shut the door, sir!" sternly uttered. The door was shut, and the libeler stood trembling before the libeled. He told his tale, and produced his certificate, which was instantly clutched by the injured merchant. "You wrote a pamphlet against us once!" exclaimed Mr.

OF THE SEVERAL LESSONS BEARING THIS OR A SIMILAR TITLE IN THE **McGuffeys** *(some of them in verse; all of them illustrating the application of the Golden Rule), this is probably the most interesting. It is also one of the few selections about businessmen in the* **Readers.** *For the most part—even in the later editions—the agrarian base of American society is implicitly represented as still predominant. And even here, the businessman is located in England, not America.*

311

First used in the 1857 edition of the Sixth Reader, this selection was demoted to the Fifth Reader in the 1879 and 1920 editions. No authorial attribution was ever furnished, but it might well have been extracted from a collection of sermons.

Grant. The supplicant expected to see his ⁺parchment thrown into the fire. But this was not its ⁺destination. Mr. Grant took a pen, and writing something upon the document, handed it back to the bankrupt. He, poor wretch, expected to see "rogue, scoundrel, libeler," inscribed; but there was, in fair round characters, the signature of the firm.

4. "We make it a rule," said Mr. Grant, "never to refuse signing the certificate of an honest tradesman, and we have never heard that you were any thing else." The tears started into the poor man's eyes. "Ah," said Mr. Grant, "my saying was true! I said you would live to repent writing that pamphlet. I did not mean it as a threat. I only meant that some day you would know us better, and be sorry you had tried to injure us. I see you repent of it now." "I do, I do!" said the grateful man; "I bitterly repent it." "Well, well, my dear fellow, you know us now. How do you get on? What are you going to do?" The poor man stated he had friends who could assist him when his certificate was obtained. "But how are you off in the mean time?"

5. And the answer was, that, having given up every farthing to his creditors, he had been compelled to ⁺stint his family of even common necessaries, that he might be enabled to pay the cost of his certificate. "My dear fellow, this will not do; your family must not suffer. Be kind enough to take this ten-pound note to your wife from me. There, there, my dear fellow! Nay, do not cry; it will all be well with you yet. Keep up your spirits, set to work like a man, and you will raise your head among us yet." The overpowered man endeavored in vain to express his thanks; the swelling in his throat forbade words. He put his handkerchief to his face, and went out of the door, crying like a child.

CXXXII.—THE GLOVE AND THE LION.

FROM LEIGH HUNT.

LEIGH HUNT, an English poet, was born in 1784. His writings, prose and poetic, are full of life and beauty.

1. KING Francis was a ⁺hearty king, and loved a royal sport,
And one day as his lions fought, sat looking on the court;

fectly at his ease, with his faculties in full play, and the full orbit of his genius forever clear and unclouded.

5. And then, the stores of his mind were inexhaustible. He had commenced life with an attention so [+]vigilant, that nothing had escaped his observation; and a judgment so solid, that every incident was turned to advantage. His youth had not been wasted in idleness, nor overcast by intemperance. He had been, all his life, a close and deep reader, as well as thinker; and by the force of his own powers, had wrought up the raw materials which he had gathered from books, with such exquisite skill and [+]felicity, that he has added a hundred fold to their original value, and justly made them his own.

CXXXVII.—A CONVERSATIONAL PLEASANTRY.

From Franklin.

Benjamin Franklin was born in 1706. While apprenticed to the printing business, he found opportunity for self-improvement, and began to write anonymously for the New England Courant, pieces which were much admired. His history as a statesman and philosopher is familiar to every American. He died in 1790.

1. Some wit of old—such wits of old there were,
Whose hints showed meaning, whose [+]allusions, care,—
By one brave stroke, to mark all human kind,
Called clear, blank paper, every infant mind;
Where, still, as opening sense her [+]dictates wrote,
Fair virtue put a seal, or vice a blot.
The thought was happy, [+]pertinent, and true;
Methinks a genius might the plan pursue.

2. I, (can you pardon my presumption?) I,
No wit, no genius, yet, for once, will try.
Various the papers various wants produce;
The wants of fashion, elegance, and use.
Men are as various; and, if right I scan,
Each sort of paper represents some man.

3. Pray, note the fop, half powder, and half lace;
Nice as a bandbox were his dwelling-place;
He's the *gilt-paper*, which, apart you store,
And lock from vulgar hands in the [+]scrutoir.

THE WRITINGS OF BENJAMIN FRANKLIN—PARTICULARLY THE PITHY maxims of Poor Richard's Almanac *(1733–1758) and the pragmatic observations in his* Autobiography *(1818)— remained popular throughout the nineteenth century. Excerpts from Franklin's writings were frequently employed in school books, but the* McGuffeys *include surprisingly few. This light piece appeared in the 1844* Fifth Reader *and was used to help inaugurate the* Sixth Reader *in 1857. It disappeared from the series, however, in 1879.*

Some of Franklin's analogies are successfully humorous, others—particularly the ninth and tenth stanzas—reflect the anti-intellectualism and sexism of his time. Franklin's pragmatic dismissal of all "our" poets in stanza nine may perhaps have been a display of assumed modesty (could he have viewed himself a poet here?), but the prejudices such verses propagated unfortunately extended beyond the bounds of his own rhymes.

4. Mechanics, servants, farmers, and so forth,
   Are *copy-paper*, of inferior worth;
   Less prized, more useful, for your desk †decreed;
   Free to all pens, and prompt at every need.

5. The wretch, whom †avarice bids to pinch and spare,
   Starve, cheat, and †pilfer, to enrich an heir,
   Is *coarse brown paper*, such as peddlers choose
   To wrap up †wares which better men will use.

6. Take next the miser's †contrast, who destroys
   Health, fame, and fortune, in a round of joys.
   Will any paper match him? Yes, throughout,
   He's a true *sinking-paper*, past all doubt.

7. The retail politician's anxious thought
   Deems this side always right, and that stark naught;
   He foams with censure; with †applause, he raves;
   A dupe to rumors, and a tool of knaves;
   He'll want no type, his weakness to proclaim,
   While such a thing as *foolscap* has a name.

8. The hasty gentleman, whose blood runs high,
   Who picks a quarrel, if you step †awry,
   Who can't a jest, a hint, or look endure;
   What is he? What? *Touch-paper* to be sure.

9. What are our poets, take them as they fall,
   Good, bad, rich, poor, much read, not read at all?
   Them and their works, in the same class you'll find;
   They are the mere *waste-paper* of mankind.

10. Observe the maiden, innocently sweet;
    She's fair *white paper*, an †unsullied sheet;
    On which the happy man, whom fate ordains,
    May write his name, and take her for his pains.

11. One instance more, and only one, I'll bring;
    'T is the great man, who scorns a little thing;
    Whose thoughts, whose deeds, whose †maxims are his own,
    Formed on the feelings of his heart alone.
    True, genuine, *royal-paper*, is his breast;
    Of all the kinds most precious, purest, best.

CLXIX.—GOD'S GOODNESS TO SUCH AS FEAR HIM.

1. FRET not thyself because of evil-doers,
Neither be thou envious against the workers of iniquity;
For they shall be cut down like the grass,
And wither as the green herb.
Trust in the LORD and do good;
So shalt thou dwell in the land, and †verily thou shalt be fed.
Delight thyself, also, in the LORD,
And He shall give thee the desires of thy heart.
Commit thy way unto the LORD;
Trust also in Him, and He shall bring it to pass,
And He shall bring forth thy righteousness as the light,
And thy judgment as the noonday.
Rest in the Lord, and wait patiently for Him.

2. Fret not thyself because of him who prospereth in his way,
Because of the man who bringeth wicked †devices to pass.
Cease from anger and forsake wrath;
Fret not thyself, in any wise, to do evil,
For evil-doers shall be cut off;
But those that wait upon the LORD, *they* shall inherit the earth.
For yet a little while, and the wicked shall not be:
Yea, thou shalt diligently consider his place, and it shall not be.
But the meek shall inherit the earth,
And shall delight themselves in the abundance of peace.

3. A little, that a righteous man hath,
Is better than the riches of many wicked;
For the arms of the wicked shall be broken,
But the LORD upholdeth the righteous.
The LORD knoweth the days of the upright,
And their inheritance shall be forever;
They shall not be ashamed in the evil time;
And in the days of famine they shall be satisfied.

4. The steps of a good man are ordered by the LORD,
And he delighteth in his way;
Though he fall, he shall not be utterly cast down,
For the LORD upholdeth him with his hand.
But the wicked shall perish,
And the enemies of the Lord shall be as the fat of lambs,
They shall consume; into smoke shall they consume away.
The wicked borroweth and payeth not again;
But the righteous sheweth mercy and giveth.
For such as are blessed of him shall inherit the earth.

THIS SELECTION IS TAKEN ALMOST DIRECTLY FROM THE KING JAMES version of the Bible. It is Psalm 37 set in verse form, with verses 12–15 and 37–40 omitted—and verses 20–22 and 23–24 inverted in sequence. Like most Biblical lessons in the McGuffeys, the source of the passage is unspecified and was probably thought unnecessary. It has been in the McGuffeys from 1844 to the present.

Although the rationale for including this particular Psalm was probably religious, rather than pedagogical, a good case may be made for it on educational grounds. It provided in advance, as it were, a satisfying rationale for students who might be troubled when they left school and found a moral world somewhat more complex than that pictured in their Readers.

The McGuffeys *employed proportionally far more lessons from the Bible than this collection (because of page limitations) can indicate. In fact, most early editions of the* Readers *carried the following prefatory remarks by McGuffey.*

From no source has the author drawn more copiously in his selections, than from the Sacred Scriptures. For this, he certainly apprehends no censure. In a Christian country, that man is to be pitied, who, at this day, can honestly object to imbuing the minds of youth with the language and spirit of the Word of God.

The student of the Bible will, it is believed, be pleased to find a specimen of the elegant labors of Bishop Jebb, and some specimens of sacred poetry, as arranged by Dr. Coit, in which the exact words of our authorized translation are prescribed, while the poetic order of the original is happily restored.

5. I have been young, and now am old,
   Yet have I not seen the righteous forsaken,
   Nor his seed begging bread.
   He is ever merciful and lendeth,
   And his seed is blessed.

6. Depart from evil and do good,
   And dwell for evermore;
   For the LORD loveth judgment,
   And forsaketh not his saints:
   They are preserved forever:
   But the seed of the wicked shall be cut off.
   The righteous shall inherit the land,
   And dwell therein forever.
   The mouth of the righteous speaketh wisdom,
   And his tongue talketh of judgment;
   The law of his God is in his heart:
   None of his steps shall slide.
   The wicked watcheth the righteous,
   And seeketh to slay him.
   The Lord will not leave him in his hand,
   Nor condemn him when he is judged.

7. Wait on the LORD and keep his way,
   And He shall exalt thee to inherit the land:
   When the wicked are cut off, thou shalt see it.
   I have seen the wicked in great power,
   And spreading himself like a green †bay-tree;
   Yet he passed away, and lo, he was not:
   Yea, I sought him, but he could not be found.

CLXX.—CHARACTER OF COLUMBUS.

FROM IRVING.

1. COLUMBUS was a man of great and †inventive genius. The operations of his mind were †energetic, but irregular; bursting forth, at times, with that irresistible force which characterizes intellect of such an order. His ambition was lofty and noble, inspiring him with high thoughts, and an anxiety to distinguish himself by great †achievements. He aimed at dignity and wealth in the same elevated spirit with which he sought renown; they were to rise from the territories he should discover, and be commensurate in importance.

Illumed with fluid gold, his near approach
Betoken glad. Lo! now apparent all,
Aslant the dew-bright earth and colored air,
He looks in boundless majesty abroad;
And sheds the shining day, that burnished plays
On rocks, and hills, and towers, and wandering streams.
High-gleaming from afar. Prime cheerer, light!
Of all material beings first, and best!
Efflux divine! Nature's resplendent robe!
Without whose vesting, beauty all were wrapt
In unessential gloom; and thou, O sun!
Soul of surrounding worlds, in whom best seen
Shines out thy Maker, may I sing of thee?

THOMSON.

CLXXXIII.—CALLING THE ROLL.

FROM SHEPHERD.

1. "CORPORAL GREEN!" the †orderly cried;
    "Here!" was the answer, loud and clear,
    From the lips of a soldier standing near;
And "here!" was the word the next replied.
"Cyrus Drew!" and a silence fell;
    This time, no answer followed the call;
    Only his rear-man saw him fall,
Killed or wounded, he could not tell.

2. There they stood in the failing light,
    These men of battle, with grave, dark looks,
    As plain to be read as open books,
While slowly gathered the †shades of night.
The fern on the slope was splashed with blood,
    And down in the corn, where the poppies grew,
    Were redder stains than the poppies knew;
And crimson-dyed was the river's flood.

3. For the foe had crossed from the other side,
    That day, in the face of a murderous fire
    That swept them down in its terrible †ire;
And their life-blood went to color the tide.
"Herbert Cline!" At the call there came
    Two †stalwart soldiers into the line,
    Bearing between them Herbert Cline,
Wounded and bleeding, to answer his name.

THE NEXT FOUR SELECTIONS WERE AMONG THOSE INTRODUCED INTO the **Sixth Reader** in 1866, and represent the most significant acknowledgment of the Civil War's occurrence that one can find in any of the McGuffeys. As in the 1866 revisions at the lower levels, care was taken to preserve the usefulness of the previous edition by adding these lessons in a block at the end. (Although it is impossible to ascertain now, it is quite conceivable that the 1857 edition did not really get shelved, but was printed concurrently with the 1866 version for different regional distribution.)

"Calling the Roll" was one of the popular war songs (another of which was "The Dead Drummer-Boy") penned by Nathaniel Graham Shepherd (1835–1869). He spent much of the Civil War traveling as a war correspondent for the New York Tribune. "Calling the Roll" was retained in all later editions of the McGuffeys—but was moved down to the **Fifth Reader**.

4. "Ezra Kerr!" and a voice said "here!"
  "Hiram Kerr!" but no man replied:
  They were brothers, these two; the sad wind sighed,
  And a shudder crept through the corn-field near.
  "Ephraim Deane!"—then a soldier spoke:
  "Deane carried our regiment's colors," he said,
  "When our ensign was shot; I left him dead,
  Just after the enemy †wavered and broke.

5. "Close to the roadside his body lies:
  I paused a moment, and gave him to drink;
  He murmured his mother's name, I think;
  And death came with it and closed his eyes."
  'T was a victory—yes; but it cost us dear;
  For that company's roll, when called at night,
  Of a hundred men who went into the fight,
  Numbered but twenty that answered "*here!*"

CLXXXIV.—THE DYING SOLDIER.

1. THE shadows of evening are thickening. Twilight closes, and the thin mists are rising in the valley. The last charging †squadron yet thunders in the distance; but it presses only on the †foiled and scattered foe. The fight is over! And those who rode foremost in its fields at morning, where are they now? On the bank of yon little stream, there lies a knight, his life-blood ebbing faster than its tide. His shield is rent, and his lance is broken. Soldier, why faintest thou? The blood that swells from that deep wound will answer.

2. It was this morning that the sun rose bright upon his hopes; it sets upon his grave. This day he led the foremost rank of spears, that had crossed the foe's dark line; then death shouted in the onset! It was the last blow that reached him. He has conquered, though he shall not triumph in the victory. His †breast-plate is dinted. His †helmet has the traces of well-dealt blows. The scarf on his breast! *she* would shrink but to *touch* it now, who *placed* it there.

3. Look on yon crimsoned field that seems to mock the purple clouds above it! Prostrate they lie, drenched in

their dark red pool; thy friends and enemies; the dead and dying; the ⁺veteran, with the ⁺stripling of a day; the nameless trooper, and the leader of a hundred hosts. Friend lies by friend; the steed, with his rider; and foes, linked in their long embrace—their first and last—the gripe of death. Far o'er the field they lie, a gorgeous prey to ruin! White plume and steel ⁺morion! saber and ⁺yataghan! crescent and cross! rich vest and bright ⁺corslet! They came to the fight as if they came to a feasting. Glorious and glittering, even in death, each shining warrior lies!

4. His last glance still seeks that banner! The cry that shall never be repeated, cheers on its last charge. Oh, but for strength to reach the field once more! to die in the foe's front! Peace, dreamer! Thy place in the close rank is filled; and yet, another waits for his who holds it. Soldier! she who sped thee on thy course to-day, shall seek thee, with her blue eyes, in the conquering ranks to-morrow; but she shall seek thee in vain! Proud heads shall bow for thee. Bright eyes shall weep for thee.

5. Heath! thou wilt be the soldier's pillow! Moon, let thy cold light, this night, fall upon him! But, morning, thy soft dews shall tempt him not! The soldier must wake no more. He is dead! The cross of a knight is on his breast! his lips are pressed to his lady's token! Soldier, farewell!

CLXXXV.—THE PICKET.

1. "ALL quiet along the Potomac," they say,
   "Except, now and then, a stray ⁺picket
   Is shot, as he walks on his beat to and fro,
   By a rifleman hid in the thicket."

2. 'T is nothing—a private or two, now and then,
   Will not count in the news of the battle;
   Not an officer lost, only one of the men,
   Moaning out, all alone, the death rattle.

3. "All quiet along the Potomac to-night,"
   Where the soldiers lie peacefully dreaming;
   Their tents, in the rays of the clear autumn moon,
   Or the light of the watch-fires, are gleaming.

"THE PICKET" FIRST APPEARED AS "THE PICKET GUARD" IN HARPER's **Weekly** *in November, 1861. The author was Ethelinda Eliot Beers, better known as Ethel Lynn Beers, whose other famous verse ("Which Shall It Be?") is included earlier in this collection (pages 197–200). The selection here became so well known by its first line that Mrs. Beers changed its title and in 1879—the day that she died—her only book was published as* All Quiet Along the Potomac and Other Poems.

Mrs. Beers's verse—written during the war—pictures a fairly universalized soldier, but one who historically had to be from the North. And so—as innocuous and safely sentimental as it seems—it was quietly removed from the Readers. In the 1879 edition, all evidence of regional favoritism disappeared, and the most noticeable Civil War poem was F. M. Finch's famous "The Blue and the Gray," which was first published in the Atlantic Monthly in September, 1867. A single stanza demonstrates why Henry Steele Commager labeled Finch's verse "a masterpiece of impartiality":

> By the flow of the inland river,
> Whence the fleets of iron have fled,
> Where the blades of the grave grass quiver,
> Asleep are the ranks of the dead;—
> Under the sod and the dew,
> Waiting the judgment day;
> Under the one, the Blue;
> Under the other, the Gray.

4. A †tremulous sigh from the gentle night-wind
 Through the forest leaves slowly is creeping,
While the stars up above, with their glittering eyes,
 Keep guard; for the army is sleeping.

5. There is only the sound of the lone sentry's tread,
 As he tramps from the rock to the fountain,
And thinks of the two in the low trundle-bed,
 Far away in the cot on the mountain.

6. His musket falls slack—his face, dark and grim,
 Grows gentle with memories tender,
As he mutters a prayer for his children asleep,
 For their mother, may Heaven defend her!

7. The moon seems to shine as brightly as then,
 That night, when the love yet unspoken
Leaped up to his lips, and when low murmured vows
 Were pledged, never more to be broken.

8. Then drawing his sleeve roughly over his eyes,
 He dashes the tears that are welling,
And gathers his gun closer up to its place,
 As if to keep down the heart-swelling.

9. He passes the fountain, the †blasted pine-tree;
 The footstep is †lagging and weary,
Yet onward he goes, through the broad belt of light,
 Toward the shade of the forest so dreary.

10. Hark! was it the night-wind that rustled the leaves?
 Was it moonlight so suddenly flashing?
It looked like a rifle:—"Ha! Mary, good-bye!"
 And the life-blood is ebbing and plashing!

11. "All quiet along the Potomac to-night;"
 No sound save the rush of the river;
While soft falls the dew on the face of the dead:
 The picket's off duty forever!

THE BRAVE AT HOME.

1. THE maid who binds her warrior's sash,
 And smiling, all her pain dissembles,
The while beneath the drooping lash,
 One starry tear-drop hangs and trembles;

Though Heaven alone records the tear,
   And fame shall never know her story,
Her heart has shed a drop as dear
   As ever dewed the field of glory!

2. The wife who girds her husband's sword,
   'Mid little ones who weep and wonder,
And bravely speaks the cheering word,
   What though her heart be rent asunder;—
Doomed nightly in her dreams to hear
   The bolts of war around him rattle,—
Has shed as sacred blood as e'er
   Was poured upon the field of battle!

3. The mother who conceals her grief,
   While to her breast her son she presses,
Then breathes a few brave words and brief,
   Kissing the patriot brow she blesses;
With no one but her loving God,
   To know the pain that weighs upon her,
Sheds holy blood as e'er the sod
   Received on Freedom's field of honor!

CLXXXVI.—THE LOST PLEIAD.

From Otway Curry.

The Pleiades are a group of seven small stars, situated in the neck of the constellation Taurus, and regarded by some astronomers as the central point round which our universe of stars is revolving.

According to fable of the ancients, the Pleiades were the seven daughters of Atlas, and were turned into stars, on account of their amiable virtues and mutual affection. Only six of the group are visible to the naked eye. The ancients supposed the seventh concealed herself, out of shame for having bestowed her love upon a mortal, while her sisters were the favorites of divine personages.

In the following beautiful poem, the lost Pleiad is represented as having gradually disappeared from the heavens to wander away, on its mighty circuit through "the deep deserts of the ancient night and far-off universe," but yet, in the coming ages, again to return, after having completed its sublime revolution.

1. Millions of ages gone,
Didst thou survive, in thy enthronèd place,
Amidst the assemblies of the starry race,
   Still shining on—and on.

"The Brave at Home" is a portion of a longer work, **The Wagoner of the Alleghanies,** *by Thomas Buchanan Read (1822-1872), a minor American poet and painter. Although* **The Wagoner** *was a poem about the Revolutionary War, it first appeared in 1862 during the Civil War—and the general, clichéd nature of such excerpts as "The Brave at Home" easily circulated as topical verses. Read's best known painting was "Sheridan's Ride," which was also the title and subject of his best known poem. That poem was written expressly for the elocutionist J. E. Murdock, who read it throughout the country for the benefit of the U.S. Sanitary Commission (a civilian group raising funds for support of military morale and health; a forerunner of the U.S. Red Cross).*

*HERE IS ANOTHER VERSE FROM SAMUEL WOODWORTH (1785–1842)—
the man who gave the world the "Old Oaken Bucket" (pages
176–77). In "The Needle," with a regular meter that suggests
a monotony in his subject, he is instructing all "ye maidens"
in the woman's proper role in life—as seen from his safe,
male perspective.*

322

II. THE NEEDLE.

THE gay belles of fashion may boast of excelling
  In waltz or cotillon, at whist or quadrille;
And seek admiration by vauntingly telling
  Of drawing, and painting, and musical skill:
But give me the fair one, in country or city,
  Whose home and its duties are dear to her heart,
Who cheerfully warbles some rustical ditty,
  While plying the needle with exquisite art:
The bright little needle, the swift-flying needle,
  The needle directed by beauty and art.

If Love have a potent, a magical token,
  A talisman, ever resistless and true,
A charm that is never evaded or broken,
  A witchery certain the heart to subdue,
'Tis this; and his armory never has furnished
  So keen and unerring, or polished a dart;
Let beauty direct it, so polished and burnished,
  And oh! it is certain of touching the heart:
The bright little needle, the swift-flying needle,
  The needle directed by beauty and art.

Be wise, then, ye maidens, nor seek admiration,
  By dressing for conquest, and flirting with all;
You never, whate'er be your fortune or station,
  Appear half so lovely at rout or at ball,
As gayly convened at the work-covered table,
  Each cheerfully active, playing her part,
Beguiling the task with a song or a fable,
  And plying the needle with exquisite art:
The bright little needle, the swift-flying needle,
  The needle directed by beauty and art.
                —*Samuel Woodworth.*

VII. SCHEMES OF LIFE OFTEN ILLUSORY.

Samuel Johnson, 1709-1784. This truly remarkable man was the son of a bookseller and stationer; he was born in Lichfield, Staffordshire, England. He entered Pembroke College, Oxford, in 1728; but, at the end of three years, his poverty compelled him to leave without taking his degree. In 1736, he married Mrs. Porter, a widow of little culture, much older than himself, but possessed of some property. The marriage seems to have been a happy one, nevertheless; and, on the death of his wife, in 1752, Johnson mourned for her most sincerely. Soon after his marriage, he opened a private school, but obtained only three pupils, one of whom was David Garrick, afterward the celebrated actor. In 1737, he removed to London, where he lived for most of the remainder of his life. Here he entered upon literary work, in which he continued, and from which he derived his chief support, although at times it was but a meager one. His "Vanity of Human Wishes" was sold for ten guineas. His great Dictionary, the first one of the English language worthy of mention, brought him £1575, and occupied his time for seven years. Most of the money he received for the work went to pay his six amanuenses. The other most famous of his numerous literary works are "The Rambler," "Rasselas," "The Lives of the English Poets," and his edition of Shakespeare. In person, Johnson was heavy and awkward; he was the victim of scrofula in his youth, and of dropsy in his old age. In manner, he was boorish and overbearing; but his great powers and his wisdom caused his company to be sought by many eminent men of his time.

OMAR, the son of Hassan, had passed seventy-five years in honor and prosperity. The favor of three successive caliphs had filled his house with gold and silver; and whenever he appeared, the benedictions of the people proclaimed his passage.

Terrestrial happiness is of short continuance. The brightness of the flame is wasting its fuel; the fragrant flower is passing away in its own odors. The vigor of Omar began to fail; the curls of beauty fell from his head; strength departed from his hands, and agility from his feet. He gave back to the caliph the keys of trust, and the seals of secrecy; and sought no other pleasure for the remainder of life than the converse of the wise and the gratitude of the good.

The powers of his mind were yet unimpaired. His chamber was filled by visitants, eager to catch the dictates of

THE TONE OF THE AUTHOR'S NOTE FURNISHED HERE SHOWS AN admirable balance between its coverage of Dr. Johnson's writings and its brief mention of his person and manner. Such balance was strikingly rare at the time it was written (1879), since by then Macaulay's warped critical view of Johnson had already started to dominate. To Macaulay (who admitted he was trying to chop down the grand old Tory, just as Johnson had humorously claimed always to give the "Whig dogs" the worst of it), Johnson was a man whose writings were no longer read, but whose eccentric life was fascinating—even if written by a mere toady (i.e., Boswell, another of Macaulay's Tory targets). Macaulay's effort at political/literary revisionism was, for too many years, very successful in America, largely because it was his short biased Life of Johnson *that was mass-reproduced for schools—not Boswell's longer and better biography.*

Johnson wrote this selection in 1760 as Idler *Number 101, one of a series of weekly essays he contributed to the* Universal Chronicle, or Weekly Gazette *from 1758 to 1760. It has appeared in every edition of the McGuffey Sixth Reader in the text shown here, which is—with only minor changes for the most part—as Johnson wrote it. Most of the changes are very slight, such as Americanizing the spelling, modernizing punctuation, etc. A curious alteration, however, occurs in the* McGuffey *version with the changing of Johnson's simple* you *and* your *to* thou *and* thy—*evidently an attempt to create an archaic flavor.*

experience, and officious to pay the tribute of admiration. Caleb, the son of the viceroy of Egypt, entered every day early, and retired late. He was beautiful and eloquent: Omar admired his wit, and loved his docility.

"Tell me," said Caleb, "thou to whose voice nations have listened, and whose wisdom is known to the extremities of Asia, tell me, how I may resemble Omar the prudent? The arts by which thou hast gained power and preserved it, are to thee no longer necessary or useful; impart to me the secret of thy conduct, and teach me the plan upon which thy wisdom has built thy fortune."

"Young man," said Omar, "it is of little use to form plans of life. When I took my first survey of the world, in my twentieth year, having considered the various conditions of mankind, in the hour of solitude I said thus to myself, leaning against a cedar which spread its branches over my head: 'Seventy years are allowed to man; I have yet fifty remaining.

"'Ten years I will allot to the attainment of knowledge, and ten I will pass in foreign countries; I shall be learned, and therefore I shall be honored; every city will shout at my arrival, and every student will solicit my friendship. Twenty years thus passed will store my mind with images which I shall be busy through the rest of my life in combining and comparing. I shall revel in inexhaustible accumulations of intellectual riches; I shall find new pleasures for every moment, and shall never more be weary of myself.

"'I will not, however, deviate too far from the beaten track of life; but will try what can be found in female delicacy. I will marry a wife as beautiful as the houries, and wise as Zobeide; and with her I will live twenty years within the suburbs of Bagdad, in every pleasure that wealth can purchase, and fancy can invent.

"'I will then retire to a rural dwelling, pass my days in obscurity and contemplation; and lie silently down on the bed of death. Through my life it shall be my settled resolution, that I will never depend on the smile of princes; that I will never stand exposed to the artifices of courts; I will never pant for public honors, nor disturb my quiet with the affairs of state.' Such was my scheme of life, which I impressed indelibly upon my memory.

"The first part of my ensuing time was to be spent in search of knowledge, and I know not how I was diverted from my design. I had no visible impediments without, nor any ungovernable passion within. I regarded knowledge as the highest honor, and the most engaging pleasure; yet day stole upon day, and month glided after month, till I found that seven years of the first ten had vanished, and left nothing behind them.

"I now postponed my purpose of traveling; for why should I go abroad, while so much remained to be learned at home? I immured myself for four years, and studied the laws of the empire. The fame of my skill reached the judges: I was found able to speak upon doubtful questions, and I was commanded to stand at the footstool of the caliph. I was heard with attention; I was consulted with confidence, and the love of praise fastened on my heart.

"I still wished to see distant countries; listened with rapture to the relations of travelers, and resolved some time to ask my dismission, that I might feast my soul with novelty; but my presence was always necessary, and the stream of business hurried me along. Sometimes, I was afraid lest I should be charged with ingratitude; but I still proposed to travel, and therefore would not confine myself by marriage.

"In my fiftieth year, I began to suspect that the time of my traveling was past; and thought it best to lay hold on the felicity yet in my power, and indulge myself in domestic pleasures. But, at fifty, no man easily finds a woman beautiful as the houries, and wise as Zobeide. I inquired and rejected, consulted and deliberated, till the

Most of the McGuffey *selections from Samuel Johnson's writings do not appear until the* Fifth *and* Sixth Reader, *probably because they are relatively complex both in diction and syntax, and because—as anyone who has tried soon learns—they are usually impossible to paraphrase or reduce without serious loss. The presence of Johnson is felt in the earlier* Readers, *however, even if he seldom receives authorial credit. Sometimes passages from his works are used to illustrate style (such as the use of parallelism and antithesis in his comparison of Dryden and Pope); at other times, lines are lifted to illustrate particular moral points (e.g., "He that would pass the latter part of life with honor and decency, must, when he is young, consider that he shall one day be old; and remember, when he is old, that he has once been young.").*

Omar's shame at "wishing to marry" is the only significant change made in the McGuffey version. Johnson's essay reads "made me ashamed of gazing upon girls"—a phrase evidently determined to be too suggestive! Even the moralistic Dr. Johnson had to be bowdlerized before he was fit for pupils of the McGuffeys.

sixty-second year made me ashamed of wishing to marry. I had now nothing left but retirement; and for retirement I never found a time, till disease forced me from public employment.

"Such was my scheme, and such has been its consequence. With an insatiable thirst for knowledge, I trifled away the years of improvement; with a restless desire of seeing different countries, I have always resided in the same city; with the highest expectation of connubial felicity, I have lived unmarried; and with an unalterable resolution of contemplative retirement, I am going to die within the walls of Bagdad."

Notes.—**Bag däd.´**—A large city of Asiatic Turkey, on the river Tigris. In the ninth century, it was the greatest center of Moslem power and learning.

Zobeide (Zo-bād´).—A lady of Bagdad, whose story is given in the "Three Calendars" of the "Arabian Nights."

In this selection the form of an allegory is used to express a general truth.

VIII. THE BRAVE OLD OAK.

Henry Fothergill Chorley, 1808–1872. He is known chiefly as a musical critic and author; for thirty-eight years he was connected with the "London Athenæum." His books are mostly novels.

A song to the oak, the brave old oak,
  Who hath ruled in the greenwood long;
Here's health and renown to his broad green crown,
  And his fifty arms so strong.
There's fear in his frown, when the sun goes down,
  And the fire in the west fades out;
And he showeth his might on a wild midnight,
  When the storms through his branches shout.

6.—6.

wants no drilling; it never ranks in the awkward squad; it has no left hand, no deaf ear, no blind side. It puts on no look of wondrous wisdom, it has no air of profundity, but plays with the details of place as dexterously as a well-taught hand flourishes over the keys of the pianoforte. It has all the air of commonplace, and all the force and power of genius.

XIX. SPEECH BEFORE THE VIRGINIA CONVENTION.

Patrick Henry, 1736-1799, was born in Hanover County, Virginia. He received instruction in Latin and mathematics from his father, but seemed to develop a greater fondness for hunting, fishing, and playing the fiddle than for study. Twice he was set up in business, and twice failed before he was twenty-four. He was then admitted to the bar after six weeks' study of the law. He got no business at first in his profession, but lived with his father-in-law. His wonderful powers of oratory first showed themselves in a celebrated case which he argued in Hanover Courthouse, his own father being the presiding magistrate. He began very awkwardly, but soon rose to a surprising height of eloquence, won his case against great odds, and was carried off in triumph by the delighted spectators. His fame was now established; business flowed in, and he was soon elected to the Virginia Legislature. He was a delegate to the Congress of 1774, and in 1775 made the prophetic speech of which the following selection is a portion. It was on his own motion that the "colony be immediately put in a state of defense." During the Revolution he was, for several years, Governor of Virginia. In 1788, he earnestly opposed the adoption of the Federal Constitution. When he died, he left a large family and an ample fortune. In person, Mr. Henry was tall and rather awkward, with a face stern and grave. When he spoke on great occasions, his awkwardness forsook him, his face lighted up, and his eyes flashed with a wonderful fire. In his life, he was good-humored, honest, and temperate. His patriotism was of the noblest type; and few men in those stormy times did better service for their country than he.

IT is natural for man to indulge in the illusions of hope. We are apt to shut our eyes against a painful truth, and listen to the song of that siren till she transforms us into beasts. Is this the part of wise men, engaged in a great and arduous struggle for liberty? Are we disposed to be of the number of those, who, having

PATRICK HENRY'S FAME AS AN ORATOR OVERSHADOWS THE CURIOUS mixture of other successes and failures in his life. In addition to twice failing as a storekeeper, he also failed as a farmer—even with help from his in-laws, who purchased slaves for him. After establishing his reputation as an orator, however, Henry's legal practice improved, and he was overwhelmingly elected Governor of Virginia for three terms (being prohibited by the state constitution from being chosen again in succession). He declined a number of other positions, including the chance to represent Virginia in the Senate and offers from Washington to serve as Secretary of State or Chief Justice of the Supreme Court. Henry's most tangible contribution to the United States in its earliest years was his prominent role in the drafting of the Bill of Rights.

Unfortunately, very little of Patrick Henry's oratory has been preserved. According to tradition, he never wrote his speeches, and the few surviving first-hand reports of listeners lack detail and—at times—offer conflicting accounts. Usually, as here, the texts of the speeches are extracted from the laudatory 1817 Life of Patrick Henry *by William Wirt (see page 225). Wirt (1772–1834) was born too late, of course, to hear any of these famous speeches, but his largely fictional recreations now stand as the traditionally accepted words of Patrick Henry.*

eyes, see not, and having ears, hear not the things which so nearly concern their temporal salvation? For my part, whatever anguish of spirit it may cost, I am willing to know the whole truth; to know the worst, and to provide for it.

I have but one lamp by which my feet are guided; and that is the lamp of experience. I know of no way of judging of the future but by the past; and, judging by the past, I wish to know what there has been in the conduct of the British ministry for the last ten years to justify those hopes with which gentlemen have been pleased to solace themselves and the house? Is it that insidious smile with which our petition has been lately received? Trust it not: it will prove a snare to your feet. Suffer not yourselves to be betrayed with a kiss. Ask yourselves, how this gracious reception of our petition comports with those warlike preparations which cover our waters and darken our land. Are fleets and armies necessary to a work of love and reconciliation? Have we shown ourselves so unwilling to be reconciled that force must be called in to win back our love? Let us not deceive ourselves. These are the implements of war and subjugation,—the last arguments to which kings resort.

I ask, gentlemen, what means this martial array, if its purpose be not to force us into submission? Can gentlemen assign any other possible motive for it? Has Great Britain any enemy in this quarter of the world, to call for all this accumulation of navies and armies? No, she has none. They are meant for us: they can be meant for no other. They are sent over to bind and rivet upon us those chains which the British ministry have been so long forging. And what have we to oppose to them? Shall we try argument? We have been trying that for the last ten years. Have we anything new to offer upon the subject? Nothing. We have held the subject up in every light in which it was capable; but it has been all in vain.

Shall we resort to entreaty and humble supplication? What terms shall we find which have not been already exhausted? Let us not, I beseech you, deceive ourselves longer. We have done everything that could be done, to avert the storm which is now coming on. We have petitioned; we have remonstrated; we have supplicated; we have prostrated ourselves at the foot of the throne, and implored its interposition to arrest the tyrannical hands of the ministry and parliament. Our petitions have been slighted; our remonstrances have produced additional violence and insult; our supplications disregarded; and we have been spurned with contempt from the foot of the throne.

In vain, after these things, may we indulge the fond hope of peace and reconciliation. There is no longer any room for hope. If we wish to be free; if we mean to preserve inviolate those inestimable privileges for which we have been so long contending; if we mean not basely to abandon the noble struggle in which we have been so long engaged, and which we have pledged ourselves never to abandon until the glorious object of our contest shall be obtained — we must fight! I repeat it, we must fight! An appeal to arms and the God of Hosts, is all that is left us.

They tell us that we are weak; unable to cope with so formidable an adversary. But when shall we be stronger? Will it be the next week, or the next year? Will it be when we are totally disarmed, and when a British guard shall be stationed in every house? Shall we gather strength by irresolution and inaction? Shall we acquire the means of effectual resistance by lying supinely on our backs, and hugging the delusive phantom of hope, until our enemies shall have bound us hand and foot? We are not weak, if we make a proper use of those means which the God of nature hath placed in our power.

Three millions of people, armed in the holy cause of liberty, and in such a country as that which we possess,

Portions of this oration are similar to Henry's other famous speech, delivered on the Stamp Act in the Virginia Legislature (May 29, 1765). Accounts of that speech vary widely, but most of them concur essentially on the well-known lines: "Caesar had his Brutus; Charles the First his Cromwell; and George the Third may profit by their example. [Cries of "Treason!"] If this be treason, make the most of it!"

This famous speech is that supposedly given by Henry to the Virginia Convention on March 23, 1775. This version, at any rate, was accepted without question by Alexander McGuffey, who chose it for the first edition of the Fifth Reader *(and moved it to the* Sixth Reader *in 1857—where it has remained). There is no authentic record of the speech, but it is recognized that his address that day had a powerful effect, and the ringing lines of the conclusion here may well have been close to what he said. They were certainly the type of expression that England's Dr. Johnson had in mind when he asked sarcastically: "Why is it that we hear the loudest yelps for 'liberty' from the drivers of the Negroes?"*

are invincible by any force which our enemy can send against us. Besides, we shall not fight our battles alone. There is a just God who presides over the destinies of nations; and who will raise up friends to fight our battles for us. The battle is not to the strong alone; it is to the vigilant, the active, the brave. Besides, we have no election. If we were base enough to desire it, it is now too late to retire from the contest. There is no retreat but in submission and slavery! Our chains are forged. Their clanking may be heard on the plains of Boston! The war is inevitable; and, let it come! I repeat it, let it come!

It is in vain to extenuate the matter. Gentlemen may cry peace, peace; but there is no peace. The war is actually begun. The next gale that sweeps from the north, will bring to our ears the clash of resounding arms! Our brethren are already in the field! Why stand we here idle? What is it that gentlemen wish? What would they have? Is life so dear, or peace so sweet, as to be purchased at the price of chains and slavery? Forbid it, Almighty God! I know not what course others may take; but as for me, give me liberty, or give me death.

NOTES.—Observe, in this lesson, the all-controlling power of emphasis in determining the falling inflection. The words "see," "hear," and "my," in the first paragraph, the word "that" in the second, and "spurned" and "contempt" in the fourth paragraph, are examples of this. Let the reader remember that a high degree of emphasis is sometimes expressed by a whisper; also, that emphasis is often expressed by a pause.

It will be well to read in this connection some good history of the opening scenes of the Revolution.

XXIII. THE MEMORY OF OUR FATHERS.

Lyman Beecher, 1775-1863, a famous Congregational minister of New England, was born in New Haven, graduated from Yale College in 1797, and studied theology with Dr. Timothy Dwight. His first settlement was at East Hampton, L. I., at a salary of three hundred dollars per year. He was pastor of the church in Litchfield, Ct., from 1810 till 1826, when he removed to Boston, and took charge of the Hanover Street Church. In the religious controversies of the time, Dr. Beecher was one of the most prominent characters. From 1832 to 1842, he was President of Lane Theological Seminary, in the suburbs of Cincinnati. He then returned to Boston, where he spent most of the closing years of his long and active life. His death occurred in Brooklyn, N. Y. As a theologian, preacher, and advocate of education, temperance, and missions, Dr. Beecher occupied a very prominent place for nearly half a century. He left a large family of sons and two daughters, who are well known as among the most eminent preachers and authors in America.

IN LYMAN BEECHER'S "NECESSITY OF EDUCATION," WHICH APPEARS earlier in this collection (pages 227–30), he demonstrated his regional pride in the West after he had moved from Boston to Cincinnati. This selection shows him somewhat defensively waving the banner of New England, but the moral and religious import of his message obviously extends well beyond a single region. "The Memory of our Fathers" entered the McGuffeys *in the 1844* Fifth Reader, *moved up to the* Sixth Reader *in 1857, and has remained there since.*

WE are called upon to cherish with high veneration and grateful recollections, the memory of our fathers. Both the ties of nature and the dictates of policy demand this. And surely no nation had ever less occasion to be ashamed of its ancestry, or more occasion for gratulation in that respect; for while most nations trace their origin to barbarians, the foundations of our nation were laid by civilized men, by Christians. Many of them were men of distinguished families, of powerful talents, of great learning and of preëminent wisdom, of decision of character, and of most inflexible integrity. And yet not unfrequently they have been treated as if they had no virtues; while their sins and follies have been sedulously immortalized in satirical anecdote.

The influence of such treatment of our fathers is too manifest. It creates and lets loose upon their institutions, the vandal spirit of innovation and overthrow; for after the memory of our fathers shall have been rendered contemptible, who will appreciate and sustain their institutions? "The memory of our fathers" should be the watchword of liberty throughout the land; for, imperfect as they were, the world before had not seen their like, nor will it soon, we fear, behold their like again. Such models of moral excellence, such apostles of civil and religious liberty, such shades of the illustrious dead looking down upon their descendants with approbation or reproof, according as they follow or depart from the good way, constitute a censorship inferior only to the eye of God; and to ridicule them is national suicide.

The doctrines of our fathers have been represented as gloomy, superstitious, severe, irrational, and of a licentious tendency. But when other systems shall have produced a piety as devoted, a morality as pure, a patriotism as disinterested, and a state of society as happy, as have prevailed where their doctrines have been most prevalent, it may be in season to seek an answer to this objection.

The persecutions instituted by our fathers have been the occasion of ceaseless obloquy upon their fair fame. And truly, it was a fault of no ordinary magnitude, that sometimes they did persecute. But let him whose ancestors were not ten times more guilty, cast the first stone, and the ashes of our fathers will no more be disturbed. Theirs was the fault of the age, and it will be easy to show that no class of men had, at that time, approximated so nearly to just apprehensions of religious liberty; and that it is to them that the world is now indebted for the more just and definite views which now prevail.

The superstition and bigotry of our fathers are themes on which some of their descendants, themselves far enough from superstition, if not from bigotry, have delighted to dwell. But when we look abroad, and behold the condition of the world, compared with the condition of New England, we may justly exclaim, "Would to God that the ancestors of all the nations had been not only almost, but altogether such bigots as our fathers were."

bound to the music of their solitary cries, to the tinkle of their gushing rills, to the sound of their cataracts! How inspiriting are the odors that breathe from the upland turf, from the rock-hung flower, from the hoary and solemn pine! How beautiful are those lights and shadows thrown abroad, and that fine, transparent haze which is diffused over the valleys and lower slopes, as over a vast, inimitable picture!

XXV. THE JOLLY OLD PEDAGOGUE.

George Arnold, 1834–1865, was born in New York City. He never attended school, but was educated at home, by his parents. His literary career occupied a period of about twelve years. In this time he wrote stories, essays, criticisms in art and literature, poems, sketches, etc., for several periodicals. Two volumes of his poems have been published since his death.

'T was a jolly old pedagogue, long ago,
  Tall, and slender, and sallow, and dry;
His form was bent, and his gait was slow,
And his long, thin hair was white as snow,
  But a wonderful twinkle shone in his eye:
And he sang every night as he went to bed,
  "Let us be happy down here below;
The living should live, though the dead be dead,"
  Said the jolly old pedagogue, long ago.

He taught the scholars the Rule of Three,
  Reading, and writing, and history too;
He took the little ones on his knee,
For a kind old heart in his breast had he,
  And the wants of the littlest child he knew.
"Learn while you're young," he often said,
  "There is much to enjoy down here below;
Life for the living, and rest for the dead!"
  Said the jolly old pedagogue, long ago.

THE IRONY OF A POEM ON A SCHOOLMASTER BEING WRITTEN BY A POET who "never attended school" is surpassed only by the fact that some enthusiastic McGuffey Readers *fans have—over the years—cited this title as a description of the dour William Holmes McGuffey! It has appeared, however, only in the Sixth Reader—over which William never had any control. First added to the series in 1866, it has been a part of all subsequent editions.*

With the stupidest boys, he was kind and cool,
  Speaking only in gentlest tones;
The rod was scarcely known in his school—
Whipping to him was a barbarous rule,
  And too hard work for his poor old bones;
Besides it was painful, he sometimes said:
  "We should make life pleasant down here below—
The living need charity more than the dead,"
  Said the jolly old pedagogue, long ago.

He lived in the house by the hawthorn lane,
  With roses and woodbine over the door;
His rooms were quiet, and neat, and plain,
But a spirit of comfort there held reign,
  And made him forget he was old and poor.
"I need so little," he often said;
  "And my friends and relatives here below
Won't litigate over me when I am dead,"
  Said the jolly old pedagogue, long ago.

But the pleasantest times he had of all,
  Were the sociable hours he used to pass,
With his chair tipped back to a neighbor's wall,
Making an unceremonious call,
  Over a pipe and a friendly glass:
This was the finest pleasure, he said,
  Of the many he tasted here below:
"Who has no cronies had better be dead,"
  Said the jolly old pedagogue, long ago.

The jolly old pedagogue's wrinkled face
  Melted all over in sunshiny smiles;
He stirred his glass with an old-school grace,
Chuckled, and sipped, and prattled apace,
  Till the house grew merry from cellar to tiles.

The lenient classroom discipline and non-theological philosophy of this "jolly old pedagogue" signal clearly that he is not to be confused with William Holmes McGuffey. The pipe and "friendly glass" serve as additional reminders that this lesson was added later in the century.

"I'm a pretty old man," he gently said,
   "I've lingered a long time here below;
But my heart is fresh, if my youth is fled!"
   Said the jolly old pedagogue, long ago.

He smoked his pipe in the balmy air
   Every night, when the sun went down;
And the soft wind played in his silvery hair,
Leaving its tenderest kisses there,
   On the jolly old pedagogue's jolly old crown;
And feeling the kisses, he smiled, and said:
   "'T is a glorious world down here below;
Why wait for happiness till we are dead?"
   Said this jolly old pedagogue, long ago.

He sat at his door one midsummer night,
   After the sun had sunk in the west,
And the lingering beams of golden light
Made his kindly old face look warm and bright,
   While the odorous night winds whispered, "Rest!"
Gently, gently, he bowed his head;
   There were angels waiting for him, I know;
He was sure of his happiness, living or dead,
   This jolly old pedagogue, long ago!

XXVI. THE TEACHER AND SICK SCHOLAR.

SHORTLY after the schoolmaster had arranged the forms and taken his seat behind his desk, a small white-headed boy with a sunburnt face appeared at the door, and, stopping there to make a rustic bow, came in and took his seat upon one of the forms. He then put an open book, astonishingly dog's-eared, upon his knees, and, thrusting

XXXI. SPEECH OF WALPOLE IN REPROOF OF MR. PITT.

Sir Robert Walpole, 1676–1745, was educated at Eton and Cambridge. He entered Parliament in 1700, and soon became a good debater and skillful tactician. He was prime minister of Great Britain from 1721 to 1742, in the reigns of George I. and George II. He was an able statesman; but has been accused of employing corruption or bribery on a large scale, to control Parliament and accomplish his purposes.

I WAS unwilling to interrupt the course of this debate, while it was carried on with calmness and decency, by men who do not suffer the ardor of opposition to cloud their reason, or transport them to such expressions as the dignity of this assembly does not admit.

I have hitherto deferred answering the gentleman, who declaimed against the bill with such fluency and rhetoric, and such vehemence of gesture; who charged the advocates for the expedients now proposed, with having no regard to any interests but their own, and with making laws only to consume paper, and threatened them with the defection of their adherents, and the loss of their influence, upon this new discovery of their folly and ignorance. Nor, do I now answer him for any other purpose than to remind him how little the clamor of rage and petulancy of invective contribute to the end for which this assembly is called together; how little the discovery of truth is promoted, and the security of the nation established, by pompous diction and theatrical emotion.

Formidable sounds and furious declamation, confident assertions and lofty periods, may affect the young and inexperienced; and perhaps the gentleman may have contracted his habits of oratory by conversing more with those of his own age than with such as have more opportunities of acquiring knowledge, and more successful methods of communicating their sentiments. If the heat of temper would permit him to attend to those whose age and long acquaintance with business give them an indis-

THIS SPEECH AND ITS CELEBRATED REJOINDER IN THE FOLLOWING lesson were regular features in most nineteenth-century American textbooks, appearing in the McGuffeys in the 1844 Fifth Reader and all editions of the Sixth from 1857 to the present. They did so much to establish the oratorical reputation of William Pitt the Elder, that it is almost a shame they did not happen the way they are presented here.

In the first place, neither Walpole nor Pitt "made" these speeches; they were written by Samuel Johnson—then a young reporter who was not even present when they spoke. Although Johnson's role was known in the nineteenth century, it is pointed out in none of the American textbook versions. To make matters worse, many of the school books credit the fictional speeches to the wrong Walpole and Pitt. The McGuffeys avoid the error of those who give the rejoinder to to William Pitt the Younger (who hadn't been born when the alleged debate occurred), but they slip in announcing the Walpole to be Sir Robert.

putable right to deference and superiority, he would learn in time to reason, rather than declaim; and to prefer justness of argument and an accurate knowledge of facts, to sounding epithets and splendid superlatives, which may disturb the imagination for a moment, but leave no lasting impression upon the mind. He would learn, that to accuse and prove are very different; and that reproaches, unsupported by evidence, affect only the character of him that utters them.

Excursions of fancy and flights of oratory are indeed pardonable in young men, but in no other; and it would surely contribute more, even to the purpose for which some gentlemen appear to speak (that of depreciating the conduct of the administration), to prove the inconveniences and injustice of this bill, than barely to assert them, with whatever magnificence of language, or appearance of zeal, honesty, or compassion.

XXXII. PITT'S REPLY TO SIR ROBERT WALPOLE.

William Pitt, 1708–1778, one of the ablest statesmen and orators of his time, was born in Cornwall, and educated at Eton and Oxford. He entered Parliament in 1735, and became a formidable opponent of the ministry of Sir Robert Walpole. He gained great reputation by his wise and vigorous management of military affairs in the last years of the reign of George II. He opposed the "Stamp Act" with great earnestness, as well as the course of the ministry in the early years of the American Revolution. In 1778, he rose from a sick bed to make his celebrated speech, in the House of Lords, in opposition to a motion to acknowledge the independence of America. At its close, he fell in an apoplectic fit, and was borne home to die in a few weeks afterward. He was buried in Westminster Abbey. Mr. Pitt possessed a fine personal presence and a powerful voice; he was very popular with the people, and is often called the "Great Commoner." He was created "Earl of Chatham" in 1766.

THE atrocious crime of being a young man, which the honorable gentleman has, with such spirit and decency,

The supposed speaker of the first passage was Horace Walpole the Elder, brother to Sir Robert Walpole, who was the First Lord of the Treasury and in effect England's first real "prime minister"—although that term was not to be recognized even unofficially for years. (To complicate matters further, there was also another Horace Walpole—Sir Robert's son—who later, in 1764, wrote what is usually considered the first Gothic novel: The Castle of Otranto; *but neither he nor William Pitt the Younger play any role in this affair.) The exchange here supposedly took place in the House of Commons on March 2, 1741, during the debate on the Bill for the Encouragement and Encrease of Seamen.*

In 1738 the House of Commons passed a resolution forbidding the reporting of their transactions in newspapers and periodicals. (Most politicians, it appears, have never really wanted to be reminded of what they said.) Samuel Johnson was at that time working for Edmund Cave's Gentleman's Magazine, *which—to circumvent the new law—started a "new" feature: the debates were reported using easily penetrated anagrams for legislators' names, and calling the whole production "Debates in the Senate of Magna Lilliputia" (as supposedly received from Lemuel Gulliver's grandson). Although others were involved, Johnson evidently worked on these debates from their inception; and he admitted having the sole responsibility for their composition from early in 1741 until 1744. These two speeches are among those he later acknowledged as his.*

Johnson never actually attended any of the debates he supposedly reported, and he seldom had more to work from (he confessed to Boswell) than "the names of the several speakers, and the part which they had taken in the debate." As he later admitted to another friend, most of the debates were "the mere coinage of his own imagination," a reluctant claim that is substantiated by comparing his "reports" with some surviving notes of legislators or auditors.

Johnson was a relatively young man at the time—just getting started as a writer in London—and he probably put a little personal zeal into Pitt's famous lines about "The atrocious crime of being a young man." According to Boswell, Johnson subsequently quit writing the debates when he discovered to his dismay that people were accepting them as factual. But other biographers indicate that Johnson showed both amusement and some pride as he heard Pitt's speeches compared favorably to those of Demosthenes and Cicero.

charged upon me. I shall neither attempt to palliate nor deny; but content myself with hoping that I may be one of these whose follies cease with their youth, and not of that number who are ignorant in spite of experience. Whether youth can be imputed to a man as a reproach, I will not assume the province of determining; but surely age may become justly contemptible, if the opportunities which it brings have passed away without improvement, and vice appears to prevail when the passions have subsided. The wretch, who, after having seen the consequences of a thousand errors, continues still to blunder, and whose age has only added obstinacy to stupidity, is surely the object either of abhorrence or contempt, and deserves not that his gray hairs should secure him from insult. Much more is he to be abhorred, who, as he has advanced in age, has receded from virtue, and become more wicked—with less temptation; who prostitutes himself for money which he can not enjoy, and spends the remains of his life in the ruin of his country.

But youth is not my only crime; I am accused of acting a theatrical part. A theatrical part may either imply some peculiarity of gesture, or a dissimulation of my real sentiments, and an adoption of the opinions and language of another man. In the first sense, the charge is too trifling to be confuted, and deserves only to be mentioned that it may be despised. I am at liberty, like every other man, to use my own language; and though, perhaps, I may have some ambition to please this gentleman, I shall not lay myself under any restraint, nor very solicitously copy his diction or his mien, however matured by age, or modeled by experience.

But, if any man shall, by charging me with theatrical behavior, imply that I utter any sentiments but my own, I shall treat him as a calumniator and a villain; nor shall any protection shelter him from the treatment he deserves. I shall, on such an occasion, without scruple, trample upon

all those forms with which wealth and dignity intrench
themselves, nor shall anything but age restrain my resentment; age,—which always brings one privilege, that
of being insolent and supercilious, without punishment.

But, with regard to those whom I have offended, I am
of opinion that, if I had acted a borrowed part, I should
have avoided their censure: the heat that offended them
was the ardor of conviction, and that zeal for the service
of my country which neither hope nor fear shall influence
me to suppress. I will not sit unconcerned while my liberty is invaded, nor look in silence upon public robbery.
I will exert my endeavors, at whatever hazard, to repel
the aggressor, and drag the thief to justice, whoever may
protect him in his villainies, and whoever may partake of
his plunder.

XXXIII. CHARACTER OF MR. PITT.

Henry Grattan, 1750–1820, an Irish orator and statesman, was born
at Dublin, and graduated from Trinity College, in his native city. By
his admiration of Mr. Pitt, the first Earl of Chatham, he was led to
turn his attention to oratory. In personal appearance, he was unpre-
possessing; but his private character was without a blemish.

THE secretary stood alone. Modern degeneracy had not
reached him. Original and unaccommodating, the features
of his character had the hardihood of antiquity. His august mind overawed majesty itself. No state chicanery, no
narrow system of vicious politics, no idle contest for min-
isterial victories, sank him to the vulgar level of the great;
but overbearing, persuasive, and impracticable, his object
was England, his ambition was fame.

Without dividing, he destroyed party; without corrupting, he made a venal age unanimous. France sunk beneath
him. With one hand he smote the house of Bourbon,
and wielded in the other the democracy of England. The

NOTE.—Nova Scotia was first settled by the French, but, in 1713, was ceded to the English. The inhabitants refusing either to take the oath of allegiance or to bear arms against their fellow-countrymen in the French and Indian War, it was decided to remove the whole people, and distribute them among the other British provinces. This was accordingly done in 1755. The villages were burned to the ground, and the people hurried on board the ships in such a way that but a few families remained undivided.

Longfellow's poem of "Evangeline" is founded on this incident, and the above selection describes the scene where the male inhabitants of Grand-Pré are assembled in the church, and the order for their banishment is first made known to them.

LXXIII. SONG OF THE SHIRT.

Thomas Hood, 1798-1845, the son of a London bookseller, was born in that city. He undertook, after leaving school, to learn the art of an engraver, but soon gave up the business, and turned his attention to literature. His lighter pieces, exhibiting his skill as a wit and punster, soon became well known and popular. In 1821 he became subeditor of the "London Magazine," and formed the acquaintance of the literary men of the metropolis. The last years of his life were clouded by poverty and ill health. Some of his most humorous pieces were written on a sick bed. Hood is best known as a joker—a writer of "whims and oddities"—but he was no mere joker. Some of his pieces are filled with the tenderest pathos; and a gentle spirit, in love with justice and humanity, pervades even his lighter compositions. His "Song of the Shirt" first appeared in the "London Punch."

WITH fingers weary and worn,
    With eyelids heavy and red,
A woman sat, in unwomanly rags,
    Plying her needle and thread:
        Stitch! stitch! stitch!
In poverty, hunger, and dirt,
    And still with a voice of dolorous pitch,
She sang the "Song of the Shirt!"

IN ADDITION TO HIS WORK ON THE LONDON MAGAZINE MENTIONED IN *the* McGuffey *note, Hood edited such other publications as* Gem, *the* Comic Annual *(which he began in 1830 and edited for twelve years), the* New Monthly Magazine, *and* Hood's Magazine. *A victim of tuberculosis, Hood's later work turns away from the wit, humor, and satire that had marked most of his career. "The Song of the Shirt" belongs to this later period, first appearing in* Punch *in 1843. It premiered in the* McGuffeys *in the 1857* Sixth Reader *and has been retained in all subsequent editions.*

"Work! work! work!
While the cock is crowing aloof!
    And work! work! work!
Till the stars shine through the roof!
It is oh to be a slave
    Along with the barbarous Turk,
Where woman has never a soul to save,
    If this is Christian work!

"Work! work! work!
Till the brain begins to swim;
    Work! work! work!
Till the eyes are heavy and dim!
    Seam, and gusset, and band,
Band, and gusset, and seam,
    Till over the buttons I fall asleep,
And sew them on in a dream!

"O men, with sisters dear!
    O men, with mothers and wives!
It is not linen you're wearing out,
    But human creatures' lives!
        Stitch! stitch! stitch!
    In poverty, hunger, and dirt,—
Sewing at once, with a double thread,
    A shroud as well as a shirt.

"But why do I talk of Death?
    That Phantom of grisly bone,
I hardly fear his terrible shape,
    It seems so like my own;
    It seems so like my own,
        Because of the fasts I keep;
O God! that bread should be so dear,
    And flesh and blood so cheap!

Hood wrote "The Song of the Shirt" in an attempt to dramatize the condition of factory labor during his time. It is perhaps the most socially conscious selection in the Readers, *demonstrating an awareness of the dehumanizing aspects of labor . . . an awareness that appears nowhere else in the* McGuffeys. *While it is just as didactic as the more traditional clichéd* McGuffey *selections, it carries an impassioned plea that is still convincing. The images may sound overly familiar today, but when these lines were written, they were anything but cliché.*

"Work! work! work!
  My labor never flags;
And what are its wages? A bed of straw,
  A crust of bread—and rags,
That shattered roof—and this naked floor—
  A table—a broken chair—
And a wall so blank, my shadow I thank
  For sometimes falling there.

"Work! work! work!
From weary chime to chime!
  Work! work! work!
As prisoners work for crime!
  Band, and gusset, and seam,
  Seam, and gusset, and band,
Till the heart is sick, and the brain benumbed,
  As well as the weary hand.

"Work! work! work!
In the dull December light,
  And work! work! work!
When the weather is warm and bright;
While underneath the eaves
  The brooding swallows cling,
As if to show me their sunny backs,
  And twit me with the spring.

"Oh but to breathe the breath
  Of the cowslip and primrose sweet!
With the sky above my head,
  And the grass beneath my feet!
For only one short hour
  To feel as I used to feel,
Before I knew the woes of want,
  And the walk that costs a meal!

"Oh but for one short hour,—
  A respite, however brief'!
No blesséd leisure for love or hope,
  But only time for grief!
A little weeping would ease my heart,
  But in their briny bed
My tears must stop, for every drop
  Hinders needle and thread."

With fingers weary and worn,
  With eyelids heavy and red,
A woman sat, in unwomanly rags,
  Plying her needle and thread:
    Stitch! stitch! stitch!
  In poverty, hunger, and dirt,
And still with a voice of dolorous pitch—
Would that its tone could reach the rich!—
  She sang this "Song of the Shirt."

LXXIV. DIAMOND CUT DIAMOND.

Édouard René Lefebvre-Laboulaye, 1811–1883, was a French writer of note. Most of his works involve questions of law and politics, and are considered high authority on the questions discussed. A few works, such as "Abdallah," from which the following extract is adapted, were written as a mere recreation in the midst of law studies; they show great imaginative power. Laboulaye took great interest in the United States, her people, and her literature; and many of his works are devoted to American questions. He translated the works of Dr. William E. Channing into French.

Mansour, the Egyptian merchant, one day repaired to the cadi on account of a suit, the issue of which troubled him but little. A private conversation with the judge had given him hopes of the justice of his cause. The old man asked his son Omar to accompany him in order to accustom him early to deal with the law.

The entire poem—especially the penultimate line's implicit condemnation of the rich—demonstrates a class consciousness that is rare in the McGuffeys. And it is very much a secular poem as well: God appears only as an expletive, and there is no promise of "pie in the sky, bye and bye." All things considered, it is surprising that such a selection ever got into the Readers, even in the later editions.

XCVIII. LOCHINVAR.

OH, young Lochinvar is come out of the west,
Through all the wide Border his steed was the best;
And save his good broadsword, he weapon had none,
He rode all unarmed, and he rode all alone!
So faithful in love, and so dauntless in war,
There never was knight like the young Lochinvar!

He stayed not for brake, and he stopped not for stone,
He swam the Eske River where ford there was none;
But ere he alighted at Netherby gate,
The bride had consented, the gallant came late:
For a laggard in love, and a dastard in war,
Was to wed the fair Ellen of brave Lochinvar!

So boldly he entered the Netherby hall,
Among bridesmen, and kinsmen, and brothers, and all:
Then spoke the bride's father, his hand on his sword —
For the poor craven bridegroom said never a word —
"Oh, come ye in peace here, or come ye in war,
Or to dance at our bridal, young Lord Lochinvar?"

"I long wooed your daughter, my suit you denied; —
Love swells like the Solway, but ebbs like its tide —
And now am I come, with this lost love of mine,
To lead but one measure, drink one cup of wine.
There are maidens in Scotland more lovely by far,
That would gladly be bride to the young Lochinvar."

The bride kissed the goblet; the knight took it up,
He quaffed off the wine, and he threw down the cup.
She looked down to blush, and she looked up to sigh,

With a smile on her lips, and a tear in her eye.
He took her soft hand, ere her mother could bar,
"Now tread we a measure!" said young Lochinvar.

So stately his form, and so lovely her face,
That never a hall such a galliard did grace;
While her mother did fret, and her father did fume,
And the bridegroom stood dangling his bonnet and plume;
And the bridemaidens whispered, "'Twere better by far
To have matched our fair cousin with young Lochinvar."

One touch to her hand, and one word in her ear,
When they reached the hall door, and the charger stood near,
So light to the croup the fair lady he swung,
So light to the saddle before her he sprung!
"She is won! we are gone, over bank, bush, and scaur:
They'll have fleet steeds that follow," quoth young Loch-
  invar.

There was mounting 'mong Græmes of the Netherby clan;
Forsters, Fenwicks, and Musgraves, they rode and they ran;
There was racing and chasing on Cannobie Lee,
But the lost bride of Netherby ne'er did they see.
So daring in love, and so dauntless in war,
Have ye e'er heard of gallant like young Lochinvar?

— *Walter Scott.*

Sir Walter Scott (1771–1832) was one of the most prominent British writers of his time, admired both for his long poems (especially The Lay of the Last Minstrel *and* The Lady of the Lake) *and his novels (among the more famous of which were* The Heart of the Midlothian, Ivanhoe, *and* Kenilworth). *He played an active role in helping to establish the* Quarterly Review *in 1809 (the Tory answer to the Whig's* Edinburgh Review), *and in 1813 he was offered the poet laureateship (which he refused, recommending that it be given to Southey).*

NOTES.—The above selection is a song taken from Scott's poem of "Marmion." It is in a slight degree founded on a ballad called "Katharine Janfarie," to be found in the "Minstrelsy of the Scottish Border."

The **Solway** Frith, on the southwest coast of Scotland, is remarkable for its high spring tides.

Bonnet is the ordinary name in Scotland for a man's cap.

Luckily for us we found a friend here,—a man who has been from the beginning one of Colorado's chief pioneers; and who is never, even in the wildest wilderness, without resources of comfort.

"You can't sleep here," he said. "I can do better for you than this."

"Better!"

He offered us luxury. How movable a thing is one's standard of comfort! A two-roomed pine shanty, board walls, board floors, board ceilings, board partitions not reaching to the roof, looked to us that night like a palace. To have been entertained at Windsor Castle would not have made us half so grateful.

It was late before the "city" grew quiet; and, long after most of the lights were out, and most of the sounds had ceased, I heard one solitary hammer in the distance, clink, clink, clink. I fell asleep listening to it.

CII. IMPORTANCE OF THE UNION.

MR. PRESIDENT: I am conscious of having detained you and the Senate much too long. I was drawn into the debate with no previous deliberation, such as is suited to the discussion of so grave and important a subject. But it is a subject of which my heart is full, and I have not been willing to suppress the utterance of its spontaneous sentiments. I can not, even now, persuade myself to relinquish it, without expressing once more my deep conviction, that, since it respects nothing less than the union of the states, it is of most vital and essential importance to the public happiness.

I profess, sir, in my career hitherto, to have kept steadily in view the prosperity and honor of the whole country, and the preservation of our federal Union. It is

THE SPEAKER HERE WAS DANIEL WEBSTER (1782-1852), PERHAPS America's most famous orator. His reputation was established primarily during his nineteen years as a Whig senator from Massachusetts, but he also served several terms as a congressman and two as Secretary of State. Both highly praised and viciously maligned for his Ciceronian eloquence and controversial positions, Webster was a larger-than-life figure who subsequently became somewhat of a folk hero. His writing and speeches were collected in eighteen volumes in 1903.

to that Union we owe our safety at home, and our consideration and dignity abroad. It is to that Union that we are chiefly indebted for whatever makes us most proud of our country. That Union we reached only by the discipline of our virtues, in the severe school of adversity. It had its origin in the necessities of disordered finance, prostrate commerce, and ruined credit. Under its benign influences, these great interests immediately awoke, as from the dead, and sprang forth with newness of life. Every year of its duration has teemed with fresh proofs of its utility and its blessings; and, although our territory has stretched out wider and wider, and our population spread farther and farther, they have not outrun its protection or its benefits. It has been to us all a copious fountain of national, social, and personal happiness.

I have not allowed myself, sir, to look beyond the Union, to see what might lie hidden in the dark recess behind. I have not coolly weighed the chances of preserving liberty, when the bonds that unite us together shall be broken asunder. I have not accustomed myself to hang over the precipice of disunion, to see whether, with my short sight, I can fathom the depth of the abyss below; nor could I regard him as a safe counselor in the affairs of this government, whose thoughts should be mainly bent on considering, not how the Union should be best preserved, but how tolerable might be the condition of the people when it shall be broken up and destroyed.

While the Union lasts, we have high, exciting, gratifying prospects spread out before us, for us and our children. Beyond that, I seek not to penetrate the veil. God grant that in my day, at least, that curtain may not rise. God grant that on my vision never may be opened what lies behind. When my eyes shall be turned to behold, for the last time, the sun in heaven, may I not see him shining on the broken and dishonored fragments of a once glorious Union; on States dissevered, discordant, belligerent; on

Examples of Webster's oratorical splendor were often selected for inclusion within the McGuffeys, *and many of the passages dealt specifically with the subject of this speech— preserving the Union. This particular lesson is found first in the 1844* Fifth Reader, *and then in the* Sixth Reader *from 1857 to the present. But as early as the 1837* Fourth Reader *Webster is represented on the subject; there, in a lesson entitled "Evils of Dismemberment," he asks:*

But who shall re-construct the fabric of demolished government? Who shall rear again the well-proportioned columns of constitutional liberty! Who shall frame together the skilful architecture which unites national sovereignty with states-rights, individual security, and public prosperity?

Webster's wish never to see the "States dissevered, discordant, belligerent," was granted, for he died before the outbreak of the Civil War. But his words lived on, deliberately retained in the McGuffeys even after the violence was underway. And the speech survived in the Sixth Reader after the war—partly because it was safely nationalistic, promoting neither North nor South; and partly because of its elocutionary possibilities.

a land rent with civil feuds, or drenched, it may be, in fraternal blood.

Let their last feeble and lingering glance rather behold the gorgeous ensign of the Republic, now known and honored throughout the earth, still full high advanced, its arms and trophies streaming in their original luster, not a stripe erased or polluted, not a single star obscured — bearing for its motto no such miserable interrogatory as, What is all this worth? nor those other words of delusion and folly, Liberty first, and Union afterwards — but everywhere, spread all over in characters of living light, blazing on all its ample folds, as they float over the sea and over the land, and in every wind under the whole heavens, that other sentiment, dear to every true American heart — Liberty and Union, now and forever, one and inseparable!

—*Daniel Webster.*

NOTE.—This selection is the peroration of Mr. Webster's speech in reply to Mr. Hayne during the debate in the Senate on Mr. Foot's Resolution in regard to the Public Lands.

CIII. THE INFLUENCES OF THE SUN.

John Tyndall, 1820–1893, one of the most celebrated modern scientists, was an Irishman by birth. He was a pupil of the distinguished Faraday. In 1853 he was appointed Professor of Natural Philosophy in the Royal Institution of London. He is known chiefly for his brilliant experiments and clear writing respecting heat, light, and sound. He also wrote one or two interesting books concerning the Alps and their glaciers. He visited America, and delighted the most intelligent audiences by his scientific lectures and his brilliant experiments. The scientific world is indebted to him for several remarkable discoveries.

As surely as the force which moves a clock's hands is derived from the arm which winds up the clock, so surely is all terrestrial power drawn from the sun. Leaving out of account the eruptions of volcanoes, and the ebb and flow of the tides, every mechanical action on the earth's sieged at Warsaw, in 1794, by a large force of Russians, Prussians, and Austrians. After the siege was raised, he marched against a force of Russians much larger than his own, and was defeated. He was himself severely wounded and captured.

Sarmatia is the ancient name for a region of Europe which embraced Poland, but was of greater extent.

CXIV. LABOR.

Horace Greeley, 1811-1872, perhaps the most famous editor of America, was born in Amherst, New Hampshire, of poor parents. His boyhood was passed in farm labor, in attending the common school, and in reading every book on which he could lay his hands. His reading was mostly done by the light of pine knots. At fifteen he entered a printing office in Vermont, became the best workman in the office, and continued to improve every opportunity for study. At the age of twenty he appeared in New York City, poorly clothed, and almost destitute of money. He worked at his trade for a year or two, and then set up printing for himself. For several years he was not successful, but struggled on, performing an immense amount of work as an editor. In 1841 he established the "New York Tribune," which soon became one of the most successful and influential papers in the country. In 1848 he was elected to Congress, but remained but a short time. In 1872 he was a candidate for the Presidency, was defeated, and died a few days afterward. Mr. Greeley is a rare example of what may be accomplished by honesty and unflinching industry. Besides the vast amount which he wrote for the newspapers, he published several books; the best known of which is "The American Conflict."

EVERY child should be trained to dexterity in some useful branch of productive industry, not in order that he shall certainly follow that pursuit, but that he may at all events be able to do so in case he shall fail in the more intellectual or artificial calling which he may prefer to it. Let him seek to be a doctor, lawyer, preacher, poet, if he will; but let him not stake his all on success in that pursuit, but have a second line to fall back upon if driven from his first. Let him be so reared and trained that he may enter, if he will, upon some intellectual calling in the sustaining consciousness that he need not debase himself, nor do violence to his convictions, in order to achieve

HORACE GREELEY WIELDED GREAT INFLUENCE IN THE NINETEENTH century, primarily through his oft-quoted editorials in the Tribune. *Some of his editorial campaigns (especially his attacks on monopolies and his support of a protective tariff and of labor organization) were too controversial to be listed in the* McGuffey *biographical statement. It is somewhat surprising, however, that there is no mention of Greeley's steady support for the homestead law and his famous words:* "Go West, Young Man!"

It should be noted that Greeley's argument here is more complex than the anti-intellectual calls earlier in the century for only a practical education. There is a bias in his rhetoric, to be sure, but his pragmatic assessment of the labor situation at that time makes his call for more vocationally-oriented training a persuasive one. Many would find his message timely yet.

success therein, since he can live and thrive in another (if you choose, humbler) vocation, if driven from that of his choice. This buttress to integrity, this assurance of self-respect, is to be found in a universal training to efficiency in Productive Labor.

The world is full of misdirection and waste; but all the calamities and losses endured by mankind through frost, drought, blight, hail, fires, earthquakes, inundations, are as nothing to those habitually suffered by them through human idleness and inefficiency, mainly caused (or excused) by lack of industrial training. It is quite within the truth to estimate that one tenth of our people, in the average, are habitually idle because (as they say) they can find no employment. They look for work where it can not be had. They seem to be, or they are, unable to do such as abundantly confronts and solicits them. Suppose these to average but one million able-bodied persons, and that their work is worth but one dollar each per day; our loss by involuntary idleness can not be less than $300,000,000 per annum. I judge that it is actually $500,000,000. Many who stand waiting to be hired could earn from two to five dollars per day had they been properly trained to work. "There is plenty of room higher up," said Daniel Webster, in response to an inquiry as to the prospects of a young man just entering upon the practice of law; and there is never a dearth of employment for men or women of signal capacity or skill. In this city, ten thousand women are always doing needlework for less than fifty cents per day, finding themselves; yet twice their number of capable, skillful seamstresses could find steady employment and good living in wealthy families at not less than one dollar per day over and above board and lodging. He who is a good blacksmith, a fair millwright, a tolerable wagon maker, and can chop timber, make fence, and manage a small farm if required, is always sure of work and fair recompense; while he or she who can keep books or teach music fairly, but knows how to do nothing else, is in constant danger of falling into involuntary idleness and consequent beggary. It is a broad, general truth, that no boy was ever yet inured to daily, systematic, productive labor in field or shop throughout the latter half of his minority, who did not prove a useful man, and was not able to find work whenever he wished it.

Yet to the ample and constant employment of a whole community one prerequisite is indispensable,—that a variety of pursuits shall have been created or naturalized therein. A people who have but a single source of profit are uniformly poor, not because that vocation is necessarily ill-chosen, but because no single calling can employ and reward the varied capacities of male and female, old and young, robust and feeble. Thus a lumbering or fishing region with us is apt to have a large proportion of needy inhabitants; and the same is true of a region exclusively devoted to cotton growing or gold mining. A diversity of pursuits is indispensable to general activity and enduring prosperity.

Sixty or seventy years ago, what was then the District, and is now the State, of Maine, was a proverb in New England for the poverty of its people, mainly because they were so largely engaged in timber cutting. The great grain-growing, wheat-exporting districts of the Russian empire have a poor and rude people for a like reason. Thus the industry of Massachusetts is immensely more productive per head than that of North Carolina, or even that of Indiana, as it will cease to be whenever manufactures shall have been diffused over our whole country, as they must and will be. In Massachusetts half the women and nearly half the children add by their daily labor to the aggregate of realized wealth; in North Carolina and in Indiana little wealth is produced save by the labor of men, including boys of fifteen or upward. When this disparity shall have ceased, its consequence will also disappear.

One might question the absolute nature of Greeley's "broad, general truth" here, and certainly it fails to address itself to whether the individual boy so "inured" is being denied the opportunity to develop an intellectual skill that might potentially be of greater value to himself and society. But such objections do not negate the basic thrust of Greeley's position, as long as his position is not viewed as suggesting that applied training in a "productive industry" become the primary goal of the educational system.

*THE POEMS OF WILLIAM CULLEN BRYANT (1794–1878) APPEAR
frequently within the pages of the* McGuffey Readers. *His
thematic range was narrow, with nearly all the poems expressing religious affirmation growing out of natural observations;
but his style was carefully restrained and demonstrated a
dignity much early American verse lacked. Although he earned
a distinguished reputation as the editor of the* New York
Evening Post *for nearly fifty years, his fame today is largely
linked with this poem and his most famous composition,*
Thanatopsis *(1817).*

CXXVII. LINES TO A WATERFOWL.

WHITHER 'midst falling dew,
While glow the heavens with the last steps of day,
Far, through their rosy depths, dost thou pursue
  Thy solitary way?

Vainly the fowler's eye
Might mark thy distant flight to do thee wrong,
As, darkly painted on the crimson sky,
  Thy figure floats along.

Seek'st thou the plashy brink
Of weedy lake, or marge of river wide,
Or where the rocky billows rise and sink
  On the chafed ocean side?

There is a Power whose care
Teaches thy way along that pathless coast.
The desert and illimitable air,
  Lone wandering, but not lost.

All day, thy wings have fanned,
At that far height, the cold, thin atmosphere,
Yet stoop not, weary, to the welcome land
  Though the dark night is near.

And soon that toil shall end,
Soon shalt thou find a summer home, and rest,
And scream among thy fellows; reeds shall bend,
  Soon, o'er thy sheltered nest.

Thou'rt gone; the abyss of heaven
Hath swallowed up thy form; yet, on my heart,
Deeply has sunk the lesson thou hast given,
    And shall not soon depart.

He, who, from zone to zone,
Guides through the boundless sky thy certain flight,
In the long way that I must tread alone,
    Will lead my steps aright.
                     —Bryant.

"To a Waterfowl" was one of Bryant's earliest poems, written in 1815 and published three years later. It was selected initially for the 1843 Third Reader, *then moved to the* Fourth *in 1857 and finally to the* Sixth Reader *in 1879. Praised by Matthew Arnold as "the most perfect brief poem in the language," it is in many respects an epitome of the selections included in the* McGuffey Eclectic Readers.

Selected Bibliography

The resources for any study of the *McGuffey Eclectic Readers* and their era are rich and varied—ranging from the *Readers* themselves (only a sampling of which could be included here) to the many studies on or relating to American history, culture, education, and morality. Although the following list includes the most important of sources consulted in preparing this book, it obviously makes no attempt to be inclusive.

Brammer, Mauck. The American Book Company: Our Heritage and Our History. Unpublished manuscript, 1969. Offices of Litton Educational Publishing, Inc., New York.

Butts, R. Freeman and Lawrence A. Cremin. *A History of Education in American Culture*. New York: Henry Holt and Co., 1953.

Cameron, W. J. *The Mind of McGuffey*. Oxford, Ohio: Miami University, 1937.

Carpenter, Charles. *History of American Schoolbooks*. Philadelphia: University of Pennsylvania Press, 1963.

Commager, Henry Steele. "McGuffey and His Readers." *Saturday Review*, 16 June 1962, pp. 50–51, 69–70.

Crawford, Benjamin Franklin. *William Holmes McGuffey: The Schoolmaster to Our Nation*. Delaware, Ohio: Carnegie Church Press, 1963.

Elson, Ruth Miller. *Guardians of Tradition: American Schoolbooks of the Nineteenth Century*. Lincoln: University of Nebraska Press, 1964.

Livengood, W. W. *Our Heritage: A Brief History of the American Book Company*. Cincinnati: American Book Co., 1947.

Minnich, Harvey C. *William Holmes McGuffey and His Readers*. New York: American Book Co., 1936.

Mosier, Richard D. *Making the American Mind: Social and Moral Ideas in the McGuffey Readers*. New York: King's Crown Press, 1947.

Neitz, John. *Old Textbooks*. Pittsburgh: University of Pittsburgh Press, 1961.

Root, E. Merrill. "What McGuffey's Readers Read." *The Review of the News*, 17 January 1973, pp. 1–14.

Ruggles, Alice McGuffey. *The Story of the McGuffeys*. New York: American Book Co., 1950.

Saunders, D. A. "Social Ideas in *McGuffey Readers*." *Public Opinion Quarterly*, 5 (1941), 579–89.

Smith, William E. *About the McGuffeys*. Oxford, Ohio: Cullen Printing Co., 1963.

Sutton, Walter. *The Western Book Trade: Cincinnati as a Nineteenth-Century Publishing and Book Trade Center*. Columbus, Ohio: Ohio State University Press, 1961.

Tope, M. *William Holmes McGuffey and a History of the McGuffey School Books; Containing Also a Phrenological Delineation*. Bowerston, Ohio: The Phrenological Era Press, 1929.

Vail, Henry M. *A History of the McGuffey Readers*. Cleveland, Ohio: Burrows Brothers Co., 1911.

Index